The two figures on the cover are fifth century mosaics from the Church of Santa Sabina in Rome. They symbolize the Church of the Jews (eklesia ex circumcisione) on the left and the Church of the Gentiles (eklesia ex gentibus) on the right. It is curious that the light shining through the window brightly illuminates the latter while casting the Church of the Jews in deep shadow, the theme of my book.

Cover-Up

How the Church Silenced Jesus's True Heirs

Lawrence Goudge

iUniverse, Inc.
Bloomington

Cover-up
How the Church Silenced Jesus's True Heirs

iUniverse books may be ordered through booksellers or by contacting:

iUniverse
1663 Liberty Drive
Bloomington, IN 47403
www.iuniverse.com
1-800-Authors (1-800-288-4677)

ISBN: 978-1-4697-8728-2 (sc)
ISBN: 978-1-4697-8730-5 (hc)
ISBN: 978-1-4697-8729-9 (e)

Printed in the United States of America

iUniverse rev. date: 7/16/2012

Permissions

Contents

Preface: All Fowl of Every Wing

In the mountain of the height of Israel will I plant it:
and it shall bring forth boughs, and bear fruit, and be a goodly cedar:
and under it shall dwell all fowl of every wing;
in the shadow of the branches thereof shall they dwell.
Ezek 17:22–23 KJV

One of the great tragedies of Christianity is that it has *not* allowed "all fowl of every wing" to dwell under its branches. Instead, hatred and heresy hunting haunt its shadows. Although the twentieth century saw some changes as ecumenism began to take God's proclamation in Ezekiel seriously—at least some Muslims, Jews, and Christians began to work together to try to bring a little harmony out of their fractured pasts—there is a long way to go.

Yet one early group held Ezekiel's vision dear: Jesus's Jewish followers. In a homily supposedly delivered in what is now Tripoli in Lebanon, Peter proclaims that although "Jesus is concealed from the Jews," and Moses is hidden from the Christians, "there being one teaching by both, God accepts him who has believed either of these."[1]

In his book *Jewish Christianity*, Hans-Joachim Schoeps points out that such inclusivity remains worthy of note even today (page 68). The Church hounded that inclusive movement out of existence, however, thus effectively destroying all hope for a tolerant world. Not only that, but the scholarly world in general continues to keep the history of Jesus's Jewish heirs plunged in darkness. Victims of a two-thousand-year conspiracy of silence, their story has lain unnoticed for far too long. It is time to change that.

Suppressing scholarly dissent is alive and well. The Israel Academy of Sciences and Humanities has denied me permission to quote from *The Jewish Christians of the Early Centuries of Christianity according to a New Source* so sadly, I have paraphrased most of this material. Unfortunately, paraphrases do not capture the authentic voices of these tenth century Jewish Christians so they must still remain hidden behind the smokescreen of scholarly censorship.

Chapter 1

The First Last Supper

Seeing the Eucharist through the Smoke

"Bad instruction ... vain boasting and other such like evils have filled the whole house of this world, like some enormous smoke ... preventing those who dwell in it from seeing its Founder aright ... What, then, is fitting for those who are within, excepting with a cry brought forth from their inmost hearts to invoke His aid, who alone is not shut up in the smoke-filled house, that He would ... open the door ... so that the smoke may be dissipated ... and the light of the sun ... may be admitted." *Clementine Recognitions* 1.15.

T his is the apostle, Peter, talking to his new disciple, Clement of Rome. In the debate that follows, Peter charges St. Paul with being the source of these errors, claiming that Paul's visions have deluded him. This debate is fiction, of course. The *Recognitions* is a "romance" written in the late second or early third century when the Clementine community was fighting bitterly against a now dominant Gentile Christianity. Through Peter, we hear their voices as they struggle to shine a light into the smoke-filled house.

The smoke has not cleared. Despite being portrayed as buffoons by the evangelists, Jesus's original disciples surely had the clearest understanding of his mission. Yet the church has thrown a smoke screen over their direct heirs, the Ebionites (from the Hebrew *Ebyon*, meaning "the Poor") and the Nazarenes, for almost two millennia. In fact, Christianity has been involved in a very real conspiracy (unlike the one concocted in *Holy Blood, Holy Grail,* which is fiction). It is time to open the door to see what is there when the smoke dissipates. What, indeed, is under the soot that smudges the face of the Poor?

An epic struggle between James, the brother of Jesus, and Paul, the self-appointed apostle to the Gentiles, was the spark that kindled the fires of this smoke screen. The word "epic" is not hype: the outcome determined the future course of Christianity, although both men died long before the dust settled. The winning Pauline faction has heavily reworked the surviving records. Nevertheless, the struggle can be teased out of them. Translators today still fudge passages that don't suit them—as I will show. Knowingly or not, they are abetting the great conspiracy.

God versus Man

In this chapter, we will focus on one aspect of the church's cover-up by solving the mystery of the Last Supper, a rite the Ebionites repudiated. Before we start, however, we must point out two matters. Firstly, Jesus's Jewish followers never thought of him as "God," whereas Gentile Christians did. Paul certainly thinks of him in that way, saying that Jesus, "subsisting in the form of God, did not think it robbery to be equal with God, but emptied himself, taking the form of a slave, being made in human likeness …"[2] This describes the incarnation of a divine being, which is and always would have been totally unacceptable to any Jew, incidentally casting doubt on whether Paul really was the Jew he claimed to be.

Secondly, a note on terminology: Jesus's followers in Judea never called themselves, or thought of themselves as, Christians. In New Testament times, they were either "Followers of the Way" or Nazarenes. They were devout, sometimes even fanatical, Jews. Consequently, I will use the term "Jesus's Jewish followers" or "Followers of the Way," until the revolt in 70 CE. Afterward, the Ebionites and the Nazarenes were the two most prominent groups, but I am going to invent a blanket name, Yeshuites, to cover all of Jesus's Jewish followers. "Christians" will be reserved for the splinter group that believed in Paul's radically revised view of Jesus's mission. I will use "Jewish Christian" in direct quotations only—and under protest, since it implies Jews who believe that Christ died for their sins. For instance: one Sunday morning in the nineteenth century, the Hart clan, my grandmother's family, startled the city of Halifax when they descended on Brunswick Street Methodist Church, converted to Christianity en masse, and were thenceforth the pillars of that congregation. Now, *they* were Jewish Christians.

Love Better than Sacrifice

Since the Last Supper is a sacrificial rite, we must examine Jesus's attitude toward sacrifice. His two most important commandments reveal his priorities:

> "Hear, O Israel: the Lord our God, the Lord is one; you shall love the Lord your God with all your heart, and with all your soul, and with all your mind, and with all your strength." The second is this, "You shall love your neighbor as yourself" (Mk 12:29–32, NRSV).

The scribe who asked Jesus's opinion on the most important commandment replies that these overshadow burnt offerings and sacrifices. Jesus approves, telling the scribe that he is close to the kingdom of God. Why, then, holding these views, would Jesus sacrifice himself as an atonement to God? Both Matthew and Luke saw the problem, deleting all reference to sacrifice in that story. After all, it made Jesus's death on the cross irrelevant. Luke, like Paul, saw Jesus's sacrificial death as the be-all and end-all of his new religion. In fact, Luke's two-part account, his Gospel and the book of Acts, portrays the benighted disciples, Peter in particular, only gradually realizing that they have a new religion on their hands. But why would the Son of God pick such dim disciples?

There is more: both Matthew and Luke removed the direct quote from the Torah, "Hear, O Israel, etc."[3], because it flatly proclaims Jesus's Jewishness. Luke's Jesus is tending toward a religion in which the Jewish God breaks his promises to his people and turns to the Gentiles.

It wasn't just words: Jesus's actions showed that offering himself as a sacrifice was alien to all he stood for. Consider this passage: "In the temple he found people selling cattle, sheep, and doves, and the money-changers … Making a whip of cords, he drove all of them out of the temple, both the sheep and the cattle."[4] It wasn't just the handsome profit the traders made. Jesus was attacking temple sacrifice, which would have ground to a halt without the traders. We see this antipathy in the *Clementine Recognitions*, which also harps on the evils of sacrifice while neglecting justice and mercy.[5] At one point, Peter tells the temple establishment that their sacrifices anger God because the time for sacrifices is past.[6] The author wrote this after the destruction of Jerusalem when the time was indeed past.

What about human sacrifice? Judaism had repudiated it centuries earlier. If God prevented Abraham from sacrificing his son, would he not spare his own?

The whole focus of Jesus's program was repent; live simply and justly. That was how the Kingdom of God would come. Only once does he tell someone to make the requisite sacrifices, when he heals a leper, but the leper had to do that to reenter society.[7]

If Jesus rejected sacrifice, why did he predict his death,[8] the reader may object. Here Mark put his own view of the mission in Jesus's mouth, a routine practice for ancient writers. Never once, however, does Mark's Jesus even hint of a sacrifice for the sins of mankind.

Jesus was focused on this world. He had a clear idea of what was going to happen—and that shortly. These are his words a couple of days before that fateful last supper:

> But in those days, after that suffering, the sun will be darkened, and the moon will not give its light, and the stars will be falling from heaven, and the powers in the heavens will be shaken. Then they will see "the Son of Man coming in clouds" with great power and glory. Then he will send out the angels, and gather his elect from the four winds, from the ends of the earth to the ends of heaven ... Truly I tell you, this generation will not pass away until all these things have taken place (Mk 13:24–27, 30, NRSV).

Mark did not make this up. That generation had already passed away when he wrote that around 70 CE. They are Jesus's words, and an embarrassment to the developing church.

Whose Last Supper?

The reader may go on to object that the night before his crucifixion, Jesus consecrated the bread with these words: "Take; this is my body;"

and the wine: "This is my blood of the covenant, which is poured out for many."[9] It is highly dubious that Jesus ever said that. Luke's text sheds some light on the matter:

> When the hour came, he ... said to them: "I have greatly desired to eat this Passover with you before I suffer; *for I tell you that I will by no means eat it until it is fulfilled in the kingdom of God.*" Then he took a cup and, after having given thanks he said: "Take this and divide it among yourselves; for I tell you that from now on I will not drink of the fruit of the vine until the kingdom of God comes." Then he took the bread, and when he had given thanks, he broke it, and gave it to them saying, "This is my body, *which is given for you* ..." (Lk 22:14–19a, NRSV, italics mine).

If Jesus won't eat until the kingdom comes, it's coming here on earth, since God already reigns in heaven. Luke's text is far different from Mark's. Mark and Luke and Matthew (which is again different) all amended their source for their last suppers.

The New Revised Standard Version (NRSV) notes that the italicized phrase, "which is given for you" is missing from "other ancient authorities." Ehrman[10] points out that Luke "*never*, anywhere else, indicates that the death itself is what brings salvation from sin." Thus later redactors tampered with Luke to turn his account into the institution of the Christian Eucharist.

And what about John? Astoundingly, his Last Supper is simply a mystical discourse. He is totally ignorant of the institution of the central mystery of Christianity. He does know the concept, however: at one point, his Jesus says that he is the bread of life and that those who come to him will never be hungry (Jn 6:35). Fine. That's acceptable as a metaphor. Then it gets less acceptable: "[Jesus] ... said to them, '... unless you eat the flesh of the Son of Man and drink his blood, you have no life in you'"[11].

There's something wrong here. That's fine in a pagan mystery religion, but no Jew would ever have said that. Including Jesus.

Let's examine the blood of the covenant. In Leviticus, God threatens anyone who eats blood—even foreigners. He will set his face against that person and "cut him off from among his people." He then repeats himself to make sure there is no mistake.[12] No ambiguity there. The law absolutely forbade ingesting any blood, not to mention human blood—or a god's blood. Thus, even aside from his distaste for sacrifice, Jesus could never have said what John reports. Small wonder then that, shortly thereafter, the evangelist notes: "Because of this, many of his disciples turned back and walked no longer with him."[13]

I'll say. Every single one of them would have left him. In fact, this originally referred to Paul, not Jesus, as I will show in chapter 8. But how embarrassing. How could John omit the most central act of Jesus, the institution of the Lord's Supper?

One clue is to be found in the *Didache*, an early manual of instruction for Jesus's followers. Its text of the Eucharist, which incidentally means "thanksgiving," is instructive. Instead of the familiar words, this rite reads:

> Begin with the chalice: "We give thanks to you, our Father, for the holy vine of your servant David, which you made known to us through your servant Jesus." Then over the particles of bread: "We give thinks to you, our Father for the life and knowledge you have made known to us through your servant Jesus."[14]

There is no body broken for you; there is no blood of the new covenant, yet it clearly states that this is the Eucharist. Note also that it calls Jesus God's servant, not his son. This would remain the basic pattern for Yeshuites and those who derived their rites from them. Some of the latter still exist.

Irenaeus illuminates this. After disparaging the Ebionites for denying Jesus's supernatural birth, he comments that they reject "the heavenly wine," believing it to be the water of the world and therefore "not receiving God so as to have union with Him."[15] These Ebionites were the direct heirs of Jesus's disciples who were practicing Jews. They drank no blood (even symbolically), nor did their spiritual descendants.

The Church and Paul's Visions

Next we must turn to Paul's visions for more light on the matter. In some passages, one must examine the Greek to get the true picture of what happened, for instance, in Paul's account of his first known visionary experience:

> For you have heard of my previous life in Judaism, how intensely I persecuted the church of God and *wasted it.* I was

advancing in Judaism beyond many of my contemporaries and was an extreme zealot for the ancestral traditions. But when the One, having separated me from my mother's womb and called me through his grace, was pleased to reveal his Son in me that I might preach Him among the nations, right off I did not confer with flesh and blood, neither did I go up to Jerusalem to consult with those who had been apostles before me, but I went away into Arabia, and later returned to Damascus (Gal 1:13–17; my translation).

I translated it myself since most other versions whitewash their saint. By Paul's own admission, he "wasted" the followers of Jesus. But the New International Version renders this "how intensely I persecuted the church and *tried to destroy* it." "*Tried* to destroy" masks the real meaning. Of the versions I consulted, only the archaic King James and the Catholic Bible gave honest translations.

Paul "wasting" Jesus's followers is graphically recounted in a much-neglected source for the origins of Christianity, the *Clementine Recognitions* (CR), which we will often consult in this work. The Clementine literature contains valuable material, the earliest layers of which may be as close to the events they describe as the Gospels, although Christian hands tampered with it right up until the infamous Rufinus (of whom more anon) rendered it into Latin. When possible, I use the less tampered Syriac version.

The Clementine authors insisted that their traditions originated with Peter and James. Is it because Peter alleges that Paul's doctrines derived from his *false* visions that so many scholars ignore these valuable documents?

Now we are getting closer to an understanding of what is going on. I will show that Paul, the man who said that the law was dead, instituted the Last Supper with its new covenant. Compare these two passages. First Paul: "In the same way he also took the cup, after supper, saying, 'This cup is the new covenant in my blood. Do this, as often as you drink, in memory of me.'"[16] Then Exodus 24:7–8 (KJV): after Moses read the book of the covenant to the Children of Israel, they promised to obey all that the Lord said. "And Moses took the blood [of the sacrificed oxen] and sprinkled it on the people, and said, 'Behold the blood of the covenant, which the Lord hath made with you concerning all these words.'"

Clearly, Paul's rite in First Corinthians is replacing the old law. Jesus would never have done that. Like many Pharisees of his time, he said that the law should be interpreted with justice and mercy. Thus if need arose he both healed and plucked grain on the Sabbath, but Paul's travesty of his mission would have appalled Jesus, as it did his brother, James, when he finally realized the full import of Paul's activities. When the opportunity arose, James forced Paul to recant and take a purification vow in the temple. I quote James: "Then everybody will know that there is no truth in these reports about you, *but that you yourself are living in obedience to the law.*"[17] (Italics mine.) An eyewitness friendly to Paul reported this.

Did Paul defy James? Why should he? He had already boasted to the Corinthians how he handled such situations:

> "To the Jews, I became as a Jew, in order to gain Jews. To those under the law I became as one under the law— though not myself under the law—so that I might gain those under the law. To those without the law [non-Jews] I became as one without the law so that I might win those without the law." [He sums his method:] "I have become all things to all men."[18]

In plain words, he was a liar. That made Saint Jerome squirm:

> "Then Paul took the men, and the next day purifying himself with them, entered into the temple, to signify the accomplishment of the days of purification, until an offering should be offered for every one of them." Paul, here again let me question thee: Why didst thou shave thy head, why didst thou walk barefoot according to Jewish ceremonial law, why didst thou offer sacrifices, why were victims slain for thee according to the law? Thou wilt answer, doubtless, "To avoid giving offence to those of the Jews who had believed." To gain the Jews, thou didst pretend to be a Jew; *and James and all the other elders taught thee this dissimulation.*[19] (Italics mine.)

That's an old political trick; smear the opposition. If Paul lied or, in Jerome's politically correct language, dissimulated, it was all James's fault.

Jesus's later Jewish followers had no such compunction. The Qaraites, a Jewish sect who considered Jesus to have been a just and pious man, alleged that Paul was famous for trickery and lying.[20] The *Tathbit* documents the lying, rendering the above Corinthians passage: "With the Jew, I was a Jew, with the Roman, a Roman, and with the Arma'i, an Arma'i."[21] The word "Arma'i" means "those who worship stars and idols," or Paul's "those without the law." Small wonder so many Christian scholars ignore the *Tathbit*, since it points out Paul's duplicity.

So Paul obeyed James, proving to the world he was still an observant Jew,[22] his last act as a free man.

Can we really say, however, that Paul invented the Christian Eucharist? Actually, his visions revealed it:

> "*For I received from the Lord* what I also handed on to you, that the Lord Jesus on the night when he was handed over took a loaf of bread, and when he had given thanks, he broke it and said, 'This is my body on your behalf. Do this in remembrance of me.' After supper, he took the cup …"[23] (Italics mine.)

In Galatians 1:11, Paul clarifies what he means by "I received from the Lord." He writes, "For I make known to you, brothers, that the gospel I preached is not according to man; for I did not receive it from any man, nor was I taught it, *but through a revelation of Jesus Christ*" (my translation). Not according to man, note. Not from Peter, not from James, but from Jesus, who is thus, at least, semidivine, a concept no Jew would entertain.

This, then, is "the Gospel" channeled by Paul. Divinely revealed, a new creation, it is the centerpiece of his new mystery religion. Consequently, the synoptic Gospels, written more than a decade later, drew on Paul for their Last Suppers. The living Jesus never proclaimed a new covenant—he died a practicing Jew. (Perhaps more accurately, a practicing Israelite. Judaism as we know it only developed after the destruction of the temple.)

Thus Paul did not create it: this rite was a visionary revelation, unlike some of those devised by people lusting for power in our time—often with tragic results. Remember the cultists who committed mass suicide expecting to board that mystic spaceship, Comet Hale-Bopp? Or the debacle at Waco?

Paul was a profoundly conflicted individual, given to violence and obsessed with ambition. He was in a highly excited state, fresh from killing Jesus's followers, still full of bloodlust when the vision on the road to Damascus struck him down. With his brilliant mind and consummate command of language, Paul created a new religion in a stroke of genius that still wields tremendous power. The idea that God became incarnate and offered himself as a sacrifice on the cross for the salvation of mankind cast a spell that overshadowed the more distant dying gods/goddesses, such as Persephone and Adonis, simply because they *were* distant and mythical. But Paul's new creation came with a price.

Peter anticipated that price. In a little-known quote, he asserts that both God's covenants—with the Jews and with the Gentile—are valid.[24] Had Peter's view prevailed, the many sects and religions might have coexisted in peace instead of spattering the world with blood.

Judaism has the honesty to openly portray the warts of its founding fathers. Jacob/Israel stealing the birthright of his brother, Esau, is a good example of this. It would be interesting if Christianity were to likewise acknowledge Paul's rough edges. He was a remarkably effective magician, cursing anyone who preached any other Gospel but his.[25] And just as in fairy tales, fate fulfilled the curse. For centuries, the church consigned to the flames anyone who dared to preach a rival Gospel, and the smoke from those fires has blurred the nature of the early church to this day. Shrouded for far too long, the Jewish followers of Jesus deserve to reemerge into the light of history.

Chapter 2

Fighters from the Cradle

The Galileans are fighters from the cradle and at all times numerous, and never has cowardice afflicted the men ... (Josephus, 1959, 192).

Small, seemingly insignificant, Galilee is one of those volcanoes of history that erupt from time to time. It spews magma into the ivied towers of scholarship as well as onto that eternally contested land. Who were the Galileans? What about Jesus? What did he come to do? Controversy roils like lava around him while, like some pagan psychopomp, he leads phantom trains in the most mystifying incarnations: Osiris? Adonis? Son of God? Jewish Messiah? King of the Jews? Itinerant cynic? Rebel? Zealot? Healer? Magician? In this chapter, I will attempt to disperse some of the haze of myth with a walk through sunny Galilee. After all, since the Jesus movement not only consisted of Galileans but also maintained a strong base there for centuries, we must have at least some understanding of their world to truly understand their movement.

"Fighters from their cradle?" That's not the idyllic Galilee of my Sunday school days, nor does it fit the peaceful scenario some scholars promote, no doubt influenced by their understanding of Jesus. So is Josephus reliable? Like all writers, he had an agenda: firstly, to toady up to his patrons, the Flavian emperors, who liberally supplied his bread and butter, and, secondly, to chronicle the recent Jewish war for a Gentile audience. In fact, a pugnacious streak did run through Galilee. It's a matter of record. Some more notable belligerents will illustrate the point.

Hezekiah was a chief of the "bandits" *(lestai)*. At the tender age of fifteen, Herod (later "the Great") caught him when he was "overrunning the district adjoining Syria with a very large gang" and executed the whole lot in 47 BCE.[26] Hezekiah's gang must be unique in the annals of banditry. The mothers of the "robbers" went to Jerusalem and complained to the king, Hyrcanus, who summoned Herod to trial! The high priests backed up these mothers of bandits, alleging that Herod and family were taking over the reins of government. They also complained that no one should be executed unless condemned by the Sanhedrin. It is curious such powerful interests would defend a "gang of robbers." In fact, the governor of Syria had to intervene to save Herod's life.

Some years after this incident, the Roman senate made Herod "King of the Jews." First he had to subdue them. Although Josephus claims that "apart from a few localities, all Galilee took up [Herod's] cause,"[27] the Galileans fought back stubbornly. Beginning his campaign by forcing his troops through a blizzard for a surprise attack on the city of Sepphoris (the capital of Galilee, only a few miles from Nazareth), he still needed several weeks to finally break the resistance of the province that had supposedly taken up his cause. It didn't end there. Thinking he had subdued it and leaving what he thought was a sufficient force behind to deal with any rising, he started off for Samaria with a large force of cavalry and infantry, intending to attack the legitimate ruler of the Hasmonean line. "His departure removed all restraint from the *habitual trouble-makers in Galilee* ..."[28] (italics mine) who, after killing his general Ptolemy, ravaged the whole country.

Those "habitual troublemakers" were really freedom fighters, supporting their legitimate rulers. They despised Herod and would resist him and his spawn, in one way or another, until the whole unsavory clan finally disappeared from the face of the earth.

The next peaceful event occurred after Herod died. When his son, Archelaus, sped to Rome to have the senate approve his succession, discontent erupted like a tidal wave over the whole country. Small wonder: Herod's magnificent architectural works had been built on the backs of groaning peasants. Galilee was no sluggard in the general mayhem, with Sepphoris again a center of unrest. Judas, the son of the above Hezekiah, broke into the royal armory there, equipped his followers, and attacked his rivals for power.[29] He was aiming at the kingship of all Judea.

Rome quickly retaliated. A legion routed all those peaceful Galileans, captured Sepphoris, enslaved its inhabitants, and burnt the city.[30] Perhaps two or three years old, Jesus would have toddled up the ridge above Nazareth to watch Sepphoris burn, along with everyone else in the village who could walk. Of the upshot, James Tabor comments:

> The trauma that gripped Galilee must have been dreadful, with dying men nailed to crosses at intervals up and down the main roads or on hillsides visible to all who passed.[31]

Tales of all that mayhem would have livened the long winter evenings in Nazareth for many a year. They had no TV; they talked.

The Zealots

Now we turn to Judas, typically surnamed "the Galilean." This noted rebel founded the Zealots, who were to have a profound effect, not only in ancient Judea, but also on subsequent history. Terrorists have, ever since, followed the pattern on the coin they struck. Perhaps it would be more accurate to say the coin of their offshoot, the Sicarii, named after the dagger, or *sica*, they concealed under their cloaks. Thus armed, they would move through a crowd toward their unsuspecting victim and stab him, a technique today's suicide bombers have honed to perfection with far more devastating results. There is a connection: the medieval assassins who so awed the crusaders were Judas's heirs, and so through to the modern era. The common thread is killing all who refuse to bow to their violent god.

Judas and his movement have been somewhat obscured. Why? Because one of Jesus's disciples was Simon the—what else?—Zealot, another Galilean. Mark sweated over that since "Zealot" was a hated name in Rome, the city where, according to some traditions, the evangelist wrote. Its armies had just brutally suppressed the Jewish Revolt. Its citizens had wildly cheered as the Triumph of Vespasian wound through its streets dragging chained Zealots to bloody deaths. It was a spectacle of almost unprecedented splendor. Although the general, Titus, "picked out the tallest and handsomest" of captive rebels for his triumph[32] Josephus concentrates on the glittering booty: "Masses of silver and gold and ivory in every shape known to the craftsman's art could be seen, not as if carried in procession but like a flowing river."[33] Blinking from the glittering stream of treasure, Rome screamed execrations at the manacled Zealots.

Thus our Evangelist had a problem. He wanted his Gospel to appeal to Rome and its empire. What to do? A devilishly clever solution! Use Aramaic: Jesus's disciple was Simon the *Cananaean;*[34] quite true and perfectly meaningless. Those who were aware of Palestinian history would likely misread it as "Canaanite," and those who weren't would just shrug. It worked for almost two millennia: the King James version on which I grew up reads, "Simon the Canaanite." In actuality, the Aramaic root is *qan'an'*, "zealous," with an added Greek ending denoting a party. Thus, Simon belonged to the party of the Zealots.

Although Luke uses the Greek word, he plays it down, writing: "Simon, who was called a Zealot.[35]" The King James's translators rendered this "Simon called *Zelotes*," leaving the Greek untranslated. They knew what it meant. Such obscurantism dogs the whole history of this provocative sect, not only in the historical works that have come down to us, almost all of which were tampered with, but among some modern scholars. Simon is the reason. For almost two millennia, the church has thrown up a smoke screen to obscure Jesus's Zealot disciple.

Before going back to the founder of the sect, we need to look at his model, Phinehas, Aaron's grandson. Out of all the brutal people in the book of Numbers, Phinehas shines. God had sent a plague into the camps of Israel. As usual, he was punishing sin, in this case, worshipping an idol, Baal of Peor. So Moses ordered the idolaters to be put to death. While the tribes still sat in mourning, one Israelite was brash enough to bring a Midianite woman back to camp for a little nooky. At this, Phinehas seized a spear and, following them into their tent, impaled them in *flagrante delicto*. That pleased God. He stopped the plague, telling Moses that Phinehas had turned away his wrath. His reward? A lasting priesthood for him and his descendants because he was *zealous* for God's honor.[36]

This gory tale inspired Judas the Galilean to found the Zealot party. It emulated its great hero throughout its history—and echoed far beyond it. We can thank Phinehas for the religious violence that plagues the world today.

From the start, the Zealots were absolutely intolerant, which is scarcely surprising. Late in his account of the war, Josephus tells us that Judas's followers mobbed those who submitted to the census of Quirinius (Luke 2 also mentions it):

> Plundering their property, rounding up their cattle, and
> setting fire to their habitations: they were no better than

foreigners, they declared, throwing away in this cowardly fashion the freedom won by the Jews at such cost, and avowedly choosing slavery under the Romans. This was a mere excuse intended to cloak their barbarity and avarice.[37]

Josephus was, of course, buttering up his patrons, the house of Vespasian.

Their central tenet: "God is to be their only Ruler and Lord,"[38] had deep roots. According to the story of Saul and Samuel, it's the way God really wanted things. Samuel was angry with the restive tribes asking for a king. He prayed. God conveniently replied that Samuel should listen to the voice of the people—an early example of God's approval of democracy—adding a threatening note: "They have rejected me from being king over them."[39] Clearly the author of Samuel was no fan of kings.

Josephus's next sentence is key; its echoes still harrow our times:

> "[The Zealots] also do not value dying any kinds of death, nor indeed do they heed the deaths of their relations and friends, nor can any such fear make them call any man Lord."[40]

This ethic guided the sect till Rome destroyed them. Yet the tenet lived on: Christian martyrs lived and died by it right down to the time of Constantine. They refused to bow to Caesar; they refused to burn incense to Caesar, and they bravely faced the consequences, just like the Zealots. Because of this refusal, Rome viewed them as traitors. How, then, did this idea enter Christianity? It's right there in the Gospels, as we shall see.

E. Mary Smallwood states[41] that the term Zealot should not be applied to the movement from its inception (by Judas the Galilean) since it only occurs in Josephus during the war in 66 CE. Absence of evidence is not evidence of absence. What about Simon the Zealot? Did she miss him because the church, emulating Mark, still tries to keep him in the dark? Mark's embarrassment proves that the Zealots were active by the twenties and thirties CE. James, confronting Paul in Jerusalem around 60 CE, tells him that there are many thousands of Jews who have believed and all are "Zealots for the law."[42] This is always translated as "zealous" or "staunch upholders" to disguise it. Thus Smallwood would have missed it unless she checked the Greek. In fact, the Zealots are almost certainly missing from

Josephus because someone, no doubt an early Christian redactor, deleted embarrassing passages. One deletion is quite glaring.

To begin: in *Antiquities* XVIII, I, 1, Josephus launches a discussion of the famous census at the time of Quirinius, immediately introducing Judas the Galilean, "who excited a fourth philosophic sect among us." He names the other three, the Pharisees, the Sadducees, and the Essenes, but omits *the name* of the fourth, Judas's sect. It never appears in the *Antiquities*, which is curious, to say the least—a nameless sect. That must be unique.

The second curious fact is that at the end of that long paragraph he writes concerning this fourth sect:

> I shall discourse a little because the infection which spread thence among the younger sort, who were zealous for it, brought the public to destruction.[43]

But instead of discoursing a little, he breaks off to discuss the other three sects. Some will object that he finally does so in Ant. XVIII, I, 6. That's true, but the logic of Josephus's sentence demands that he do it immediately, not later. By itself, we could ignore this uncharacteristic lapse, but he never tells us what happened to Judas. And that is damning. Josephus slavers over the gory ends of his other detested "brigands," yet they were all minor compared to Judas. He puts Judas and his movement in a class by itself:

> All sorts of misfortunes also sprang from these men, and the nation was infected with this doctrine to an incredible degree ... there were also very great robberies and murder of our principal men ... the sedition at last increased so high, that the very temple of God was burnt down by their enemies' fire. Such were the consequences of this ... For Judas and Sadduc, who excited a fourth philosophic sect among us ... filled our civil government with tumults at present, and laid the foundations of our future miseries ...[44]

Josephus heaps *all* the woes of first-century Judea on Judas's shoulders yet leaves his fate in total silence. And his sect is unnamed. Why?

Perhaps if we turn to the *Jewish War*, we'll find out a little more. No. Someone has excised it even more violently. Considering Josephus's allegations that the sect caused the war, we would expect to find at least as full a treatment as in the *Antiquities*, but there's only one lonely paragraph about Rome sending out Coponius as prefect when it deposed Herod's son, Archelaus. It is utterly mute on Quirinius, whose hated tax caused the uprising. All we have left is:

> In his time a Galilean named Judas tried to stir the natives to revolt, saying that they would be cowards if they submitted to paying taxes to the Romans, and after serving God alone accepted human masters. This man was a rabbi with a sect of his own, and was quite unlike the others.[45]

Okay. Let's hear about it.

But no. Again he goes on to discuss the other three sects in some detail. About Judas and his sect, all we learn is the juicy tidbit about cattle rustling and arson quoted earlier. It occurs almost at the end of his account, quite out of sequence, when the Roman juggernaut is about to storm Masada in its final cleaning-up operations. The clincher is a sentence that I purposely omitted earlier. Coming just before the cattle rustling, it reads:

> The fortress was Masada, occupied by the Sicarii under the command of an influential man called Eleazar, a descendant of the Judas who had persuaded many Jews, *as recorded earlier,* not to register when Quirinius was sent to Judea to take a census.[46] (Italics mine.)

Say what? It's not there now. Comb the *Jewish War* as you will, you will find no earlier mention of Quirinius. In fact, there is nothing about Judas persuading many Jews not to register either. Unless Josephus had a memory lapse, which is highly unlikely given the importance of this material, someone has tampered with this text. We only learn Judas's fate from the mouth of Gamaliel: "After him Judas the Galilean arose in the days of the census and drew away some of the people after him; he also perished and his people were scattered."[47] One would assume that Rome killed him, but Josephus never tells us so. His fate has disappeared.

Who removed this material and why? Was it too close to Jesus's formative years? Did it even mention him? He was at least ten years old at the time of the census, although he might even have been thirteen.

Since Sepphoris (easily seen from the heights above Nazareth) was the administrative center of Lower Galilee, the action was likely hot and heavy around him and the Holy Family. However, what so disturbed Christian redactors must remain a mystery unless an untampered version of the *War* surfaces from some desert cave. Incidentally, Bart Ehrman's *Misquoting Jesus: The Story behind Who Changed the Bible and Why* gives weight to my claim. If they edited out any Good News that didn't "fit," would they be faithful to Josephus?

It's sad. The uprising over the census, occurring when Jesus was at an impressionable age, must have influenced his life and work, either for or against armed revolt, the preponderance of opinion favoring against. In any case, we will see later that Jesus expected God to institute the kingdom—righteousness, not violence, would be the trigger.

Before saying farewell to the Zealots, there is more material to illuminate this study. Some of the Sicarii fled to Alexandria when Jewish resistance collapsed in 70 CE. Such a subversive movement soon alarmed the authorities, who rounded up six hundred of them. Josephus tells us that their fortitude caused universal astonishment:

> Subjected to every form of torture ... for the one purpose of making them acknowledge Caesar as lord, not a man gave in or came near to saying it ... But nothing amazed the spectators as much as the behaviour of young children; for not one of them could be constrained to call Caesar lord.[48]

This kind of fanaticism echoed down to the Middle Ages, when unnumbered "heretics" went up in flames.

Keeping this in mind, we turn to Polycarp, an early Christian martyr who met his end around the middle of the second century CE. While escorting him to the arena to face a bloodthirsty crowd, the captain of the police tried to persuade him, asking what harm there was in saying, Caesar is Lord. Polycarp pulled a Hollywood film actor stunt, maintaining a pregnant silence to build up the suspense. Finally he simply refused to do it.[49] He went to his death (accompanied by the requisite miracles—his body giving off the odor of incense, for instance) for refusing to call Caesar "lord."

No one can miss the similarity between the deaths of that early Christian martyr and the last Zealots. With that I will return to the peaceful Galilee of myth. Rome crucified Judas's sons in 48 CE. His grandson, Menahem, was a leader of the Zealots in the revolt, 66–70 CE,[50] and Eleazar, the chief of the Sicarii, whom we met earlier, was also a descendant. That's a lot of revolution for a peaceful people, although one family is prominent. Note that alone out of Josephus's four sects of Jewish philosophy, the rabid nationalists both arose and kept their base in Galilee.

Just because violence infests a culture does not mean that everyone participates, or even approves. Peter lived in the same world where oppression fueled peasant rage at callous governments, yet his shilly-shallying in the Gospels reflects a man trying to bring harmony to the table. In Acts, he tries to reconcile the two opposing parties over the strict observance of the law and may well have influenced Jesus's stern brother James for the happy outcome (Acts 15). And then there is the Peter of the Clementines who said that both of God's covenants were valid. It's a consistent picture, evoking a real man who fished on the Sea of Galilee so long ago.

Galileans could be violent, like Simon the Zealot, or peaceful, like Peter.

The Physical Setting

> The whole area is excellent for crops or cattle and rich in forests of every kind, so by its adaptability it invites even those least inclined to work on the land. Consequently every inch has been cultivated by the inhabitants and not a corner goes to waste. It is thickly studded with towns, and thanks to the natural abundance the innumerable villages are so densely populated that the smallest has more than fifteen thousand inhabitants.[51]

Fifteen thousand? Josephus, you're padding your numbers again. Archaeological excavation shows that four hundred people at most lived in Nazareth at that time.[52]

With that, I'm going to scuttle the nonsense that's been floating around about Nazareth—and the word "Nazarene." A little settlement of perhaps three hundred souls was Jesus's home, and it has nothing to do with Nazirites, those people who made a vow and set themselves apart in God's service. The root of the word Nazareth is NCR (*nun-tzadhe-resh*). Nazirite, on the other hand, comes from the root NZR (*nun-zayin-resh*). Their sounds are entirely different: "Nazarene," Notz-REE vs. "Nazirite," na-ZEER. It is inconceivable that na-ZEER could have morphed into Notz-REE. Confirmation comes from outside the New Testament. First examine Acts 24:5, where the agent of the high priest refers to Paul as "a ringleader of the Nazarene sect." Again Jewish rabbinical writings call Jesus's followers *Notzerim*, obviously from the same name the Jewish establishment uses in Acts. Again this is spelled with a *tzadhe*, indicating an origin from Nazareth; a *zayin* would be necessary if it came from Nazirite. Even recording these traditions a century or so after the fact, Jews knew their *zayins* from their *tzadhes*.

Poor muddle-headed Epiphanius also knows better. He tells us that the Nazarenes got their name from Jesus the Nazarene (because he grew up in Nazareth), not from *Naziraeans*, which means "those who are sanctified."[53]

St. Helena did not create Nazareth in an empty field to give Jesus "the Nazirite" a home, as the faddists insist. There was a village—archaeology shows it. It was small, covering an area of about four hectares, with no paved streets or public structures from the early Roman period.

> "On the outskirts of the village, traces of terracing have been found, as has evidence of a vineyard tower. Inside the village, wine-pressing vats with straining depressions, fermenting vats, and depressions to hold storage jars, along with grinding stones and silos are complemented by simple locally made pottery and household items. A few stone vessel fragments have been found."[54]

There was even a *mikveh* (ritual bath), which Jesus's neighbors would have used.[55] So much for Nazareth not existing. It is worth checking the book cited (Crossan and Reed). It has a beautiful painting of the Nazareth of Jesus's time with all the features listed and discussed.

Speaking of ritual baths, archaeology records that Galileans observed other Jewish rules, such as abstaining from pork, using stone vessels for rituals, and burying their dead in cist graves. There are no *mikvaot* in Capernaum—they had the lake. Ritual bathing had to be in living water, as in the case of John the Baptist. It is hardly surprising that using living water survived in the baptismal rites of the Ebionites. The *Didache* (the manual of instruction for Jesus's followers) says its readers must baptize "in living water." Peter likewise says: "But every one of you shall be baptized in ever flowing waters."[56]

The city of Sepphoris sits on a hill. Clearly visible from the ridge above Nazareth, you could walk there in an hour, something Jesus would have often done. Either he or his father (Matthew 13:55 and Mark 6:3 disagree) was a *tekton,* usually rendered carpenter, although it actually meant someone with broad skills in the building trade. Since Herod Antipas transformed Sepphoris from a sleepy provincial town to "the ornament of all Galilee" during Jesus's youth, their services would have been needed for that massive project.[57] The Gospels never once mention Sepphoris, but, on launching his career, Jesus had good reason to shun Herod's power centers, particularly after Herod executed John the Baptist.

Jesus stayed close to the borders to proclaim his kingdom. Thus he could make a quick getaway if needed. His stories are full of country activities: fishing and seeding and weeding and such. He knows, however, about the rich clothing of rulers. He knows about the courts of law—and the importance of avoiding them. His is a pastoral world although certainly not an idyllic one. We will examine that later, but first, John the Baptist.

Chapter 3

Yahya Proclaims in the Nights,
Yohana on the Night's Evenings

To make an end of sins, and to make reconciliation for
iniquity, and to bring in everlasting righteousness (Daniel
9:24, WEB).

Q umran gave birth to an idea that would profoundly affect all
human history: the idea of a Messiah. He did not look at all
like the one we know. For Qumran, John the Baptist, and Jesus,
the Messiah would, after some apocalyptic turmoil, rule over an earthly
kingdom of righteousness.

Isaiah planted the seed. After the famous "Unto us a child is born,"
the prophet predicts:

> Of the increase of his government and of peace there will
> be no end. He will reign on David's throne and over his
> kingdom, establishing and upholding it with justice and
> righteousness from that time on and forever. The zeal of
> the Lord of hosts will do this.[58]

Note its focus—peace, justice, righteousness—a focus that would ring
its changes down the ages, but whereas the institutional church (as opposed
to many ordinary Christians) lost this focus in the swamps of power, the

Yeshuites would cling stubbornly to it, finally passing the torch to later heretical groups who nourished it even to our own day. However, the prophet Daniel first developed Isaiah's hope after Antiochus IV Epiphanes desecrated the temple in 167 BCE. The Qumran sectarians watered it in the desert until it became a great tree whose branches sheltered bright visions of a new kind of kingdom. These visionary birds took wing as John the Baptist brought their message to the people. Later, Jesus would develop them even more radically.

No Mortal Ruling over You

We must sort out what John was about. The evidence is conflicted to say the least. Heretic that I am, I'm going to start with the Slavonic Josephus. Heretic, because most scholars allege that Josephus did not write it. Later hands certainly tinkered with it, but I firmly believe that the basics go back to the original author. For one thing, they illuminate one of those famous silences in the *War*. Why is Josephus mute about John, a man who made such an impact on first century Judea? He records many minor blips such as a visionary called the Egyptian leading an aborted march on Jerusalem. He left no followers. John left many, although the church buried most traces of them.

Even in their obscured state, the Slavonic passages hold a truer course through the politics of the times than the Gospels, which tiptoe around the many abuses of Rome.

The Slavonic version of the *War* contains three references to John, four to Jesus, and one to the early Christians, all of which are absent in the Greek version. I will summarize most of the first passage since Josephus's prose is verbose and tortuous. The text introduces an unnamed man clad in only his hair and pelts. There follows the most important paragraph, which I quote:

> "He came to the Jews and summoned them to freedom, saying, God has sent me that I may show you the way of the law wherein you may free yourselves from many holders of power. And there will be no mortal ruling over you, only the Highest who hath sent me. And when the people heard this, they were joyful."[59]

As in the Gospels, all Judea went out to him. He plunged them into the Jordan, telling them to stop doing evil, and a ruler who would "set them free" would be their reward. Some reviled him. Others believed.

Arresting him, Archelaus interviewed him in the presence of the doctors of the law, asking him who he was. He replied that the Spirit of God led him, that he lived on "cane and roots and tree-food" (so as to be ritually pure). When they threatened to torture him if he would not stop, he retorted that they should stop doing evil and turn to God.

A scribe named Simon objected that they read the scriptures every day: But you who came "from the forest like a wild animal" dare to teach us and mislead the people? When Simon rushed at him intending to beat him, the "wild animal" said he would not explain the mystery that lives in them. They were bringing a terrible calamity upon themselves. Then he simply walked out, crossed over to the other side of the Jordan, and continued to baptize. (End of summary).

Most important for our purposes are John's promises: he summoned them to freedom; that freedom was from those who held power (i.e., Rome and Rome's tools in Judea); he promised there would be no mortal ruling over them, only God. Where have we seen that concept? Why, in the precepts of Judas the Galilean, of course. Small wonder that material disappeared from the western version. It was a simple task for Christian redactors to omit it when copying the work. Since the Evangelists (or possibly, later hands) removed the politics from John's mission, they had to bring Josephus's *War* into line too.

They had to disguise John's mission because Jesus initiates his by proclaiming: "The Kingdom of God is at hand." If a man promoting Zealot ideals has just baptized him, then that kingdom was to be a theocracy smack here on earth. That was not the right program for the Evangelists, who were in the process of moving the kingdom up to heaven. The hopes of those who later redacted the *War* were even more firmly fixed on the sweet bye and bye, so they tinkered in the here and now.

The only other alternative is that some forger inserted this material into the Slavonic Josephus. Motive? None springs to mind. No Jew would have had the slightest reason to insert it, particularly in such an awkward spot, during the aborted reign of Archelaus. An Ebionite would have put it where it should be, during the prefecture of Pilate, and would have named the Baptist. No pagan would have cared. No Christian created it, although I suggest a Christian tampered with it.

The damning evidence has, like Satan's pitchfork, more than one prong. Firstly, the tamperer removed John's name in an attempt to make him anonymous. Why would a forger insert a narrative modeled on John but omit his name? Again, no motive presents itself, but Christian redactors had an obvious motive: scandalized by the politics of John's message, they disguised the man. Thus the western redactors cut out the whole passage and the Slavonic redactors cut out the name. All for the great cause of distancing John—and Jesus—from politics.

Their second ruse was to distance John from Herod Antipas. How? Haul their "wild man" in to face his brother, Archelaus, instead. But they had a problem: where to put the passage. Awkwardly, they had to insert it before his reign even began, since it spans but one sentence in the *War*. If Archelaus, who came to the throne in 3 BCE, dragged this unnamed clone in, he could scarcely be the baptizer of Jesus, unless he had a far longer career than other sources claim. A clever ploy, and it worked. This chronological anomaly is why many scholars dismiss the Slavonic passages.

The last anomaly is that this wild man is proclaiming Zealot ideals ten years before the rise of Judas the Galilean, a highly unlikely scenario. Nonetheless, with a nameless John moved to the beginning of Archelaus's reign, the manipulators severed all connections with Jesus.

This Zealot ideal must have been contagious. Let's revisit those who embraced it: Judas the Galilean, the first to refuse to call any man "Lord"; John the Baptist; Simon the Zealot (Jesus's disciple); Judas the Zealot (or Sicarius), aka Judas Iscariot; James of Jerusalem (Jesus's brother); and the fanatic martyrs in Alexandria, capped by that early Christian martyr, Polycarp. Following the lead of those early obscurantists, modern translators continue to disguise, delete, or otherwise obscure these facts, i.e., rendering "zealot" as "zealous." This is conspiracy, and it's alive and thriving. Keep this in mind.

Now contrast the above with the account in Ant. XVIII.v.2. Again, to spare the reader Josephus's painfully circuitous prose, I'm going to summarize: Aretas wiped out Herod's army around 34 CE. Typically, many Jews thought God had punished him: that's why losing sides always lost. And why was God punishing him? Because he slew John the Baptist. John had commanded the Jews to exercise virtue, both through piety toward God and righteousness, and only then come to be baptized. John would baptize them, not for the remission of sins, as in the Gospels, but for the purification of the body after right living had purified the soul. It struck a chord; crowds flocked to him. Fearing that John just might "raise a rebellion" (since the crowds did anything he advised), Herod decided to kill him, "to prevent any mischief he might cause." Chop, chop. Note that there is not even a whiff of John fulminating at Herod for his incestuous marriage or striptease dances by amorous stepdaughters.

Josephus Belies the Evangelists

We'll get back to Salome and her seven veils. But first, Josephus's John insists that people amend their lives before baptism. Mark 1:4 contradicts this: "John, the one baptizing in the wilderness, came proclaiming a *baptism of repentance for forgiveness of sins*," (my translation). Not one word about righteous living. It is almost as though he knew the tradition Josephus drew on and was refuting it. Luke 3:3 echoes Mark, but goes on to the exhortations to live righteous lives. Although Josephus bends the truth when it suits his purposes, there is no obvious reason why he should do so here, unlike the Evangelists, whose communities practiced a baptism opposed to John's, at least as Josephus presents it. Except, perhaps, for Matthew. He tells us that John arrived in the wilderness of Judea, proclaiming, "Repent, for the kingdom of heaven has come near."[60] That almost fits Josephus's version: almost, because Matthew has typically removed the kingdom up to heaven. If Josephus presents John's program accurately, then the Evangelists altered their material to suit their own perspectives.

We have to be careful of all texts, of course. Despite fundamentalist protestations, the word of God comes to us through the minds of men and women, of course, although the church later silenced women's voices.

Let us turn next to a curious nonsequitur passage in John's Gospel: "There was therefore a questioning of John's disciples with a Jew about purifying. And they came to John and said..."[61] Much like politicians, "they" evade the issue: they don't ask about purifying, they tell John that Jesus is baptizing. Again, like a true politician, John replies that he is not the Messiah! No one asked him that.

All these nonsequiturs are quite peculiar. What seems to be missing is the Baptist's program. Since he was purifying the people through baptism and thus rousing the ire of the temple authorities, I suspect that, in response to the question over purifying, John would have claimed that temple sacrifices were irrelevant.[62] John's practice was identical to that of the Dead Sea Scrolls: "And when his flesh is sprinkled with purifying water and sanctified by cleansing water, it shall be made clean by the humble submission of his soul to all the precepts of God."[63] Righteousness and piety were the keys.

This is implicit in Matthew. When the temple priests come to John, he exclaims, "You brood of vipers! Who warned you to flee from the wrath to come? Bear fruit worthy of repentance."[64] Clearly temple sacrifice is useless.

The original passage in John worried later redactors. If sacrifices were irrelevant, why would Jesus die on the cross? So someone deleted this material, leaving us with an awkward gap. Incidentally, there is a modern sect, the Mandaeans, who not only claim descent from John's disciples but live along the lines of John's program. Like my Puritan ancestors, they stress righteousness and piety. They also practice frequent ritual bathing in the lower Euphrates, which they call the Jordan.

Why the Jordan?

John's choice of location leads in a new direction. Here is Crossan's interpretation:

> Josephus has no mention of what is most politically explosive about John's rite: people cross over into the desert and are baptized in the Jordan as they return to the Promised Land. And that is dangerously close to certain millennial prophets, well known to Josephus and seen in detail in chapter 8 above, who, in the period between 44 and 62 CE, invoked the desert and the Jordan to imagine a new and *transcendental conquest* of the Promised Land.[65] (Italics mine.)

Among those prophets was Theudas, who claimed he would command the Jordan to part and his followers would have easy passage (to the Promised Land). Since this would have magically reenacted the crossing under Joshua that led to the conquest of Canaan, Theudas expected divine intervention. Instead, the governor of Judea cut them to pieces.

Crossan seems unaware of the Slavonic Passage that backs up his claim: "And when he [John] had thus spoken, he went forth to the other side of the Jordan," where he continued to baptize.

Nowhere does Josephus connect John with the Desert of Judea where many Essenes lived. As intimated above, John's program closely matches theirs. According to Josephus, an initiate into the order had to swear "that he will practice piety toward God and observe justice toward men."[66]

That's exactly what John demands! The famous Qumran scrolls, found fewer than thirty miles from where John was baptizing, contain rules that further confirm the similarity. Anyone who failed to observe even one letter of the law risked expulsion. The rule demanded the ultimate in piety. There was one big difference though: John took his message to the people. The Scroll Essenes lived in monastic rigor. Still, could there be a connection?

Shimon Gibson, who wrote *The Cave of John the Baptist*, is contemptuous of the idea. They excluded; he included, he points out. In any group I've ever been in there are widely divergent opinions on any matter you wish to name. Groups splintered regularly. John might well have been an Essene, and then decided that if decades of rigorous righteousness above that barren sea had not moved God to act, it was time to go out and bring ordinary people into the picture too. Maybe that would catch God's eye.

But there may have been less difference than we think, simply because the exclusive monastics of Qumran dominate our understanding of the Essene movement. Both Philo of Alexandria and Josephus, however, tell us that many Essenes lived ordinary, if righteous, lives among the people. The monastics adopted children: otherwise they would have gone extinct for lack of procreation. The second order, the one that lived in the community, encouraged marriage, according to Josephus, although they frowned on recreational sex, much like many later Christians. Considering the range of attitudes, John could easily have sprung from the Essenes, although the question can never be settled.

In any case, it is incontrovertible that they agreed on what was necessary to fulfill the prophets. Take this passage in the Dead Sea Scrolls: "Men of falsehood who walk in the ways of wickedness … shall not be cleansed unless they turn from their wickedness …"[67]

John said just that. Both believed that repenting and turning from evil would bring about God's reign of justice. Belief in that reign gripped the nation—and would lead to its destruction.

Ascetics in the Wilderness

> I stand in the strength of my Father …. I have built no house in Judea. [Statement of John according to the *Mandaean Book of John the Baptizer*, Book 19.]

Judas Maccabaeus set the pattern. He, with nine others, fled their Seleucid overlords into the desert, where they lived like the wild animals, eating nothing but wild plants to avoid defilement.[68] Note the similarities with the Baptist: life in the wilderness, fending for themselves, eating wild food, avoiding defilement. The Maccabaeans were protesting Antiochus IV Epiphanes setting up the "abomination of desolation" (an idol of Zeus) in the temple in Jerusalem. Ironically, Antiochus had added Epiphanes (manifestation of God) to his name, an insolence probably not lost on Judas the Hammer or his father, Mattathias.

Soon after that desecration, Mattathias slaughtered a Jew who was about to offer a sacrifice on the pagan altar. The book of Maccabees praises Mattathias for his zeal for the law, emulating the famous Old Testament zealot, Phinehas.[69] When the Maccabees finally smashed the power of the Seleucid Empire, they established a precedent that would fatally shape the subsequent history of Judea.

Power tends to corrupt, as Lord Acton so astutely observed. The Maccabees (or Hasmoneans, as they are often called) were no exception. Lusting for sacred as well as secular control, they displaced the rightful priestly line of Phinehas, igniting a new resistance movement: the Essenes. We have already noted that John's insistence on righteousness echoed theirs. Here we should note their attitude toward temple sacrifices as expressed in the Community Rule: "They shall atone ... for sins of unfaithfulness, that they may obtain loving-kindness for the Land *without the flesh of holocausts and the fat of sacrifice.*"[70] (Italics mine.) This recalls Jesus and his followers repudiating sacrifice as discussed in chapter 1.

Judas and his mates were not alone in eating only wild plants. We meet it again in the ubiquitous Josephus:

> When I was informed that one, whose name was Banus, lived in the desert, and used no other clothing than grew upon trees, and had no other food than what grew of its own accord, and bathed himself in cold water frequently, both night and day, in order to preserve his chastity, I imitated him in those things, and continued with him three years.[71]

That costume evokes the fig leaves of Eden.

Born in 37 CE, Josephus places this monastic flirtation before his nineteenth year—around the mid-fifties, just when Paul was active. Note the obsession with chastity. Paul was in tune with his times.

Compare Banus to our unnamed Baptist of the Slavonic text: "I live on cane and roots and tree food."[72] Both *hasids* (holy men), like Judas Maccabaeus, shared a wild-food diet. Many scholars believe that John's diet of locusts in Matthew 3:4 was really carob pods. According to the Ebionite Gospel, John ate honey cakes resembling the manna in the wilderness,[73] again a vegetarian diet.

A sect called the Rechabites followed similar rules. Their ancestor Jonadab, son of Rechab, commanded them:

> You shall never drink wine, neither you nor your children; nor shall you ever build a house, or sow seed; nor shall you plant a vineyard, or even own one; but you shall live in tents all your days ...[74]

Never build a house. In this section's head quote, Yahya (John the Baptist) proudly claims just that "I built no house in Judea." Was John drawing on Rechabite tradition?

Let us look at Luke. An angel appears to Zechariah, telling him that his wife Elizabeth will bear a son. He should name him John. The angel then decrees that he must never drink wine or strong drink.[75] Only Luke alleges that John was to be set apart *at birth* to observe either a Rechabite or a Nazirite rule. For the latter, those rules are set forth in Numbers 6:2–21: the Nazirite must not drink wine or any fermented drink, or vinegar, thus avoiding any grape product; "No razor shall come upon his head." In all traditions, when John emerges to summon Israel to righteousness, he appears to be observing a Nazirite rule, hair uncut (as well as unkempt in Josephus). In John's defense, barbers were rare in the Judean Desert. The Rechabite rule was lifelong while the Nazirite vow was only for a certain period. To compensate, the Rechabites could eat their wild food under tamed hair.

Luke adds: "And the child grew and became strong in spirit and lived in the deserts until he showed himself to Israel."[76] Nazirites didn't have to live in the desert, but, as we saw, the descendants of Rechab were nomads, dwelling in tents. Like John, they never drank wine; neither did they sow seeds nor plant vineyards. The Baptist, then, fits most Rechabite traditions. Since a Gentile evangelist would not dream up these Jewish ideas, Luke must have drawn on a Jewish source, although we have no way of knowing what that was.

Another interesting connection is Jeremiah's use of this clan. Rebuking the people of Judah, the prophet quotes God as saying:

> I have spoken to you again and again, yet you have not obeyed me ... Therefore ... I am going to bring on Judah and on everyone living in Jerusalem every disaster I pronounced against them. I spoke, but they did not listen. I called but they did not answer.[77]

The old refrain, of course. God caps it by addressing the Rechabites:

> "You have obeyed the command of your forefather
> Jonadab ... and have done everything he ordered ...."
> Therefore, this is what the Lord Almighty, the God of
> Israel says: "Jonadab son of Rechab will never fail to have
> a man to serve me."[78]

Was John looking back to this model?

And what about the Essenes? The Internet is a wonderful resource, witness the Suda project, which is translating an anonymous Greek encyclopedia (c. 1000 CE) called the Suda Lexicon. Just this morning, this item turned up: "Essenes: Jews, ascetics, who differ exceedingly from the Pharisees and scribes with reference to their mode of life; progeny of Jonadab, son of Rechab the righteous ..."[79] Whatever the rest of the world thinks of Essene origins, this lexicon firmly traced them back to the Rechabites.

In that connection, let's look at the Damascus Rule. It says that there are the "three nets of Satan." First: fornication; second: riches; third: profanation of the temple. It then instructs all Essenes to keep away from unclean riches acquired from the temple treasure.[80] Obviously, they considered the temple polluted. Other passages show that they looked to God's intervention to expel the sinful occupants there. That would have fulfilled Jeremiah's prophecy.

Recapping, we find that the Rechabites, the Essenes, and the lone hasids, Banus and John, shared a common pattern: they avoided pollution by eating natural foods and refraining from wine (except, perhaps, for the Essenes; it's unclear); all opposed the temple in Jerusalem, which they saw as sinful. The continuous practice of righteousness was essential. If you think that looks grim, you are right: "Whoever has guffawed foolishly shall do penance for thirty days," somberly proclaims the Community Rule.[81] I wouldn't have lasted an hour.

The Essenes gave birth to the *idea* of *messiah*. Judea had had no anointed kings for centuries. Although the Hasmoneans assumed kingly powers, they did not use the term *messiah*. Michael Wise points out that the mid-first-century BCE saw "texts concerned with the messiah"[82] suddenly proliferate. In his view, Qumran's Teacher of Righteousness was the prototype of all future messiahs, including Jesus, and his movement the prototype of all the countless millenarian movements that have arisen since his time, up to those who tried to hitch a ride to Heaven's Gate on Comet Hale-Bopp.

All this will be important for our study of Jesus, for the ground he shared with the Essenes—and where he broke new ground, ground that his followers tenaciously defended despite centuries of persecution.

The Roots of the Man Who Ate Tree Food

Whatever the source of Luke's special material on the Baptist, he molded it to suit his own program. The myth making is transparent: to a once-barren mother comes a son of high promise. Thanks to Luke, we now have the three "barren" mothers, Sarah, Hannah, Elizabeth, bearing three mythic sons, Isaac, Samuel, and John, all precursors, note. Isaac would father Israel (Jacob), the founder of the nation; Samuel would anoint Israel's prototypical Messiah, David; John would be the voice of one crying in the wilderness: "Prepare the Way of the Lord." For the Gentile Luke, "the Lord" being Jesus. No Jew would have had such an idea: the Lord here meant God, and God only.

Everything about Luke's John is subservient to Jesus; his father, Zechariah, is a priest descended from Abijah, lowly compared with his mystical Davidic line for Jesus. When Mary rushes off to see Elizabeth, her relative asks why this visit from "the mother of my Lord."[83] Such a visit should, of course, have been the other way around: John's father is only a human priest but the Holy Spirit "comes upon" Mary to engender Jesus. A stroke of genius: all other resurrecting gods were begotten through normal, though quite divine, sex. Luke's Jesus is engendered sexlessly and spiritually. This would have profound effects on the sexual attitudes of the church. Had the Ebionite view won, we might have been spared the massive sexual neurosis that has gripped Western civilization for the better part of the last two millennia. Jesus's original followers denied such pagan scenarios. No mythic origins grace their Gospels. Epiphanius remarks:

> And ... they say that Jesus was begotten of the seed of a
> man, and was chosen; and so by the choice of God he was
> called the Son of God from the Christ that came into him
> from above in the likeness of a dove. And they deny that
> he was begotten of God the Father ...[84]

Where might you find a prophet blessing God because he has redeemed his people, Israel? In Isaiah? No, it's in the New Testament. And who does the prophecy name? Jesus? No. Zecharias is prophesying over his newborn son.[85]

John? John has redeemed his people? That's not what the Gospels say.

There's more. The Baptist's father prophesies that God

> has raised up a horn of salvation for us in the house of
> David, his servant, as he spoke through the mouth of his
> holy prophets from of old, salvation from our enemies
> and from the hand of all who hate us, to show the mercy
> promised to our fathers, and to remember his holy
> covenant, the oath that he swore to Abraham, our father,
> to render us without fear, delivered out of the hand of
> our enemies, that we might serve him in holiness and
> righteousness before him all our days.[86]

How can that be John? Surely a "horn of salvation in the house of David" should refer to Jesus. But Zechariah is not prophesying about Jesus. And why is he prophesying things that didn't happen? Neither John nor Jesus delivered Israel from the hands of its enemies. So what is going on? Luke must be quoting a source, some earlier Baptist traditions that saw John as the expected Messiah. Luke simply forgot to bring it into line with his own Christology. Zechariah is prophesying a Messiah, not a transcendent Christ. *Recognitions* backs up my claim.[87] In it, one of the Baptist's disciples asserts that John is the Messiah, not Jesus, just as Zechariah predicts.

Why then does John deny that he is the Messiah? Scholars point out that the Evangelists were embarrassed that John baptized Jesus, so they demoted him. The fourth Gospel omits Jesus's baptism entirely.

There is something that no one to my knowledge has noticed: the last thing you are going to admit to the authorities is that you are an aspiring Messiah. That would be courting a death sentence. Like negotiating a tightrope, you must keep a delicate balance: you want the people to know but the authorities not to know. So it's hardly surprising that when the authorities were around, John would deny that he was the Messiah. Thus arises the famous tension between hiding and revealing. Jesus will face it later on.

Back to Zechariah's prophecy. It harks back to Hannah's paean when she dedicates her son, Samuel, to God's service at Shiloh, at the climax of which she cries: "He will give strength to his king and exalt the horn of his anointed."[88] The standard explanation of "horn" is that it means "strength." I am going to be heretical again and suggest that, at the very least, it carries overtones of the horn used in anointing. The ferocious aurochs, ancestor of modern cattle, roamed the ancient world with that aura of power embodied in their horns. What more potent vessel to anoint a king? Samuel fulfils Hannah's prophecy when he anoints David with a horn of oil, after which *"the Spirit of the Lord came upon David in power."*[89] The symbol is complex, and what better model could Luke's Zechariah have chosen?

Now compare Zechariah's prophecy to the Slavonic Josephus:

> God has sent me that I may show you the way of the law wherein you may free yourselves from many holders of power. And there will be no mortal ruling over you, only the Highest who hath sent me.[90]

Just what Zechariah predicts: God has sent a Messiah to deliver his people from its enemies so that Israel might serve Him in holiness and righteousness. However, at the end of Acts, Luke steals Israel's God and gives him to the Gentiles.

Considering that he's going to take the promise away, why is it here? That's a mystery I can't solve. Elsewhere, he extensively revises his sources; in the "agony," for instance, Luke's Jesus is imperturbable from his first prayer in the garden to this final surrender to his Father's will on the cross. Compare the agonized Jesus of Mark[91] (or the even more frenzied Jesus of Hebrews 5:7, who offers up loud cries and tears to the one who could save him from death).

The Elusive Mandaeans

Although the black abysses of history swallowed up John's followers, there is a curious survival in the dying marshes of Iraq, kept alive by the highly endangered Mandaeans. They claim to be descendants of the original followers of John, and there is no reason why it couldn't be true despite the sneers of many scholars. Unfortunately their works are late (and thus dubious as history), but the odd nugget glitters among the dross, such as Yohana's boast that he built no house in Israel.

In chapter 18 of the Mandaean *Book of John*, the writer recounts that Elizar had a vision in the night: "A star appeared and stood over Enishbai

(Elizabeth). Fire burned in Abâ Zâba (aged father) Zakhrià (Zechariah)."[92] Here Elizabeth, like Mary, is impregnated from on high with John. This book does not draw on Luke. He uses the Greek form, *Elisabet* (Greek has no "sh" sound), whereas the Mandaean form would have come from the Hebrew *Elisheba*, with the "l" mutating to an "n" and the loss of a vowel.

In Elizar's vision, a star falls into Jerusalem, and the sun shines in the night. The cosmos goes wild: earth groans "out of season" and whirls giddily through the heavenly spheres. Finally, the earth "opens her mouth and speaks." Obeying its cosmic command, the high priest sends to Lilyukh for an interpretation. The result, not surprisingly, angers him since it prophesies woe to the Torah because Yohana (John) will be born in Jerusalem. Furious, Elizar orders old father Zakhria to get out of Jerusalem. Not in the least cowed, Zakhria smacks Elizar on the pate, saying (cut down to the bare bones): your mother is a whore. Then off they go together, apparently lit by mystical lights.

This charming scene could possibly reflect the conflict between John and the temple priesthood. Of course, the New Testament is somewhat more restrained: John doesn't smite anyone on the pate although he does call the priests a brood of vipers. However, we should note that the charge of whoredom is not unique; in the Scrolls, the Essenes charge that the "Princes of Judah" wallow in it[93] aptly, since the Herods were notoriously promiscuous. This material hints that John inherited his opposition to many holders of power from his father, whose parents named him for the revolutionary prophet who so influenced messianic thought, including that of Jesus, as we shall see.

This happened in Jerusalem when "Elizar" was high priest. Archelaus appointed Eleazar ben Boethus to that post in 4 BCE. This contradicts Luke, who has both John and Jesus born while Archelaus's father still ruled. Nonetheless, John could have been born after Jesus. Luke designed his birth fables to show the spiritual primacy of Jesus. Anyone who would bend history ten years to put the census of Quirinius back into Herod's reign (an impossibility we will examine in the next chapter) wouldn't hesitate to do the same with John's birth date—if it suited his purposes.

If the Torah will disappear in Jerusalem because of the birth of Yohana, he is diametrically opposed to the Baptist we know. Perhaps the Mandaean work refers to the Jews being banned from the city, which Hadrian rebuilt as the pagan city, Aelia Capitolina, thus precipitating the Bar Kochba revolt. There is, however, a hint of John's concern for righteousness: wantons cease from their lewdness, although the New Testament John stresses social justice: tax collectors, don't collect more than your due, etc., while ignoring sexual laxity.

In summary: the Mandaean book of John draws on an independent source because (1) Elizabeth and Zechariah's names derive from Jewish forms rather than the Greek of Luke; (2) the Mandaeans place John's conception in the first or second year of Archelaus's reign, whereas Luke places his birth during the reign of Herod; (3) John's birth is announced to the high priest, Eleazar, in a vision instead of an angel coming to Zechariah; (4) the Mandaean John stresses sexual purity, while Luke's John stresses social justice.

Mandaean sacred scripture echoes other New Testament passages. In the Right Ginza, we read:

> Give alms to the poor and be a guide to the blind (104). If you see one who hungers, feed him; one who thirsts, give him to drink one who is naked, clothe him (105). All that is hateful to you, do not do to your neighbor (150).[94]

This negative golden rule must draw on Jewish or earlier Ebionite documents rather than the later and more challenging Jesus of the Gospels.

The Roots of Oppression

Returning from that excursion into myth-haunted marshes, we now turn to the driving force of John's career. What was the way of the law that would free Judea from its oppressors? That's easy. Again and again, Yahweh unleashes foreigners onto Israel to punish her for her sins and then restores her as a reward for just behavior. Dip anywhere in the prophets. Let's look at the revered Isaiah: after chewing out Jerusalem for forsaking the Lord and graphically picturing the ensuing devastation, he brings comfort, promising that Zion will be redeemed with justice, her penitent ones with righteousness.[95] Again in this same chapter God says (O how I love my old King James version):

> Bring me no more vain oblations; incense is an abomination to me; the new moons and sabbaths, the calling of assemblies, I cannot away with; it is iniquity, even the solemn meeting.[96]

So there!

Such prophetic passages would have burned themselves into the minds of both the Baptist and Jesus. Steeped in sacred writ each Sabbath, they would have known not only the law, but the prophets and the history of Israel. They would know Jeremiah's prophecy that the Lord would restore his people to their homeland when "search will be made for Israel's guilt, but there will be none ... for I will forgive the remnant I spare."[97] Then they would hear in the book of Ezra how Cyrus fulfilled that prophecy and sent their ancestors back to Judea.

They would also remember how, against formidable odds, the upright Maccabees pounded their Seleucid overlords—how they won their freedom, cleansed the temple, and rededicated the state to God's service. Since throughout history God enslaved Israel for injustice and freed it for righteousness, John's way of the law was to emulate the Maccabees. The people must repent and lead righteous lives, and then, repeating sacred story, they would drive the hated Romans and their toadies from the land, dedicating it once again to its rightful ruler, God. That was just what Josephus's Herod feared—John raising a rebellion with all those righteous folk at his beck and call.

The center of John's message was a quote from Isaiah: "A voice of one calling: 'In the desert prepare the way for the Lord; make straight in the wilderness a highway for our God.'"[98] All four Gospels quote that prophecy. How moving the passage; but the Evangelists perverted it. When Isaiah cried: "Comfort ye, comfort ye my people," he wasn't predicting a Greek-style "Christ" whose followers—to their shame—would persecute that very people for nearly two millennia. "Speak tenderly to Jerusalem," he goes on. And what he speaks is that her service has been completed and her sin paid for. After the passages so beautifully rendered in Handel's aria culminate in "the rough places plain," he says that the glory of the Lord will be revealed. Isaiah means the Lord God, and the Lord God only; this would have absolutely been John's understanding of the passage. And that of Jesus and his followers, the Followers of the Way. It was also a touchstone passage for nearby Qumran.

It struck a chord with the people: they flocked to John. This, of course, led to a head-on collision with the temple authorities, who, in the nature of things, had to make their accommodation with Rome. Heads would roll, they knew, if insurgents ejected their overlords. The priests were traitors, their daily sacrifice in the temple for the welfare of the emperor a visible sign of their treason. Heads did roll forty years later when the rebels seized

Jerusalem. After rolling those heads, the rebels replaced the false high priest with one from the authentic line, descended, through Phinehas the Zealot, from Aaron the priest.

In contrast to Matthew, Luke's John flings "you brood of vipers!" at the crowds in general, rather than at the temple establishment, thus disguising its political implications. The people were in expectation, Luke tells us, questioning in their hearts whether John was the Messiah.[99] Hardly vipers, the crowds would have been faithful Jews looking for deliverance from their oppressive overlords. The land groaned, crushed by its double taxes, sacred and secular.

Judaism Divided

Since all the sects—Sadducees, Pharisees, Essenes, and Zealots—will figure in this book, I'm going to examine briefly the stresses and strains in first-century Judaism. It was anything but monolithic. First the power group, the Sadducees. This aristocratic party had dominated the temple from at least Hasmonean times. Their name comes from Zadoc the priest, whose descendants had monopolized the high priesthood for centuries. Being rich, they were ultraconservative, holding strictly to the written Torah, rejecting "the traditions of the elders," which were to become such a bone of contention between Jesus and the Pharisees. Since they were both ultraconservative and politically powerful, the oppressed peasantry hated them. Although they acknowledged only the Torah, they were lax religiously—thus rousing the ire of the Essenes. When Rome destroyed the temple in 70 CE, they vanished.

The Pharisees, in contrast, held both religious power and the allegiance of the people. Generally, they were a lay group whose learning and piety commanded respect. Respect alone, of course, does not give power; that must have lain in their numbers. Certainly the Sadducees had to accommodate them to some extent, often with ill grace. Still, there was a wide spectrum of attitudes within all these different groups. "Every man is a sect of one," as someone (I don't remember who) once observed. Pharisees thus ranged from the ultraconservative to the extremely liberal. Two famous rabbis illustrate this: Rabbi Shammai was a rigid ultraconservative; Hillel, like the Mandaeans, asserted that the law simply means not doing to others what you don't want done to yourself. The Pharisees developed the twofold law, the Torah and the traditions of the elders. Following Hadrian's destruction of Jerusalem, they would codify those traditions in the Mishnah.

The Essenes out-right-winged even Rabbi Shammai. I don't know where the Torah interdicts guffawing foolishly, or even if, but the Essenes demanded absolute adherence to its precepts. The Community Rule asserts:

> Every man ... who deliberately or through negligence transgresses one word of the Law of Moses, on any point whatever, shall be expelled from the Council of the Community and shall return no more ...[100]

As fundamentalists so often do, however, they turned around and convicted themselves. We noted earlier that

> [members of the community] shall atone for guilty rebellion and for sins of unfaithfulness that they may obtain loving-kindness for the Land without the flesh of holocausts and the fat of sacrifice.[101]

That's not what the Law of Moses says, not by a long shot. It requires a lot of the flesh of holocausts and plenty of the fat of sacrifice. Although the Ebionites likewise rejected sacrifice, they, following Jesus, thought the law should be interpreted intelligently, much like the Pharisees and the authors of the Mishnah.

Senator Joseph McCarthy would have detested them—the original bogeymen:

> [The Essenes] are communists to perfection, and none of them will be found to be better off than the rest: their rule is that novices admitted to the sect must surrender their property to the order, so that among them all neither humiliating poverty nor excessive wealth is ever seen, but each man's possessions go into the pool and as with brothers their entire property belongs to all.[102]

The scrolls from Qumran's caves backed up Josephus: the Community Rule states that new recruits must bring *all their possessions* into the Community of God.[103] There they would be distributed according to need.

In contrast to the Zealots, Qumran maintained a rigid hierarchy. Nowhere do we find the idea: call no man "Lord," although a hymn in the War Rule ends: "Sovereignty shall be to the Lord and everlasting dominion to Israel."[104] That, however, was eschatological hope, not present reality. God and his hosts of angels would intervene to tip the scales in the epic battle against the forces of evil. Only then would the age of righteousness be ushered in, an idea present in the New Testament, even if disguised.

One last thing: the Qumran sectarians referred to themselves as the poor: *Ebionim*,[105] the name Jesus's followers would later adopt.

Back to John's Program

Learned and pious, he was also poor. Like the Essenes, he demanded a communist lifestyle: "The man with two tunics should share with him who has none, and the one who has food should do the same,"[106] he told the crowds. Since a loner cannot practice a communist lifestyle, he had disciples. Long active, cherishing their traditions, these followers were quite numerous, according to the Syriac version of the *Clementine Recognitions*.[107] In one exchange with Jesus, according to Mark, the high priests were afraid to deny that John was a prophet because "they feared the crowd, for all men held that John really was a prophet."[108] Paul was surprised to find them as far afield as Ephesus. Rapidly correcting their "errors," he baptized them, and they all went into ecstasy.[109]

Not only were the disciples of John widespread and active, in the Clementines, they "proclaimed their master as Christ."[110] When the author wrote that, John still had a following, and that following contradicted the Evangelists—except for a thirteenth-century Hebrew version of Matthew. In it, Jesus remarks: "For all the prophets and the law spoke concerning John."[111] Compare the received text: "For all the prophets and the law prophesied until John came."[112] In the thirteenth-century version, Jesus seems to imply that John is the Messiah promised by the prophets. There is no qualifying phrase, whereas our version cautions: "Yet the least in the kingdom of heaven is greater than he."[113] It is clear that someone tampered with Matthew to shove the Baptist into the shade.

Few other traces of John's followers have survived to our time, although the heresiologists note many baptizing sects flourishing in the early centuries of our era, some at least deriving from John. We have already noted the Mandaeans of Iraq, although some scholars disparage the idea. But then some people are obsessed with the notion that all traditional material is baseless, although archaeology has again and again exposed that bias—from the days when Schliemann first dug up Troy till Manfred Korfmann's recent discovery that Homeric Troy was huge: between four and eight thousand people lived there. Not only that, but a catastrophic war destroyed the city.[114] Scoffers never learn.

John was aware of the dangers. We read earlier in the Slavonic Josephus that "he went forth to the other side of the Jordan, *and while no one dared rebuke him,* that one did what he had done also heretofore." The original may well have said, "No one dared arrest him," since it seems some rebuking went on. That was in Perea ruled by Herod Antipas.

Herod's area? Ah, but our little kinglet's capital was Tiberias, several days' journey from this remote corner of his realm. Since John was addressing the people of Judea and Jerusalem, it may well have taken some time before Herod heard of these goings-on, particularly if John used the convoluted (or perhaps disguised) language we find in Josephus. However, the import of freeing the people "from many holders of power" would not be long lost on government spies although spies—then and now—are, at times, quite out of it.

There's good reason why Herod's watchdogs might have been dozing: the land had been dozing too, at least on the surface. After Quirinus crucified Judas the Galilean's Zealots, twenty years passed with little incident. Again, it's unwise to argue from absence of evidence. The hills crawled with bandits, a great majority of them displaced by the double load of sacred and secular taxes. None had any doubt as to why they had lost everything. Itching to overturn their oppressors, all they needed was the right leader. Surviving Zealots must have plotted while waiting for the right moment and the right man.

That's why John's message fell on receptive ears. How long it took Herod to tumble to the threat we will never know, but there is an unnoticed (except by me) clue in John, who ingenuously writes: "And John was also baptizing in Aenon near Salim, because there were many waters there."[115]

Really? Had massive crowds of repenters baptized the Jordan dry? Hardly. The Evangelist is trying to cover something up—and that something is politics. John had moved out of Herod's jurisdiction into the Decapolis. The pagan Decapolis, note. Others may disagree, pointing out that there are abundant springs around Aenon. Yes, there are, and so what? The Jordan still flowed, powerfully symbolic in the hearts of all Jews. Their ancestors had crossed this river, perhaps at the very spot where John had been baptizing, into the Promised Land. And as we saw, Crossan suggests that John was symbolically reenacting sacred story, much like the Australian aborigines reenact their Dreamtime. Things must have gotten too hot down by the Dead Sea, so he fled to Aenon.

Sacred story was real to those ancient peoples in ways we can scarcely understand, certainly not at a gut level. The best analogy is fundamentalist Christians, who are convinced that everything in the Bible is literally true. Scientific materialism did not exist. It would never have crossed their minds that the Exodus and the conquest of the Promised Land were founding myths rather than literal history. (Of course, there's a lot of myth in all history, and do we literally believe it? And there are many today who think fiction is fact; witness *The Da Vinci Code*, which is a novel!) The ancient Judeans would have been mystified by the distinction; they didn't have two categories—sacred and actual. The Bible simply told their history. It is not surprising then that only a few years after Herod lopped off John's head, another charismatic leader tried to reenact it. We have already mentioned him—Theudas. If God would separate the Jordan for Joshua,[116] why not for him? Gamaliel tells the Sanhedrin:

> For before these days Theudas arose, giving himself out to be somebody, and a number of men, about four hundred, joined him, but he was slain and all who followed him were dispersed and came to nothing.[117]

Those who followed not only firmly believed sacred story but that God would magically intervene again to save his people. And so John sent those righteous masses over Jordan into the Promised Land. When there were enough, God would help them as he had the Children of Israel.

If this was his plan, moving to Aenon must have been a political flight. Jesus would do the same, fleeing either into Gaulanitis (the modern Golan), which Herod's meek and mild brother, Philip, ruled, or like John, into the Decapolis, where the Gadarenes got mad at him for driving their swine into the sea, and even to the region of Tyre where he called that poor woman a dog. Pagan areas were barren stomping grounds for Jewish messiahs.

Who Lies about John's Fate?

History is silent as to how Herod got him. Perhaps a midnight raid across the Jordan. Illegal, but what was that to a Herodian? Why would anyone in the Decapolis care? In any case, Herod got him somehow, and thereby hangs a tale. And it is a tale, because it contains an impossibility:

> But Herod the ruler, who had been rebuked by [John]
> because of Herodias, his brother's wife, and because of all
> the evil things that Herod had done, added to them by
> shutting up John in prison.[118]

The problem? Herod executed John several years before he married
Herodias. He executed him because he feared an uprising just as Josephus
says, yet, for almost two millennia, Salome's swirling veils have titillated
everyone. Those veils are actually hiding the facts. Even Eisenman had an
agenda, so he jiggled the dates to get Herodias back in there. But she won't
go. And this is why.

Herod Antipas's incestuous marriage to Herodias, who was both his niece
and the wife of his brother, Herod Philip, cannot have taken place before 34
CE at the earliest. When Herod executed John around 29 CE, he was still
married to his first wife, the daughter of Aretas, the Arabian king of Petra. The
proof? Josephus recounts that Herod's brother, Philip,[119] died in 33 CE. Only
after that does he recount how Aretas attacked Herod for repudiating of his
daughter.[120] This can be further proved by another key date in this real drama,
the aftermath of the death of the Emperor Tiberias in 37 CE. The events of
this drama can be stretched over a period of four years, but not the eight years
needed to have Herod married to Herodias in 29 CE. Let me explain.

Sometime around the time of the death of Philip in 33 CE, Aretas's
daughter learned that Herod intended to divorce her. Tricking him into
sending her to Macheras (where John had met his end four or five years
earlier) she quickly got one of Aretas's generals to spirit her away to "Arabia."
Let's suppose that she got there sometime in 34 CE. Next, according to
Josephus, both rulers raised armies; let's allow a year for them to get
organized, which is ample. After the harvest in 35 CE would have been
a good time for the battle in which Aretas destroyed his erstwhile son-in-
law's army, retiring to Petra in triumph. Now Herod, the crowned kinglet,
was not one to sit around and sulk; he complained to the emperor, who
was, perhaps, disporting himself, as was his wont, on the Isle of Capri. Let's
say that Tiberias learned of Herod's debacle sometime in 36 CE, again
ample time for the complaint to reach him.

> "Very angry at the attempt made by Aretas," Josephus
> tells us, Tiberias "wrote to Vitellius to make war upon
> him, and either to take him alive, and bring him to him
> in bonds, or to kill him, and send him his head."[121]

Let's again allow a generous length of time for Vitellius to mobilize his two legions and march from Syria to Judea. Finally we find him with Herod in Jerusalem celebrating an unnamed festival (possibly Shavuot [Pentecost], which is in late May or early June) while his troops with their pagan ensigns continued down the coast to avoid breaking Jewish law. Since Tiberias died at Misenum on March 16, 37 CE, that gives two and a half months for the news to reach Jerusalem. With Caligula on the throne, Vitellius's orders are obsolete. He sends his army back, leaving Aretas's head intact. We can imagine a bemused governor of Syria watching poor Herod retire with his tail between his legs to his little satrapy in Galilee. (That was apparently too much for the ambitious Herodias. Smarting from the humiliation of defeat and green-eyed over the honors Caligula had heaped upon her brother, Agrippa, she managed, after much nagging, to send her reluctant husband off to Rome to ask the emperor to raise him from kinglet to king. Bad move—Caligula and Agrippa had been through a lot together and were fast friends. True to Herod's forebodings, his expedition landed the ill-fated couple in exile in Lyons, victims of the Curse of the House of Herod, which would soon strike down Agrippa too, despite imperial support.)

The times I have allowed are generous; you cannot stretch all that action back to 29 CE, which would double the time.

Some try. They dismiss Josephus's chronology, claiming that Herod brought Herodias back in 29 CE (while she was still married to his brother Philip) to be chewed out by J the B in 30 CE. But Aretas's daughter would have had to have fled to her father in 29 CE at the latest. Would it really take six years for Aretas to get himself mobilized to attack and destroy Herod's army? When you're going to beat up the creep who disgraced your daughter, you get the job done. You don't sit around and dither for six years. According to Josephus, they both raised armies immediately after the daughter's flight.

There's more. All sources agree that Herod executed John during Jesus's ministry. Pilate executed Jesus later. Rome recalled a disgraced Pilate in 36 CE, a year before the projected date for John's execution. After a precipitous massacre of Samaritans, Vitellius ordered Pilate to go to Rome, but before he reached it, Tiberius was dead.[122] The emperor's timely death thus saved two skins: Pilate's and Aretas the Arab's—years after the deaths of John and Jesus.

Guilty of many things, Herodias was innocent of John's death. The guilty parties are those who framed her, then and now: the Evangelists and their heirs, modern scholars defending the status quo no matter what the cost. These schemes only confirm that John died because Herod was not about to let God usurp his throne, insignificant as it was.

Here is the scenario I propose to account for the creation of the myth of Herodias: Tensions increased in the sixties CE. While the Yeshuites patiently awaited Jesus's return to usher in the kingdom of God, the Pauline faction envisioned a quite different outcome: their Jesus would return any moment, blasting to earth, celestial trumpets blaring; after which he would damn the wicked and grant bliss eternal to the worthy.

Earthly versus heavenly kingdoms were a lethal mix. Since John's politics implicated Jesus in earthly hopes, they had to go. Enter some bright storyteller of the Pauline persuasion. Inspired by Herod's messy matrimonial adventures, he decided to drag John into them. Who would check the dates? Certainly not Matthew or Mark, who both seized on the story.

Either Luke had not heard of Salome's swirling veils, or it didn't suit his agenda. He simply says that John had rebuked Herod because of Herodias, his brother's wife, "and all the evil things he had done," so he shut him up in prison.[123]

The fourth Gospel is even more taciturn, although it happily spouts vast tracts of verbiage elsewhere. John's John is almost as otherworldly as his Jesus: a voice crying in the wilderness, preparing the way for "God, the only begotten Son who is in the bosom of the father."[124] John the Evangelist is big on being in bosoms, spiritually of course. Herod was too fond of physical bosoms to besmirch the otherworldly light that bathes John's Gospel. His name never crosses John's lips.

Of course, it would be so sad to lose that wonderfully salacious story of lust among the Herods, a story that so inspired Oscar Wilde and Richard Strauss. Not to worry, we won't. Old myths never die; they don't even fade away. The conspirators did their work well. Like Judas, Herodias still stands convicted of a crime she didn't commit.

The church has ignored the evidence of John's revolutionary message for almost two millennia; likewise, an almost unanimous chorus of New Testament scholars rejects any Zealot component in Jesus ministry despite at least one Zealot in the ranks. Fortunately for them, they don't have to reject the "ten thousand" Zealots for the law in Jerusalem in 60 CE; a long line of translators have done their work for them. Sixteen hundred years ago, good old Jerome set the standard: his Vulgate Jews are "emulators" or "imitators" of the law, a double deception: with one small word, he robbed

Jesus's followers of both politics and passion. In the list of apostles in Acts 1:13, he simply used the Greek word *Simon Zelotes*. A deeply learned scholar, Jerome knew what these words implied. Thus the true nature of those epoch-shattering movements has been beclouded in doublethink from start to finish. (In Acts, it is *Simon o Zelotes*: Simon the Zealot.) Curiously, the Ethiopic text of the *Epistula Apostolorum* (section 2) lists not Simon but Judas *Zelotes* as one of the apostles. Is that mysterious appellation, *Iscariot*, another cover-up? Is that why Mark chose him for his myth of a betrayal in the ranks? Or to smear all Jews under that name?

Judas was not alone. The Pauline faction betrayed John and Jesus—as well as their followers, who never gave up their hope that God would one day destroy oppressive governments for all time, an ideal that Gentile Christianity tried to smother, replacing it with handouts. Handouts are not the good news to the poor.

Chapter 4

In the Silences of Josephus

hen Jesus was two or three, the stench of burning rebels spread throughout Jerusalem. Smoke reddened the eyes of the watchers—or was it their grief? And why the human pyre? As Herod lay dying, some fanatical law students had clambered down ropes from the temple roof to the great gate, reached the golden eagle the king had erected there, and hacked it down. Not only was it the symbol of Rome, it was a "graven image," prohibited by the Torah. Herod was not prepared to go gentle into that good night. Rising from his deathbed like an avenging angel, he made a bonfire of the men.[125]

We have TV; they, the grapevine. This story would have been told again and again during the long, lamp-lit evenings, particularly in lands under the Herodian thumb. On those festive trips to Jerusalem when Jesus was a child, Mary and Joseph would surely have pointed out the archway where the imperial eagle had, if only for a moment, been humbled. Since his family seems to have been deeply devout, the students' zeal for the law, highlighted by the Herodian soap opera of murder and incest, would surely have burned itself into his mind. In fact, the golden eagle episode may well have been a formative factor in his later bravery in the face of oppression.

A Dilemma

For us, the word "Christ" evokes a sacrificial savior, a concept that would have mystified Jesus and his fellow Jews. Mystified because they would have known of the mystery religions of the pagans, who both surrounded them and lived among them. In the city of Byblos, only some sixty miles north of Galilee, the citizens annually mourned the death of Adonis, their dying god:

> Throughout the land they perform solemn lamentations. When they cease their breast-beating and weeping, they first sacrifice to Adonis as if to a dead person, but then, on the next day, they proclaim that he lives and send him into the air.[126]

Mark tells us that Jesus was once in Sidon, a pagan city not far from Byblos. He would surely have been aware of these and similar rites.

I should have said that the idea of the Christian "Christ" would have scandalized, not mystified, the Jews. For them, such a "christ" would have been simply an updated Adonis, even more offensive than the imperial eagle on the gate, which had, at least, not been worshipped.

But what about that prophetic passage so movingly realized in Handel's *Messiah*: "He was despised and rejected, a man of sorrows and acquainted with grief ... Surely he hath borne our griefs and carried our sorrows?"[127] The second Isaiah here personifies an exiled Israel as a man. It was taken out of context and applied to a "christ" who was entirely foreign to the Jewish temperament.

Since both these words—Christ and Messiah—bear an indelible ideological burden, I am going to substitute the Aramaic equivalent, *Meshikha*, throughout the remainder of this book. Meshikha also means "anointed." It meant the one who would deliver Israel: that is, free it from its oppressors, the Romans and the Herodians, and bring in God's reign of justice on earth, specifically in Israel. This hope is summed up in a postresurrection statement:

> Jesus the Nazarene ... was a prophet powerful in work and in word ... our chief priests and rulers delivered him to the judgement of death and crucified him. But we had hoped he was *the one who was about to save Israel* ...[128]

This was the expectation of Jesus's uncle Cleopas, the brother of Joseph, according to that very Gentile Evangelist, Luke. I translated it myself to make this quite clear: Uncle Cleopas, who had come to Jerusalem along with the rest of Jesus's supporters, expected Jesus to deliver Israel from the Romans *right then and there.* That's the construction—"was about to redeem Israel."

Yet every translation I checked removed the immediacy from this statement. Why? Because it shows that Uncle Cleopas (and the whole throng) followed Jesus to Jerusalem with that hope in their hearts. As already noted, Luke was often more open about the politics of Jesus's ministry than the other gospelers. The church wanted that disguised, so every translator from Jerome to our time has meekly obeyed. Except me.

We can be sure that Jesus did not tell his uncle, "I'm not the Meshikha everyone expects; I'm a divine one, off to Jerusalem to offer myself as the universal sacrifice to replace the daily ones in the temple. I'm just bringing you folk along to watch." Of course, the Evangelists make out that Jesus did say he was going up to Jerusalem to die, and that the disciples were stupid; they just didn't get it. That was part of the conspiracy, the conspiracy to smother the beliefs of Jesus's Jewish followers. But *they* still believed in the traditional Meshikha when the Evangelists wrote the Gospels—and up until they were persecuted out of existence in the fifteenth century.

The Birth Prophecies

The Magnificat is a curious paean, celebrating the ancient hope of deliverance, curious since Jesus did not fulfill its prophecies. Luke did not compose these words: "[God] has succored his servant Israel, remembering his mercy, as he said to our fathers, to Abraham and to his seed forever,"[129] but that's what his Mary sings. For Luke, God had transferred that promise to the Gentiles.

Neither Jew nor Gentile would have written the Magnificat after 70 CE, when that hope lay shattered in the aftermath of the disastrous Jewish revolt: the temple destroyed, Israel scattered, and a remnant of rabbis trying to pick up the pieces in the coastal city of Yavneh. "Succored," after all, means "gave help in difficulty or distress." We saw the Zealots promise it in the last chapter. Yet Mary prophesies that Jesus will do just that, and Uncle Cleopas expected it as well. Why is it here in this Gentile Gospel? Bishop Spong suggests that, along with Zechariah's prophecy and Simeon's blessing on the newly circumcised Jesus, it is a psalm from a "Jewish Christian" religious play.[130] In any case, the source must be the literature of Jesus's Jewish followers.

Mary proclaims that God has brought down rulers from their thrones and lifted up the humble.[131] Echoes the Slavonic Josephus: John will free people from "holders of power." Whoever wrote this paean modeled much of it on Hannah's song of thanksgiving at Samuel's birth, but Hannah never promises to bring down rulers. The closest is "Yahweh makes poor, and makes rich. He brings low, he also lifts up."[132] That's just Yahweh spinning the wheel of Fortuna.

Belying the Magnificat, his own village folk reject Luke's Christ at the beginning of his career (because Luke portrays him as insulting them). From then on, his trajectory is away from the Jews. They howl for his death before the tribunal of Pilate,[133] and, as we shall see, the Evangelist ends his two-part epic, Luke-Acts, with Paul's claim that God has abandoned Israel and turned to the Gentiles.[134] Paul's God does not keep his promises. This did not pass unnoticed among Jesus's Jewish followers. In one of his speeches in the Clementine Homilies, Peter remarks, "If He changes His mind, who is steadfast?[135] So why does Luke begin his work with broken promises?

The last Magnificat promise that did not come true (but was very much in the forefront of Jesus's career) was: "He has filled the hungry with good things but has sent the rich away empty."[136] Jesus reiterates this later: "Blessed are you who are hungry now, for you will be filled," and "But woe to you who are rich, because you have received your consolation."[137] Luke was a champion of the poor, a stance that Jesus's Jewish followers would have shared. Later they proudly bore the name "Poor," the Ebionites. Thus everyone would have enough, an ideal that has seldom been attained.

To close this brief look at these survivals of Ebionite literature in Luke's infancy narrative, let us meet another prophet: Simeon, a righteous man who was "expecting the consolation of Israel." Luke's source tells us that the Holy Spirit told him he would see the "Christ of the Lord" before he died. Here is his moving benediction when he took the infant Jesus into his arms:

> "Now, Master, let your servant go in peace according
> to your word; because my eyes have seen your salvation
> which you have prepared before the face of all the peoples,
> a light for a revelation to the Gentiles and a glory for your
> people, Israel."[138]

It is sad that over the next few centuries, that light blinded the Gentiles to the glory of God's people, Israel, thus bringing Simeon's prophecy to naught.

More Myths: The Census under Quirinius

"Now it came to pass in those days that a decree went out from Caesar Augustus to take a census of all the inhabited world. This was the first census when Quirinius was governor of Syria."[139]

Surely someone else has exposed this fable, but if so, I haven't seen it: *there was no Roman census in Judea during Herod's reign.* Only Herod levied taxes, not Rome. The proof is staring us right in the face: Varus, not Quirinius, was the "governor" of Syria when Herod died, continuing in that capacity until at least 4 CE. Jesus would have been at least eight when Rome sent out Quirinius to replace Varus.

The events leading up to the census were these: having come into both a kingdom and a fortune after Herod's death, Archelaus, the typical son of a self-made man, indulged himself in riotous living and vicious oppression. Although he had learned such at his father's knee, he lacked the latter's ruthless political skills to pull it off. That was all Rome needed: it deposed him in 6 CE, imposing direct rule and dispatching Quirinius to count Judean heads (not the heads of the whole world, note). Those are the plain facts. Remember Josephus's cryptic remark that Eleazar, the commander of the Sicarii, was a descendant of the Judas who had persuaded many Jews, "as recorded earlier," not to register when Quirinius was sent to Judea to take a census. That highly censored passage about Judas the Galilean follows immediately after the fall of Archelaus,[140] not before the death of Herod.

Although fuzzy on dates, Luke did have an agenda. He was writing sacred story where "spiritual truths" trump facts, in this case Luke's determination to make Jesus fulfill the famous prophecy:

> But thou, Bethlehem Ephrathah, though thou be little among the thousands of Judah, yet out of thee shall he come forth unto me that is to be ruler in Israel; whose goings forth have been from of old, from everlasting.[141]

How those words peal out from the King James version!

Was Jesus Really Born in Bethlehem?

Bethlehem at the time of the census was an ingenious idea: it distanced Jesus's birth, both physically and temporally, from the Zealot uprising under Judas the Galilean. Matthew likewise invented a tale of a birth in Bethlehem, but both are tales, and irreconcilable. That the genealogies don't match is the least of the problems. The holy family doesn't even have the same home. Luke sets them off on a five-day trek from Nazareth to Bethlehem with poor Mary in the last stages of pregnancy, a hazardous undertaking to say the least. Afterward, "having finished all things according to the law," i.e., circumcision in Bethlehem after eight days, followed a little later by Mary's purification in Jerusalem, Luke's happy parents simply return to Nazareth.

How is it that John knew nothing of any birth in Bethlehem? In one debate, some Jews ask, "How can the Christ come from Galilee? Does not the scripture say that the Christ will come from David's family and from Bethlehem, the town where David lived?"[142] Had the birth stories been true, everyone would have known them when John wrote, precisely because they did fulfill the famous prophecy. But they didn't know. Thus we glimpse sneers at Jesus's true birthplace, sneers still remembered in John's community, if glossed over elsewhere. And with that, on to Matthew's tale.

Unhampered by Luke's bogus census, he creates an elegant solution, smacking Mary and Joseph right down in Bethlehem from the get-go. Joseph is a native son, David his ancient sire. Then Matthew brings on the Magi asking Herod, "Where is he that is born king of the Jews?" An alarmed Herod consults the scribes, who cite the famous prophecy, suitably modified by the Evangelist:

> And you, Bethlehem, in the land of Judah, are not at all the least among the rulers of Judah. For out of you shall come forth a governor who will shepherd my people, Israel.[143]

"Shepherd my people, Israel." That's not what Micah said, but it better fits Matthew's community of Jewish followers of Jesus. Again note the irony: Israel was not shepherded—except into exile and death. Still, Matthew's solution is brilliant; Mary need make no arduous trek in the last stages of pregnancy. Not only does the prophecy flow naturally from the story line, but Herod, the Magi, the massacre, and the flight make an unforgettable drama that has rung its changes down the ages and will continue to weave its spell until humanity brings down the apparently inevitable—and quite unbiblical—apocalypse on its own head.

Unfortunately the massacre is too good to be true. Josephus, who never missed a chance to slaver over Herod's cruelties, would have relished that one, the slaughter of every baby boy in Bethlehem. Of course, the king *did* murder children: his own. The unfortunate Alexander and Aristobulus went around 7 BCE, and the treacherous Antipater followed in 4 BCE, so why not spread the blessings around? Let's say that Jesus was born in 6 BCE. It would have fitted well in grisly sequence: Herod's sons in 7, the Boys of Bethlehem in 6, or perhaps 5, Antipater in 4, just days before, itching and worm-eaten, he himself died a miserable death, a climax worthy of Shakespeare.

Herod was, of course, paranoid about his shaky claim to the throne. He married (and murdered) a Hasmonean princess to try to legitimize his claim to the throne. According to Julius Africanus he also burned all the genealogical records. Poor Herod: he thought he might appear of noble origin if no others could trace their lineage back to the patriarchs.[144] What a waste. Everyone knew he was an Idumaean, not a Jew. What it did do, however, was to make it impossible for anyone to prove descent from Aaron or Zadoc or David.

Since Herod's fears were common currency, Josephus would never have ignored such a bloodbath in Bethlehem, that town so sacred to Jewish history. Indeed, had Matthew's story been true, there wouldn't have been a Jew anywhere in the world who would not have known of it.

Now we must turn to a source that has been virtually silenced. It first appeared in a lecture by Shlomo Pines published in Jerusalem in 1966, *The Jewish Christians According to a New Source.* This document is entitled *Tathbit Dala'il Nubuwwat Sayyidina Mahammad,* "The Establishment of Proofs for the Prophethood of Our Master Mohammad." Pines tells us that the tenth-century author 'Abd al-Jabbar incorporated and adapted for his own purposes writings that reflected "the views and traditions of a Jewish Christian community ..."[145] I will refer to this document as the *Tathbit.*

The scholarly establishment violently attacked Pines for this paper, and then quashed it in a conspiracy of silence. It is out of print and rare and, as pointed out earlier, the publishers refused me permission to quote from it. Until recently, only Jewish scholars such as Hyam Maccoby discussed it.

In 2004, Gabriel Said Reynolds published a book that dismisses Pines's view, claiming that everything in the *Tathbit* is of Muslim origin. Reynolds alludes to apocryphal Gospel quotations contained in text but never explains why Muslim scholars would cherish and recopy at least two, if not more, apocryphal Christian Gospels for four centuries. Small wonder, since the likelihood is nil.[146] I found no listing for an English translation of the *Tathbit*. On checking with his publisher, Brill, I found out why. There was none then. However, in 2010, Reynolds published selections from it.[147] I have only had time to scan through parts of it, but I suspect I could count on my fingers the number of people who know that it contains excerpts from otherwise unknown apocryphal Gospels—excerpts that would be invaluable for comparative New Testament studies.

Most Christian scholars have maintained a thunderous silence, no doubt because the *Tathbit* contains an alternative view of the development of Christianity through the eyes of "Jewish Christians." This is a shame. In this work are the voices, views, writings, and Gospel quotes of Jesus's Jewish followers. Our other surviving sources are hostile reports by the church fathers, with one major exception, the Clementine literature. For the rest, manuscript bonfires illumined many a night.

Why has the establishment silenced those voices? Why the conspiracy? For one thing, Jesus's original followers firmly believed that he died trying to institute a world of justice. They were appalled at the idea of his death being a bloody sacrifice to God to atone for our sins—the central tenet of Pauline Christianity. If Jesus were going to come back, he would have done so long ago to dispose of this idea once and for all. It would never have occurred to him, or his brother James, or Peter, that his heavenly Father would commit such incredible parental abuse (with thanks to Bishop Spong for pointing out the abusive aspect of the atonement). Besides, God had banned human sacrifices centuries earlier.[148]

Some scholars defy the norm. In *The Ways That Never Parted*, John Gager writes, "we need to be conscious of what recent cultural critics have called 'master narratives,' in particular their power to distort our picture of the past."[149] Gager points to one fallacy of that "master narrative": "*The evidence for the persistence of various strands of Jewish Christianity is overwhelming ...*" Carleton Paget's claim that "evidence for the existence of such [Jewish Christian] sects beyond the fifth century is almost nonexistent" [is] *manifestly without merit*, as Crone and numerous others have shown."[150] (Italics mine.) These voices still cry unheard in the wilderness, but with this book I am adding mine.

Back to the ignored *Tathbit*. It contains a fascinating quote from an apocryphal Gospel about Joseph's jaunt to Egypt. Interestingly, it knows of no Herodian massacre. It tells us that eight days after circumcising Jesus, Joseph took his wife and son to Egypt where they stayed for twelve years. Then they returned to Jerusalem.[151]

Perhaps the gospel they referred to is the original Ebionite Gospel on which Matthew's community based their later version. (Howls from scholars here.) It cannot be the other way around: in Matthew there is nothing about circumcision. They stay in Egypt at the most three years, returning on hearing of Herod's death, when they avoid not only Jerusalem, but also Judea, because Joseph is afraid of Herod's son, Archelaus. At any rate, Jesus's Jewish followers in the East also remembered a visit to Egypt with, apparently, no reason given. (Unless Muslims kept copies of apocryphal Nazarene Gospels in Tehran's archives, as Said seems to assume. Orthodox Christians certainly didn't.)

Where did Matthew's Magi come from? Persia? That was their original homeland. Pliny tells us a little about this tribe of seers.[152] Among other tittle-tattle, he tells us that one of their ploys was claiming that the gods did not "obey or appear to those with freckles," which was why poor Nero got excluded. And so we learn that Nero had freckles, something we'd never guess from looking at his statues. But Tiridates, who was apparently both the king of Armenia and a magus, brought the Magi with him and initiated Nero into their magic banquets. Thus the Magi paying homage to Jesus, the new "King of the Jews," would not have appeared as particularly unusual to readers of Matthew's Gospel.

However, the newly conquered Tiridates had not come willingly: Nero brought him and his train to appear in his triumph. Magi didn't just up and say, "Let's go and pay homage to this or that king." This particular event may have been the germ of Matthew's idea—Jesus is one-upping Nero, and the timing is just about right. If he wrote his Gospel around 80 CE, that gives fifteen years for the earlier story to have made the rounds of empire and, considering Nero's notoriety, juicy tidbits about him, including his freckles, would have been a staple of the Roman grapevine.

"You'll never guess what I heard yesterday about Caesar Nero!"

"No! What?"

"Magi came all the way from Armenia to pay homage to him, and do you know why the gods are so mean to him?"

"Do tell."

"His freckles, my dear, that's what the magi say, his freckles!"

"Goodness gracious, who would have thought?"

But the implications are profound: why would these famous magicians come all that way to pay homage to a newborn king of the Jews, a king who would never rule over them, a king, in fact, who could be no more than a Roman patsy in an insignificant state?

Matthew is raising Jesus to mythic proportions. At the very least, he is a divinely appointed king, since the heavens foretell his birth. But something is quite out-of-whack: Jesus never fulfills the Magi's prophecy; he never becomes the king of the Jews. Nor, back to Luke, does he fulfill Gabriel's prophecy to Mary that he would reign over the house of Jacob forever in *an everlasting kingdom.*[153] That puts a millennial spin on the old prophecies. Yet how could Luke even think he would reign over the house of Jacob, let alone for a millennium? After 70 CE, that house was scattered to the winds.

Both Evangelists are struggling to fit the emerging mythology of Jesus as a dying god into the Jewish prophetic tradition, and a very uncomfortable fit it is. Ezekiel would have had a fit, not to mention all the other prophets, including Moses, who slew Israelites for lesser lapses. After all, the Children of Israel only worshipped a cow. To worship God's Son was an unthinkable blasphemy.

God's Son, Joseph's Son, or Bastard?

> Cerinthus ... represented Jesus as having not been born of a virgin, but as being the son of Joseph and Mary according to the ordinary course of human generation, while he nevertheless was more righteous, prudent, and wise than other men. (Irenaeus: *Against Heresies*, Book I, chapter XXVI).

In the beginning, they bickered about it; then they swept it under the rug. The Ebionites claimed that Joseph was the father ("he was begotten of the seed of a man ... And they deny that he was begotten of God the Father ..."[154]). Other Jews, as well as pagans, claimed that Jesus was illegitimate: fathered by a man, not a ghost, holy or otherwise. Traces of an irregular birth cast a shadow on every source: Matthew; Mark; Luke; John; Jewish written traditions; allegations by Celsus, the Christian basher; and the furious rebuttals of the outraged church fathers.

Matthew and Luke handle this stubborn fact in different ways, but it is clear in both Gospels: Mary was unmarried both when she conceived and when she bore Jesus. Matthew cites a [mis]translation of that famous passage in Isaiah that a virgin will conceive and bear a son.[155] It is common knowledge that the original Hebrew of Isaiah read "a young woman," not a virgin. Whatever Jesus's parenthood, Joseph acknowledged him after he was born, according to Matthew (and somewhat more ambiguously in Luke), so legally he was no longer illegitimate. But rumors of bastardy dogged him throughout his career. We must pursue this, not because sex sells but because of its impact on the nature of Jesus's mission and that of his followers.

To begin, a hot exchange in John's Gospel. Jesus is arguing with some Jews. He claims that his teachings will set them free,[156] reminiscent of the Slavonic Baptist: a way that would free them from holders of power. His opponents argue they don't need to be freed: they are Abraham's descendants and have never been slaves of anyone. (That's peculiar. What about Egypt?) After Jesus admits that they are the seed of Abraham, the clash comes: "I speak what I have seen with my father [God], and you do what you heard from your father [who he later identifies as the devil],"[157] Jesus retorts.

Now the hackles are up. They deliver their grand slam: "We were not born of fornication."[158]

Let's analyze that. Did they really take Jesus seriously? That the devil had busily seduced their mothers? Hardly. A not so meek Jesus had just insulted them. Since they aren't protesting dalliance with the devil in the family tree, their remark can only be a snide crack at Jesus's questionable birth.

It's clearer in Mark, in a passage he didn't invent since it smears Jesus's parentage. When Jesus comes to preach in Nazareth, the villagers say, "Is this not the carpenter, the son of Mary ..."[159] The names of legitimate men were *always* distinguished by a patronymic, e.g., Bartholomew, "son of Tolomai; Barabbas, "son of the father." Here Mark, in the earliest and hastiest Gospel, implies that Joseph did not publicly acknowledge Jesus.

Matthew and Luke rectified that. Matthew writes, "Is this not *the carpenter's son*? Is not his mother called Mary?"[160] (Italics mine.) All perfectly legitimate now and quite in line with: "Joseph ... took [Mary] as his wife, but had no marital relations with her until she had borne a son; and *he named him Jesus*."[161] (Italics mine.) Since Matthew was a Jew, writing for a Jewish constituency, he was careful to look after the legal niceties.

Incidentally the above shows that Mary did not remain a "virgin," since Joseph only refrained from marital relations until after Jesus was born. The Bible tells me so. It tells me again in Galatians: "God sent his son, born of a woman,"[162] Paul writes. A woman, not a virgin. Had Paul, who was obsessed with sexual abstinence, heard even a rumor of the virgin birth, he would have broadcast it far and wide.

Anyone wishing to study this matter further should consult Schaberg, 1987. She is a very concerned, balanced writer, struggling with difficult material. More concise and very readable, James Tabor treats it thoroughly, since he is concerned with the royal pretensions of Jesus's family.[163]

If Mark's villagers were that offhanded about this matter, it was quite old hat in Nazareth. Jesus had lived with this stigma since birth.

I'm convinced that this very fact—his irregular birth and the consequences of growing up with it in a small village—inspired him to reverse ideas, to turn the world topsy-turvy, which is the touchstone of authenticity for the sayings attributed to him in the Gospels. He must have been a feisty and bright little child who matured into a feisty and original thinker. Don't be led astray by the institutional church's meek and mild image, which was fostered by early scribes tampering—for instance, where originally Jesus gets angry at a leper who says, "If you choose, you can make me clean."[164] It was a simple matter for later scribes to slightly amend the Greek word for "anger," rendering it "pity." Such tiny weeds in the fields of scripture yielded our saccharin Sunday-school Jesus. The meek and mild do not drive out temple bankers, and he must have had the backing of a large number of supporters, to get away with it, who were likewise not so meek and mild. I'm planting a seed. Watch it grow.

Can We Know Anything about Jesus's Youth?

And how did Jesus grow? Whether Joseph legally acknowledged Jesus or not, he must have been a devoted father. Since tradition suggests he was an older man, my fantasy is that he fought in the Galilean resistance movement; when Herod crushed it in 40 BCE, he fled across the Jordan into the Decapolis, where he plied his trade as a *tekton* (not just a carpenter, but one having general construction skills) in exile. When Herod got into murdering his own family in a big way, Joseph had the dream Matthew records[165] and hied him back to Nazareth; and there was Mary, needing a husband. Finally after years of loneliness and exile among pagans, he found happiness. Whatever the background story, Jesus always spoke lovingly of fathers—as opposed to mothers, of whom he has little good to say. For a negative instance, see:

> When he was saying this, a woman in the crowd raised her voice and said to him, "Blessed is the belly that bore you and the breasts that gave you suck." But he said, "Rather

blessed are those who hear the word of God and keep it."[166] (My unbowdlerized translation.)

Jesus seems rude here (with not even a nod to the blessing of his mother) to make a point he stresses elsewhere: compared with keeping God's word, family is unimportant.

Education

I'm going to tackle one of the big names. Don't get me wrong, John Dominic Crossan is a brilliant scholar who has made a towering contribution to the study of Jesus and early Christianity. Nonetheless, even the best scholars have biases. Submitting his material to the evidence of cross-cultural anthropology in the introduction to his book *The Historical Jesus*, Crossan finds that "peasants are usually illiterate" (page XII) and therefore Jesus couldn't read. I'm not so sure. Cross-cultural anthropology is a very inexact "science," to say the least. Jesus was an individual born into a highly unusual culture–one that enshrined the education of children in the law. In Deuteronomy, just two verses after the revered *Shema* that Mark's Jesus quoted: "Hear, O Israel, the Lord our God, the Lord is one,"[167] we read:

> And these words which I command you this day shall be upon your heart; and you shall teach them diligently to your children, and shall talk of them when you sit in your house, and when you walk by the way and when you lie down, and when you rise. And you shall bind them as a sign upon your hand, and they shall be as frontlets between your eyes. And you shall write them on the doorposts of your house and on your gates."[168]

This was a sacred trust, enshrined in sacred writ. Unlike many others, I believe Josephus when he claims that Jews honored that trust:

> For ignorance he left no pretext. He appointed the Law to be the ... necessary form of instruction, ordaining ... that every week men should desert their other occupations and assemble to listen to the Law and to obtain a thorough and accurate knowledge of it ...[169]

With a little exaggeration, Josephus goes on to claim that if anyone asks a Jew about his laws, he will tell them more readily than he will tell his own name; this is because they are instilled into him from earliest childhood.[170] I don't just believe Josephus out of pure faith: we will shortly see *that Jesus had just this kind of familiarity with Holy Writ*. Which, of course, doesn't prove that he could *read*. But …

In Crossan's work with Jonathan Reed, *Excavating Jesus, Beneath the Stones, Behind the Texts,* he takes pains to point out the evidence for Jewish ritual practice in Galilee: proper ritual containers for food, correct burials (even in the Nazareth of Jesus's time), absence of pig bones in domestic refuse, and ritual baths. They point out that well over three hundred stepped immersion pools (Jewish ritual baths) have been excavated, mostly in Judea, Galilee, and Golan.[171] If three hundred have been excavated, there must have been thousands. All these are physical remains of the practice of the law. You cannot practice the law unless you know it, and to know it, you have to learn it. All over Galilee, people must have read the Torah and read it regularly, just as Josephus avers.

There is other evidence, much contested by the pooh-poohers. The *Baba Batra* in the Talmud tells us that Yehoshua ben Gamla ordained that teachers should be set up in every district and that children should be entered at the age of six or seven years.[172] Since Ben Gamla was a high priest shortly before the destruction of the temple (63–65 CE), this is after Jesus. But that is not all. Another text refers to an earlier time: "And Shimon ben Shetach ordained three things: … and that the children should go to school …"[173] If true, this could have affected Jesus, since ben Shetach was the brother of Queen Alexandra, who was active in the sixties and seventies BCE. Another Talmudic text maintains that hundreds of schools existed in Jerusalem prior to its destruction, which Hezser dismisses contemptuously as "unlikely to contain any historical truth."[174]

This is carrying things a bit far. Long dismissed as fable, Herodotus's "Amazons" have actually been dug up (although amputated breasts, if such existed, have long since crumbled into dust) and numerous other examples show that the ancients were not always the fabulists scholars like to make them out to be. I've already mentioned Troy. Perhaps "hundreds of schools" is suspect, but there must have been some in Jerusalem. How else could aspiring scribes learn? Later, Hezser refers to a passage from the messianic Rule of the Congregation from Qumran,[175] which rules that boys are to be instructed in the Book of Meditation and taught the precepts of the Covenant for ten years.[176]

"If this text is more than a merely theoretical ideal and reflects some reality, one must assume that the children obtained an elementary education before they could advance to the subjects listed here,"[177] (Italics mine.)

she comments, again parading her scholarly skepticism. Moving beyond Jesus's time, she cites a passage that claims that five hundred schools or "houses of scribes" existed in Bethar at the time of the Bar Kochba revolt,[178] the inference being that scribes taught students in their houses, rather than in formal buildings.

Despite the lateness of the texts (except for Josephus and Qumran) this is a significant body of evidence for the high priority of teaching children the Torah. For instance, Hezser notes:[179]

> Similarly Josephus writes that the Torah "orders that [children] shall be taught letters, and shall learn both the laws and the deeds of the forefathers, in order that they may imitate the latter, and, being grounded in the former, may neither transgress nor have any excuse for being ignorant of them."[180]

Being taught letters may mean reading, not writing. Perhaps only scribes actually learned to write. Hezser asserts:

> The focus on the reading of the Torah in Jewish elementary education seems to have been customary at least since the last centuries of the Second Temple. The connection between teaching one's children letters and their prospective *ability to read the Torah is repeatedly emphasized in Greek Jewish writings and by Josephus.*[181] (Italics mine.)

This would apply to Jesus. Then there are the examples. We are told that, while passing places of teaching, people overheard children reciting the Torah. The Mishnah ruled that if the noise of teaching disturbed their sleep, neighbors had no right to object. Their sleep? When did they teach? Hezser cites Martial, "even before the first cock-crow the teacher's angry shouts and lashes can be heard and the neighbors ask for sleep."[182] That was, of course, in Rome. The ancients must have been keen on learning to root their children out of bed before dawn. Another story tells how the "nations of the world" came and asked a famous philosopher, Abnymos of Gadara (the town with the notorious swine):

> "Can we conquer this nation?" He said to them: "Go and make the rounds of their synagogues and study houses. If you find there children chirping out loud in their voices, you cannot conquer them."[183]

There can be no doubt that Jesus's childish voice, too, loudly chirped out the Torah.

Judging from their later activities, Jesus's family must have been devout; and if Joseph was a tekton, reasonably well-to-do, but only because of the timing of a particular building project. You may remember that Herod Antipas transformed nearby Sepphoris into his capital and the "ornament of all Galilee" during Jesus's childhood and youth. Such a huge project would have needed a multitude of skilled builders. The Protevangelion of James possibly retains a memory of that when it tells us that when Mary's sixth month had come, Joseph returned from his building houses abroad, which was his trade.[184] (Sepphoris is only about three miles from Nazareth.)

The villagers might well have met in Joseph's home. "Synagogue" usually meant a meeting, not a building, at that early period. Few actual "synagogues" have been found dating to the first century in the northern area. Wherever they met, Jesus and his younger brother, James, were surely avid students—the latter's reputation for learning suffuses virtually all sources.

Let's examine the boys in turn. First there's the old Sunday school story of a worried Mary and Joseph finding their son in the temple in Jerusalem, astounding the teachers with his intelligence at the tender age of twelve.[185]

Most scholars simply dismiss this as a Lukan invention. However, he must have drawn on a Jewish source, since a variant crops up in tenth century Iran. The *Tathbit* records that

> it is said in the Gospel ... Joseph entered his house and asked Maryam: "Where is the boy?" ... She said to him: "I thought he was with you." And he said: "I thought he was in the house and beside you." Both were worried, being afraid that he was lost, and they went together to search

for him. And Joseph the Carpenter said to Maryam: "Take one road, and I shall take another. Perhaps one of us will find him." And they went full of anxiety. Maryam, his mother, found him and said: "My son ... we were anxious ... Where were you and with whom? Your father is full of anxiety on your account." He said: "I was in Jerusalem, and I studied."[186]

Two independent Gospel stories. Given the evidence I will present of Jesus's intimate knowledge of scripture, there must be a grain of truth to these traditions.

There is a third story, although from adulthood. John asserts that Jesus astounded his hearers in Jerusalem with his learning: they wondered how he knew letters, "having never learned?"[187] And a rather mysterious fourth, which we read in the story of the woman taken in adultery. There Jesus stooped down and *wrote* with his finger in the earth.[188] This story is a later addition some scribe inserted in the sixth century. Its source, however, is almost certainly Jewish. According to Eusebius, Papias used to tell a story of a woman who was accused of many sins before the Lord, which was in the Gospel according to the Hebrews.[189] Born around 70 CE, Papias knew John the Elder (author of the Gospel of John?). He also claimed to have asked those who knew the original disciples what they had said, and recorded it in five books. Unfortunately, those books are all gone.

Now the evidence from Jesus's teaching. Let me fulfill my promise about a hot little seed. When asked what the Kingdom of God was like, Jesus said, "It's like a mustard seed. It's the smallest of all seeds, but when it falls on prepared soil, it produces a large plant and becomes a shelter for birds of the sky."[190] Surely his listeners must have scratched their heads and said (to themselves, if not to him), "Say what? Mustard? That lanky weed? Birds sheltering in it? Get real. Besides, it drives us farmers crazy. We spend hours pulling it out so it won't choke the wheat." (Growing up in Nova Scotia, I did just that—before the plague of pesticides.)

The (unmentioned) crop was the Romans and Herod and their toadies oppressing Judea. Those pernicious weeds that would choke them out were people preparing to bring in God's rightful kingdom. He who has ears, let him hear. But don't tell Herod.

I love this parable. It is just so brilliant, and it has stumped everyone but me for two millennia. Of course, if I were to be truly humble, I would admit I have not checked every known interpretation, but they are mostly by Christians brainwashed by the official line that Jesus was spreading a kingdom of "heaven." For instance, note the cozy interpretation of the Jesus Seminar:[191] "This is parody. For Jesus, God's domain was a modest affair, not a new world empire." And then they almost get it: "The parable ... is also antisocial in that it *endorses counter movements* and ridicules established tradition."[192] Yes! Yes! You're almost there! Think outside the box.

And what has all this to do with Jesus's learning? Well, not only is it hiding a subversive political message, but it's a witty takeoff on scripture. Compare it with it source, this majestic passage from Ezekiel:

> Thus saith the Lord God;
> I will also take of the highest branch of the high cedar
> and will set it;
> I will crop off from the top of his young twigs a tender one,
> and will plant it upon an high mountain and eminent:
> In the mountain of the height of Israel will I plant it:
> and it shall bring forth boughs, and bear fruit, and be a goodly cedar:
> and under it shall dwell all fowl of every wing;
> in the shadow of the branches thereof shall they dwell.[193]

This is Ezekiel's allegory of Israel restored after the Babylonian exile. A towering cedar on a mountaintop is what Jesus's hearers would have expected, not a weed in a field. Had Jesus heard this prophecy only once on a dozy Sabbath day, it would have gone in one ear and out the other. Only someone well versed in scripture could have dreamed up such a brilliant parody. It certainly did not come from a cabal of scholars cobbling together a mythical Jesus.

So much for the prophets. Now for the law.

> "Now what I am commanding you today is not too difficult for you or beyond your reach. It is not up in heaven, so that you have to ask, 'Who will ascend into heaven to get it and proclaim it to us so we may obey it?' Nor is it beyond the sea, so that you have to ask, 'Who will cross the sea to get it and proclaim it to us so we may obey it?' No, *the word is very near you; it is in your mouth and in your heart* so you may obey it."[194] (Italics mine.)

Here is Jesus's commentary on this passage as recorded in Thomas:

> Jesus said: "If those who lead you tell you this: 'Behold, the kingdom is in the sky,' then the birds of the sky will come first before you. If they should tell you this: 'It is in the sea,' then the fish will come first before you. Rather, the kingdom is of your inner eye ..."[195]

Trust Jesus to add that witty touch: watch out! The birds will beat all you pie-in-the-sky types. Heaven is, of course, exactly where Matthew puts his kingdom. Who knew? Flocks of birds have been flapping up to heaven ahead of the church for almost two millennia.

You can't play around with scripture unless you know it well. Even the Lord's Prayer is based on a passage from Proverbs. That's for later. But these examples (there are more) demonstrate why Jesus's contemporaries were so impressed with his learning, just as recounted in those Gospel stories. It is also incontrovertible that, not only were his followers deeply steeped in scripture (at least the author of the Clementines was), but their reverence for Jesus's knowledge crops up again and again.[196]

Now James, who led Jesus's followers from 30 to 62 CE. After Jesus's death, he was highly respected and wielded considerable power in Jerusalem. We saw that in his confrontation with Paul as well as his embarrassing assertion (to translators) that Jesus's followers were all zealots for the law. You have to know the law to be a zealot for it. Furthermore, most sources refer to James as the "bishop" of the assembly, including the Clementines and Eusebius, that state historian of Christian origins. No unschooled man would have left such a universally recognized legacy.

Hegesippus, a second century author, tells us that when the priestly hierarchy hauled James up before the assembled people, demanding that he deny his faith in Christ, he refused. They killed him because of the universal respect he commanded, *"because of the height which he had reached in a life of philosophy and religion."*[197] Perhaps the text exaggerates how learned James was, but if he had as firm a grip on scripture as his brother, it fits.

None of this proves that Jesus and James could read. Devout Jewish boys would have learned scripture by heart (just as devout Muslims have done and still do), but someone in Nazareth had to read. Their knowledge of scripture didn't descend like a dove—and they knew their scripture. As is the way of the world, the better off were able to give the gift of learning to their children. When Joseph toiled away helping turn Sepphoris into the ornament of all Galilee, he would have made many contacts. Who better than his sons, Jesus and James, to benefit from this, thus meriting the learning not only attributed to them in those later sources but evident in their lives? In fact, both were able and confident leaders, as though they had learned the ropes early on. Perhaps that simple accident of history, the rebuilding of Sepphoris, by enabling Joseph to educate his sons, had a profound impact on the history of the world.

Julius Africanus tells us that the family compiled a genealogy, traveling about the countryside expounding it.[198] Paul confirms it: the brothers of the Lord traveled about with their sister/wives.[199] Cynic that I am, however, I wonder if they perhaps made the genealogy up. There was nothing to stop them. As we saw in the last chapter, Herod destroyed the records. On the other hand, since everyone knows everyone else's business in little villages, if they suddenly decided to claim descent from David, the Nazarenes would have laughed them out of town. Surely Matthew and/or Luke drew on those genealogies. The family also kept a chronicle, a book of days, which may well have outlined Jesus's career.

Unlike Jesus, however, James was not witty. His epistle advises: "Let your laughter be turned to mourning ..."[200] He followed his own advice, his knees as knobby as a camel's from all that praying. But I'm getting ahead of myself.

What Else We Might Infer about Jesus's Childhood

Before we examine the event that precipitated Jesus's career, let's take a moment to examine what his childhood might have been like. Devout and studious on the one hand, but with an impish sense of humor, I expect he would have been a most popular boy. Warding off the odd slur about his birth would have honed his repartee skills, which were considerable.

How I envy him: I always get those *bon mots* the next day; sometimes they're quite clever—or would have been had they come on the spot. I stand in awe of Jesus's coups. One in particular precipitated a memorable event in my youth. After supper, we had evening worship. Each of us took turns reading scripture while deep reverence reigned over the table. Once it fell to me to read the passage in which Jesus's mother and brothers came to fetch him home because they thought he was mad. When a messenger told him that they were waiting outside, "he answered them, saying, 'Who is my mother, or my brethren?' And he looked round about on them which sat about him, and said, 'Behold my mother and ...'" I doubled up in helpless laughter at the idea of Jesus calling all those men his mother. Totally inappropriate, of course, but I was only thirteen. The scene is still vivid. I glanced around at Father, Mother, and Aunt Mabel watching me in the dim light of an October evening, waiting for me to get a grip on myself, which I quickly did and went on, "and my brethren! For whosoever shall do the will of God, the same is my brother, and my sister, and mother."[201]

It's pure Jesus. From that uncomfortable memory I get a sense of how it would have struck his listeners. I suspect I'm not alone; it probably hit a few funny bones in Galilee too. But Jesus's quick reaction fascinates me. With that simple announcement, he grabs everyone's attention, memorably making a point that is central to his mission, one that ties in perfectly with that of the Baptist: righteousness leads to the kingdom.

Before we move on, the Jesus Seminar claims that this passage reflects the tension between Jesus's relatives, some of whom were leaders, and the disciples, who were not, the situation in the "Christian community prior to 70 CE."[202] The Seminar is blissfully unaware that Jesus's followers *in the Palestinian movement were not Christians.* This group of theologically trained scholars can't see that because it strikes at the very core of the Christian myth: that Jesus founded a new, salvation-based movement through his sacrificial death on the cross. He did not. In any case, pedestrian minds do not come up with witty quips. This goes right back to Jesus, not to a disgruntled Evangelist inventing snide remarks about Jesus's family.

Now to an item in Jesus's childhood we touched on earlier: the revolt of Judas the Galilean. Jesus would have been between the ages of ten and thirteen then. You will remember my quote from the *Jewish War*: "The fortress was ... occupied ... under the command of an influential man called Eleazar, a descendant of the Judas who had persuaded many Jews, *as recorded earlier*, not to register when Quirinius was sent to Judea to take a census."[203] And I pointed out that there's a gap: someone removed that earlier passage.

Now I'm going to quote from a book by a heretic I have come to treasure: G. R. S. Mead. His *Gnostic John the Baptizer*:[204]

> In describing there the events which led up to the outbreak of the revolt, [Josephus] treats of all the other religious and political movements in Palestine, even the most insignificant, contemporary with the beginnings of Christianity, and yet he says not a single word about the Baptist or Jesus. This is a very striking and puzzling

omission. Where precisely we should expect to find such mention, and where far greater opportunities occur for bringing it in than in *The Antiquities*, we are confronted with "*the silence of Josephus.*"

What actually confronts us is the "silenced Josephus." Christian scribes transmitted all his works. Not only did someone pare down the census-inspired revolt, the *War* says not a word about Jesus or John the Baptist. There has to have been explosive stuff there, but it is all gone beyond recall.

Despite the maimed Josephus, we can be absolutely sure that the revolt against foreign taxation made a deep impression on a devout Galilean youth, a boy just moving into his idealistic teens. Surely Jesus would have given considerable thought to the rape of the land, *Eretz Israel*, and to those who tried, and failed, to stop it. It is hard for us in the privileged West to understand the kind of oppression he endured. Still, could we imagine ourselves, just for a moment, as that Jewish boy, so bright and thoughtful, watching an angry rebellion swirl about him? Would we not wonder what might succeed where Judas the Galilean failed? Or would we just decide there'd be pie in the sky bye and bye? And let the birds beat us there?

Forests covered the hills ringing Nazareth when Jesus was born.[205] During his youth, they disappeared. Perhaps he helped plant the vines and olive trees that supplied Herod's rapacious court as well as upper classes of nearby Sepphoris. With no refrigeration, cities depended on the local countryside for produce. He would have seen the slow impoverishment of the *am ha-aretz*, the people of the land, and the displacement and desperation of those who could no longer pay the taxes.[206] He must have known some of them. They pepper his stories, particularly the disgruntled day laborers who eked out a precarious existence in the fields and vineyards of the rich. Along with other Nazarenes, Joseph's income probably suffered when Herod built an even more impressive capital, Tiberias, in 17 CE. That was too far to commute. Thus at about the age of twenty, Jesus may have experienced privation for the first time in his life. Tiberias meant more drain on Galilee's resources—its peasantry now supporting not one, but two cities, on top of paying the temple tax.

Transformation

Eretz Israel indeed groaned under its burdens. Yet aside from the odd bandit crawling the hills, we hear of no unrest until John appeared in all his hairiness to rouse a restless populace. Small wonder so many newly impoverished folk flocked to learn about a way that would free them from those who leeched the land dry. The prophet's fame spread to the north; the very air crackled with the expectation of deliverance, as Luke noted.[207] Many Galileans went to the Jordan, some joining his movement, according to the Fourth Gospel. And few people would have more influence on history than an unknown carpenter who felt drawn there along with the rest.

For Jesus's early followers, this was the defining moment of his career. Let us begin with a quote from the Ebionite Gospel:

> And on this account they say that Jesus was begotten of the seed of a man, and was chosen; *and so by the choice of God he was called the Son of God* from the Christ that came into him from above in the likeness of a dove …[208] (Italics mine.)

Here God made Jesus the Meshikha through the agency of the dove, not through a virgin birth. Again I must stress that the Ebionites were Jesus's and James's direct heirs, so we need to take their views very seriously indeed.

With that in mind, here is Luke's account of the event:

> Now when all the people were baptized, and when Jesus also had been baptized and was praying, the heaven was opened, and the Holy Spirit descended upon him in bodily form like a dove. And a voice came from heaven, "You are my Son, the Beloved; with you I am well pleased."[209]

The NRSV goes on to note that other ancient authorities read, "You are my Son; today I have begotten you." Now according to Ehrman:

> The verse was quoted a lot by the early church fathers in the period before most of our manuscripts were produced. It is quoted in the second and third centuries everywhere from Rome, to Alexandria, to North Africa, to Palestine, to Gaul, to Spain. And in almost every instance, it is the other form of the text that is quoted ("Today I have begotten you").[210]

Ehrman then alleges that the ending, "with you I am well pleased," was a scribal emendation to combat adoptionist heretics. Yes, those terrible heretics, Jesus's first followers! And originally Luke agreed with those heretics; in fact, they were probably his source as in so much else in his Gospel. Clearly, until at least the third century, Christians were free to believe that God adopted Jesus as his son at his baptism. Nicaea would change that.

Why has the church played down this crucial moment in Jesus's life? The Feast of the Baptism of Our Lord is tucked in on January 7, overshadowed by the high feast of the Epiphany the day before. The Ascension of the Lord is celebrated on May 25, and the Conversion of St. Paul on January 25. Why is Paul's transforming experience highlighted on a celebratory day, a twenty-fifth, while Jesus's baptism founders in the wake of the Magi? Had the adoptionists won (those who believed, like the Ebionites, that God adopted Jesus as his son at his baptism in the River Jordan), it would have been a high church festival indeed. Did the church drop this feast into that black hole to shame the Ebionites? (Or perhaps it was ashamed that John baptized Jesus.)

Now let's turn to the account of Mark for another insight:

> And it came to pass in those days that Jesus came from Nazareth of Galilee and was baptized in the Jordan by John. And immediately going up out of the water, he saw the heaven being rent and the spirit coming down to him as a dove; and there was a voice out of the heavens, "You are my son, the beloved; in you I am well pleased." And immediately the spirit thrusts him forth into the desert.[211]

How graphic: "He saw the heavens being rent." It takes a very special scene to get Mark's attention; he likes to get on with his fast-paced story. Again I translated this passage literally, not only to show the implicit violence of spirit possession but to capture the rush of immediacy, the sudden change in tense: *"[It] thrusts him ..."* This is trance.

The Evangelist would scarcely invent a story in which the Son of God is ignominiously pushed around by a spirit—and not even a holy one at that! Surely he is drawing on a tradition handed down by those first disciples, a story not even they would have invented, an experience Jesus must have described to his inner circle. Spirit possession does not befit the divine Son of God. Therefore the account must be true.

It's still an embarrassment. Here's how the NIV conspirators gentle it: "At once the spirit sent him out into the desert," which disguises the possession. Yet they claim that they are faithful to God's infallible word. I don't think so. Not here. It's a venerable tradition. Long ages before, Matthew softened it too: "Then Jesus was led up by the Spirit ..."[212] All so very civilized. Luke elevates it, making sure we know what sort of "spirit" it was: "Jesus, full of the *Holy* Spirit, returned from the Jordan and was led by the spirit into the wilderness ..."[213] When writers make such emendations, both ancient and modern, something is making them squirm.

Morton Smith, in *Jesus the Magician,* tipped me off to the implications of Mark's account. Naturally, mainstream scholars heap contempt on Smith's ideas, although it is indisputable that Jesus repeatedly employed magical practices, especially in Mark, which must be how Peter remembered it according to Papias' account (which we will look at in the next chapter). Although this is only peripheral to my theme, it does point toward something important: Jesus's charisma. Meshikhas rose like weeds in first century Palestine, flourished like weeds for a season, were cut down like weeds for their trouble, and vanished like smoke into the autumn air. But the prolific seeds of two pesky mustard weeds refused to be burnt on the garbage heap of history: the movements founded by the Baptist and Jesus. None of the powers of the first century, neither temporal nor demonic, could crush those infestations. Why did these two movements, unlike all the rest, refuse to die?

One thing was charisma; both men inspired devoted followers. John, however, could not match Jesus, whose career spawned a bewildering maze of religious ideas. Not only that: his death sparked an explosion of visions. His practices may have inspired them, since there are hints of other trance experiences in the Gospels, such as the transfiguration and the woman taken in adultery.

He was far more volatile than the church paints him. The stresses of his early years probably fueled this volatility. On the one hand, his stories are full of images of fatherly care—therefore, Joseph obviously showered him with love. On the other, he had to field the taunts about his irregular birth that haunted him throughout his life.

Like bees swarming to the queen who holds the key to their future, crowds converged on John. The excitement would have infected Jesus like everyone else: this wild man of the desert promised both freedom from their hated overlords and the long-awaited reign of justice. When I call up this scene in my mind, I can actually feel the air crackle. A hot sun beats down into this tropical pocket of earth, the lowest spot on the planet. While the crowds chatter, the rest of creation is silent in the midday heat. Jesus enters the Jordan; John plunges him under. He goes into an ecstatic trance and in that trance hears God's voice echoing a scrap of his beloved scripture: "You are my son; today I have begotten you."

What words for a man haunted by a tainted birth! Thrust by the spirit, he sets off on a journey of self-discovery.

Chapter 5

The Barefoot Heralds

Saul is told, "David is in Naioth in Ramah." And Saul sends messengers to take David, and they see the assembly of the prophets prophesying, and Samuel standing, set over them, and the Spirit of God is on Saul's messengers, and they prophesy—they also. And they declare it to Saul, and he sends other messengers, and they prophesy—they also; and Saul adds and sends messengers a third time, and they prophesy—they also. And he goes there to Naioth in Ramah, and the Spirit of God is upon him—him also; and he goes, going on, and he prophesies till he comes in to Naioth in Ramah; and he strips off—he also—his garments, and prophesies—he also—before Samuel, and falls down naked all that day and all the night; therefore they say, "Is Saul also among the prophets?"[214]

Ah, the beauties of the Hebrew Bible. Its prose treads in a trance-like beat, its mesmeric refrain: "They also, him also, he also" evoking an aged seer, Samuel, casting spells to trap David's enemies. So I tried my hand at rendering it into English. I can't say "translated" since I have no Hebrew whatsoever; rather I adapted Young's literal translation. I couldn't help but notice, during my research, how the poor prudish NIV cringed. They stripped off the word "naked," writing: "He lay that way all day and all night ..." What wicked thoughts might not a naked old Saul lying there evoke?

What has Saul to do with my story? Some scholars claim that no one remembered the events of Jesus's life and that the Evangelists modeled their account on Old Testament stories. If so, Saul's trance is the lone passage Mark might have drawn on for the spirit thrusting Jesus into the desert. Even so, it's not a great fit. Saul's motives scarcely inspire emulation. Mark's baptismal account, and its aftermath, must go back to Jesus's recollections of his vision quest in the wilderness.

(I believe that trance literally happened. In moments of intense emotion, I have heard words from the sky—literally. Once I even heard choirs of angels singing up there. I'm better now, though.)

A vision quest? Yes. Worldwide shamanic literature parallels Mark's account: the heavens open; voices speak out of the sky. The helping animal (a dove descending); the spirit-driven trance; wrestling with evil, often terrifying forces. Mark tells us: "And he was in the desert forty days being tempted by Satan, and he was with the wild beasts, and the angels ministered to him."[215] Any shaman would recognize that as a spirit journey. Similar accounts abound in Mircea Eliade's *Shamanism*.

Afterwards, how does Jesus attract followers? By his ministry of healing, the prime function of a shaman. And how does he heal? Applying spittle, laying on of hands, expelling demons—traditional techniques all. Not only that, but he passes these on. Peter becomes a healer too.

As noted earlier, trance was rife in the early church. There was something in Jesus's program that encouraged it. The Pentecost event and Saul on the road to Damascus are the most famous, but they are not unique. Paul assumes that his assemblies will go into trance and speak in tongues. I earlier mentioned him baptizing some Ephesians who did just that. He once boasted that his proclamation was "in demonstration of spirit and of power,"[216] *power* here meaning a spiritual entity. Paul claims to be possessed by Christ's spirit and not just in metaphor. "But when the One ... was pleased to reveal his Son *in* me ...," Paul writes to the Galatians,[217] a passage that has distressed many a translator. Again, "But we have the mind of Christ,"[218] and "it is not longer I who live, but Christ who lives in me."[219]

Possession dogs Jesus's career. In John, people accuse him of having a demon, but the most fascinating passage is: "And when his family heard it, they went out to seize him, for they said, 'He is beside himself.'"[220] This is even more damning because both Matthew and Luke delete it. Yet the stories must have been widely known. The rumors persisted long after Jesus's death. In an anti-Christian polemic, Celsus wrote around 177 CE:

> It is by the names of certain demons, and by the use of incantations, that the Christians appear to be possessed

of miraculous power. And it was by means of sorcery that Jesus was able to accomplish the wonders which he performed ...[221]

Thus we are going back to Saul and Samuel and the ecstatic prophets of Naioth. Such traditions range from the blowing snows of Lapland to the steaming jungles of Colombia.

Because this is uncomfortable material, I suggest there is more history in these Gospel accounts than some believe. Fortunately, a number of historians are beginning to agree. It used to be an article of faith among some New Testament scholars that by the time the Gospels were written, everyone had forgotten what Jesus said and did—except for some pithy aphorisms. Authors then combed scripture, inventing the rest of the story on that pattern. However, the earliest parts of Thomas were written around 60 CE, and the material he shares with Mark must predate that. So the first material must have been written down no later than the mid-fifties.

Eyewitnesses were still living then who most assuredly remembered what happened: Jesus's brother, James; their cousin, Simeon, son of Cleopas (Jesus's cousin); Peter; John; and the real Mark (as opposed to the later Gentile redactor of Mark) are the most notable. Since the disciples met at Mark's mother's house soon after Jesus's death, Mark was probably there too. Five prominent survivors who were in Jerusalem when Pilate crucified Jesus. They were not in their dotage. They remembered.[222]

Eusebius cites as a "firm tradition" that after the death of James,

> "those of the apostles and disciples of the Lord that were still alive, assembled from every place, together with those who were of the family of the Lord according to the flesh ... to discuss whom they should choose as worthy to be the successor to James and voted unanimously for Simeon bar Cleophas."[223]

The heirs of this group had their own Gospels, those of the Hebrews, the Nazarenes, and the Ebionites. The ancients never suggest that the events of Passion Week in these Gospels differed from our own. These were the traditions of the people who were there when it happened. Jesus's relatives were still prominent in the church when the first drafts of the Gospels were written. In fact, they were prominent in the Jerusalem church until the debacle of 130 CE, according to Eusebius, who had no love for the Hebrew faction. Were Jesus's family and his disciples so muddleheaded that they forgot the events of his life?

There is another aspect to this. One of the few remaining fragments of that almost-muzzled church father, Papias, tells us that Mark recorded Peter's memoirs. Again some scholars are beginning to take this seriously.[224] Of course, just as in the Clementines, a Gentile hand heavily reworked Mark, but *all* the Evangelists veneered their Jewish sources—and all their sources were Jewish. The living Jesus had no Gentile disciples. Papias's claim suggests that the baptismal story in the second Gospel is based on what Jesus told Peter, who then told Mark.

There is something quite thoughtful about another of Papias's remarks: "For I considered that I should not get so much advantage from matter in books as from the voice which yet lives and remains."[225] Here he tells us how he questioned those who had known the apostles, asking what Peter or James or John had said. Many preachers still traveled widely, reporting what they knew of Jesus and his disciples. That itinerant tradition goes back to the earliest days of the church.

Unfortunately, except for a few fragments, Papias's works vanished into the smoke. Again, Eusebius gives us the clue:

> [Papias] gives also other accounts which he says came to him through unwritten tradition, certain strange parables and teachings of the Saviour, and some other more mythical things. To these belong his statement that there will be a period of some thousand years after the resurrection of the dead, *and that the kingdom of Christ will be set up in material form on this very earth.* I suppose he got these ideas through a misunderstanding of the apostolic accounts, not perceiving that the things said by them were spoken mystically in figures. For he appears to have been of very limited understanding, as one can see from his discourses.[226] (Italics mine.)

Eusebius sneers at Papias for believing in the earthly reign of justice that Jesus promised.[227] The church agreed with Eusebius, so Papias's works vanished into smoke.

Desert Trance, Desert Plans

We noted in the chapter on Galilee that Herod's death ignited uprisings throughout the land—Varus burning Sepphoris to the ground while the holy family watched, sparking stories that must have illuminated many a winter night. Ten years later, the Zealot storm engulfed Galilee. Jesus's family possibly saw Zealots burn the houses of those who submitted to Rome. They would certainly have heard that God was the only rightful ruler of Israel. They would surely have known the slogan "Call no man master." These experiences would have etched themselves into the mind of a religious and idealistic boy.

Imagine those Galilean Sabbaths, devoted to the things of God. As the first star appeared in the night sky over Nazareth, did a *hazzan* mount up on a roof to blow the first notes on the shofar, warning the workers to come in from the fields? Later, at intervals, two more would sound, after which flames began to flicker in every home in the village. Observant of the law, the women had already prepared the dried fish, dates, figs, and bread that would be eaten cold at the evening meal. In the morning the families would rise and, fasting, gather to hear a leader read and comment on some passage of scripture. That was a long time for children to go without food. Did Jesus's stomach ever rumble? Did his mind ever wander to the midday meal that awaited them after synagogue? Perhaps the people discussed the selected passage, since there would have been no doctors of the law in country places. In a devout household such as Mary and Joseph's, what better way to while away those long Sabbath afternoons than with tales of a sacred and heroic past? Story, then as now, played a prominent part in people's lives, and this was their story. Perhaps some of the other villagers gathered together with them; radicals, supporting the Zealots, would have taken one side; conservatives, the other. Arguments would no doubt have been hot and heavy, as they are in Jesus studies to this day. From their later history, it seems clear that Jesus's family were in the radical camp.

Jesus would have known that famous passage in the Psalms: "You are my son, today I have begotten you."[228] The Psalmist sang just before: "The rulers take counsel together against the Lord and his anointed..."[229] These rulers, then, conspired against God's son, *the anointed governor of his people.*

Caught up in the ecstasy of baptism, hearing those words from the skies would have sent him into a wild spin. If God had chosen him, then God's world had gone topsy-turvy indeed. In that topsy-turvy world, Jesus's teaching and parables would put the last in first place, just as God had promoted a boy with a tainted birth from that nowhere village, Nazareth. There *is* a biblical precedent: Ezekiel said that all the trees would know that God had felled the high tree and lifted up the low.[230] For Ezekiel, that was Israel rising from the dust—but if a nation, why not a man? Little wonder that the spirit thrust him forth into the desert, thrust him into that very place where Israel was to prepare the way of before God. That's why John was there. That's why Jesus went there—instinctively.

A famous parable begins as a man goes down from Jerusalem to Jericho. From Jerusalem's Mount Scopus, you can see (just south of Jericho) the Dead Sea—it's that close. Yet our parable man descended from the relatively well-watered upland into the depths of a far different world. The lowest place on earth at two hundred fifty meters below sea level, the wilderness of Judea is the smallest famous desert on earth. This desert is remarkably beautiful, especially when viewed from the more favored heights. Nonetheless, not a good place to get lost. Here, fasting for forty days (according to story), Jesus would have come down to earth. Joy would have alternated with fear. What should he do now?

Whether he had been John's disciple or coworker is a question no one can answer, but the similarity of their programs suggests that Jesus learned from him. All the Gospels except Luke imply that he was working outside Galilee until John was arrested as a subversive. Matthew tells us that on hearing that, Jesus immediately went to Galilee.[231] Now he had a dilemma: how to proclaim his message yet evade Herod.

This leads us to a blind spot. Some scholars discuss the tension between revealing and hiding in Mark as though it were a literary device. Duh. Rulers pounce on aspiring *Meshikhas*. So what strategy does Jesus adopt? Parables: letting those with "ears to hear" know that he plans to institute God's reign while disguising the import of that reign from Herod and, later, the temple priesthood. Some people who asked what the kingdom of God is like were surely spies laying traps. Thus revealing and hiding is not a literary device; it's a strategy for self-preservation.

Because Jesus shines. Here is one of my favorites (in my own words): "How shall I compare the Kingdom of God? It's like yeast a woman hid in fifty pounds of flour until it was all leavened."[232] The yeast is Jesus's message, "repent," which will infiltrate the fifty pounds of flour, "Israel." Just wait till this swelling lump of righteous dough bursts its bounds, engulfing all those "holders of power."

I must thank the Jesus Seminar, whose knowledge of scripture is far broader than mine. They point out that Abraham tells Sarah to prepare fifty pounds of flour for God's messengers who have come to announce that she will bear a son.[233] Fifty pounds of flour, it seems, is a suitable amount to celebrate an epiphany.[234] Then they note that "hiding" leaven in flour is an unusual way to express the idea of mixing yeast and flour. Indeed. Jesus was making a point: the woman is *hiding it so it can work its magic secretly.* Jesus likewise conceals his kingdom message in a parable while Herod blithely goes about his business until it's too late. He who has ears to hear, let him hear.

Again:

> "There was a judge in a certain city who didn't fear God, and didn't respect man. A widow was in that city, and she often came to him, saying, 'Defend me from my adversary!' He wouldn't for a while, but afterward he said to himself, 'Though I neither fear God, nor respect man, yet because this widow bothers me, I will defend her, or else she will wear me out by her continual coming.' The Lord said, 'Listen to what the unrighteous judge says. Won't God avenge his chosen ones, who are crying out to him day and night ...? I tell you that *he will avenge them quickly.*"[235] (Italics mine.)

Jesus is convinced that God will redeem Israel, "his chosen ones," quickly, if they will only cry out to him day and night. The Gospels often recount his long and arduous prayers. (Brother James did likewise.) Meanwhile, Herod's spies would be scratching their heads, just as many other listeners would. How dare he compare God to an unrighteous judge? Welcome to Jesus's clever topsy-turvy world.

Only Luke records this parable: the revolutionary implications are all too plain. Remember Uncle Cleopas's expectation that Jesus was about to redeem Israel? Now look at a passage in Acts 1:6–7 (my translation):

> So coming together, they asked him, "Lord, is it at this time that you will restore the kingdom to Israel?" He said, "It is not for you to know the times or seasons which the Father has placed in his own authority."

That's twice that Luke clearly shows the disciples expecting Jesus to oust the Romans and restore Israel. We will later see that Gamaliel understood the aims of Jesus's followers in just that way. (With many thanks to Maccoby.[236]) We will also see the crowds expecting the same thing in the Slavonic Josephus.

Why is Luke so open? Because his two-part work is a polemic against Jesus's original disciples. When Luke wrote, their heirs, the Nazarenes, still believed that God would establish his kingdom on earth. To counteract that, Acts shows a benighted Peter, the "rock," gradually realizing that he'd been too dim to see what Jesus was about. He was Luke's perfect dupe, always swinging from one pole to the other. I've always loved Peter; he reminds me of me. However, Luke's grand scheme is why he, unlike all the other Evangelists, dares reveal the revolutionary import of Jesus's career, as (mis)understood by his disciples. Even the Thessalonians accused Paul of "acting contrary to the decrees of the Emperor, saying that there is another King named Jesus."[237] That's treason.

Parables as a code was a brilliant idea. They are memorable, particularly if they upset tradition, and Jesus thrived on upsetting tradition. Pithy stories with such twists would have caused a buzz in Galilee, no doubt also contributing to the later success of the movement, since they undermined the establishment under which the land groaned.

But Jesus needed to sort one thing out, which may be the key to the long period of self-examination, forty days or not. His dilemma? Why had Judas the Galilean failed? And the Essenes who had waited in vain for so long? What about John the Baptist?

Look at their respective programs: Judas the Galilean claimed that if they were zealous for God in resisting the census, God would help them. Didn't work. Qumran had segregated itself in holy loneliness for over a century, and God had not acted. John the Baptist went public, promising God would free them from their overlords. Herod cut off his head.

So how about the boy with the stigma? He decided, perhaps while wrestling in the desert with his own demons, that he must bring the masses to righteousness for God to deliver Israel. John's good work had brought the already righteous into the fold. He, in contrast, would go to the unrighteous: the tax collectors, the whores. Not only to them but to all those who were debarred from the temple: the halt, the blind, the maimed, and, of course, the illegitimate. He would defy the law. He had to because of his birth. Conservatives resisted him, both for who he was and for those who he included. This powerful idea kindled the inclusivity that Jesus's followers—at their best—have embraced throughout history.

The Rube from Nazareth Defies Convention

Next: how to catch people's attention. "Can anything good come out of Nazareth?" Nathaniel sneers when Philip tells him that Jesus is the one foretold.[238] The Pharisees scoff as well: "Search, and see that no prophet has arisen out of Galilee."[239] Nazareth was just about as nowhere as you could get. In the fourth century, Epiphanius notes that it was just a village in Jesus's youth, implying that it was, by his time, much larger.[240] So how was a Galilean from an obscure family in an obscure hamlet to get himself noticed?

He had models. Galilee was notorious for oddball *hasids* (holy men), Honi the Circle Drawer being a worthy example. He thought himself God's son too. Praying for rain, he got a gentle shower. He chided God— he wanted rain that would fill the cisterns and pits. He got a raging downpour for his trouble. Undeterred, he asked for a rain of blessing and graciousness. God obliged.[241]

Such gall angered the authorities. A prominent Pharisee of the court of Queen Alexandra, Simeon ben Shetah, threatened to ban Honi because of his overfamiliarity with God. In the end, however, Honi, like Jesus, died for defying authority. Honi and Jesus were far from unique.[242] Jesus's offbeat thinking was in the mainstream of the northern tradition, a proud one in the land the Israelites called the "Circle of the Unbelievers" (Gelil ha-Goyim).

Healing was another part of this tradition. Hanina ben Dosa supposedly healed Gamaliel's son from a distance,[243] much like Jesus and the centurion's boy.

Jesus healing on the Sabbath has the ring of authenticity. It is quite in line with his conviction that you go the law one better—in this case, doing good on the Sabbath. Illness is a complex matter: sufferers who feel empowered are often healed. Mark notes with some embarrassment that Jesus failed in Nazareth, which implies that he did heal elsewhere. John's message drew the crowds. In contrast, Jesus gained fame as a charismatic healer. That's why the crowds flocked to him. From that springboard, he launched his campaign for the kingdom of God.

To Set Themselves Free from the Roman Hand

The Slavonic Josephus throws the master narrative out the window. Remember John the Baptist's promise? Compare the hopes around the (anonymous) Jesus: "And many from the folk followed him and received his teachings. And many souls became wavering, *supposing that thereby the Jewish tribes would set themselves free from the Roman hands.*[244] (Italics mine.)

That's it! That sentence is why the Western version of the *Jewish War* is silent about Jesus. The Slavonic hand chose instead to delete names, leaving Jesus and John anonymous. Taking a different tack, the Evangelists disguised Jesus's plan to free Israel from its oppressors, even going so far as to show him looking more favorably on Romans than on Jews, although he would have met few Romans in Galilee. Rome's puppet, Herod Antipas, still ruled. Delete. Expunge names. Disguise motives. Those early Christians kept themselves busy!

"Now after John was arrested, Jesus came into Galilee, proclaiming God's good news and saying, 'The time has been fulfilled and the kingdom of God has drawn near; repent and believe in the good news.'"[245] Is Jesus so sure that the time has been fulfilled because of John's arrest? Tabor[246] cites a passage in Zechariah in which Yahweh says, "Strike the shepherd, and the sheep will be scattered; and I will turn my hand against the little ones."[247] The prophet goes on to say that a third will be left alive. God will put them into the fire to refine them.

Here we have the apocalyptic refining that precedes God instituting the kingdom of justice on earth. In the final week of his life, Jesus consciously fulfilled the prophecies in the chapter of Zechariah that follows this. Thus seeing John as the prophesied shepherd is quite possible—even probable.

Mark's Jesus chose Capernaum to launch his campaign.[248] Why Capernaum? With just three miles to Gaulanitis, you could flee Herod's clutches quickly. Being on the lake, you could escape by sea. It was also the farthest lakeside town from Tiberias, Herod's new capital and the seat of his power. Not only did Jesus plan ahead, he made trips to Bethsaida (in Philip's territory) and across the Sea of Galilee into the Decapolis. Scouting? Or fleeing? We may never know, but eventually he did have to flee.

Luke's Two-Part Epic

Luke has a different chronology. His Jesus goes to Nazareth, where he reads a Christianized version of Isaiah 61:1–2. With his conspiracy to de-Judaize Jesus already in full swing, Luke stops his quote with "to proclaim a year acceptable to the Lord,"[249] cutting off the next line of the prophecy, "and the day of vengeance of our God ..."[250] Originally, the whole passage promised to restore Israel, not only freed from foreign rule but with those foreigners serving God's people. Jesus comments on Luke's modified prophecy: "Today this scripture has been fulfilled in your hearing."[251]

After all have spoken well of him, even marveling that "Joseph's son" should speak such gracious words, Jesus insults them: no prophet is acceptable in his hometown. During the famine in Elijah's time, Jesus says, there were many widows in Israel; the prophet was sent not to them, but to a widow in Sidon. Then he reminds them of the many lepers in Israel in Elisha's time, but the prophet cleansed only Naaman the Syrian."[252]

This is no way to drum up support for a mission. Luke is mythologizing, and mythologizing ineptly. His Jesus begins his ministry by hinting that the mission will go to the Gentiles, a prophecy Luke fulfils at the end of Acts. The Evangelist is also maligning the Jews, at least by implication, and not only the Jews, but the good folk of Nazareth, making them reject Jesus. After such unprovoked insults, the villagers naturally try to throw him off a cliff. The problem? There is no cliff. At best, they could have taken him up a hill and rolled him down again.

We've already noted another reason for Luke's angry attack on the Nazarenes. When he wrote, Jesus's relatives were still keeping the family records there. Since they had the "wrong understanding" of Jesus's mission, Luke disparaged the whole lot. After describing Herod's destruction of the genealogical records, Julius Africanus goes on to say:

> A few of the careful, however, having obtained private records of their own, either by remembering the names or by getting them in some other way from the registers, prided themselves on preserving the memory of their noble extraction. Among these are those already mentioned, called *Desposyni*, on account of their connection with the family of the Saviour. Coming from the Jewish villages of Nazareth and Cochaba, they traversed the rest of the land and expounded the preceding genealogy from memory and from the book of daily records as faithfully as possible.[253]

The daily records of Jesus's immediate family! Oh, to find those in some Palestinian cave! But note: *Desposyni* means "the family of the ruler" (related to our "despot"). Not the "family of the Saviour." They were known in Palestine as the family of the *ruler*. That clearly tells us what Jesus's aims were and possibly why those records were destroyed. And why Luke maligned the Nazarenes.

Thus Luke launches Jesus's career on the wrong foot from the get-go. His overarching plan required this hostile reaction at the launch. His two books, Luke and Acts, trace an epic sweep from initial rejection and misunderstanding in Nazareth followed by opposition during his career, through a tentative acceptance after his crucifixion (Gamaliel's defense in Acts 5), through Peter's vision from God that all foods are clean and thus that the law is no longer in effect (a vision Luke sets in the largely pagan city of Caesarea as a bridge to the world of the Gentiles). The Gentiles can now freely share the "good news." Enter Jesus's brother, James the Just, to resist; his imposition of the four Noahide rules on Gentiles; Paul's ignoring the restrictions; Peter's shilly-shallying (no doubt historical); the final confrontation with James leading to Paul's arrest and removal to Rome. There he summons the city's Jews to hear him speak. Listening to him expound his vision of Jesus's mission, some believe, some don't. Just before they leave, Luke puts this curse into Paul's mouth (ending, as he began, with Isaiah):

> "The Holy Spirit was right in saying to your fathers
> through Isaiah the prophet:
> *'Go to this people, and say,*
> *You shall indeed hear but never understand,*
> *And you shall indeed see but never perceive.*
> *For this people's heart has grown dull,*
> *And their ears are heavy of hearing,*
> *And their eyes they have closed;*
> *Lest they should perceive with their eyes,*
> *And hear with their heart,*
> *And turn for me to heal them.'*
> Let it be known to you then that this salvation of God has
> been sent to the Gentiles; they will listen."[254] (Italics mine.)

And with that chilling indictment, Luke closes his perfectly unified account, begun by the Jews rejecting Jesus and ended by God rejecting them—chilling because it launched the holocausts of two millennia. As Peter counters: "If [God] changes His mind, who is steadfast?"[255] But the Church swept that under its rug.

Luke laid the groundwork: this was the conspiracy that stole the God of the Jews and eventually turned him into the triune God of Gentile Christianity. We will be following this trajectory after dealing with Jesus's career, as we continue to try to piece together what he was really about and thus what his followers believed.

An Enigma

> "A sower went out to sow his seed. And as he sowed, it fell along the path; it was trodden down and the birds of heaven devoured it. And other seed fell on the rock, and growing, it withered because it had no moisture. And other seed fell in the midst of thorns, and as it grew, the thorns choked it. And other seed fell on good soil; growing, it produced fruit an hundredfold." (Lk 8:5–8, my translation.)

I chose Luke's version, although in some ways I prefer Thomas because he leaves the parable an enigma whereas Luke more or less copies Mark's lame explanation. I omitted that. But an enigma? you ask. This is so stale.

Now it is. But not then. The peasants, who were Jesus's hearers, would have sat up in shock: what idiot would scatter seeds on a path? What fool on a rock? What wastrel on thorns? Today no farmer, even in our overfed first world, wastes seed in such places. So what is Jesus's point, aside from getting the peasants' attention?

The key is the kingdom movements of Jesus's time: the wasted seed refers to three of them. Firstly, Judas the Galilean's zealots went out into the open road, urging people to resist the Roman census. Rome soon trampled them under foot and devoured them. Secondly, the Essenes withdrew to the barren stones rimming the Dead Sea. After decades of seeding the land with their lonely piety, God's kingdom still languished in the desert waste. Thirdly, John the Baptist sowed among the thorns—Rome's toadies, the temple priesthood, and Herod's spies—openly promising to free the people from many holders of power. The thorns choked him. Jesus, as earlier noted, learned lessons from them all. He was one canny customer and wasn't going to be caught in any of those traps. That's where the tension between hiding and revealing comes in. He hides his seed in good soil; no one notices until it ripens and yields the fruit of the kingdom. Seed in rich soil, weeds sheltering birds, yeast hidden in a lump of dough. Jesus was a riot.

Good soil? Yes, he knew he had good soil. He had heard peasants groan under Herod's mounting exactions and long for deliverance. He had watched the people flock to John. Luke knows: "As the people were filled with expectation, and all were questioning in their hearts concerning John, whether he might be the Messiah …"[256] James Tabor points out that many Jews were convinced that Daniel's prophecy of seventy weeks of years[257] was nearly up. Thus the deliverance of Israel was at hand.

Tabor also convincingly argues that the three-year schedule in the fourth Gospel is the actual span of Jesus's ministry rather than the one year the synoptic Gospels allow. It certainly makes sense—one year is scarcely enough time for Jesus to establish himself as a potent force not only in Galilee but in Judea, where he gained some very influential supporters, according to all sources.

The *Tathbit* backs this up. "They say" that the Jewish authorities disputed with Jesus *for three years*, then brought a suit against him with the Roman authorities.[258]

Who are "they"? "A sect among the Jews considers that Jesus … was the son of Joseph the Carpenter … a just and pious [man]," it tells us.[259] 'Abd al-Jabbar speaks of them in the present tense. Since this is what the Ebionites believed, this sect, living in what is now Teheran in the late tenth century, is closely related to the Yeshuites, who didn't disappear in the fifth century as the master narrative claims.[260]

The Sign of Jonah

Although often regarded as mysterious, nothing could be more obvious than the meaning of the sign of Jonah. Here's how Matthew handles this material from Q (briefly, Matthew and Luke use analogous material that must come from a common source. Scholars have termed it "Q" for *Quelle*, the German word for source): the scribes and Pharisees ask for a sign. Jesus answers, "An evil and adulterous generation seeks for a sign; but no sign shall be given to it except the sign of the prophet Jonah … The men of Nineveh … repented …"[261]

Jesus directs this diatribe at the tools of Rome. Now recall the story: when Jonah finally preached against the city of Nineveh because of its wickedness, he declared that in forty days, Nineveh would be overturned.[262] So what did the Ninevites do? They listened. They repented. The king even issued a decree: let everyone call urgently on God. Let them give up their evil ways and their violence. Who knows? God may yet relent.[263]

They did, so God spared them. All God's people have to do, Jesus is saying, is to emulate the Ninevites: repent, and God will deliver them just as he did Nineveh. However, if you believe that Jesus's mission was to save mankind by dying on the cross, what has the sign of Jonah got to do with it? Nothing. Isn't that mysterious?

Despite Jesus's efforts, the Jewish War broke out a few decades later. Repentance had died under the crushing exploitation of both Rome and the temple. Soon after it began, the rebels burned the record office, thus destroying the bonds of the moneylenders.[264] Had the rebels prevailed, the peasantry would have been freed from the unbearable burden of debt. Instead, Rome crushed them all: lenders and debtors.

Jesus Would Have Burned Them Too

It's so nice, the Lord's Prayer. We get a holy glow. We should, instead, be sitting on pins and needles because every time we say, "and forgive us our trespasses, as we forgive those who trespass against us," we do indeed need forgiveness: we have been duped by the conspiracy, the conspiracy to betray one of Jesus's deepest convictions. Forgiveness because we have adapted Jesus's message to fit our comfortable pew. Jesus actually said: "Forgive us our debts as we also have forgiven our debtors."[265]

Jesus meant it, "debts," not sins or that fuzzy circumlocution "trespasses." To squelch any doubt that Jesus meant what he said, Luke confirms it elsewhere: "Give to everyone who begs from you … love your enemies, do good, and lend, expecting nothing in return."[266] This is not just one of Luke's fancies. The long-lost *Didache* 1.5a tells us: "To everyone asking of you give, and do not ask for it back, for the Father wishes that gifts be given to all from his own bounty." The Gospel of Thomas also confirms Luke 6:35: "Jesus said, 'If you have money, do not loan it at interest; rather give it to him from whose hand you will not get it back.'"[267]

It's wonderful that we recovered the suppressed Gnostic material from the sands of Egypt as well as the Jewish "Christian" *Didache,* which surfaced in the nineteenth century. They add immeasurably to our understanding of the early history of Jesus's followers. Without them, we would only have had Luke's record of this saying. These two independent sources show that it must go back before the sixties CE. Three streams of Jesus's followers would not have independently invented it; in fact, it is so shocking, it must be from Jesus's own lips. The *Didache* 1.4b illuminates the brutal reality of life in first century Judea: it points out that if someone takes what is yours, there's no point in asking for it back, since you cannot get it anyway. A lawless world.

The Jesus Seminar notes that the debt saying in the Lord's Prayer arose out of the plight of the oppressed poor, whose debts were "probably overwhelming."[268] Indeed they were, and their rage at this burden erupted again and again over the next forty years, culminating in the insurgents burning the record office.

This brings up another parable. Although recorded only in Luke (who had a thing about debt), it is again so shocking that it must be from Jesus's lips. It tells how a rich man caught his manager squandering property. In a scene out of Enron, his employer asked for an accounting. Like the Enron conspirators, the manager found a way to ingratiate himself with his master's creditors:

> "So, summoning his master's debtors one by one, he asked the first, 'How much do you owe my master?' He answered, 'A hundred jugs of olive oil.' He said to him, 'Take your bill, sit down quickly, and make it fifty.' Then he asked another, 'And how much do you owe?' He replied, 'A hundred containers of wheat.' He said to him, 'Take your bill and make it eighty.' And the master commended the dishonest manager because he had acted shrewdly."[269]

Uncomfortable as this parable is, it fits in with forgiving debts. Jesus's hearers would have sat up and taken notice.

Jesus was not just a backwoods bumpkin: he was familiar with financial transactions as well as forgery. He could well have learned about such scribal skullduggery while working in Sepphoris, or if he was an itinerant *tekton*, at any number of places, perhaps even Tiberias, since that was Herod's next project.

Such malpractice was not rare. Hezser notes that rabbinic sources frequently mention erasures in papyrus documents. She goes on to quote a ruling: "One whose writ of indebtedness was blotted out, witnesses give testimony about it, and he comes to a court and they draw up his confirmation."[270] On the following page she tells of a man who tried the opposite to the parable: since someone owed him money, he changed his bill from fifty to eighty. They caught him; he got only thirty.

I was deeply moved this morning. I cried as I read in the *Toronto Star* that the G-8 has just "forgiven" the billions in debt of eighteen countries; those crushed countries groan under the same burdens as did those first century Judean peasants. One reason why this happened is that the churches of the world united at the turn of the millennium to pressure them to proclaim a "jubilee year," to forgive these debts. It's quite wonderful that the responsible part of the world church has rediscovered what Jesus was really about and is acting on that knowledge. Many non-Christian lobbyists have done their part too, but it is heartening that Jesus's vision is still alive and flourishing as we approach the two thousandth anniversary of his ministry, which will be somewhere in the ballpark of 2027–30.

This jubilee year action reminds us that Jesus wasn't original. His source is Deuteronomy 15, the Year of Canceling Debts, which was ideally to happen every seventh year. At this time, every creditor should cancel all loans made to other Israelites.[271]

So what is Jesus doing? *He's going the law one better again.* You don't just cancel debts every seventh year. You cancel them period. In Matthew, the Lord's Prayer rides fast behind all of Jesus's other "improvements" of the law: not killing or not committing adultery is not enough, not getting divorce or not swearing falsely is too weak, not an eye for eye but forgive, get buck naked in court when sued for your coat,[272] and love your enemy. (We'll explain the buck-naked later.) All that separates them is the condemnation of praying like hypocrites.[273]

Of course, Jesus's ideas on debt would never work; which just goes to show that he was human.

Radical Sharing

But there was more than canceling debt. Check these two passages. First the familiar one: "Blessed are you poor, for yours is the kingdom of God."[274] *Not will be, is,* that strange idea that the kingdom is right here but unseen by the blind. And how? Turn to Acts 4:32 for the second: "Now the multitude of those who had believed were one in heart and soul. No one claimed any of his possessions for his own, but they had all things in common." (My translation.)

And there it is—Jesus's followers launched the first communal society. No wonder Mark's rich young man, on hearing the cost, went away sadly because he owned so much.[275] Yet the "multitude" willingly shared everything when they joined the Followers of the Way, later known as the Ebionites, the Poor.

This is such a significant event in political history we need to stop and savor it. Could Jesus's society really be the fount from which communist societies flowed? Mind-boggling—but not quite true. As we saw in chapter 3, the Essenes were there first:

> And if it be his destiny ... to enter the company of the community, his property and earnings shall be handed over to the Bursar of the congregation who shall register it to his account and shall not spend it for the Congregation."[276]

Should you doubt that the Dead Sea scrolls are Essene documents, Josephus tells us that the Essenes are "communists to perfection."[277]

A third source, Philo of Alexandria,[278] confirms both Josephus and the Scrolls as to their communist focus. Since the likelihood of two separate and deeply religious legalistic sects practicing communism in first century Judea is vanishingly small, Qumran must have been an Essene community.

Oh dear. The Essenes have the honor (or blot, depending on your politics) of being the first communists. Jesus was just a copycat. The establishment will now throw up its hands and cry, "There was no connection between Jesus and the Essenes."

I beg to differ. He was obviously familiar with the religious ferment that was going on around him. Even in the backwaters of Galilee, not only did he hear about John the Baptist, but he was so impressed that he trekked several days to be baptized.

Philo tells us that the Essenes lived in many cities of Judea "and in many villages and in great and populous communities."[279] Josephus concurs: they have not one city but large colonies everywhere.[280] Having once been an Essene,[281] Josephus knew whereof he spoke. Even Pliny in faraway Rome knew about them, placing them west of the Dead Sea above (north of?) Engedda (En Gedi).[282]

How could Jesus not have known about this sect that was everywhere? With his temperament, he would surely have found out everything he could about their ideas. Having done so, he made improvements, as he did with just about everything he touched. For instance, the Damascus rule states: "No madman, or lunatic, or simpleton, or fool, no blind man, or maimed, or lame, or deaf man, and no minor, shall enter into the community ..."[283]

Trust Jesus to buck convention and invite them all into his kingdom. But the communist plot? Jesus lifted it whole. Even he, with his wild imagination, could find no way to go further than giving up all your worldly goods. Well, your life. But scribes probably added that later after the crucifixion.

Although first with the practice, the Essenes were not first with that idea; that honor (or dishonor) goes to the Greeks. In his Politics, Aristotle tells us:

> In the opinion of some, the regulation of property is the chief point of all, that being the question upon which all revolutions turn. This danger was recognized by Phaleas of Chalcedon, who was the first to affirm that the citizens of a state ought to have equal possessions. He thought that in a new colony the equalization might be accomplished without difficulty, not so easily when a state was already established; and that then the shortest way of compassing the desired end would be for the rich to give and not to receive marriage portions, and for the poor not to give but to receive them.[284]

Ideas! The Greeks were big on them. Phaleas, however, never brought his to fruition, so the fame (or infamy) of the Essenes is secure. Surely they invented the idea on their own: they spurned all pagan thought. Philo of Alexandria claims that, although devoted to moral philosophy, they studied only the Torah.[285]

The Essenes share another common thread:

> Not only is their table in common but their clothing also. For in winter they have a stock of stout coats ready and in summer cheap vests, so that he who wishes may easily take any garment he likes, since what one has is held to belong to all and conversely what all have one has.[286]

Just what the Baptist ordered: whoever has two coats must share with anyone who has none, and whoever has food must do likewise.[287] Would John and the Essenes have come up with these ideas independently? You won't find them in the Torah. And what of Jesus? He went them and the law one better: "And if anyone takes you before a judge for your tunic, give him also your cloak."[288] Jesus was a hoot; that would have left the red-faced defendant clad in just belt and sandals—radical sharing to the nth degree. (Oh, oh. You get naked in court before you love your enemy.[289])

The Essenes were exclusionists. As such, they left but faint scratches on the scrolls of history, at least until Qumran. And therein lies the power of Jesus's wildly inventive mind. He founded a society of the Poor that, like him, refused to die, despite two millennia of suppression.

Since this society was active shortly after the resurrection, this was Jesus's work, not an imitation of the Essenes by a "multitude" of believers.

There's one more aspect of radical sharing we must examine: Jesus's revolutionary relations with women. Luke names three of them who walked with him and the twelve as they "went journeying from town to town and village to village, proclaiming the kingdom of God."[290] This may be why people gossiped that Jesus made friends with tax collectors and sinners,[291] "sinners" here being the politically correct word for prostitutes or fornicators. (Later, we will find it plainly stated in an apocryphal Gospel that the establishment still keeps in the dark.) In his world, as in the Middle East today, women traveling around with men who were not their husbands would be considered such. "I have not come to call the righteous, but sinners"[292] was Jesus's clever rebuttal.

So Jesus had women disciples. After his death, there were women apostles as well as women in other responsible roles until an increasingly male-dominated church reined them in. Thereafter, these women shared the fate of the Nazarenes: the church did everything in its power to write them out of history. Have you ever heard of Thecla, a disciple of Paul who both evangelized and baptized? No. Of course not.[293]

We will see these empowered women resurrect in the Middle Ages. Incidentally, it is a myth that Hippolytus called Mary Magdalene "Apostle to the Apostles." This appears in a work attributed to him that dates from the Middle Ages. Still, the risen Jesus told her to announce his resurrection to his disciples,[294] so she has every bit as much right to be called "apostle" as Paul, who Jesus also appointed in a vision. Sometimes the church has called her an apostle—when not calling her a whore.

Paul would later co-opt Jesus's career, expressing it in that powerful myth of the ancient world: the dying and resurrecting god (or goddess, in the case of Persephone), who brings life to the people. Originally, of course, this was the life-giving grain—in Paul's vision, the salvation of mankind. The tension between these two, the institutional church with Paul's mystery religion versus the Ebionites holding to Jesus's radical social program, would shape Western history. It was the latter's poverty and sharing that prompted St. Anthony and St. Francis to reject worldliness and found radical monastic communities (I use "radical" in its original sense, going back to the roots of Christianity as lived by the primitive church). Karl Marx was not immune either.

You Cannot Serve God and the World

Power struggles are the curse of humanity. As they neared Jerusalem, James and John approached Jesus privately and asked if they might sit, one on his left, the other on his right, in his kingdom. When the rest learned of this wheeling and dealing behind their backs, sparks flew. So Jesus addressed the whole group: "You know that the rulers of the nations lord it over them, and their great ones have authority over them. It is not so among you."[295] Obviously they are not jockeying for position in some apocalyptic Kingdom of Heaven. Note the tense: "*It is not so among you.*" Jesus is founding a state in which no one is to be called lord. Remember the Zealots?

There is another pertinent saying. First from Q: "No household slave can serve two lords; for either he will hate the one and love the other, or he will hold fast to the one and the other he will despise."[296] As is, this recalls the Zealot motto: either you serve God or you serve man.

Q didn't like that. It called for diversionary tactics, so it added, "you cannot serve God and *mammon*,"[297] (Italics mine.) an obscure Semitic word probably meaning "wealth." Those who don't use plain English (actually plain Greek) are usually up to no good. Remember Simon the *Cananaean*? Most Jews would have glanced over their shoulder when they heard that word, but *mammon*? They would have scratched their heads. Scribal skullduggery stalks the land.

Thomas does not add this mystifying sentence.[298] This is one of the clearest examples of how the Evangelists removed the politics from Jesus's message: those who serve Rome—the temple priesthood, for example—cannot serve God. Those who serve God will not serve Rome. Had Thomas known Q's addition, he would most certainly have included it since, of all the Evangelists, he most vehemently opposes commerce: "Businessmen and merchants will not enter the places of my Father,"[299] is his addition to the parable of the reluctant guests. Thus his omission of the "*mammon*" statement shows that it was not there in the first place.

The Hebrew Gospel of Matthew shines another ray of light into the smoke screen: "No one is able to serve two masters ... You cannot serve

God and the world."[300] Just what the Zealots believed. And no "mammon" anywhere. Why should it be? For the peasants Jesus was addressing, wealth was not even in the cards. I'm going to stick my neck out: this particular passage goes right back to the original Hebrew Gospel of Matthew that the church fathers so often sneered at. *Because it doesn't disguise Jesus's political aims.*

One more passage. After condemning the scribes and Pharisees for their lordly ways, Jesus tells his disciples:

> "But you are not to be called rabbi, for you have one teacher and you are all brothers. And call no one your father on earth, because you have one father—the one in heaven. Neither be called leaders, because you have one leader, the anointed."[301]

I suspect that the last sentence originally read, "None of you are to be called lord, for you have one Lord, and that is God," rather than "one leader, the anointed." Jesus always shunned the word "the anointed" for the reasons we have seen, so Matthew surely has changed the text. Whether read as *"leaders"* or "lords," the import is the same.

Jesus is founding a nonhierarchical society: no one is to lord it over another, and no one is to be called rabbi or father or leader. Although this particular passage is peculiar to Matthew, the attitude is implicit in his repudiation of the sons of Zebedee. How quickly the church turned a deaf ear to Jesus's explicit instructions. "Father" soon became the accepted term for a priest. Were the Ebionites able to resist? It's doubtful: it's not our nature. Like our closest cousins, the chimps, and our more distant cousins, the hens, we establish pecking orders. Sad and universal. But Jesus's vision was a noble one that has inspired reform throughout history—as it still does today.

Even Josephus, the emperor's arch-toady wrote, "[God] ordained our government to be ... a Theocracy, by ascribing the authority and the power to God ..."[302] Here, Josephus agrees with the Zealots, forgetting his earlier contempt for their views. This is treading dangerous waters, but the Flavian emperors would never have read that book since it is a defense of Judaism.

And don't forget James of Jerusalem. Obscured by historians though it is, James died because he was the head of the many thousands of Zealots in Jerusalem and thus a political threat to his assassin, Ananus, that temple high priest and tool of Rome.

Nor Polycarp, who died for the Zealot ideal: refusing to call Caesar "Lord." Whether he, like the Zealots, believed that God was the only rightful ruler is not clear, but he was obeying Jesus's directives, disguised as they are in the surviving records. Later, we will see that Gentile Christians inherited the Zealots' fanatic intolerance. However, the Zealots and Polycarp were at opposite poles: violence versus nonviolence. We will learn Jesus's attitude on the Mount of Olives.

The Party

Forget the grim Zealots. Let's party!

Jesus must be one of the few reformers who liked to live it up. It's just radical sharing: the fellowship of good times, of banqueting and even—dare I say it—drinking, a side of Jesus that most churches ignore. (The church I go to celebrates Jesus's sociability.)

It's in the Gospels. Again and again he parties with his followers, often with the rejects of society, something that endears him to me since it's how I've often felt. The children sitting in the marketplace is a case in point, but there is an important variant that is still in the shadows. This is from the *Tathbit*:

> In [the Gospel] Christ says, "Compare the sitting of this evil tribe to children sitting in the market-place [who] are called by their companions: We sang for you and you did not dance, and we wailed for you, and you did not weep. John came to you, who did not eat or drink. And you said: He does not eat or drink and the Son of Man came to you, an eater and a drinker, and you said: He is an eater and a drinker who goes into the houses of fornicators and keeps company with sinners.[303] (cf. Mt 11:16–18 and Lk 7:31–34.)

Although all versions imply that Jesus drinks heartily, nowhere does he deny that he likes his wine. But the meaning is clearer in the *Tathbit*. In the canonical Gospels, the children call to their playmates. John and Jesus are almost a new thought. In the *Tathbit*, Jesus and John are the "companions" who call the others to wail or to dance. Spurning John, they do not weep for their sins. Spurning Jesus, they condemn him for partying with fornicators. Shades of countless Christians ever since. A partying Jesus? Not in my church!

The *Tathbit* says what it means: fornicators—those "loose" women who traveled around with Jesus and his disciples and supported them with their own money. Again I must stress that we can be absolutely sure that neither Muslim nor Gentile Christian kept this apocryphal Gospel alive to appear in the late-tenth century.

Despite Gospel smears, Peter was true to his master. In the apostle's last homily before his death, he exhorts his listeners to continue the communal, caring society Jesus instituted. He knows they will do this, he tells them, if they fix love in their minds. And what method does Peter recommend? Why, the partaking of food together. "See that ye be frequently one another's guests," he tells his audience.[304]

Both Jesus and Peter, therefore, call their followers not to those sober-sided meetinghouses of my Puritan ancestors but to a feast of joy in God's kingdom. The Ebionites held that vision dear: we will see Jerome sneer at them for expecting a thousand years of "voluptuousness" when the prophecies are fulfilled.

Barefoot Heralds

In the Sermon on the Mount, Jesus says:

> "Do not worry about your life, what you will eat or drink; or about your body, what you will wear ... Look at the birds of the air; they neither sow nor reap nor gather in barns, and yet your heavenly Father feeds them. Are you not much more valuable than they? ... And why do you worry about clothes? See how the lilies of the field grow. They do not labor or spin. Yet I tell you that even Solomon in all his splendor was not dressed like one of these. If God so clothes the grass of the field, which is here today and tomorrow is thrown into the fire, will he not much more clothe you, O little-faiths?"[305]

Although this is from Q, we also find these ideas in Thomas. This was the bait. And they bit. Why?

Because the Judean peasantry, their faces ground into the mire, were willing to try anything. They had nothing to lose. Matthew bluntly states that Jesus had compassion on them because they were distressed and prostrate.[306]

Why? Josephus tells us:

> The whole area is excellent for crops or cattle, and rich in forests of every kind, so by its adaptability it invites even those least inclined to work on the land. Consequently every inch has been cultivated by the inhabitants and not a corner goes to waste."[307]

The problem? The peasants were like carts carrying twice as many bricks as they were designed for: they groaned under the double load. The cost of Herod Antipas's grandiose schemes, expanding Sepphoris and then creating a new capital, Tiberias, on top of the temple tax had bled the land dry, forcing many into unpayable debt. Banditry followed. Jesus's teaching and parables describe these conditions, and he promised relief: "Blessed are the poor, for yours is the kingdom of God. Blessed are those who hunger now, for you will be satisfied. Blessed are those weeping now, because you will laugh."[308] But every coin has a flipside. Jesus threatens the oppressors: "But woe to you, you rich ones, because you have your consolation. Woe to you who are full now, for you will hunger. Woe, the ones laughing now, for you will mourn and cry."[309] Small wonder they crucified him.

The "distressed and prostrate" passage is unique to Matthew. He understood the misery in Galilee as the other Evangelists did not because Galilee was his home. He may even have written in Capernaum. The Jesus movement survived oppression and persecution because it was born in oppression and offered hope for deliverance from that oppression.

The Baptist and Essenes promised the same thing, yet there was something unique about Jesus's teaching, a compassion that echoes the Buddha. The Essenes were not big on that. It was not just the Yeshuites. All Christians worth their salt care about those who suffer, just as Jesus did. The support Christians gave each other awed the ancient world. Peter knew. Closing his final speech in Caesarea, he urges his listeners to be compassionate to all.[310] The church triumphant, as opposed to countless numbers of ordinary Christians, has not always heeded.

Jesus first had to separate the sheep from the goats. When someone once said he would follow Jesus, he replied, "Foxes have holes, and the birds of heaven nests, but the Son of man has nowhere that he may lay his head."[311] We don't learn whether the would-be follower was up to sleeping under the stars, but he may, like the rich man, have turned sorrowfully away.

Jesus trusted both human nature and God. Our Lord's Prayer goes: "Give us this day our daily bread …" It was in my mother's crumbling King James Bible that I saw a reference to Proverbs. It read: "But give me only my daily bread." Intrigued, I read the whole passage. This is Agur son of Jakeh's prayer: "Keep falsehood and lies far from me; give me neither poverty nor riches, but give me only my daily bread. Otherwise, I may have too much and disown you …"[312] Is this not another way of saying, "Do not bring me to the test" or the older version, "Lead me not into temptation?" Again Jesus's had an intimate knowledge of scripture. Agur's prayer may have influenced ours.

"Give me neither poverty nor riches," so Jesus sends out his brave souls:

> "Go nowhere among the Gentiles and enter not any Samaritan city. Go rather to the lost sheep of Israel …. Provide no gold, silver or brass in your belts, nor a wallet for the way, nor two tunics, nor sandals, nor a staff; for worthy is the workman of his food."[313]

Jesus is emulating the Essenes: "When they travel they carry no baggage at all, but only weapons to keep off bandits."[314] Jesus's followers don't even take weapons.

The campaign of the sandalless twelve was the first act in an epic drama, a drama that beats anything Broadway has ever offered: no show has run for almost two millennia. In scene after scene, reform movements have struggled with a rich and complacent church, while subplots wind through the checkered history of politics, one of the most famous involving the millenarian Karl Marx. Jesus's followers barged out into the rough and tumble of the world, a world they were convinced that they could change beyond recognition. In fact, they did, but not in the way they had hoped.

First a summary, then the implications. The society (the Ebionites, or the Poor) that Jesus created in that backwater, Galilee, was the Kingdom of God here and now, which totally rejected material values, not only wealth but power structures: they were to share everything in common. Although the Essenes invented this program, it had little impact until Jesus sent it out into the real world, where it created a slow bang, the waves of which spread out from Galilee into Judea, from thence into the whole Roman Empire. Its waves still rock power elites today.

What caused this impact? It offered an alternative to the poverty and exploitation ordinary folk endured in the empire. Rome was slow to grasp this, but when it did, it began the persecutions Christians endured for centuries although, like most oppressors, it disguised its reasons. "It's a superstition," was a common charge. Closer was: it's sedition against Rome—Christians refuse to call Caesar "Lord." It was actually sedition against the very foundations of society. It was *the way of the law wherein you may free yourselves from many holders of power,* to quote the disappeared passage from Josephus. State persecution ended when that consummate politician, Constantine, brilliantly co-opted the church into becoming an arm of power, backed by the proto-Catholic party that was already slavering to gain that power—betraying everything Jesus had stood for.

That was a dark moment, a moment the Cathars would later condemn. Since power corrupts, that church swiftly became the persecutor, as underdogs tend to do when they suddenly pop up on top. As time passed, it lusted after total power, eventually even trying to usurp temporal rulers.

> And leading [Jesus] up, he showed him all the kingdoms of the world ... And the devil said to him, "To you I will give all their authority and glory because it has been given to me and I can give it to whomever I wish; so if you will worship me, I will give it all to you." Jesus said, "It is written, 'You shall worship the Lord your God, *and serve him only.*"[315] (Italics mine.)

And serve God only. Jesus's struggle with his demon yielded his program: a society of equals ruled by God.

Not so the church: it bowed—and ruled. True to his promise, the devil rewarded it. But the devil's deals always have a catch.

Chapter 6

Mount of Olives, Please Split!

At that same hour, some Pharisees approached [Jesus] saying: "Depart and go away, because Herod wants to kill you" (Lk 13:31, my translation).

In the Grain Fields

Herod had a split personality. Compare the above quote to his reaction after the arrest: "And Herod, seeing Jesus, rejoiced greatly; for he had long wished to see him, having heard about him and hoped to see him perform a sign."[316] Maybe he didn't so much rejoice as gloat, "Now I've got the bastard. Now I'll kill him." He certainly didn't want to see a Houdini kind of sign, the sort of disappearing act Jesus had pulled on the people of Nazareth.

Luckily, Luke lacked a good editor. Lucky also that ten chapters separate these items; later redactors missed the contradiction. But why the switch? In the second passage, the Evangelist is gearing up to blame the Jews for the crucifixion. So he paints a kindly Herod (compare the John the Baptist myth: seduced by his sexy niece, the tetrarch sorrowfully cuts off John's head). That's where the benign Bible Pilate comes from too—as opposed to the bloodthirsty Pilate of history.

Back to the head quote. How does Jesus react on learning that Herod wants to do unto him as he did unto John? He makes a smart crack:

"Go tell that fox this: 'Behold, I expel demons and make cures today and tomorrow and on the third day I will be perfected ... It is not possible for a prophet to perish outside Jerusalem.'"[317]

That defangs the fox, doesn't it? In the divinely prophesied plan, Herod is powerless. So our brave hero casually goes and dines with a prominent Pharisee. Luke's Jesus is one cool customer.

There was once, I believe, a different upshot. On hearing that someone wants to kill them, most humans flee or hide. This would be the logical place for the grain fields story Luke shares with Mark and Matthew.[318] Passing through the grain fields on the Sabbath with Jesus, the disciples pluck some heads of grain to eat. When some Pharisees, who are apparently trailing along on this little Sabbath outing (thus breaking the law), ask Jesus why they are breaking the law on the Sabbath, Jesus retorts: when David and his companions were hungry, they entered the house of God and ate the consecrated bread which, by law, only the priests could eat.

Note the precedent: the high priest gives David the bread when he is fleeing Saul.[319] *Jonathan has just warned him that the king wants to kill him—* just what the Pharisees warned Jesus. When in peril, you can put the law aside. This was standard practice. The Maccabees ignored the Sabbath if they were attacked. Others who had not were massacred. Shlomo Pines concurs, noting that when the Gospels show Jesus healing or his disciples plucking grain on the Sabbath, it is a case of dire need and therefore justifiable.[320]

One necessity is fleeing pursuit. Normally, people prepared food for the Sabbath. Those in flight could not.

Why Would Jesus Go to Tyre?

Few commentators wonder why Jesus is so often in Gentile territory. He tells his disciples not to go "among the Gentiles or enter any town of the Samaritans. Go rather to the lost sheep of Israel." Nonetheless, the possessed swine swarm into the sea in the pagan Decapolis.[321] Why is Jesus there? Do pagans care about a Jewish kingdom of God? Not one whit. And Samaria. Violence could erupt at any time there. Why, then, does Jesus travel through Samaria so often when the preferred route was along the Jordan? The Gospels claim that Jesus is fleeing the crowds who want to be healed. Healing is great publicity, and Jesus understood publicity.

The reason is: he is avoiding Herod. Shortly after learning of John's death, Jesus says to his disciples, "Come by yourselves privately to a desert place and rest a little."[322] So they take ship—to Philip's territory. There are no desert places on Herod's side, whereas the eastern shore is riddled with hiding places. The crowds find him anyway, which precipitates the feeding of the five thousand.

Then he sends his disciples by boat to Bethsaida, which is in Gaulanitis (beneath the modern Golan Heights), still outside Herod's jurisdiction. Shortly after that, they head for the hills, up through the Gaulanitis to the district of Tyre,[323] where Jesus insults the Syro-Phoenican woman, suggesting that to heal her daughter would be "to take the children's food and throw it to the dogs."

What's he doing among the dogs? The Gospels never explain. Again, upon his return he takes a circuitous route through the non-Jewish Decapolis. Scholars often claim that Mark had a poor grasp of Palestinian geography.

Actually, those scholars have a poor grasp of Jesus's program. Mark was drawing on Peter's memories, and Peter knew why Jesus took that route: to avoid Herod's lands. Shortly afterward, Jesus makes the cryptic comment: "Beware of the leaven of the Pharisees and of Herod."[324] Since leaven was sometimes used as a metaphor for evil,[325] this may refer to the traps Jesus's enemies were laying for him, particularly Herod but also the Pharisees, who were spying for the temple authorities.

A little later, Mark begins his predictions (put in Jesus's mouth) of Jesus's death. Jesus was aware of the danger. Knowing that Herod was planning the same fate for him as for John the Baptist, Jesus was on the run. I can think of no other reason why he would go Phoenicia, where "the dogs" were not going to repent for a Jewish Kingdom of God. In John, he doesn't spend much time in Galilee either; he's often in Jerusalem, goes through Samaria, is on the far side of the Jordan when Lazarus dies, and again feeds the five thousand in the pagan Decapolis.

While he skulked in foreign lands, his program was on hold. Or perhaps not. Had he sent out his sandalless heralds when he himself was already in hiding? It doesn't look so from the Gospels, but their chronologies contradict each other. When Papias tells us that, having been Peter's interpreter, Mark wrote down what he remembered of Peter's words, he goes on: "It was not, however, in exact order ... For he neither heard the Lord nor accompanied Him."[326]

Signs of the Times?

Since Jesus spent much of his career avoiding Herod's long arm, when and why did he decide to go as the prophesied Messiah to Jerusalem?

Josephus records two possible precipitating events. The first: Pilate sneaking the army ensigns into Jerusalem during the night.

> When day dawned this caused great excitement among the Jews; for those who were near were amazed at the sight, which meant that their laws had been trampled on—they do not permit any graven image to be set up in the City—and the angry mob was joined by a huge influx of people from the country. They rushed off to Pilate in Caesarea, and begged him to remove the standards from Jerusalem and to respect their ancient customs. When Pilate refused, they fell prone all round his house and remained motionless for five days and nights.[327]

Notice the size and intensity of the reaction. Traders and others traveling about the country would have brought this news to Galilee, where it would have been the talk of the countryside. And if Josephus exaggerates, you can imagine what the grapevine would have done. The denouement was a surprise, however. On the sixth day, Pilate

> took his seat on the tribunal in the great stadium and summoned the mob on the pretext that he was ready to give them an answer. Instead he gave a pre-arranged signal to the soldiers to surround the Jews in full armour, and the troops formed a ring three deep. The Jews were dumbfounded at the unexpected sight, but Pilate, declaring that he would cut them to pieces unless they accepted the images of Caesar, nodded to the soldiers to bare their swords. At this the Jews as though by agreement fell to the ground in a body and bent their necks, shouting that they were ready to be killed rather than transgress the Law. Amazed at the intensity of their religious fervor, Pilate ordered the standards to be removed from Jerusalem forthwith.[328]

This looks like Pilate the wimp of the Gospels. Or did he realize that an unprovoked massacre might anger the emperor and lead to his recall? (That actually happened six years later.)

He often ignored Jewish sensibilities. He minted a coin that year, 30 CE, bearing a *lituus*, a curved crook used by Roman augurs. Although Rome often used this pagan symbol on coins outside Palestine, no prefect but Pilate used it in Judea. For both the standards and the coin, he could scarcely have been ignorant of the precedents. It's almost as though he was baiting his subjects.

It may have been politically expedient to back down over the ensigns, but Pilate stiffened his will for the next crisis.

> After this he stirred up further trouble by expending the sacred treasure known as Corban on an aqueduct fifty miles long. This roused the populace to fury, and when Pilate visited Jerusalem they surrounded the tribunal and shouted him down. But he had foreseen this disturbance, and had made the soldiers mix with the mob, wearing civilian clothing over their armour, and with orders not to draw their swords but to use clubs on the obstreperous. He now gave the signal from the tribunal and the Jews were cudgelled, so that many died from the blows, and many were trampled to death by their friends as they fled. The fate of those who perished horrified the crowd into silence.[329]

In the *Antiquities,* Josephus records these uprisings immediately before the crucifixion of Jesus. In that passage, not one word remains about sedition, just that Pilate crucified him.[330]

From the size of the crowds, it is probable that the Jews rioted at a festival. If it was Hanukah, the celebration of the purification of the temple after the Maccabaeans trounced their Seleucid overlords, it would explain their readiness to riot. This must be the event Jesus hears about in which Pilate mingled the blood of Galileans with their sacrifices.[331] Had Pilate shed blood twice in Jerusalem in such a short time, Josephus would surely have recorded it.

If Jesus based his expectations on the Daniel prophecies, he may have interpreted those disturbances as the sign:

He shall make a strong covenant with many for one week,
and for half of the week he shall cause sacrifice and offering
cease; and upon the wing of abominations shall come one
who makes desolate, until the decreed end is poured out
on the desolator.[332]

Pilate first desecrated the Holy City (pagan ensigns), then desecrated
a sacrifice (Corban was a sacrificial offering offered to the temple by the
Jews). Then his massacre desolated the city. At this time of heightened
expectation, those signs would have been all he needed. This was the
prophesied moment: the decreed end would be poured out on the
desolator—Rome in the person of Pilate.

If the massacre was at Hanukah, Jesus would have had about four
months to get his followers organized. Having warned them to keep their
lamps well oiled and their wicks trimmed, ready for the bridegroom's
entrance, that would have been ample time. And so secretly, perhaps
with the password "the Kingdom now," the news spread like smoldering
grassfires throughout Galilee. We read that Jesus went through one town
and village after another teaching as he made his way to Jerusalem.[333]
Again he traveled through Samaria, where he was safe from Herod.[334]

To the Holy City

Although the following is speculation, it is based on the sources we
have. No definitive reconstruction is possible: too much information
is missing. I believe, however, that mine best fits the data. The trip to
Jerusalem and the ensuing events kept me thinking and rethinking for
years, but as I mused about it and studied the original sources again and
again, things began to fall into place. Events like these are etched into the
participants' minds; they talk about them again and again, particularly
events as momentous as Jesus's death and resurrection. The details would
have gotten skewed a bit (John's account differs significantly from that
of the other Evangelists), but the general outlines would have been well
known. Earlier I listed some of those who were still alive when the first
accounts were first written. We also know from Paul's letters that not only
had Jesus's brothers and original disciples traveled widely, but they had sent
emissaries abroad—to Galatia, Corinth, and Rome—to counteract Paul's
doctrines. In fact, that's why Paul wrote most of his letters: to refute the
Jerusalem party. Since Paul's interpretation of the passion and crucifixion

was not that of James and Jesus's original disciples, the events surrounding it would have been a hot topic.

So this ragtag band set off quietly and unobtrusively. Perhaps it wasn't as small as one might think. Or as disorganized. Or as unified. All groups factionalize, witness James and John, all agog on this very road to Jerusalem for the best places in the kingdom.

Why did they go so early? Jesus entered in triumph five days before Passover. I suggest it was because the main body of Roman troops was still at their winter quarters in Caesarea and would only arrive in Jerusalem in time for Passover. Others will object that there was always a garrison guarding the temple. If so, it would have been small. Except for minor blips, the land had been quiet for almost twenty-five years, ever since Rome had put down Judas the Galilean. Historians record times of trouble, not when the land is quiet. Peace does not make news. During the quarter century between the census revolt and the demonstrations against Pilate, Josephus has little to say: changes in the high priesthood, Herod's building activities, troubles in Parthia, the poisoning of Augustus's son, Germanicus. Exactly the conditions to make a governor complacent, particularly one who had successfully quelled a riot, a riot with no hint of rebellion.

Pilate may have been sitting smugly in Caesarea, gloating over having just taught the Jews a lesson. Martin Sicker confirms my views:

> The early period of Roman administration in Judaea was marked by two principal deficiencies: the poor quality of its governors and the inadequacy of the military forces permanently assigned to maintain order in the country. Vespasian, personally familiar with the consequences of these failings, undertook to make significant improvements on both counts ... Since any internal challenge to Roman authority in Judaea was likely to arise in Jerusalem, the bulk of the legion was to be stationed there *rather than in the distant administrative capital at Caesarea.*[335] (Italics mine.)

There we have it. Jerusalem was inadequately garrisoned in Pilate's time. Even thirty-five years later, when revolt erupted in 67 CE, the lack of foresight is astounding. Despite increasing unrest during those decades, a rabble of disorganized, factionalized, internecinely feuding rebels held Rome at bay for three years. If Rome hadn't been ready for trouble then—it had, after all, ample warning—the complacency of the administration in 30 CE must have been lax in the extreme.

Pilate was a curious prefect. Although bloodthirsty when aroused, he could be peculiarly indecisive. He had little reason to suspect that the winds of rebellion were blowing across the land. The two disturbances he had dealt with were spontaneous reactions, not organized resistance. Herod had quietly dealt with John the Baptist. Rome was not even involved because it was outside its jurisdiction. Jesus had been mainly active in Galilee, again outside Rome's jurisdiction. That might have been part of the plan: Jesus was smart, a lateral thinker. Herod and Pilate were apparently at odds, so if Herod's Galilee was restive, what was that to Pilate? Nothing. Not his worry.

Until Holy Week, Jerusalem seems to have known little of Jesus. (In John, he was well-known, but John is late and has a particular agenda.) Matthew, who drew on native traditions, writes: "As he entered Jerusalem, the whole city was shaken, saying, 'Who is this?' The crowds that accompanied him answered, 'This is the prophet Jesus from Nazareth of Galilee.'"[336]

Thus far, his plan had worked; he had taken the city by surprise. He needed to. He had some key things to do there unmolested.

To Fulfill What Was Spoken by the Prophet

Those key things were to fulfill some prophecies to bring in the kingdom of God. The first is the most famous: he sent two disciples to fetch an ass for his triumphal procession.[337] This fulfills Zechariah 9:9: "Rejoice greatly, O Daughter of Zion ... Lo, your king comes to you, triumphant and victorious is he, humble and riding on an ass, on a colt, the foal of an ass."[338] And so we get Matthew's hilarious picture of Jesus riding on both at the same time.[339] Was Thomas mocking Matthew when his Jesus comments that you cannot mount two horses?[340]

This scene sits very uncomfortably with Pauline Christology. The problem is the cry of the crowds: "Hosanna, blessed is the one coming in the name of the Lord; blessed is the coming kingdom of our father, David!"[341] *The coming kingdom of our father, David?* That is flatly political, an earthly kingdom. If Mark was mining prophecies, Zechariah's was the wrong one for a dying savior. There are passages the Evangelists could have used. For instance, Daniel 9:26: the Messiah will be cut off, or Zechariah 12:10–11: weeping for the one they have pierced. They didn't, though.

Even the great mystagogue, John, reports a political scene. The crowds' first shout is identical to Mark's. He is not copying, though. The cry goes on: "Even the King of Israel!"[342] Again, the King of Israel reigns on earth. John tries to get around the problem, claiming that Jesus's benighted disciples didn't understand until he "was glorified," presumably that the crowds were screaming metaphors. Calling one who will die on the cross to save mankind "the King of Israel" is a lame metaphor at best.

Matthew strikes out all references to the kingdom of David or the King of Israel. His kingdom has migrated to the sky, where it was to stay for millennia. Except among the heretics.

When I was a church choir director, I used to crease my brow on Palm Sunday. This story is a travesty of the upshot. Why is it there? The only solution that makes any sense is that Mark (and John) reported what happened, which Peter and others remembered with crystal clarity. It could not endear Mark's cause to Roman converts. Rome had just won a costly war suppressing those who tried to reestablish "the kingdom of our father, David." Thus it must have been too well known for Mark to omit it. Jesus willingly accepted it. Therefore it must have been his goal.

Writing for a Gentile audience, Luke had no such qualms:

> As [Jesus] was now approaching the path down from the Mount of Olives, all the multitudes of the disciples, rejoicing, praised God with a great voice for all the powerful deeds they had seen, saying: "Blessed is the coming one, the king in the name of the Lord! *Peace in heaven,* and glory in the highest places."[343] (Italics mine.)

Luke's kingdom has also migrated to heaven in this inept Pauline Christian adaptation. Since the original Mark learned the story from Peter, he well knew what Zechariah had prophesied: that this *triumphant and victorious king* would have "dominion from sea to sea and from the river to the ends of the earth." An ambitious program, but one that was expected to happen right here, not in heaven. In contrast, Luke's Jesus weeps over the fate that will befall Jerusalem forty years later. He has abandoned his earlier plans to right earthly wrongs. Now it's just business as usual for those who weep and are hungry. So much for Luke's Beatitudes.

Given the embarrassing message of the crowd, Mark's account rings true. Watching a delirious, palm-waving mob, led by a man on a donkey (you have to see a man riding a donkey to realize how silly he looks), shouting incomprehensible Aramaic, Roman passersby would have joked together, poking each others' ribs in glee. The temple authorities would, of course, have been alarmed, but explaining the threat to Roman soldiers would have been fruitless. "That rabble? Where are their arms? You're out of your minds!" After all, exuberant tumult at a festival was normal. If a real problem arose, Pilate had already shown his cunning.

Two Swords against the Might of Rome

Before going on to the other prophesies, I need to backtrack a little. First, the rich man seeking salvation. When Jesus tells him he must give away all his possessions and come and follow him, he has far too many possessions. Watching him go, Jesus remarks: "It is easier for a camel to go through the eye of a needle than a rich man into the kingdom of God."[344]

For some reason his poverty-stricken disciples are astonished! Who can be saved then? Jesus tells them that it may be impossible with men, but *"all things are possible with God."*[345] This thread—what God can do—runs through all of Jesus's thought. Surely only God could enable this ragtag band of Galileans to defy Rome.

Before going out to the Mount of Olives, Jesus asks what weapons they have (only in Luke do we get this whiff of rebellion). Two swords, they say. Jesus says, "It is enough."[346] The Jesus Seminar dismisses this as a Lukan invention: "There is nothing ... that cuts against the social grain, that would surprise or shock his friends, or that reflects exaggeration, humor, or paradox."[347] Really? That must be one humorless seminar. Two swords against the might of Rome? That strikes me as funny. Their problem is that the master narrative says he's going to Jerusalem to sacrifice himself as the universal Paschal Lamb. Why any swords?

Smoke and mirrors lurk in these dark woods. According to Luke, the incident of the swords fulfills Isaiah's suffering servant passage. The prophet actually wrote that he was one of *"the rebels,"*[348] which Luke renders: "He was reckoned with the lawless men,"[349] not the same thing at all. Next we turn to Jerome's Vulgate. Perhaps inspired by Luke's "emendation," he renders Isaiah's Hebrew into Latin as: *"et cum sceleratis reputatus est"* ("and was reputed with the wicked").[350] It is no surprise, then, that the King James reads, "And he was numbered with the transgressors," using that pious and archaic word still beloved of modern translators who, in spite of proper access to the sources, use it to mask the meaning of the Hebrew.

Thus Jesus's rebel intent disappears from both Isaiah's prophecy and its supposed fulfillment in Luke. The master narrative wins again.

Let's shine a beam through these smudge-fires. Two people carrying swords does not make Jesus lawless. People carried weapons to defend themselves from brigands. Remember, Essene travelers carried them. It would only make him lawless if he were leading them in some illegal act such as rebellion or robbery. Robbery, of course, is not in the running. Jerome realized that. So how did he translate Luke? *"Et quod cum iniustis deputatus est."*[351] By no stretch of the imagination could his disciples carrying two swords "reckon him with the unjust." The prophecy makes no sense now. It only works when the Hebrew is translated properly, as "the rebels."

Cover-up. Luke, Jerome, and countless other translators masked the meaning of this passage. It was too close to the truth.

Ask and Ye Shall Receive

Two swords against Rome is like kids playing war games. Jesus is turning the world upside-down again. Then there is that other set of rather childlike sayings: the "ask and ye shall receive" complex. The Gospels are laced with them, the first in the Sermon on the Mount. Laying out his future program, Jesus says:

> "Ask and it will be given you; seek and you will find; knock and the door will be opened to you. For everyone asking, receives, and the seeking one finds, and to the one who knocks, it shall be opened."[352]

Not only does Luke copy this material from Q, but the same idea is found in Mark, John, and in Thomas (not once but three times).[353]

Mark gives it a setting, one that suits his propaganda. Passing a fig tree on the way into Jerusalem, a hungry Jesus curses it because it is not bearing fruit. Mark even notes that it is not the season for figs! Next day, the tree has "withered away from its roots."[354] This is Mark's mean-spirited parable of the fate Judea will suffer forty years hence. It certainly doesn't redound to Jesus's credit. (Luke changes it from an actual event to Jesus telling a parable with the same point. His Jesus is no longer churlish.)[355]

When the disciples comment on the withered tree, Jesus says:

"Have faith in God. If anyone says to this mountain, 'Go throw yourself into the sea,' and does not doubt in his heart but believes that what he says will happen, it will be done for him. Therefore ... whatever you ask for in prayer, believe that you have received it, and it will be yours."[356]

I remember coming home from Sunday school one sunny day in May, ruminating on this passage. I glanced up at the ancient mountains that line the north shore of Nova Scotia's Cobequid Bay, wondering if it might work. Curiously, had we taken a Sunday afternoon drive inland, we would have followed the course of Folly River as we climbed Folly Mountain, perhaps to picnic on the shores of Folly Lake. I decided I didn't have enough faith to toss mountains into the sea, so I went home to a cold lunch instead. Just as well. It would have sent a massive tsunami down the Bay of Fundy.

The Fourth Gospel also knows the tradition of asking and receiving. John's Jesus, having suffered inflation to Godlike status, now takes the credit: "I will do whatever you ask in my name, so that the Father may be glorified in the Son. If you ask anything in my name, I will do it."[357] Delighted with Jesus as fairy godmother, John has him repeat it those magical three times.[358]

All branches of the tradition contain this complex of sayings yet even then, they must have made many people uncomfortable. Now recall the conclusion to Jesus's parable about continuous pleading:

> "Listen to what the unrighteous judge says. Won't God avenge his chosen ones, who are crying out to him day and night ...? I tell you that he will avenge them quickly."[359]

From his teaching, we know that Jesus was profoundly steeped in scripture. Year after year, at Passover, he would have heard:

> Moses answered the people, "Do not be afraid. Stand firm and you will see the deliverance the Lord will bring you today. The Egyptians you see today you will never see again. The Lord will fight for you; you need only to be still." Then the Lord said to Moses, "Why are you crying out to me? Tell the Israelites to move on. Raise your staff and stretch out your hand over the sea to divide the

watei so that the Israelites can go through the sea on dry ground. I will harden the hearts of the Egyptians so that they will go in after them. And I will gain glory through Pharaoh …"[360]

Thanks to Cecil B. DeMille, we all know what happened next. Many people still maintain that this story is literally true. Along with all his Jewish contemporaries, Jesus would have believed the same. This was their history, not their myth. Examples could be multiplied: Joshua leading the Children of Israel through the Jordan;[361] the Lord delivering Jericho into Joshua's hands;[362] the Lord moving the heart of Cyrus to allow the captives to return to Judah.[363] At key points, God intervened in history.

The prophets had also promised these things, including Hannah:

"It is not by strength that one prevails; those who oppose the Lord will be shattered. He will thunder against them from heaven; the Lord will judge the ends of the earth. He will give strength to his king and exalt the horn of his anointed."[364]

Remember also the beloved Isaiah 40? "O Zion, that bringest good tidings, get thee up into the high mountain … Behold, the Lord God will come with strong hand, and his arm shall rule for him."[365]

Such passages could be multiplied over and over. This was sacred history, sacred prophesy. No one doubted them. Now Jesus was going to put them to the test.

The Lord Is the True God. The Nations Cannot Endure His Wrath[366]

Jesus had gone up to Jerusalem confident that God would help them. He knew his prophecies well. From his baptismal experience, he was convinced that God had chosen him as his anointed. Therefore, God would act. How else was he to establish "the kingdom of our father, David"? The high priestly establishment was just as corrupt and bound to the oppressors as it had been under Seleucid rule. Against all odds, Judas Maccabaeus and his motley band of insurgents had brought down their once mighty empire and freed Israel, with God's help, of course. Like the Maccabees, Jesus had called Israel to repentance. The time was ripe.

Could Jesus really have been so naïve? Not only does all that data above point to it, but he was in good company. In the chapter on John the Baptist, we noted Theudas trying to magically reenact the entry of the Children of Israel into the Promised Land. There were also

> "deceivers and imposters, under the pretence of divine inspiration fostering revolutionary changes, they persuaded the multitude to act like madmen, and led them out into the desert under the belief that God would there give them tokens of deliverance."[367]

Crossan cites nine cases. Among the most notable is the Egyptian "false prophet." After collecting a following of "about thirty thousand dupes," this "fraud" led them by a circuitous route through the desert (imitating sacred history) to the Mount of Olives. From there, he intended to force an entrance into Jerusalem, overpower the Roman garrison and seize supreme power. Felix the Procurator sent out the troops. Rome survived another sacred attempt on its sovereignty.[368]

The mythic past was real. Otherwise, Judean history from Judas the Galilean through the bar Kochba revolution is incomprehensible. Repeatedly, leaders arose to deliver Israel, expecting God to intervene. In the War Rule, the Sons of Light would only win when the hosts of God joined battle: "*The assembly of gods and the hosts of men shall battle*, causing great carnage ..."[369] Heartened by the shouts of the multitude and the clamor of the gods, the sons of light will defeat the company of darkness. God will redeem his people.

If this was Jesus's plan, and I am convinced that it was, he was in good company. Now, let us return to the prophecies.

The Anointing

According to Daniel, seventy weeks were "*to bring in everlasting righteousness ... and to anoint the most holy [one].*"[370] Jesus must be anointed to fulfill Daniel.

This presents problems: the Bible contradicts itself. Richard Bauckham points out that in Mark, the woman who anoints Jesus before the crucifixion is anonymous (although it happens in Bethany).[371] John, however, names her: Mary of Bethany. Bauckham's explanation is that names would have incriminated the people involved when Mark wrote, but by John's time, it didn't matter. They were all dead and could not be prosecuted for aiding and abetting a rebel. He also notes that Mark puts the anointing in the middle of Passion Week to mask its meaning, whereas John places the action immediately before the triumphal entry, but then tries to hide its messianic import by having Mary anoint Jesus's feet. In none of the four Gospel accounts is this a messianic anointing.[372] All the Evangelists disguise the revolutionary aspect of this incident. Luke even moves it to the middle of the ministry.

Since a Messiah (or Christ, to use the Greek term) must be anointed, the Evangelists were in a quandary. They use the word "Christ" freely but get red in the face over the how. Mark's Mary may have originally anointed him as the Messiah with later redactors turning this political act into a symbolic one. As we have it now, Jesus says that she has anointed his body for burial. That *was* a waste of money since he would have washed it all off before they buried him two days later. In any case, she didn't anoint his body. Matthew follows Mark closely, but Luke turns the woman into a sinner, who apparently uses the avails of prostitution to buy an expensive alabaster jar of nard to pour, not over Jesus's head but on his feet. The whole scene is surreal: first she weeps enough tears to wash his feet (that's a lot of crying). She then wipes them with her hair (did she forget to bring a towel?) before pouring the expensive ointment over them.

Later, we will see how Acts sheds a different light on Jesus's anointing. An Ebionite Gospel will clarify it even more.

Here is the scenario as I see it: because of Daniel's prophecy, all Israel anxiously awaits the Messiah. While Jesus is skulking in the borderlands, Pilate fulfills the desolation prophecy. But, as quoted above, he must be anointed. The Bethany family undertakes the task, and a very risky one it is indeed.

Trust Jesus to have himself anointed by a woman, not a male priest. He possibly could have. He had at least three allies in the Sanhedrin: Nicodemus, Joseph of Arimathea, and Gamaliel. But for Jesus, the last would be first. He chose a laywoman.

Zechariah Fulfilled

Having been anointed and ridden into Jerusalem on an ass, one would expect Jesus to go on to the next step. But what happens? Mark tells us he entered the temple and looked around. *It now being late,* he went out to Bethany with the twelve.[373]

Why this anticlimax? How could Mark have been so inept?

He wasn't. He was drawing on Peter's memories. Either Jesus hadn't planned very well or the whole business had taken longer than expected. They should have arrived earlier. The traders had all left, so he had to return the following day for his next step:

> And entering into the temple, he began to cast out those selling and those buying in the temple, and the tables of the moneychangers and the seats of those selling doves he overturned, and he did not permit anyone to carry a vessel through the temple.[374]

Jesus is fulfilling Zechariah's last prophecy: "And there shall no longer be a trader in the house of the Lord of hosts on that day."[375] On what day? Why on the day when the Lord will become king over all the earth,[376] the day Israel is delivered from foreign oppression and "everyone that survives of all the nations that have come against Jerusalem shall go up year after year to worship the King, the Lord of hosts ..."[377] Even Thomas may have a memory of this event: Jesus says, "Buyers and traders may not go into the places of my father."[378]

Here, at least Matthew should have crowed: To fulfill what the prophet Zechariah spoke. It's not there. Why? Because it predicts an earthly kingdom of God. All four Evangelists pass over this in silence.

Jesus could be relatively certain he would get away with it. As noted, he had friends and supporters in Jerusalem and environs. He knew how Pilate operated, even if he was already in town. He would have known that earlier the prefect had carefully organized his troops beforehand in Caesarea, and then sprung a surprise on the demonstrating Jews. It is worth looking at the account in the *Antiquities*:

> However, the Jews were not pleased with what had been done about this water; and many ten thousands of the people got together, and made a clamour against him, and insisted that he should leave off that design. Some of them also used reproaches, and abused the man, as crowds of such people usually do. So he habited a great number of his soldiers in their habit, who carried daggers under their garments, and sent them to a place where they might surround them. So he bade the Jews go away ...[379]

All of this took time and organization. Having heard the story, Jesus took his chances.

If God still did not act, he could fade away to Bethany to continue his plan.

In John, Jesus evicts the temple traders at the onset of his career, rather than at its climax.[380] Did the Evangelist separate these events because he was aware that Jesus was fulfilling a prophecy and wanted to obscure it? If so, he succeeded. Most scholars seem unaware that Jesus was fulfilling a prophecy. (However, I was surprised to read in 2006 that James Tabor had also cracked the code.)

Now he has ridden into Jerusalem on an ass and expelled the traders. Would God act? It seems not yet.

The crowds were intimidating, so the temple stalled for time. The priests may have needed definite proof that Jesus was planning sedition to convince Rome to act. If the Roman contingent in the Antonia fortress that overlooked the temple court noticed anything, they must have assumed it was an internal squabble and would not get involved unless it grew to threatening proportions. Passover, when they would be on high alert, was still days away. The Fourth Gospel tells us:

> So the chief priests and the Pharisees gathered the council, and said, "What are we to do? For this man performs many signs. If we let him go on thus, every one will believe in him, and *the Romans will come* and destroy both our holy place and our nation."[381]

This may not be John's invention. Joseph of Arimathea or Nicodemus could well have told Jesus's followers what had gone on in the Sanhedrin. Both men were clandestine supporters of Jesus. In fact, there was another spy according to the *Clementine Recognitions*.[382] It tells us that Gamaliel belonged secretly to their group and by their counsel was in the Sanhedrin. Gamaliel did defend them in Acts. That's two independent witnesses to Gamaliel's support. Thus there were three people in the Sanhedrin who could, and almost certainly did, tell Jesus's brother, James, what went on in council (if not Jesus himself during that week) although it would've called for the utmost discretion.

Jesus played his trump card. On the night before Passover (according to John), he shared a meal with his disciples.

At that supper, Jesus says: "I will never again drink of the fruit of the vine until the day that I drink it new in the kingdom of God."[383] Could

Jesus mean he will drink the fruit of the vine in heaven? Hardly! Luke is even clearer: "I will not drink of the fruit of the vine until the kingdom of God comes."[384] No ambiguity there. It matches Jesus saying, "There are some standing here who will not taste death before they see the kingdom of God has come with power."[385] By 70 CE, this was a total embarrassment: many of Jesus's hearers had died. Therefore, Jesus surely said it. *The kingdom of God is to be right here on earth.* The promise at the beginning of his career is about to be fulfilled:[386] the kingdom has drawn very near.[387]

The kingdom of God has come with power. The Greek has an immediacy that is missing in most translations. It is now less than twenty-four hours until the beginning of Passover, the rite that commemorates God's deliverance of his people from bondage.

And so, with utmost confidence, Jesus set off after supper with his disciples for the vigil to end all vigils.

On the Mount of Olives with the Slavonic Josephus

For fresh insights into this vigil, back to the Slavonic Josephus. It reveals things missing from the Gospels, although I believe they were there before redactors edited them out. Here the silenced Josephus speaks. A later hand has altered his voice, but I'm a heretic: some of it goes back to Josephus:

> Now it was his custom often to stop on the Mount of Olives facing the city. And there also he avouched his cures to the people. And there gathered themselves to him of servants a hundred and fifty, but of the folk a multitude. But when they saw his power, that he accomplished everything that he would by word, they urged him that he should enter the city and cut down the Roman soldiers and Pilate and rule over us. But that one scorned it.

> And thereafter, when knowledge of it came to the Jewish leaders, they gathered together with the High-priest and spake: "We are powerless and weak to withstand the Romans. But as withal the bow is bent, we will go and tell Pilate what we have heard, and we will be without distress, lest if he hear it from others, we be robbed of

our substance and ourselves be put to the sword and our children ruined." And they went and told it to Pilate. *And he sent and had many of the people cut down* [italics mine; the reason will become evident later]. And he had that wonder-doer brought up. And when he had instituted a trial concerning him, he perceived that he is a doer of good, but not an evildoer, nor a revolutionary, nor one who aimed at power, and set him free. He had, you should know, healed his dying wife.

And he went to his accustomed place and wrought his accustomed works. And as again more folk gathered themselves together round him, then did he win glory through his works more than all. The teachers of the Law were [therefore] envenomed with envy and gave thirty talents to Pilate, in order that he should put him to death. And he, after he had taken [the money], gave them consent that they should themselves carry out their purpose. And they took him and crucified him according to the ancestral law.[388]

First, let's look at Mead's book. He quotes a scholar who claims that

these pieces were very different from those of all other ancient Christian forgeries known to us. His main contention throughout this very thorough enquiry is that the author ... must be ... a Jew and not a Christian. There is no evidence of direct dependence on early canonical Christian literature ... In so far as there is agreement with the Gospels or Acts, it is only in respect to the barest generalities ... the writer is not simply fabricating freely out of his imagination. *He has traditional material of some sort to go on* [italics mine] ... He is not a hostile critic by any means; on the contrary, he is in general sympathetic. Indeed he regards both John and Jesus as outstanding personalities, even astonishingly so, and his sympathies are enlisted for them because he thinks they have both been most unjustly done to death. His attitude is thus in general that of a friendly Jewish outsider—a very difficult part for a convinced Christian to play ... He, however, nowhere asserts that Jesus was the Messiah. Frey's main contention … is that the writer worked on Jewish general popular oral sources; in other words, *he had at his disposal traditions proximate to the occurrences, and therefore worthy of attention as giving a picture of an early outside view of nascent Christianity.*[389]

One century later, this Slavonic material is still ignored. Why? Because it's Jewish. And written by a Jew who is "not a hostile critic." No Jew would have interpolated this into Josephus's account later than the eighties of the first century. By that time, Jews and Christians were bitter enemies. That leaves only one option: this interpolator must have been an Ebionite or another Jew who sympathized with Jesus's aims, and they made them while Josephus was still alive. They should be taken seriously in the study of early Christianity. But they are not.

Here is what I think Josephus might have written.

> Now it was his custom often to stop on the Mount of Olives facing the city. And there he avouched his cures to the people. And there gathered themselves to him of servants a hundred and fifty, but of the folk a multitude. When knowledge of it came to the Jewish leaders, they went and told Pilate what they had heard, and Pilate sent and had many of the people cut down. And he had that wonder-doer brought up. And when he had instituted a trial concerning him, he ordered that he should put him to death. And they took him and crucified him.

Now I'm going to look at what I think the Ebionite inserted—bit by bit.

> But when they saw his power, that he accomplished everything that he would by word, they urged him that he should enter the city and cut down the Roman soldiers and Pilate and rule over us. But that one scorned it.

Christians did not insert this: they were hiding any hints of rebellion. Now compare John 6:15: Jesus, realizing the crowd was about to take him by force to make him king escaped into the mountain by himself. The same situation, except John moves it to the Decapolis. That in both these passages Jesus avoids force suggests that he had *some other plan*.

Next, summarized in plain language: When the Jewish leaders learned what Jesus was doing, they consulted the high priest. Fearing that they would be robbed of their substance, put to the sword and their children ruined, they went and told Pilate. Compare John 11:45–8, 53 (part of which we noted earlier):

> Many of the Jews therefore, who had come with Mary and had seen what he did [resurrected Lazarus], believed in him; but some of them went to the Pharisees and told them what Jesus had done. So the chief priests and the Pharisees gathered the council, and said, "What are we to do? For this man performs many signs. If we let him go on thus, everyone will believe in him, and the Romans will come and destroy both our holy place and our nation." So from that day on they took counsel how to put him to death.[390]

Look at the common elements. In the Slavonic Josephus, he cured people. In John, he raised Lazarus from the dead. In both, the Jewish leaders heard of these things. In both, they assembled the council. In both, they are concerned that the Romans will destroy them. In the Slavonic Josephus, they go immediately and tell Pilate, but Pilate lets him go; eventually they have to bribe him to consent to Jesus's death; in John, they plot how to kill him.

Can all this be coincidence? To agree so closely both in content and sequence, these texts must have drawn on a common earlier tradition. Only the details vary, as one might expect after the lapse of decades. As I've pointed out, the disciples had access to information as to what went on in the Sanhedrin, which would explain why these two accounts follow the same lines.

Moving on:

> "And when he had instituted a trial concerning him, he perceived that he is a doer of good, but not an evildoer, nor a revolutionary, nor one who aimed at power, and set him free. He had, you should know, healed his dying wife."

This looks like a later Christian revision. Compare it with an incident found only in Matthew 27:19. During the trial, Pilate's wife sent him a message: a dream had forewarned her that he should have nothing to do with Jesus.

In both passages, Pilate's wife influences his "clemency." Their differences suggest that they are independent inventions attempting to justify Pilate's out-of-character behavior.

To summarize: after Pilate released Jesus, he returned to the Mount of Olives and continued to "win glory through his works." This roused the envy of *the scribes* (temple authorities, no Pharisees here), who bribed Pilate with thirty talents to put Jesus to death. He accepted, allowing them to crucify him. (Thirty talents? Matthew had the high priests bribe Judas with thirty pieces of silver. Curious.)

As in the Gospel of Peter, the Jews, not Roman soldiers, crucify Jesus. This is fiction. Only Romans under Roman orders crucified criminals and only for the crime of insurrection.

The Gospel of Peter knows nothing of any betrayal by Judas: "Now it was the last day of the unleavened bread … But we, the *twelve* disciples of the Lord, wept and were grieved …"[391] This is on the day of resurrection, yet Judas is still one of the twelve. The Apology of Aristides is likewise innocent of any betrayal. "Jesus … had twelve disciples … he died and was buried; and … after three days he rose and ascended to heaven. Thereupon these twelve disciples went forth throughout the known parts of the world."[392] "These twelve"—not eleven plus a new appointee. Paul concurs: the risen Jesus appeared to the twelve.[393] Remember that the Ethiopic text of the *Epistula Apostolorum* lists Judas *Zelotes* as one of the apostles. The betrayal is a myth, as Jewish authors have pointed out.[394]

With that, consider the first Mount of Olives paragraph: the assertion that when his followers wanted him to rule over them, Jesus scorned the idea. Compare that with the passage from John, which we looked at earlier. When Jesus goes across the Sea of Galilee, a great crowd follows because of "the signs that he did on the sick."[395] After they go up into a mountain, John comments: "And the Passover, the feast of the Jews, was near."[396]

Jesus feeds the crowd. "Then Jesus took the loaves, and having given thanks, he dealt them out to those reclining there; so also the fish …"[397] The Last Supper in First Corinthians uses similar words "took the loaf." Next both passages use the exact same Greek phrase, "and having given thanks." Both are also tied in with the Passover.

When the people saw the sign that he had done, they began to say, "This is indeed that prophet who is to come into the world." When Jesus realized that they were about to come and take him by force to make him king, he withdrew again to the mountain by himself.[398]

Passover has nothing to do with the events John recounts. Why is it there? John is distancing Jesus from any suggestion of a messianic revolt in the events leading up to his arrest. That is why he took this material and moved it to the early part of Jesus's mission, just as he did the cleansing of the temple. It has several elements of the story the Slavonic Josephus tells of the Mount of Olives: a mountain, crowds impressed by the healings, the crowd wishing to make him a king (of the pagan Decapolis? Not likely), Jesus avoiding that. I believe that both of these stories draw on a common source.

Where Are Those Earthquakes When You Need Them?

It was down to the crunch now. The agony in the garden was an agony of praying: praying that God act on Zechariah's key passage:

> Then the Lord will go forth and fight against those nations as when he fights on a day of battle. On that day his feet shall stand on the Mount of Olives ... [which] shall be split in two from the east to the west ... and you shall flee as you fled from the earthquake in the days of Uzziah king of Judah. Then the Lord your God will come, and all the holy ones with him .... *And the Lord will become king over all the earth ...*"[399]

Thus Jesus, like John, expected "a new and transcendental conquest of the Promised Land."[400] Jesus was to be the Meshikha, God's regent on earth.

Mark's Jesus agonizes from start to finish. As the night wore on, it probably grew much more dramatic than Mark allows. However, in one of the suppressed Gospels preserved in the *Tathbit*, there is a tradition that the agony *was* more intense: "Jesus ...did not cease to go on with praying, imploring, supplicating and weeping."[401] The Epistle to the Hebrews echoes this: "Jesus offered up prayers and supplications, with loud cries and tears, to him who was able to save him from death."[402] The agony in the garden was truly an agony, an agony of praying that God would do his part and fulfill Zechariah's prophecy. If he did not, Jesus knew the outcome.

I'm not alone in my heresy:

> On the theory outlined here, however, there was great reason to pray and to stay awake, and there was great reason to avoid temptation. Jesus was not waiting passively in the Vale of Gethsemane for his arrest. He was expecting an awesome miracle and the appearance of the glory of God: but he must have felt that this manifestation would depend, to some extent, on his own worthiness and that of his disciples.[403]

It didn't happen. Was there a division among Jesus's followers? Did some of them, led by Barabbas and perhaps another Judas, decide to ride the crest of the wave and revolt, since the Mount of Olives had not split nor had the hosts of heaven come storming across the skies to deliver Israel? In any case, we know a revolt occurred. We know because of something Peter told Mark, something later redactors forgot to cross out.

"Now there was one named Barabbas, bound with the rebels, who had committed murder in *the* rebellion."[404] (Italics mine). This is immediately after Pilate interrogates Jesus. The implication is clear: this rebellion and Jesus's arrest and trial were part and parcel of the same thing.

Matthew dropped the rebellion like a hot potato. He writes: "And they had then a notable prisoner, called Barabbas."[405] No mention of rebellion, let alone "*the* rebellion." Simply a notorious prisoner, crime unnamed. Luke chose another solution, simply saying that Barabbas was imprisoned for some rebellion happening in the city.[406] That severs it from Jesus. Obviously, Mark's records of Peter's memories contained much that is forever lost, but there is just a smidgen in the Slavonic Josephus, the sentence I italicized earlier: "When knowledge of it came to the Jewish leaders, they went and told Pilate what they had heard, and Pilate sent and had many of the people cut down." Involved in rebellion, they died; that's exactly what Mark implies.

S. G. F. Brandon highlights the absurdities of Jesus's trial—once we have divested it of its Christian overtones. Mark tells us that the temple authorities delivered a Jewish man, accused of sedition, to Pilate. This man,

> who claimed to be the Messiah and was recognized as such by his followers, had recently attacked the Temple

establishment, and was so powerfully supported by the people that he could not be arrested publicly. The Roman governor interrogates the prisoner about the charges, but can elicit no answer from him. After describing the governor's surprise at the prisoner's silence, the account of the proceedings abruptly ends without any mention of a decision. Attention is then switched to a completely different situation. The governor is now faced by a Jewish crowd demanding the release of an unspecified prisoner, in accordance with what is alleged to be the governor's annual practice. The governor, who for some unexplained reason has become convinced of the innocence of the prisoner with whom he is dealing, and the malevolence of the Jewish authorities toward him, offers the crowd the release of this prisoner. But the Jewish authorities are now surprisingly able to persuade the crowd, which they had formerly feared, to ask for the release of another prisoner who had been captured in a recent insurrection, which had caused the death of some of the Roman forces. The governor, who had strangely resorted to the amnesty custom to save an innocent prisoner instead of releasing him on his own authority, frustrated by the manoeuvre of the Jewish authorities, then asks the crowd what he is to do with the innocent prisoner, whose innocence he publicly acknowledges. The crowd replies that he is to be crucified. So the Roman governor obeys, and orders the scourging and crucifixion of a man whom he had declared to be innocent and desired to save.[407]

Backed by thousands of soldiers, Pilate interacting with the temple authorities and a rabble in such a way is, Brandon says, "patently too preposterous… for belief."[408]

There is more. Jesus tells Caiaphas that he is the Meshikha.[409] Ripping his clothes, the high priest cries, "Blasphemy!" But Jesus has not blasphemed. He has admitted that he plans to overthrow the regime. Matthew "corrected" that. His Jesus admits nothing about being the Meshikha.

Luke treats this material differently: when Jesus admits that he is the Son of God (a traditional title for the Meshikha), the council says it needs no more testimony. They have heard it from his own lips.[410] Taking him to Pilate, they lay the charge: "We found this man perverting our nation and ... *saying that he himself is Christ [the Meshikha], a king.*"[411] (Italics mine.) What could be clearer?

John seems quite confused here. First, Ananas interrogates Jesus. Getting nothing out of him, he sends him to the high priest Caiaphas (his son-in-law). Now it's like the Grand Old Duke of York, who marched ten thousand men up to the top of the hill and marched them down again. Nothing happens. *In the other sources, Jesus admits that he is the Meshikha before Caiaphas.* Someone removed it.

They take him to Pilate, who asks if he is the King of the Jews,[412] although the Evangelist neglects to tell us why the prefect would think that.[413] Jesus claims that his kingdom is not of this world. John has set up an impossible situation: Jesus can't be the king of heaven, since that would put him above God (the idea of the Trinity lay far in the future). So what world, or rather what otherworld, is he claiming to be king of? Poor John! He's boxed Jesus into a paradox.

Speaking of claims, what document do you think would have asserted that Herod and Pontius Pilate assembled along with the Gentiles (i.e. the Romans) and the people of Israel against Jesus, who God had anointed? I stress: Herod and Pontius Pilate are the instigators. The people of Israel come last, no leader named. It contradicts the picture painted in the Gospels of a benevolent Pilate trying to save Jesus. Rather, he and Herod initiate the action.

In view of the evidence I've assembled, you might imagine this comes from an Ebionite Gospel. No. It's in Acts,[414] part of a prayer of thanksgiving offered by Jesus's followers after the Sanhedrin has released Peter and John, perhaps around 36 CE. This prayer suggests that Christian redactors seriously skewed the Gospel narratives of the trial. Luke here allows us a glimpse of the political implications of Jesus's career. He must have drawn this prayer from the traditions of Jesus's followers and didn't notice that it flatly contradicts the account in his first book. This is *not* a Lukan creation.

Is this why the evangelists disguised Mary of Bethany's anointing in so many different ways? The prayer states that God anointed Jesus. For Jews, that meant one thing: he claimed to be the Meshikha, God's temporal agent, ruling for him on earth. And if Jesus was God's anointed, Pilate didn't need to conspire with anyone. That was treason pure and simple, and the penalty for treason was crucifixion. Remember the Sanhedrin's charge:

"We found this man perverting our nation *and forbidding us to give tribute to Caesar,* and saying that he himself is Christ a king."[415] (Italics mine.)

We have a contradiction. Remember the spies of the chief priests asking Jesus a trick question: is it lawful to pay tribute to Caesar? Jesus asks them whose title a denarius bears. "Caesar," they reply. Jesus turns the tables with his reply: "Then give to Caesar the things of Caesar and to God the things of God."[416] Get an editor, Luke. These two passages (fewer than three chapters apart) flatly contradict each other.

So Pilate nailed Jesus to the cross, inscribing his crime, "the king of the Jews" about his head, the crime Mark's Jesus admitted. The prefect also crucified two of the other rebels (*lestai*) with him. Translators render this Greek word "bandit," but it is the term Josephus uses for freedom fighter. Rome thus ended Jesus's attempt to create a kingdom of righteousness. The powers of this world were not to be brought to their knees thus. One aches to imagine what Jesus was thinking as he hung there dying: "My God, my God, why hast thou forsaken me?"

But, of course, Jesus was an adept at turning the world topsy-turvy. Even death could not change that.

Chapter 7

Without the Shedding of Blood

Master and Lord, who ... [has] granted us humble sinners ...
the grace to stand at your holy Altar *and to offer to you this
dread sacrifice without shedding of blood for our own sins
and those committed in ignorance by the people.* —"Prayer of
Offering of St. James," from the Divine Liturgy of James
the Apostle and Brother of God[417] (Italics mine.)

On the first Sunday after Christmas, the bones of the "Brother
of God" (wherever they lie scattered) shudder. They shudder
because, on that day, the Divine Liturgy of James the Apostle
and Brother of God is celebrated in Jerusalem. They shudder because the
title "Brother of God" would have been anathema to the real James. They
also shudder because this liturgy, in its present form, celebrates the Father,
the Son, and the Holy Spirit, "the one simple and undivided Trinity." That
would have appalled him, as it did all the Nazarenes.

Nonetheless, it is considered to be the oldest Christian liturgy, some
asserting that it dates back to 60 CE. Parts of it are primitive. Before
entering the sanctuary, the priest intones: "Send forth your good grace
upon us ... so that ... we may offer you gifts, presents, fruits, for the
removal of our sins, for the forgiveness of all your people ..." Why offer
gifts? That's why Christ died. This must be a remnant of an earlier form
of the rite, reflected in the "sacrifice without shedding blood for the sins
of the people," quoted above. This seems to repudiate Paul's Eucharist.

It is true that many early masses speak of the unbloody sacrifice as if denying complicity in Jesus's death—yet Jesus's death *was* bloody, and communicants are now going to drink that blood. Something peculiar is going on. I suggest it harks back to earlier Yeshuite practice. In any case, this prayer evokes the James of church history, his knees as callused as a camel's from praying in the temple for "the forgiveness of the people."

There's more. The priest asks for enlightenment that, "We may be seen to be not only hearers of the spiritual songs, but also doers of good deeds ..." This echoes the strife we will examine shortly wherein Paul claims that faith saves, versus James's rebuttal: it is works. To my knowledge, the stress on sacrifice without blood and doing good deeds is absent from modern liturgies with their Pauline focus. (I may be wrong. I have not researched liturgies in depth.)

And more. This liturgy celebrates James's home assembly: "We make this offering to you, Master ... *for the holy and glorious Sion, the mother of all the Churches ...*" Sion (or Zion) is the old center of Jerusalem. Rome later challenged that title, claiming it for itself, as we will see in the chapter on Constantine. Pope John Paul II, however, recently ceded it back.[418]

It is sad that we no longer possess the untampered text. It would have illuminated the thoughts and beliefs of Jesus's original followers. But as proto-Catholicism gained power, the conspiracy to muffle its opponents kept pace until, at the Council of Nicaea, that party won (although shakily, and it took centuries to bring the other factions to heel). Thereafter, the church triumphant rewrote or disappeared everything that did not conform to its dogma. The orthodox East, however, allowed the "Brother of God" to stand, whereas the West demoted James to "cousin" when it decided that Mary was a "perpetual virgin." The Holy Family would have been astounded.

Holy Family Relations

Did the Evangelists also betray Jesus's family by painting them hostile? Many scholars think so. The family was prominent among the Nazarenes, and his brother Jude, as noted earlier, kept family records and chronicles which, along with everything else Yeshuite, disappeared after the Catholic triumph. Since that family, known as the *Desposyni* (the king's relatives) opposed the salvationist doctrine of the Pauline faction, the Evangelists blackened their memory, so the reasoning goes. That's likely true. They painted the disciples as stupid, so why not the family? However, I expect that family was like any other family, with squabbles and splits, discords and alliances. There were, after all, at the least seven siblings, the sisters unnamed in the Gospels.

First a little speculation. When Jesus returned to Nazareth to preach, it appears that the villagers had not seen him for a long time:

> He ... came to his hometown, and his disciples followed him. On the Sabbath he began to teach in the synagogue, and many who heard him were astounded. They said, "Where did this man get all this? What is this wisdom that has been given to him? What deeds of power are being done by his hands! *Is not this the carpenter, the son of Mary* and brother of James and Joses and Judas and Simon, and are not his sisters here with us?" And they took offence at him. Then Jesus said to them, "Prophets are not without honor, except in their home town, and among their own kin, and in their own house."[419] (Italics mine.)

I noted earlier that, as an itinerant *tekton*, he had learned all about invoice rigging, something he would not have learned in Nazareth. Perhaps, having become skilled in construction as a youth, he had decided to leave the stultifying atmosphere of a village of perhaps three hundred people who still called him the "son of Mary." Perhaps he left James to be the head of the family when Herod began building his new capital, Tiberias, where his skills would have been in great demand. That could explain why he is an itinerant when we first meet him as an adult, who has been away long enough for the villagers to say, "Hey, isn't that Jesus, the son of Mary?" Note also Jesus's snide comment about his own kin: his own family was apparently cool to him.

The following reconstruction of the family dynamics is based on surviving sources. After that transforming experience at the Jordan, Jesus begins to go about the Galilean countryside telling people to repent because the kingdom of God is at hand. His family, who had perhaps heard that John the Baptist had been arrested, are understandably alarmed. Setting out to "seize him" since he is "beside himself," they are met with that response (noted earlier) that is pure Jesus: *This is my family: those who do the will of God.* That put them in their place.

His career proceeds. His success is astounding, perhaps partly because he is a charismatic healer but certainly because, as Luke puts it, "the people were expecting, all were debating"[420] about the Meshikha. The soil is well prepared. With Galilee groaning under Herod's exactions, the land is agog with messianic hopes. We followed Jesus fleeing Herod across the border into Phoenicia, close enough to keep in touch with his supporters but out of harm's way. As the chosen moment nears, excitement mounts. An impressive groundswell of support, disguised as a Passover pilgrimage, begins to converge on Jerusalem.

Up to this point, Jesus's family seems to have been watching from the sidelines. Now they get caught up in the mass mania. They, too, would have hated their oppressors. Or alternatively, they decide: it looks like he's going to pull this off, so we'd better not be left on the sidelines. *Just imagine, we'll be the royal family!* (Which, as we have already seen, came true, despite the crucifixion.) In the march on the Holy City, they too jockey for position. Things still aren't right. The *Secret Gospel of Mark* (which is a brilliant forgery if it's not authentic) remarks: "And [Jesus] comes into Jericho, and the sister of the youth whom Jesus loved and his mother and Salome were there, and Jesus did not receive them."[421] Why would a forger concoct this rejection of his mother? It seems more likely to be genuine, pointing to stresses the Gospels hint at, perhaps a power struggle within the family. In any case, for Mary, this is her son. As mothers all know, there's a powerful bond. She patiently follows at a distance. Then disaster: Pilate crucifies Jesus. Mother and son are reconciled as he hangs on the cross, at least in John's account.

The *Tathbit*, however, preserves a related, but opposite picture. It quotes a Gospel crucifixion scene in which Mary brings her sons, James, Simon and Judah, to the foot of the cross. Jesus rejects them, saying: "Take your sons, and go away."[422]

This fragment from a lost Gospel, still available in tenth-century Teheran, portrays family relationships that harmonize with the *Secret Gospel of Mark*. We can see it in the canonical Gospels if we look.

At the marriage in Cana, when Mary hopefully tells Jesus that they have run out of wine, Jesus replies (according to the prettified NIV), "Dear woman, why do you involve me? ... My time has not yet come,"[423] a peculiar rendition. The text actually reads: "What's that to me and you, woman? My hour is not yet come" (my translation). It's every bit as rude in Greek, and there's no "dear woman" anywhere in sight.

Here I must point up the NIV's hypocrisy. After recounting the qualifications and the work of all the translators, the checkings and revisions, not just once but twice by two different bodies, they tell us that three times they revised the Bible, each time making sure they remained faithful to the original.[424] It assures us that all the translators were convinced the Bible was the Word of God and thus infallible.[425] If the Word of God is "infallible," you don't make Jesus nice to his mother when he was rude. Of course, it was the NIV that downplayed Paul's destructiveness, as we saw earlier. God's heroes must be flawless. And the Son of God must be polite to his mother.

John gives us a glimpse of the brothers' hostility. As the Festival of Booths approaches, they snidely urge him to go to Judea to show off his works. John adds that they did not believe in him.[426]

However, the whole family commits itself in the drama's last act. They'd come all the way, welcome or not, and so after the ascension, we learn that the disciples returned to Jerusalem, where they "joined together constantly in prayer, along with the women and Mary the mother of Jesus, and with his brothers."[427] Perhaps it was there, in that electric atmosphere, that the resurrected Jesus appeared to James as recounted in 1 Cor 15:7. Since either James or Peter told Paul this, it is their recollection of what happened. The Gospel accounts, written decades later, say nothing about James's vision. They had already demoted him to James the less. Their agenda was to put the family in the background.

There is, however, another reference to James's vision. Jerome recorded it in his *Lives of Illustrious Men: James, the Brother of our Lord* (Jerome had apparently not heard that James had been demoted to a cousin). He tells us that the Gospel of the Hebrews says: "But the Lord, after he had given his grave clothes to the servant of the priest, appeared to James (for James had sworn that he would not eat bread from that hour in which he drank the cup of the Lord until he should see him rising again from among those that sleep)" and again, a little later, it says, "'Bring a table and bread,' said the Lord." And immediately it is added, "He brought bread and blessed and brake and gave to James the Just and said to him, 'my brother eat thy bread, for the son of man is risen from among those that sleep.'"[428]

These documents reveal a normal family—as opposed to a "Holy Family." People change. Family dynamics change. Jesus's family was no different, especially considering the earth-shaking events surrounding Mary's son.

The Holy Church

The same is true of Jesus's followers. Until recently, the establishment lapped up Luke 4:32: "Now the company of those who believed were of one heart and soul," claiming there were no conflicts in the primitive church. An early church father, Hegesippus, seconded Luke, claiming "until then [the postapostolic age] the Church remained a pure and uncorrupted virgin."[429] He is speaking of heresies, but he implies that there was no significant strife among the early Christians. Eusebius too strives to make the apostolic age peaceful. Surely Peter and Paul never fought: he cites Clement's claim that when Paul argued with Cephas (Aramaic for rock, or Peter[430]), it was another Cephas, not the Peter of the Gospels.[431] Clement made that up. There's only one man nicknamed "Rocky." And he fought with Paul.

Real associations, as opposed to mythic, are riddled with stress, personality conflicts, and power struggles. After the death of charismatic leaders such as Alexander the Great, Mohammad, or Madame Blavatsky, their followers are particularly vulnerable. Christianity was no exception.

Who Inherited Jesus's Mantle?

In the beginning, although Acts does not specify any leader, it implies that it is Peter. He initiates choosing a replacement for Judas;[432] he is the spokesman for the mysterious events at Pentecost;[433] he addresses the crowd after healing the cripple at the Gate Beautiful;[434] for this, he is arrested along with John and then threatened and released;[435] he catches Ananias and Sapphira in their lies and watches both of them die by God's hand in retribution;[436] finally, he is the spokesman defying the high priest after the second arrest.[437]

In Acts 8, the ground begins to shift: "Now when the apostles at Jerusalem heard that Samaria had accepted the word of God, they sent to them Peter and John."[438] The assembly would never have sent their leader on such a mission.

A little later, after the infamous Caligula appointed his friend Herod Agrippa as his puppet king of Judea, the latter imprisoned Peter. On his escape, the apostle went to the house of Mary, the mother of John Mark, where he described his experiences. He then asked them to tell all this to "James and to the brothers"[439] before leaving town until Caligula's puppet died a very public and colorful death in 44 CE.[440] In this offhand way, with no explanation, Luke makes the transition he could not avoid: from here on, James leads Jesus's followers with a firm hand.

Matthew is explicit, claiming that Jesus appointed Peter (on this rock I will build my church[441]), but since this passage appears nowhere else, it probably indicates that the Matthean community viewed Peter as their founder. Not so the Gospel of Thomas:

> The disciples said to Jesus, "We know that you will depart from us. Who is to be our leader?" Jesus said to them, "Wherever you are, you are to go to James the righteous, for whose sake heaven and earth came into being."[442]

Eusebius backs up Thomas:

> Clement in the sixth book of the *hypotyposes* adduces the following: "For," he says, "Peter and James and John after the ascension of the Saviour did not struggle for glory, because they had previously been given honor by the Saviour, but chose James the Just as bishop of Jerusalem."[443]

He later lists the "bishops" of Jerusalem in order, beginning with James[444] (until 130 CE, all are "Hebrew," i.e., Jewish followers of Jesus). Peter is conspicuously absent. James is the leader, the "bishop" of the "mother of all the churches," from the beginning. This also agrees with the *Clementine Recognitions*.

We will never know exactly what happened. In spite of Clement's claim of utter selflessness in the choice of James, I suspect he did some sugar-coating. It's just too neat. Would James and John, who had jockeyed for power on the road to Jerusalem, cede power to Jesus's brother a few weeks later because Jesus had already given them honor? He'd put in their places, rather. Aside for the natural propensity of humans to strive to dominate, I suspect there was a power struggle. From all our sources, James seems the polar opposite of Jesus (and Peter, who leaned toward Jesus "reformed" view of Judaism)—rigidly conventional.

And Who Was James?

Since James was the first leader of the Yeshuites, we must examine his character. I once studied Carl Jung with a liberal Christian minister who was quite distressed because his son had embraced fundamentalist Christianity. Again I have a friend who never talks politics with her brother: she's left, and he's far right. If Jesus was liberal, and brother James conservative, that's not unusual. Having been tarred by society, I question that society; so I understand when Jesus welcomes its rejects. James, on the other hand, might well have had a self-righteous streak: he was conceived legitimately.

As noted earlier, Jesus both challenged authority and upset the worldview of his hearers: the last shall be first, ask the rejects to your party, and the kingdom is like a weed etc., the sort of stuff to infuriate the fundamentalist mentality, which fiercely defends the status quo. That was James: "For whoever keeps the whole law and yet stumbles at just one point is guilty of breaking all of it."[445] Ow! Jesus would *not* have approved. Perhaps James ousted Peter, who was much more in tune with Jesus's ideas, then imposed his authority on the infant Nazarene movement. There's a full spectrum: James, rigid traditionalist, Peter, waffling experimenter, and Paul, the revolutionary adapting his "Christ" to a mystery religion, pagan style. All stemming from the intractable career of an unconventional maverick.

We sense James's controlling nature in the New Testament, especially in the passage I have gone back to again and again, Acts 21:20, in which he states that Jesus's followers in Jerusalem are all zealots for the law. His control is clear in the Clementines as well. Peter charges the elders in Tripolis:

> "Wherefore, above all, remember to shun apostle or teacher or prophet who does not first accurately compare his preaching with *that of James*, who was called the brother of my Lord, and to whom was entrusted to administer the church of the Hebrews in Jerusalem ... even though he come to you with witnesses ..."[446] (Italics mine.)

A far cry from "You know that the rulers of the Gentiles lord it over them .... It is not so among you" of Jesus.

Let us turn to the Jerusalem Council.[447] As in many movements, the Way contained both right and left wings, the left holding to Jesus's progressive views of the law, as opposed to the rigid fundamentalists, who stressed its strict observance. Some of the latter had gone down to Antioch insisting that new converts be circumcised; that is, Gentiles must obey the whole law. Not surprisingly, this caused no little dissension. The Antioch Church delegated Paul and Barnabas to go up to Jerusalem to discuss the issue. After a (no doubt) more heated exchange than Luke cares to record, James ruled that Gentile converts need only obey four "Noahide" laws: to refrain from food polluted by idols, from fornication, from animals that have been strangled, and from blood, not particularly onerous task. This is the only time James appears flexible, but he was actually adhering to standard Jewish practice. Curiously, Irenaeus, quoting James's rulings, ends with the Golden Rule: "And what they do not wish to be done to themselves do not do to others."[448] Jesus would have approved. However, it is clear that James is the undisputed leader. The final decision rests with him. He made a wise decision, since that council was a power struggle that could easily have split the movement in two.

The *Clementine Recognitions* also makes this clear: "The Church of the Lord which was constituted in Jerusalem was most plentifully multiplied and grew, being governed ... by James, who was ordained bishop in it by the Lord." [449] This independent witness confirms Eusebius that James was the first bishop.

The *Recognitions* later reports the apostles and the Sanhedrin. Peter alleges that if the Jews do not cease from sacrifices, the temple will be destroyed and the abomination of desolation shall stand in the holy place,[450] a passage probably written after Rome built a temple to Jupiter on its ruins after 130 CE. Although James is absent, when the apostles report the discussion to him, he makes no objection.[451] Epiphanius quotes from the *Anabathmoi* (Ascents) *of James* that he "preaches against the temple and the sacrifices ..."[452] but this is late and questionable.

Other traditions stress James's reputation for devoutness. In the same passage where he notes James's camel-callused knees, Hegesippus claims that he "drank no wine or strong drink, nor did he eat flesh; no razor went upon his head; he did not anoint himself with oil, and he did not go to the baths."[453] Phew! So that's why he died a virgin at the age of ninety-six.[454]

Ninety-six? Epiphanius, who makes that claim, is mythologizing. James died around the age of sixty and three centuries were to pass before Epiphanius "virginalized" him. Later, the church makes the whole family chaste, even poor old St. Joseph. St. Thomas Aquinas, though not the first with the claim, was the most influential. The "angelic doctor" asserted that Joseph had to be a virgin because saints do not fornicate.[455] I guess before they become saints doesn't count: St. Augustine fornicated vigorously for almost two decades.

Forged or Genuine: James's Letter

Let's imagine Jesus's brother around the mid-fifties CE. At the height of his power, he heads a burgeoning movement of Jesus's followers in

Jerusalem. They have an uneasy standoff with the temple authorities, one that will erupt into violence later, but, at the moment, the authorities are just watching. Until the Son of Man comes striding across the sky on the clouds, James is simply waiting patiently (or not). Probably not, if the stories of callused camel knees are true. Meanwhile, down in Caesarea by the sea, poor Felix the procurator must be quite exhausted with putting imposters to death every day, as Josephus tells us.[456]

James has his own revolt to quell. He has sent emissaries to Galatia to counteract Paul's teaching that the law is dead. In the scene we are imagining, one of these emissaries has just returned bearing a copy of a furious epistle of Paul. As the leader of the Nazarenes reads, he frowns: not only does Paul claim that the law is dead, but that faith in James's brother, Jesus, brings salvation. His eyes blaze as he reads that no one can be justified by works of the law: "The many who rely on works of the law are under a curse!"[457] James stands up and strides about. "Consider Abraham: 'He believed in God, and it was credited to him as righteousness!'"[458] He reads, then exclaims, "This is outrageous," and calls for his scribe. Soon he is dictating his rebuttal as the scribe translates his words into fluent and elegant Greek. Thus was born the Epistle of James. "Was not Abraham our father justified by works, when he offered his son Isaac upon the altar?"[459] he writes, refuting Paul's claim.

Eusebius doubts the authenticity of this epistle, pointing out that not many of the ancients mentioned it.[460] Little wonder! It refutes both Pauline Christianity and its claim that believing in Jesus saves, not works. That's why it was disputed: it is "heresy" from start to finish. Martin Luther tagged it on as an appendix in his 1536 translation. Despite its trouble staying in the Bible, it hung on.

Almost as offensive to the proto-Catholic party is its Jewishness. Not only does the author refer to "Abraham, our father," but he opens with, "To the twelve tribes in the dispersion, greeting."[461]

Another offensive passage:

> Anyone who speaks against a brother or judges him speaks against the law and judges it. When you judge the law, you are not keeping it but sitting in judgement on it. There is only one lawgiver and judge, the one who is able to save and destroy.[462]

James is, of course, countering Paul's assertions. Its very offensiveness argues for its authenticity. If this letter had been forged after the destruction of Jerusalem, it would never have made it into the canon. The Gentile church then held the power the scattered Nazarenes had lost. How it managed to get in at all remains a mystery. Some churches must have venerated so much that it survived all attacks. Contrariwise, Paul's passionate denunciations in his letters to Galatia, Rome, Corinth, and even Philippi show that those who sided with Jerusalem wielded considerable power. Some of these may have originally been "God-fearers," Gentiles who had not fully embraced Judaism but worshipped with the Jews in the synagogues. Whoever and wherever they were, they kept this epistle alive. We will never know how.

Some scholars claim that no Aramaic speaker could have written such fluent Greek. We don't know that. The Bar Kochba cache of letters shows that some Aramaic speakers could *only* write Greek, and they apologized for it.[463] Besides, we know that Paul dictated some (if not all) of his letters. Raymond E. Brown[464] is among the scholars who believe that, since this letter expresses the ideas of James, it was either dictated to a scribe or written by one of James's followers. Almost all the letters that have survived from Roman Judea were dictated to scribes,[465] so James would have been simply following the norm.

The author is a spokesperson for the Poor. For instance:

> For if there enters into your synagogue a gold-fingered man splendidly arrayed and there enters also a poor man in shabby clothing, and you look on the one in splendid clothing and say, "Sit here [in this good seat]" and say to the poor man, "You, sit under my footstool," have you not … become judges with evil thoughts? Has not God chosen the poor in the world to be rich in faith and to be heirs of the kingdom?[466]

Again I translated it myself because most others render "synagogue" as "meeting" or "assembly" or some such circumlocution. Although the word does literally mean "meeting," it denotes, then as now, a Jewish meeting. Gentiles called their assemblies *ecclesia*. Why the dishonesty? Because "synagogue" shows that the Mother Church in Jerusalem was Jewish?

This document, whether written by James or a close associate, is of prime importance for our understanding of the early Ebionites (the Poor) while James still lived and ruled.

Having said that God has chosen the *poor* to be heirs of the kingdom, James speaks about the oppression by the rich; then writes: "Don't they blaspheme the honorable name by which you are called?"[467] I quoted the World English Bible because it is faithful to the original. Others bend the infallible word of God to imply that the honorable name is Jesus. The context clearly shows that this honorable name is *"the Poor"* or *Ebionites.*

James was prescient. Eusebius bad-mouths the heirs of Jesus's first followers thus: "For the name of Ebionites indicates the poverty of their intelligence, for this name means 'poor' in Hebrew."[468]

James's opposition to Paul permeates every page. In the first chapter, he urges his readers to be "doers of the word, and not hearers only,"[469] contradicting Paul's claim that salvation comes through faith, not works. A gentle rebuke follows:

> If anyone thinks himself religious, not bridling his tongue
> but deceiving himself in his heart, his religion is worthless.
> Religion clean and undefiled before God the Father is this:
> to visit orphans and widows in their affliction, and keep
> himself unspotted from the world.[470]

We will see later that, with one exception, the only time Paul takes any interest in the poor is in response to James's requests.

Although this epistle lacks Jesus's lively wit, it is not unimaginative. When I read: "Every good giving and every perfect gift is from above and comes down from the Father of lights, in whom there is no place for change or for shifting shadows."[471] I can imagine it coming from Jesus's brother. Again, the passage we looked at earlier is a lively evocation of a snob bowing and scraping to the bejeweled man. Note also this passage:

> Behold also the ships, so great, yet driven by strong winds;
> and they are guided by a very small rudder where the
> helmsman directs; so also the tongue is a little member
> and boasts of great things.[472]

As the rudder turns the ship, the tongue wags the man, an imaginative metaphor, although others claim James read it elsewhere (interestingly, they don't say where). I agree with Eisenman that this passage is directed at Paul. One of his inflammatory passages matches it well. Paul has just charged that if someone comes and proclaims a different Jesus, one that he himself had not proclaimed or a Gospel that they had not received, the Corinthians "well endure" it:

For I reckon I don't come at all behind the "super-apostles" ... For such are false apostles, deceitful workers, transforming themselves into apostles of Christ. And no wonder, for Satan transforms himself into an angel of light. It is no great wonder then if his ministers masquerade as ministers of righteousness; their end will be *according to their works*.[473] (My italics and translation.)

According to their works? That's a curious charge from the man who claims that works don't matter. Works vs. faith was a key issue between the two men, thus Paul is making a backhanded slur that many translators try to obscure. Apostles were a very restricted and elite group, originally referring only to the twelve. Therefore, the slur is directed at the originals in Jerusalem, including James, than whom none could be more "super," as we saw earlier. Note Paul's tongue boasting that he is their equal.

In chapter 4, James shifts away from Jesus's central concerns. He asks, "Whence come your wars and your fights? Is it not the pleasures soldiering in your members? You desire but you don't have."[474] This is what one would expect from a James who, later legend claims, was a lifelong Nazirite; that is, set aside from his mother's womb, vowed to purity for life. There is, of course, a possibility that Mary might have vowed her second son as a Nazirite to atone for her sin, at least in society's eyes. Even if raped, she would still have been stigmatized. Yet Jesus paid almost no attention to this sort of thing. There's only the one passage (in Matthew) where he claims that anyone who lusts after a woman has already committed adultery in his heart,[475] and that is suspect.

Jesus would have approved of James warning the rich of their miseries to come: "Listen! The wages of the laborers who mowed your fields, which you kept back by fraud, cry out, and the cries of the harvesters have reached the ears of the Lord of hosts ..."[476] Then he pronounces his indictment: "You condemned, you murdered the righteous man; he does not resist you."[477] Is this directed at those who killed his brother?

After exhorting them to be patient in suffering, he evokes the prime hope the Ebionites held from first to last, a hope that still refuses to die: "Strengthen your hearts, because the presence of the Lord has drawn near."[478] It's the same verb and the same construction that Jesus uses in Mark when he says that the kingdom of God "has drawn near."[479] Gentile Christianity too, as we shall see, believed early on that Jesus would return and establish the reign of justice here on earth, although that was later declared heretical.

God Destroyed Jerusalem because of James's Assassination?

Although overshadowed by that of his brother, the death of James was one of the great deaths of history. It initiated an epic event. Later the church tried to hide it, but Jerome noted it in his *Lives of Illustrious Men*:

> Josephus also in the 20th book of his Antiquities ... records the tradition that this James was of so great sanctity and reputation among the people that the downfall of Jerusalem was believed to be on account of his death.[480]

Origen and Eusebius also knew it. As with the section on Judas the Galilean that disappeared from the *Jewish War*, someone has removed this "offensive" material from the *Antiquities*. Origen complains that Josephus should have said the city fell because of the crucifixion of Christ. When that became dogma, Christian redactors simply omitted the offending passage.

Although scholars have contended interminably over this item, early Christian writers and redactors did that sort of thing. Read Rufinus and weep:

> In my translation I should follow as far as possible *the rule observed by my predecessors*, and especially by that distinguished man whom I have mentioned above, who, after translating into Latin more than seventy of those treatises of Origen which are styled Homilies and a considerable number also of his writings on the apostles which a good many "stumbling-blocks" are found in the original Greek, *smoothed and corrected* them in his translation, that a Latin reader would meet with *nothing which could appear discordant with our belief.* His example, therefore, we follow, to the best of our ability ...[481] (Italics mine.)

Note that Rufinus is following the example of others, some even distinguished, who also "smoothed and corrected." Of course heresy stalked Origen (betraying the master narrative was dangerous) but censorship was, and is, alive and well whenever texts belie the party line. Oh to find those ancient writings with their stumbling blocks intact.

Back to James. This disappeared passage has startling implications: could Jesus's brother have been so influential that people believed his assassination brought down the Jewish state? Why not? They believed that God destroyed Herod's army to punish him for executing John the Baptist. Again and again, Josephus chronicles this idea: after Honi the Circle Drawer refuses to curse one faction of Jews against another, they stone him to death; God sends a hurricane, thus ruining the whole country's crops.[482] In another passage, it is Josephus's own opinion:

> Now Jesus [not the Jesus of the New Testament] was the brother of John, and was friend of Bagoses [a general in the army of the Persian king, Artaxerxes], who had promised to procure him the high priesthood. In confidence of this support, Jesus quarrelled with John in the Temple and so provoked his brother [the reigning high priest], that in his anger his brother slew him ... However God did not neglect its punishment; *but the people were on that very account enslaved and the Temple was polluted by the Persians.*[483] (Italics mine.)

Josephus's God was quick to revenge, a view still dear to many people today.

Josephus almost certainly knew James. When the high priest engineered the latter's assassination, Josephus was twenty-five. He had studied extensively in Jerusalem during his early youth. In his autobiography, he claims that he had attained such eminence in the intricacies of Jewish Law that even senior priests consulted him. During the four years preceding the death of James, he lived in Jerusalem as a Pharisee. Considering Josephus's intimate knowledge of the ins and outs of the temple establishment and how prominent both these men were, they must have crossed paths on many occasions. He was in the city when Ananas assassinated James. Therefore any information he gives is of the highest value, always, of course, with the caveat that he is toadying to his patrons, the Flavians, and that later hands "smoothed and corrected" his work.

Eusebius writes: "[James] was by all men believed to be most righteous because of the height which he had reached in a life of philosophy and religion."[484] How did the second child of a peasant family from the backwoods of Galilee attain such eminence? Remember Joseph was a *tekton*, who surely helped rebuild Sepphoris and, being the caring father we see in Jesus's glowing references, he would have ensured that his children got the best upbringing he could afford. If James was a Nazirite, he had to learn the law. Since there were scribes in Sepphoris, he could well have "sat at their feet" (as Paul did at those of Gamaliel) and learned his scripture well. His letter cites, or quotes, eleven books of the Hebrew Bible. Given the brilliance of Jesus's mind, one would expect that the rest of the family were smart, and the James of church tradition as well as his imaginative letter exemplify this. All the sources, Acts, Josephus, the Clementines, and the church fathers, agree that he achieved great power, influence, and renown in Jerusalem. Yet his astounding career is almost unknown.

The Climax of an Illustrious Life

It was a long career. For over thirty years, the Way acknowledged him as leader. There's an enigma: Most high priests during that time were related to Caiaphas, who wanted to crucify Jesus. That powerful family would not have forgotten that, nor that Rome crucified him as a rebel.

As in all ruling families, Caiaphas had enemies. One of those may have been Gamaliel. Acts and the *Recognitions* either imply or state that he was a secret ally of the Way: he even dared defend Jesus's followers before the Sanhedrin.

Some claim that the *Clementine Recognitions* are dependent on Acts, but I disagree. Varying widely, they almost seem to recount separate events. Among other things, James is the leader in the *Recognitions*, whereas in Acts the Sanhedrin arrests Peter and John for "proclaiming in Jesus the resurrection of the dead." In the *Recognitions*, Caiaphas politely requests that they come and discuss whether Jesus is the "Christ."[485] There could scarcely be a greater contrast.

In Acts, Gamaliel cites the examples of the rebels, Theudas and Judas the Galilean, before saying:

> "Keep away from these men ... because if this ... undertaking is of human origin, it will fail; but if it is of God, you will not be able to overthrow them—in that case, you may even be found fighting against God."[486]

In the *Recognitions*, Gamaliel cites no examples, merely stating, "If what they are engaged in be of human counsel, it will soon come to an end; but if it be from God, why will you sin without cause, and prevail nothing?"[487] The ideas are close, but the words are far different.

In Acts the Sanhedrin orders the disciples to be flogged, whereas the Ebionite Recognitions, hostile to Paul, portrays an intense but not unfriendly debate, the disciples condemning animal sacrifice. In Luke's work, the martyr Stephen only condemns sacrifices that were offered to idols.[488] Shortly afterwards, they take him and stone him while Paul holds the cloaks of the stoners. Later, in the very next paragraph, we will see *Recognitions* gives Paul a far different role.

In Acts the council orders a vague number of apostles flogged before releasing them and ordering them not to preach in the name of Jesus.[489] In the *Recognitions*, Paul irrupts into the proceedings, stirring up trouble and actually throwing James headlong down the temple steps before killing a number of Jesus's followers. In contrast, the Paul of Acts doesn't begin his persecutions until after the stoning of Stephen,[490] who doesn't appear in the Clementines. Only later do we learn that murder was included in Saul's activities when the frightened Damascenes ask if this isn't the man who "had destroyed the ones invoking Jesus name in Jerusalem."[491] In the Clementines, followers of the Way flee to Jericho en masse;[492] in Acts, they are "scattered throughout Judea and Samaria."[493] In light of these many contradictions, the two accounts must draw on independent sources. This was the first major attack on the Way after the crucifixion, an event not easily forgotten, even though the details became garbled (perhaps intentionally) in the two very different versions.

Acts and the Clementines agree in sending Paul to Damascus with letters from the high priest. However, in Acts Paul's letters authorize him to bind any followers of Jesus he finds in Damascus and bring them back to Jerusalem. There's a problem. The high priest has no authority to do such a thing. Damascus was in the province of Syria: Paul would have to negotiate that with the governor.

The *Recognitions* presents a more believable scenario: Gamaliel tells the disciples that Paul has a commission to arrest Jesus's followers anywhere, but he is off to Damascus because he believes that Peter has fled there.[494] If Paul could convince the governor that Peter was a wanted rebel, then he might get permission to bring him back for trial.

This still leaves us with the conundrum of James's long reign in Jerusalem. The atmosphere for the first decade after Jesus's death appears to have been distinctly unhealthy for his followers. According to Acts 12, Herod Agrippa I killed James, the brother of John, and imprisoned Peter shortly before his death in 44 CE. The following year, however, during the great famine of Claudius's reign, Saul and Barnabas brought food relief to the elders in Jerusalem. Perhaps this severe famine distracted the authorities. The queen of Adiabene relieved the city at the time, procuring "a great quantity of corn" from Alexandria and a "cargo of figs" from Cyprus, distributing them to "those who were in want of it."[495] We hear no more of persecution in the capital until James's assassination over fifteen years later.

In contrast to a seemingly quiescent Way, Josephus records (as noted earlier) that things were getting "worse and worse continually," with Felix busily catching and killing insurgents every day.[496] Despite that, he found time to get up to his neck in high-priestly intrigues, managing to bribe a friend of the high priest, Jonathan, to bring some Sicarii into Jerusalem under the guise of worshipping God where,

> mingling themselves among the multitude, they slew Jonathan, and as this murder was never avenged, the robbers [read: insurgents] went up with the greatest security to the festivals after this time ... [they] slew certain of their own enemies ... and slew others not only in the remote parts of the city, but in the temple itself also.[497]

Considering the open violence, perhaps it's not surprising that the Way, quietly waiting for the Son of Man to come in on the clouds, was left alone.

Then came the high priesthood of Ananus, another of Caiaphas's in-laws. It was in 60 CE that James insisted that Paul prove he was still subject to the law. Paul would not likely forgive that humiliation. It was not in his nature. In fact, he could not even forgive himself, as we shall see. After extremists hatched a plot against his life, Paul managed to get himself moved under heavy guard to the safety of Caesarea. Later that year, Ananus came to prosecute. His attorney accused Paul of agitating Jews everywhere and of being a ringleader of the sect of the Nazarenes.[498]

Now let's turn to some curious material. In Acts there are hints that he was implicated in revolutionary talk. As noted earlier, the Thessalonians haul him up before the city magistrates accusing him of acting "contrary to the decrees of Caesar, saying that there is another king, Jesus."[499] After his arrest, he protests, "Neither against the law of the Jews, not against the temple, nor against Caesar have I offended at all."[500] The first two phrases rebut charges his foes had lodged against him. For the last, had no one charged him with sedition, he need not deny it. Again Luke lets us glimpse political undertones that are masked elsewhere.

Did Paul turn state's evidence? Did he tell Ananus that Jerusalem was swarming with Zealots under James's command? If so, the latter would have had no doubt what to do. Zealots had but one aim: to overthrow the state. Shortly after the new procurator, Festus, arrived, Ananus returned to Caesarea to continue his suit, giving Paul a new opportunity to disclose the aims of his enemy, James. A single word would have done the trick. The recent Sicariot assassination of Jonathan (the Sicarii were offshoots of the Zealots), whether engineered by Felix or not, would not have been lost on Ananus ben Ananus. However, Festus had more integrity than his happy predecessor. And so Ananus bided his time, no doubt keeping a close watch on James. Then Festus died.

Ananus struck. Now was the time to root out those closet Zealots. Writing perhaps around 150 CE, Hegesippus tells us what Josephus does not: how Ananus engineered the assassination. James was winning far too many people to the belief that Jesus was "the Christ." "Many even of the rulers believed" (the Sanhedrin who governed religious matters), which caused "a commotion among the Jews and Scribes and Pharisees, who said that there was a real threat that the whole people would be looking for Jesus as the Christ."[501] This is the same scenario: the Christ (Meshikha) would expel Rome and institute the kingdom of justice. So the Scribes and Pharisees took James to the pinnacle of the temple and asked him a weird question that need not concern us here. However, the following quotation gives the game away:

> And [James] answered with a loud voice, "Why do ye ask me concerning Jesus, the Son of Man? He sitteth in heaven at the right hand of the great Power, and is about to come upon the clouds of heaven." And when many were fully convinced and gloried in the testimony of James, and said, "Hosanna to the Son of David," these same Scribes and Pharisees said again to one another, "We have done badly in supplying such testimony to Jesus. But let us go up and throw him down, in order that they may be afraid to believe him."[502]

Nothing could be clearer (after a little analysis). I chose the archaic translation because it renders the immediacy: Jesus is "about to come on the clouds of heaven," a detail Hegesippus does not suppress despite a century having passed with it unfulfilled. This was no small matter, since James was so highly esteemed. The response, "Hosanna [*Save us*] to the son of David," is how the crowds hailed Jesus on his entry into Jerusalem. Hegesippus, a Christian of Hebrew extraction, understood this: the assembled Jews were voicing their yearning for deliverance from political oppression.

Five years later, this ferment of expectation would explode into the disastrous Jewish revolt. Vermes tells us that the Essenes arose at the time when the Jews expected God to deliver Israel as the prophets foretold.[503] You will remember that Luke said the same thing. A hymn from Qumran foretells God's help: "That the slain may fall by the mysteries of God ... For the King of Glory is with us; *the host of his spirits is with our foot-soldiers and horsemen* ...[504] (italics mine.)

Christian sources are not as detailed as the scrolls, but as noted in the previous chapter, Jesus shared the idea. Here is a prophecy that recalls the Scrolls:

> "But in those days, after that affliction, the sun will be darkened and the moon will not give its light, and the stars will be falling out of heaven, and the powers of the heavens will be shaken; and then they will see the Son of Man coming on the clouds with great power and glory. And then he will send his angels and he will assemble his chosen ones from the four winds, from the ends of earth to the ends of heaven ... Truly I tell you, this generation will not pass away before all these things have taken place."[505]

How cosmic the scale! It eclipses the scenario in the War Rule quoted above. In it, the cosmos remains on track. Meanwhile, until the powers of the heavens are shaken, Jesus sits at the right hand of the great Power waiting for the moment no one knows.

Ananus didn't like the sound of that dead Meshikha looming in the heavens. With a land swarming with Josephus's "impostors," this was an explosive situation. Any unusual event—an eclipse of the sun, the appearance of a pretender—could precipitate an eruption in such a highly charged Judea. Small wonder Ananus determined to crush the flagship, James and his chief associates, while he had the chance. According to Josephus, the chief priest hauled them up before the Sanhedrin. After accusing them of breaking the law, he delivered them to be stoned.

Some of the "the most fair-minded" citizens petitioned King Agrippa to censure Ananus. Others went to meet Albinus to complain that it was unlawful for the high priest to assemble a sanhedrin without the governor's consent. In response, Albinus wrote to Ananus, threatening to punish him. At that, King Agrippa took away his high priesthood.[506] Soon after, Ananus met the end he had feared. The Zealots assassinated him after taking over the city in the great revolt.

Josephus never tells us what laws Ananus charged James with breaking. He and his fellow "zealots for the law" would have been the last people to have been "breakers of the law" (Ananus's charge)[507] in the sense of the Torah. Therefore, it must have been Roman laws against sedition, even if the Son of Man was still waiting in the wings. James was a very real threat at the head of his large organization. That was his sentence of death.

"Because of his exceeding great justice he was called the Just, and Oblias, which signifies in Greek, 'Bulwark of the people' and 'Justice' ..."[508] Hegesippus wrote. His successor and cousin, Symeon bar Cleopas, had nothing like his stature, and thus began the long decline of Jesus's Jewish followers. After the destruction of Jerusalem in 70 CE, the primacy of its assembly vanished into the mists of history. James was a powerful figure. It's sad that the church has pushed him into the shadows, demoting him to the status of "James the Less" because his Christology and staunch Jewishness was embarrassing. James "the greater" is actually the shadowy one, almost an echo of his more prominent brother, John. However, it is fascinating that our James is beginning to reemerge into his proper place as a key figure in the early history of Christianity.

A mystique still surrounded James in the fourth century. To build up our confidence, Eusebius recounts that, in the city of Paneas (Caesarea Philippi, the city to which Jesus had fled to escape Herod), he saw a statue said to be of Jesus healing the woman with an issue of blood. This is understandable, he claims, since

> [he] learned also that the likenesses of his apostles Paul and Peter, and of Christ himself, are preserved in paintings, the ancients being accustomed, as it is likely, according to a habit of the Gentiles, to pay this kind of honor indiscriminately to those regarded by them as deliverers.[509]

Having assured us that such things are genuine, he tells us the chair of James was also preserved to his day, "the brethren who followed him in succession" had maintained it."[510] That's pretty miraculous in itself, considering the two destructions Rome visited on Jerusalem.

And with such questionable relics, we regretfully leave the tale of James. Unlike Jesus, he would soon disappear behind the smoke screens of history. He was just too Jewish for the church.

Chapter 8

A Cuckoo in the Nest

Seizing a strong brand from the altar, [he] set the example of smiting. Then others ... were carried away with like readiness. Then ensued a tumult ... of the beating and the beaten. Much blood is shed; there is a confused flight, in the midst of which that enemy attacked James, and threw him headlong from the top of the steps; and supposing him to be dead, he cared not to inflict further violence upon him. But our friends lifted him up, for they were both more numerous and more powerful than the others; but, from their fear of God, they rather suffered themselves to be killed by an inferior force, than they would kill others.[511]

"That enemy" is Paul exploding into the affairs of the Way—according to the *Clementine Recognitions*. Like the Book of Acts, it is history fictionalized. Or memory fictionalized. These two documents are firmly polarized: the Clementines detest Paul; Acts idolizes him. The "truth" will never be known but, by comparing the two accounts, we can construct a tentative outline.

In both, a confrontation in the temple ends in violence: in Acts, the stoning of Stephen; in the Clementines, an attempt to kill James. They agree that Saul then persecuted Jesus's followers. Some he scattered abroad; others he killed.

Then came the vision on the road to Damascus. The problem was that Paul's visions contradicted what the living Jesus had taught.

In the Clementines, Peter flatly rejects them. "And how did [Jesus] appear to you," he asks Paul, "when you entertain opinions contrary to his teachings?"[512] Questioning the validity of apparitions, Peter asserts that only the teachings of those who worked with Jesus are true.

Almost plaintively, the Clementines then suggest that if Jesus had truly appeared to Paul, *he should not oppose Peter.*[513] This may be a direct reference to Paul's assertion: "When Cephas came to Antioch, I opposed him to his face, because he was condemned."[514] (That phrase upsets translators. "Self-condemned," "blamed," "in the wrong," they write; anything but what Paul actually said.) Our Clementine Peter rebuts the charge; had Paul really seen Jesus, he would not revile the truth proclaimed by Peter, *"as if I were ... a person that was condemned,"*[515] (italics mine), the same word translators shun. Finally Peter says: "If you really wish to work in the cause of truth, learn first of all from us what we have learned from Him, and, becoming a disciple of the truth ..." to which Simon/Paul responds: "Far be it from me to become his or your disciple."[516] Paul always went his own way.

Schoeps points out that Peter's speech contains all the arguments Paul attacked in his epistles. He claims that the author of the Clementines had Paul's epistles and Acts in front of him when he wrote.[517] These works thus shed light on the Syrian Ebionites opinion of Paul and his visions. (The epistles, fine, but I question Acts: the stoning of Stephen [Acts] versus the attack on James [Clementines] precipitates Paul's persecution. That's not copying.)

Bad-mouthing Paul's visions has not endeared the Clementines to most historians. Although the self-proclaimed apostle cast a dark shadow down the centuries, many magic wands have sprinkled gold dust across it. This chapter will examine the shadow lurking under the glitter. Peeling back the gold dust, we will find some of it counterfeit.

Paul and Caiaphas

After admitting to wasting the assembly of God,[518] Paul implies he did so because he was an extreme zealot for his ancestral traditions. There's something wrong here. With many Pharisees in their ranks, the Way did not threaten ancestral traditions. What it threatened was high-priestly power. Paul is working for Caiaphas, the bitter enemy of the Way, when he appears on the scene. Having (perhaps) engineered Jesus's arrest years before, Caiaphas has hired Paul to destroy his followers.

We're going to take a new look at Paul's commission: the Syriac version of *Recognitions*. Gamaliel is absent. A Nazarene "plant" reports what went on the Sanhedrin:

> He told us how the enemy, before the priests, promised Caiaphas the high priest that he would massacre all those who believe in Jesus. He departed for Damascus to go as one carrying letters from them so that when he went there, the nonbelievers might help him and might destroy those who believe.[519]

"As one carrying letters." In this version, almost certainly closer to the original than the Latin, Paul has no bogus commission from Caiaphas to arrest Nazarenes in Damascus, which, as pointed out, he could not do. Here he simply promises Caiaphas to massacre Jesus's followers there. Kill—not bring them back bound to Jerusalem. The letters will only help him gain supporters for his nefarious plan. That isn't copied from Acts.[520] And it makes sense, as Acts doesn't.

Caiaphas knew full well that the masses opposed him. Spies had probably told him that some of the Sanhedrin, Gamaliel, Nicodemus, and Joseph of Arimathea, as well as many Pharisees, favored the Way. If it had gained the strength that Acts and the Clementines claim, he must have felt the temple trembling beneath his feet. He needed to act, but how, with such prominent opposition in his own camp? Did he secretly hire Saul to head the mob that wreaked destruction among its leaders and scattered their followers, while he himself stayed in the background until the deed was done? Threatened leaders have always hired thugs to do their dirty work.

More Plots

According to Acts, Nazarene opponents arrested Stephen for saying that Jesus of Nazareth would destroy the temple "and change the customs Moses delivered to us."[521] The destruction of the tainted temple runs through all these documents (Qumran despised it). Three independent sources attribute this prediction to Jesus.[522] The temple symbolized the sell-out to Rome, the oppression of the people, something Caiaphas and his cronies must have known. So he brought in Stephen for questioning and got the upshot he wanted: a lynch mob, and then a persecution that uprooted the Way from its power base in Jerusalem and (temporarily) broke its hold on the people.

The Clementines could scarcely be more different: the Sanhedrin and the Way debate quite amicably. James is just about to convince the assembled Jewish powers to be baptized when Paul, backed by his mob, instigates a riot. That aborted mass conversion is no doubt a fantasy of these later Jewish followers of Jesus. Nonetheless, realizing that the tide of sentiment was turning against him, Caiaphas may well have signaled Paul to do what they had previously agreed upon, and a murderous riot ensued.

Christianity Was Born on the Road to Damascus

Although the church celebrates its birthday on Pentecost, it was actually born on the road to Damascus. Had Paul not had that transforming experience, the history of Jesus's followers would have been far different—how different we can never know, but it would likely have remained a largely Jewish millennial movement. Although Paul is reticent about his visions, he does speak briefly about the experience that utterly changed him from persecutor to promoter. Here are Paul's accounts of his transforming experience. The first:

> "But when he who had set me apart from my mother's womb and called me by his grace, was pleased to reveal his Son in me so that I might preach him among the Gentiles ..."

Then he goes on:

> *"I did not immediately confer with flesh and blood neither did I go up to Jerusalem to those who were apostles before me, but I went immediately into Arabia and later returned to Damascus. Then after three years, I went up to Jerusalem to visit Cephas [Peter] and stayed with him fifteen days, but of the other apostles I saw none—except James, the Lord's brother. Now of these things I write you, behold, before God, I do not lie. Then I went to Syria and Cilicia and I*

was still unknown to the assemblies of Judea in Christ. But they only heard it said: 'The one who persecuted us before now preaches the faith he was then destroying.'"[523] (Italics mine.)

The italicized passage contradicts Acts, which says he went to Damascus, not Arabia. Which account is true we will never know.

Since Paul did not know Jesus in the flesh, his reports are either secondhand or visionary. Peter's reminiscences when Paul visited him in Jerusalem[524] are the likely source of the resurrection appearances listed below. Peter seems likely since he had that little weakness, boastfulness: his sighting comes first. That's not the Gospels' truth: they all give women pride of place. Again, memories get rearranged, and the stresses those people suffered in the wake of Jesus's horrific death would have skewed recollections even further. I do like Peter, with his charming foibles.

Paul's second mention of his visionary encounter adds little information:

> For I delivered to you as of first importance what I also received: That Christ died for our sins according to the scriptures, and was buried and that he has been raised on the third day according to the scriptures, and that he was seen by Cephas [Peter], then by the twelve; afterward he was seen by over five hundred of the brothers at one time, of whom the majority remain until now, though some fell asleep; afterwards he was seen by James, then by all the apostles; and lastly of all, even as if to an abortion, he was seen by me also. (My literal translation.)[525]

Most translators render "As if to an abortion" as "As if to one untimely born." That is so much more polite, and neatly disguises the self-loathing that surfaces from time to time in Paul's writing.

Abortion as a Metaphor for a Conflicted Soul

We need to look at that because from it flows the great church dogma: we are all so hopelessly evil that only God's grace can save us. This directly contradicts Jesus, who told his listeners to be perfect[526] "even as your heavenly Father is perfect,"[527] and expected it, since only thus could the kingdom of God be achieved. This insistence on Pauline grace was to plague the church throughout much of its history. The Yeshuites' stubborn belief that humans could become perfect only survived underground. The Cathars (the Perfect) almost certainly got this idea from Jesus's early followers.

Grace assuaged the conflicts in Paul's soul. Their depths are evident in Romans 7. After asserting that Christians are "dead to the law through the body of Christ," he writes:

> "While we were living in the flesh, sinful passions worked in our members through the law to bear the fruit of death. Now we are discharged from the law ... we serve in the newness of the spirit."[528]

Like James's "pleasures soldiering in your members," sinful passions working in our members means sex: Paul's passions bear the fruit of death. All babies will one day die. This dichotomy between the flesh and its passions, which are evil, and the spirit, which is good, is Greek. It is not Judaic. In the beginning, God looked on his creation and found it good, and that included licit sex. Yet Paul claims that he trained as a Pharisee. Maccoby[529] examines this enigma. I'm not going to.

Humans love a scapegoat. Paul blames the law for his problems:

> I would not have known sin except through the law. Also I did not know lust except if the law had not said, "You shall not lust." But sin, taking advantage of the commandment, wrought in me every lust, for without the law, sin is dead.[530]

Hardly. He is referring to: "You shall not covet," with that old-fashioned verb rather similar to lust except that it has an added connotation, "without regard to others' rights." Here is that commandment:

> You shall not covet your neighbor's house; you shall not covet your neighbor's wife, or his manservant or his maidservant, or his ox or his ass or anything that is your neighbor's.[531]

From his works, we know a lot about Paul: his neighbor's house did not tempt him. He bragged how he worked for his own keep and asked nothing of anyone else. That covers menservants and maidservants, oxen and asses, or anything that belonged to others. Everything, that is, but the wife.

He goes on:

> "For we know that the law is spiritual; but I am of the flesh, sold into slavery under sin. I do not understand what I do; for I do not do what I want, but what I hate. But although I do what I wish I didn't, I agree that the law is good. For I know that nothing good dwells in me, that is, in my flesh, for I wish for that which is good, but I cannot do it. For I practice not the good I wish to do, but the evil I don't want to do. But if what I wish not to do is what I do, *it is not longer I that do it, but the sin that dwells in me.* I find, then, this law: when I wish to do the good, the evil is present. For I delight in the law of God in my inner man, but I see a different law in my members warring against the law of my mind, taking me captive by the law of sin that is in my members. Wretched man that I am; who will deliver me from this body of death? Thanks be to God through Jesus Christ our Lord."[532] (My translation and Italics.)

It isn't "the devil made me do it," it's "the sin that dwells in me." Paul's disobedient member led him to seek a scapegoat. And with the help of St. Augustine, his neurosis would become dogma.

St. Augustine was furious that his member rose whether he would or no. He tells us that, at sixteen, "the thorn bushes of lust grew rank about his head"[533] (like any other sixteen-year-old boy). He next condemns his father's delight at seeing his son's erection at the baths whereas he should have been teaching him to be chaste and pursue God instead.

Urging chastity on a teenage boy amid the bushes of lust is like telling a spider not to spin. The saint pursued a lecherous career until his early thirties, when he exchanged earthly mistresses for Mistress Church. Now he did what his father didn't: wrote diatribes against sexual gratification,[534] causing untold guilt to countless generations, including me. Between them, Paul and Augustine fathered the church's hatred of sexuality that has so crippled Western culture for millennia. Sexual suppression, however, always erupts somewhere. The antics of the Jim Bakkers and the Jimmy Swaggarts provide some comic relief, but the notorious sexual abuse of children is one of the great—and ongoing—shames of the church. I'm getting preachy, but a healthier attitude toward sexuality, and an openness about its sometimes dark powers, would make this a much less disturbed world.

Did the Ebionites get caught up in this? "Avoid the fleshly and bodily passions," the Didache tells us.[535] We will see later that the whole culture went mad over chastity at that time.

Paul's career had a deep impact on the Yeshuites. Here is the *Tathbit*'s alternative to the account in Acts:

> This Paul was a villainous wicked Jew, actively committed to evildoing, a helper of the wicked one who stirs up schisms and *seeks power and dominance* ... (Italics mine.) While he was a Jew, he was called Sha'ul. He helped (to persecute) the Christians. Then he left Jerusalem and was absent for a long time. He returned to Jerusalem and began to help the Christians against the Jews. He told (the Christians): "Say this and do this. Dissociate yourselves from them (the Jews) and get closer to the peoples that are hostile to the Jews." Thereupon the Jews said: "How did you become a Christian and what induced you (to go) in this (direction)." He said: "The Lord, may He be blessed and exalted, induced me (to do) this. My story is that I left Jerusalem, intending (to go) to Damascus. Then the night in its darkness came upon me, a strong wind blew and I lost my sight. Thereupon the Lord called me, saying: 'Will you beat the miserable and harm the companions of my Son.' I said to Him: 'O Lord, I have already repented.' He said to me: 'If this is as you say go to the Jew Hayim the Cohen in order that he should give back to you your sight.' I went to him and apprised him (of this matter). Thereupon he drew his hand across my eyes and there fell therefrom something like egg-shells and like the scales of a fish, and I (could) see as I used to do. God called upon me (to come) to Him in heaven, and I sojourned with Him in heaven fourteen days and He instructed me in many

matters. About you He told me bad things which I will not repeat to you.'"[536]

Pines suggests that 'Abd al-Jabbar's source might have had access to a life of Paul,[537] which would explain its differences from the (three) accounts in Acts. Paul tells the story from his own point of view: the night of darkness came upon him, and a strong wind blew. This is how a man suddenly blinded would experience it. It is not copied from Acts, which has flashing lights, not darkness, and mentions no wind,[538] something people often feel during such psychic events. Acts presents an outsider's view, an outsider who saw (or imagined) the lights as opposed to the one who was plunged into darkness.

In the *Tathbit*, God sends Paul to Hayim the Cohen, who heals him by passing his hand across Paul's eyes, after which Paul goes to heaven for fourteen days. In Acts, Jesus tells Paul to wait. "The Lord" sends a disciple named Ananias to Paul, who lays his hands on him to heal him. Paul then mingles with Jesus's followers in Damascus before going to Jerusalem, where he spends time with the apostles.[539] As we saw earlier, Paul tells an entirely different story. "I did not confer with any human being nor did I go up to Jerusalem." Rather he went to Arabia.[540] Luke tries to make Paul part of the movement from the very start, which contradicts all other sources.[541]

It is unquestionably "scurrilous," to quote Pines, but no more scurrilous than the Gospel of Matthew's myth of a mob of Jews lusting for Jesus's death: "His blood be on us and on our children."[542] Untold millions of Jews have been slaughtered because of that line.

Or Paul's scurrilous attack on Moses after God gave him the law (we will look at that when Paul struggles with Jerusalem). It is hardly surprising that Yeshuites should retaliate in kind. Political correctness was an idea as yet unborn.

This passage brings us back to the scholarly skullduggery around the *Tathbit*. Although the full text is still unavailable in English,[543] in note 186, Pines wrote:

In this preliminary study not all the quotations from the Gospels occurring in our texts can be given. *These will be found in the full translation of these texts, which I have already completed,* and, of course, in the edition of the Arabic text, which is planned for the near future.[544] (Italics mine.)

That was in 1966. What happened? Abd al-Karim Uthman published the Arabic text[545] that same year. Why is this important material, although already translated, unavailable in English? Despite all my efforts, such as asking both Pines's publishers (they took a year to answer) and the Shlomo Pines Society, nothing. In 2011, I discovered why: the establishment suppressed it. It was never published.

This needs to be rectified. Fortunately, quite a bit can be culled piecemeal from Pines's collected works—with much labor. Unfortunately, Reynolds's 2010 translation is only excerpts.

Reynolds thinks that the above account "comes from a Christian converted to Islam who made it up with the help of some Jewish anecdotes about Paul, the New Testament accounts of Paul and his own somewhat coarse imagination …" [546]

There are no Jewish anecdotes about Paul. The Talmud ignores him. As for Acts, Jesus appears and tells him to go into Damascus and wait. Because of a separate vision, Ananias comes and restores Paul's sight.[547] Why would any Christian, Jew, or Muslim turn that into God sending Paul to Hayim the Cohen (Jewish priest) for healing? Reynolds's claim is imaginative at best.

The *Tathbit* claims that Paul had "a passion for dominion,"[548] which the establishment would rather not hear. Nevertheless, "a passion for dominion" describes Paul very well. On learning that his flock is wavering under pressure from James's emissaries, he writes to the Galatians: "As we have previously said, I also say again now, if anyone preaches a gospel to you beside the one you received, let him be accursed!" [549] Faced with a similar situation in Corinth, he threatens to take a big stick to his flock.[550] Paul, in his passion for dominion, was trying to wrest control of the movement from Jerusalem, which disagreed with him on Jesus's mission.

Paul's Contested Apostleship

Paul used the word apostle in a wider sense than did the Jerusalem church. He calls Andronicus and *Junia* prominent apostles.[551] How that woman stuck in the craw of the church! Since the twelfth century it has frantically claimed that Paul is actually speaking of Junias, not Junia. Nonsense! After an exhaustive search of the ancient literature, Bernadette Brooten states, "We do not have a single shred of evidence that the name Junias ever existed."[552] The church failed to turn Junia into a trans man.

Paul never tells us how he began his missionary work. Acts, however, says the church in Antioch had a visionary moment: the Holy Spirit said, "Separate to me Barnabas and Paul for the work to which I have called them." [553] So they laid their hands on them and sent them off.

Let's examine the term "apostle." It means "one sent out," understood by the original apostles as "one sent out by Jesus." The world is full of self-made folk, but sending yourself out is a bit iffy. Luke dared not claim that Jerusalem had sent Paul out, even though its power lay shattered when he wrote. Thus the Antioch assembly had to do. Paul did claim that the "seeming pillars" gave him and Barnabas the right hand of fellowship in order that they should "go to the Gentiles." [554] The church assumes that here James, Peter, and John confirmed Paul's apostleship. If so, they regretted it.

We can safely take the Holy Spirit's words with a grain of salt. Paul would just have to do with Luke's senders: Simeon called Niger, Lucius of Cyrene, Manaen, Herod Antipas's foster brother, (what was *he* doing in the movement?) none of whom were authorized by Jerusalem either. [555]

Paul is silent about any laying on of hands. "Paul an apostle, *not from men nor through man* but through Jesus Christ and God the father …" [556] (Italics mine.) The headings of First and Second Corinthians and Romans ring variations on that claim—that Jesus sent him out: the Jesus of his visions.

Jerusalem eventually contested his claim. He exclaims:

> "Am I not free? Am I not an apostle? Haven't I seen Jesus our Lord? Aren't you my work in the Lord? *If to others I am not an apostle*, yet at least I am to you; for you are the seal of my apostleship in the Lord." [557]

Who but Jerusalem would have challenged his right to be called an apostle? It was *the* center of power in the early movement. Paul grows more intense in his next epistle:

> "If indeed another one coming proclaims another Jesus whom we did not proclaim, or if you receive a different spirit that you did not receive or a gospel different from the one you received, you and yours. For I don't believe that I come behind these super-apostles." [558]

Those super-apostles could have been none other than Peter, James, John, and the rest of the twelve who grace the walls of the refectory of Santa Maria delle Grazie in Milan (unless you believe that the lissome youth who listens so demurely to Peter's question in Leonardo's fresco is Mary Magdalene—heresy indeed!). The *Recognitions* backs up Jerusalem's claim: Peter states that more than twelve apostles is as unthinkable as thirteen months in a year.[559] (He didn't know about the Mayans.)

The reason Paul's epistles stress his divine call becomes evident in this passage:

> "But what I do I will keep on doing, that I might cut off the occasion of those who desire *to boast that they work on the same terms as we do.* For such are false apostles, deceitful workmen, transforming themselves as apostles of Christ. And no wonder: Satan transforms himself into an angel of light. It's no great wonder then if his ministers also disguise themselves as ministers of righteousness whose end will be according to their works."[560] (Italics mine.)

Paul's claim to be an apostle of Christ Jesus through the will of God,[561] as opposed to the servants of Satan, is a scurrilous slam at his Jerusalem opponents—who were appointed by the living (as opposed to a visionary) Jesus. Small wonder Jesus's Jewish followers saw him as a cuckoo in the nest.

The Clementines say as much. Preaching in Tripolis, Peter adds a new twist to the temptation story. He says that the "prince of wickedness," having been rejected by Jesus, sent false prophets into the world who would speak in the name of Christ, but do "the will of the demon."[562] He immediately follows that with the same stricture we saw in the *Homilies*:

> "Believe no teacher, unless he bring from Jerusalem the testimonial of James the Lord's brother." [To make doubly sure, he repeats it:] "unless, I say, he brings a testimonial thence, [he is by no] means to be received."[563]

Found in both the *Homilies* and the *Recognitions*, this puts James into about as super a position as you can get. This item goes right back to the source. How can we know? Paul addresses it. "For we are not as the many, hawking the word of God, but as of sincerity, but as of God, before God in Christ, we speak."[564] I translated this literally because even Young's "literal" version fudges it: having claimed to speak as of God, in the very next sentence—which has been assigned a new chapter to divest it of its context—Paul wonders if he has now commended himself to the Corinthians: "Surely we do not need, as some do, *letters of recommendation to you* ..."[565] And there we have it! He does not have the required documents from Brother James. And Peter is on his case.

The success of Pauline Christianity must have galled the Yeshuites deeply. Must have? Did. We have their word for it, in texts saved by Muslims. In chapter 1, I quoted: "Similarly the Christians have claimed that the Jew Paul has worked miracles and this in spite of his being known for his tricks, his lying and his baseness ..."[566] Paul himself notes that he is treated as an impostor, yet claims to be "true."[567] Against that claim, you may remember from chapter 1 how poor Jerome agonized over Paul's public admission of lying, blaming it on James. I leave to readers to make up their own minds.

So what was this divinely appointed apostle doing that so alienated Jerusalem? A tenth century Jewish author, Ya'qub al-Qirqisani, who lived in what is now Iraq, notes a sect that held similar views to the Jewish followers of Jesus who lived there. After noting that the Temple authorities tried to kill Jesus, Qirqisani writes that the sect claims that *Paul established the Christian religion as we have it*, teaching that Jesus was divine and that the law was abolished.[568] (Italics mine).

Tenth century Iraq! And Yeshuites still recalled what Paul and James fought over.

Paul's Eucharist

You will remember that Jesus revealed the Eucharist to Paul. With fear and trembling at the risk of being lumped with the crazies, I broach the admittedly distant possibility that Paul got the idea of Jesus shedding his blood to save mankind from the Mithraic mysteries. A Mithraic liturgy survives on the walls of a second-century Mithraeum under Santa Prisca in Rome. After mentioning a young bull that Mithras carried on his "golden shoulders," we read, "And you saved us after having shed the eternal blood."[569] We have, of course, no evidence that these words predate Paul.

However, according to Plutarch (Pompey 24), Pompey found pirates offering strange sacrifices at Olympus (a pirate stronghold in southern Asia Minor) in 67 BCE, where:

They celebrated secret rites or mysteries, among which were those of Mithras. *These Mithraic rites, first celebrated by the pirates, are still celebrated today.*[570] (Italics mine.)

Plutarch later notes[571] that Pompey settled some of his twenty thousand prisoners in Cilicia, where Paul's native Tarsus lay.

So Plutarch tells us that Mithraism arose among rebels in the area of Paul's native city. Since the shedding the bull's blood was a spring fertility sacrifice (the slaughtered bull's tail often sprouts a head of grain) to ensure the growth of life-saving crops, Paul could have borrowed the idea of being saved by the eternal blood from Mithraism rather than the opposite.

There is also evidence in the church fathers. After quoting the institution of the Last Supper, Justin Martyr comments:

> Which the wicked devils have imitated in the mysteries of Mithras, commanding the same thing to be done. For, that bread and a cup of water are placed with certain incantations in the mystic rites of one who is being initiated ...[572]

Since he claims that the virgin conception of Perseus was the devil imitating the conception of Jesus[573] (centuries before it happened, a demonic device indeed), the Mithraic rite could precede Paul's as well.

This is all hypothetical. Both Justin Martyr and Prisca liturgy date from the second century CE. Nonetheless, the shedding of blood in fertility rites has deep roots in the vast silences of prehistory. Human sacrifice was the norm until it became repugnant. Gods were a different matter: we earlier noted that Adonis died each year when a boar gored him in the groin—then rose again the next day. The strength of such rites is their connectedness to the earth. No one who underwent the moving initiations at Eleusis could ever forget that the life-giving grain was the staff of life. We would do well to regain that aspect of those rites today.

It is no secret that Paul's rite updates these ubiquitous mystery religions of the Near East. Replacing the crops whose seeds die in the earth, Jesus's death brings eternal life. Jesus is "the first-fruits of those who have fallen asleep,"[574] a harvest thanksgiving shifted from earth to heaven. The other mystery religions honored our connectedness to earth. We lost that in Paul's rite.

The *Didache*'s Eucharist, however, retains it, invoking the "fragment" that was once scattered on the mountains, referring to the grain.[575] Were we to return to this understanding, Communion would be a sacred reminder of the holiness of all creation. The church to which I belong has done this: we give thanks for the gifts of the earth and to those who have labored to bring it to us instead of the body and blood of Christ. Luckily, they don't burn heretics any more.

There can be absolutely no doubt that Paul saw Jesus as a dying god:

> But we speak of God's wisdom in a mystery that has been hidden, which God foreordained before the ages for our glory, which none of the powers [*archons*] of this age [*aion*] has known; for if they had known it, they would not have crucified the Lord of Glory. But as it is written, "How many things that the eye has not seen, nor the ear heard, nor has arisen in the heart of man, has God prepared for those who love him." But *God revealed it to us through the Spirit* ...[576] (My translation and italics.)

Note that in this passage (which can still send chills up my spine) Paul tells us that God revealed a mystery to him in a vision. Yet this vision had a pagan slant. "Which God foreordained before the ages" does not come from a Jewish worldview. Jews did not divide history into ages as did the Greeks, whose ages of gold, silver, bronze, and heroes culminated in this present age of iron: the worst of all (which is obvious from the state of the world today). Paul and the Greeks shared this Indo-European idea along with the Persians and the Norse.

Note also that the death of "the Lord of Glory" is a mystery. Coffman faces this head-on in his commentary on this passage, although he claims that Christianity far exceeds the Greek mysteries since God foreordained it before creation.[577] Most modern translators find this embarrassing, translating *mysterion* as "secret and hidden" [NRSV] or "secret" [NIV], thus divorcing Paul from his context. This reflects Protestant unease with the concept, a problem that does not affect Catholicism. Among its strengths is that it has remained true to its roots. It is a mystery religion: in the hushed atmosphere of the Mass, each communicant partakes of the actual flesh of the god.

Such an idea scandalized the Yeshuites of the *Tathbit*. Not for them a dying god. Jesus clearly stated that he was an envoy of God: God had sent him, as He had the prophets before him.[578] (Due to their influence, Mohammad would later maintain the same thing.) To underline the point, the *Tathbit* quotes a saying from another apocryphal Gospel: "A man said to him: 'O Good one: teach me.' And Christ said to him: 'Do not say this to me. For there is nothing good except God.'"[579] Compare Jesus's response to the rich man in Mark 10. In both texts, Jesus clearly says he is not God.

The Year the Eucharist Was Born

I can pinpoint almost to the year Paul's first proclamation of his Eucharist. This is because of a fascinating clue in the Patristic literature. Let us begin, however, with Acts:[580]

> Some time later Paul said to Barnabas, "Let us go back and visit the brothers in all the towns where we preached the word of the Lord and see how they are doing." Barnabas wanted to take John, also called Mark, with them, but Paul did not think it wise to take him, because he had deserted them in Pamphylia and had not continued with them in the work. They had such a sharp disagreement that they parted company. Barnabas took Mark and sailed for Cyprus."

And why did Mark desert them? Epiphanius gives us the fascinating clue:

> Immediately after Matthew, Mark, who was a follower of St. Peter in Rome, was entrusted to set forth the Gospel and, after he wrote, he was sent forth by St. Peter to the area of Egypt. He happened to be one of the seventy-two, who were scattered abroad upon the word that the Lord said, "Unless someone eats my flesh and drinks my blood, they are not worthy of me,"[581] as the proof would be clear to those who read the gospel …[582]

Firstly, Eusebius tells us plainly that Mark neither heard Jesus nor followed him, although he later accompanied Peter.[583] Thus Mark could not have been scattered abroad by anything Jesus said. No Gospel names him. Some think he is the mysterious young man with only a linen garment who was following Jesus after his arrest. When they tried to seize him, he fled naked, leaving his garment behind.[584] That's just a guess. He doesn't appear until Acts, at first indirectly: on his escape from prison, Peter goes to the house of Mary, the mother of John Mark, some years after the crucifixion.[585]

Secondly, Epiphanius is a sloppy scholar. Jesus sends out the "seventy-two" to preach repentance.[586] They return with joy, gloating that even demons submitted to them. They were not scattered abroad; they were sent. Epiphanius has muddled this up with a passage in John. When Jesus says that those who eat his flesh and drink his blood will be raised up on the last day, some of the disciples murmur that it is a difficult teaching to accept. Shortly thereafter, the Evangelist comments: "Because of this, many of his disciples turned back and no longer walked with him."[587]

There is, however, someone John Mark never did "turn back" to walk with: Paul. Here is the passage: "From Paphos, Paul and his companions sailed to Perga in Pamphylia, where John left them to return to Jerusalem."[588]

Luke is silent about why John left them, but in the later fracas that led to the split between Paul and Barnabas, Luke's Paul alleges that John Mark is unreliable. Barnabas disagrees. Paul and Barnabas part while the latter takes Mark on the entirely separate mission.[589] If it was in Perga that Paul first promulgated the rite of eating the body and drinking the blood of Jesus, that would be why Mark, who was a practicing Jew, left him—on two counts: [1] laying the law aside would have been unacceptable (Jesus instituting a new covenant), [2] no Jew would drink blood of any kind. The law prohibits it.

Epiphanius concludes: "Likewise, after [Mark] returned back, he was deemed worthy by Peter to evangelize …"[590] Since Peter (as we shall see) opposed Paul, this fits perfectly with his returning from accompanying Paul because he refused to eat the flesh and drink the blood of Christ.

Luke keeps him in the background. No Antiochenes commission Mark with Saul and Barnabas. Luke first notices him in Cyprus, making a backhanded remark that they had brought John along as their attendant.[591] Since Paul was a tent-maker who boasted that he supported himself on his missions, why would he bring a servant? Papias did say that Mark wrote down Peter's reminiscences about Jesus. Being a scribe, he could, like Paul, have supported himself.

Epiphanius must have garbled the memory of John Mark, leaving not Jesus but Paul when the latter led his followers in eating the body and drinking the blood of a sacrificed Christ.

But the date, you ask? According to most chronologies, this happened in 45 CE, fifteen years after Jesus's "last supper," at the start of Paul's first missionary journey. And that, if my deductions are correct, is when the world first heard that Jesus had instituted a new covenant. Remember, the *Didache's* Eucharist has no body or blood of Christ. And the Fourth Gospel has no Eucharist at all. Had Jesus instituted it, it would have been in both.

Trouble in Jerusalem

While John Mark returned to Jerusalem, Paul and Barnabas continued their eventful first missionary journey, during which Paul managed to get himself stoned in the town of Lystra, now just one of the many tells (mounds) strewn across the Turkish plains. I once stood on its summit, musing. It was an eerie experience imagining the populous city where a mob once dragged this man outside the walls and left him for dead. But he was one tough customer—he lived to tell about it, noting it among many perils he endured in his contentious career.[592] After all his troubles, he returned to Antioch, and what was his reward? More trouble from Jerusalem. Perhaps John Mark reported back to James, who then sent men to Antioch insisting on full submission to the law. We will never know who alerted James: Paul left behind him many angry Jews who could well have made pilgrimages to Jerusalem.

Ah, scholars! Sometimes I shake my head in disbelief; sometimes I laugh. How gravely they discuss the disparities between Acts' and Paul's accounts of the first Jerusalem council. Many decide there must have been two councils; how else to explain such gross discrepancies?

The Bible may be the word of God, but Luke and Paul were human, subject to that universal human foible: manipulating facts in one's favor. Anyone who has been in a heated argument knows how contenders bend "facts" to shore up their argument. Scientists look for the simplest solution. In this case, Luke presented the tradition he received from his point of view, and Paul recounted his memories from his perspective.

In Acts 15, some of the "circumcision party" came down to Antioch. In the ensuing dissension, Paul, Barnabas, and some others were delegated to return to Jerusalem about the question.

Looking at the Jerusalem Council from Paul's point of view, we find him claiming that he went up because of a revelation.[593] There he met those "who seemed to be something,"[594] his put-down of James, Peter, and John. He likes this idea so much that he emphasizes it:

> "Knowing the grace given to me, James and Cephas [Peter] and John, *the ones seeming to be pillars*, gave the right hand of fellowship to me and to Barnabas, that we should go to the Gentiles but they to the circumcision …"[595] (Italics mine.)

Translators try to hide Paul's sneers, substituting "acknowledged pillars," or even, in Young's "literal translation," "esteemed pillars"! That's not even close to literal! The establishment wants to maintain the myth that everything was nice and cozy between Paul and Jesus's original apostles.

There's a deeper reason for the smoke screen. Why would Paul sneer at Jesus's chosen apostles? He's trying to minimize their importance. (These are the "super-apostles" he later maligns in Second Corinthians.) Their emissaries brought their "gospel" to the Galatians to confute Paul's. The Galatian epistle repudiates the law. James's "zealots" were having nothing to do with that.

Acts paints an entirely different picture of the Jerusalem Council. As noted earlier, that council did indeed add something to him: the four Noahide rules: to refrain from food polluted by idols, from fornication, from animals that have been strangled, and from blood.[596] Abstinence from fornication was Paul's great obsession so he embraced that point. "The body is not for fornication but for the Lord."[597] Fornication launches his tortured discussion of sex in First Corinthians six and seven.

With that off his chest, he turns to James's first rule: avoiding food that had been offered to idols,[598] a rule that galled him:

> "Therefore, about eating food sacrificed to idols. We know no idol really exists … and that there is no God except one …. But not all men have this knowledge; some are so accustomed to idols that they think they are eating food offered to idols, and since their conscience is weak, they are defiled. But food will not commend us to God; if we don't eat, we are no worse; if we do eat, we are no better."[599]

Next, he briefly dismisses food as irrelevant, since God will destroy both food and the stomach.

He reveals how much it galled him in the next chapter, which we looked at earlier: "Am I not free," etc., the implication being that he refuses to be bound by Jerusalem and its rules. He underlines his freedom by pointing out that he, unlike the other apostles and Jesus's brothers, works for his keep. He preaches the Gospel because an obligation was laid upon him (by the visionary Jesus): "Woe is me if I do not proclaim the good news."[600] With this higher obligation, he is "free of all men,"[601] which, of course, includes any directives from James.

Having established his independence, he lists the sins of the Children of Israel in the desert. Then:

> "What am I saying then? That an idolatrous sacrifice is anything or that an idol is anything? No. What they sacrifice, they sacrifice to demons and not to God. I don't want you to become sharers with demons. You cannot drink the cup of the Lord and the cup of demons. You cannot partake of the table of the Lord and the table of demons."[602]

He has done an about-face on food offered to idols. Idols that don't exist suddenly become demons, an idea the church later embraced with great enthusiasm.

He never touches on things strangled. Perhaps it was a nonissue.

But abstaining from blood. Did James aim this at the Eucharist that Paul "received from the Lord: [Jesus] took the cup also after supper, saying, 'This cup is the new covenant in my blood'"?[603] If so, Paul ignores that rule: it would invalidate his Eucharist. He must have gagged over agreeing to it in the first place, but he needed James's blessing to legitimize his work. I leave it there, with Paul and his Corinthians drinking the Lord's blood in direct defiance of the Jerusalem Council.

The council did not trust Paul. It sent two of its own members to Antioch with a letter clearly stating the agreement. Luke tells us that the Christians there "rejoiced at the exhortation."[604] This is Luke showing what a happy little group of Christians they were.

Paul's Struggles Continue

The conflict with Jerusalem continued. Paul writes:

> "For you, brothers, became imitators of God's churches in Judea … You suffered the same things from your own fellow-tribesmen as they did from the Jews, who both killed the Lord Jesus and the prophets, and chased us out; they do not please God and are contrary to all men, hindering us from speaking to the Gentiles so that they may be saved. Thus they always fill up the cup of their sins. But wrath has come upon them at last."[605]

Many scholars claim that someone interpolated the last line: "Wrath has come upon them at last" since it must refer to the destruction of Jerusalem. It could just as well refer to the Passover riot when Cumanus was the procurator. A soldier, standing on the parapet above the temple courts, turned his backside toward Passover crowds below and loudly broke wind. In the riot that ensued, Cumanus sent in the troops. Thousands died. James almost certainly witnessed it, and Paul wrote First Thessalonians at just about that time, the shocking event still fresh in everyone's minds.

Other scholars dismiss this whole passage. Surely Paul would not bad-mouth the Jews.

Why not? He does it elsewhere. After a scurrilous attack on Moses receiving the tablets of the law on Mount Sinai, he alleges that Moses veiled his face so that the Children of Israel would not see that the law was being done away with[606] (thus imputing duplicity to Moses!). "But their thoughts were hardened … Even until today, whenever Moses is read, a veil lies on their hearts."[607]

We humans project our own failings on others. Remember the quote in the *Tathbit*: "With the Jew I was a Jew, with the Roman a Roman, and with the Arma'i an Arma'i," the Ebionite version of "to the Jews, I became as a Jew … to those outside the law, I became as one outside the law …"[608] What more natural, then, to impute duplicity to Moses?

The man who would defame Moses and the Jews would write the Thessalonians' passage. Again, defending himself against the circumcision party, Paul turns nasty, wishing that those who insist on it "would castrate themselves!"[609] Despite Christianity's ongoing cover-up, Paul happily bad-mouthed those who stood in his way.

Jesus versus Paul on Social Justice

After getting the right hand of fellowship from the "seeming pillars" of the church, Paul tells his readers that they asked only one thing: that he remember the poor; "indeed, I was eager to do this very thing."[610] Why was he eager to do that? Search his whole authentic corpus, and you will find precious little concern for the poor. The one exception is:

> "When you come together, it is not to eat the Lord's Supper. Each of you takes his own supper without waiting for anyone else, while one is hungry, another is drunk. Don't you have houses in which to eat and drink? Or do you despise God's assembly and shame those who have nothing? What shall I say to you? Shall I praise you? No I will not praise you."[611]

Nowhere else does he show any concern for the hungry.

Because Paul's apathy over the poor is in such profound contrast to Jesus's program, which was to right the wrongs of the poor, the oppressed, and the rejects of society, we need to take it very seriously indeed. Could Paul's visionary Jesus have lost interest in these things once he got to the other world and replaced them with a new set of spiritual priorities? Paul condemns:

> "Fornication [note that this is first on his list], uncleanness, lewdness, idolatry, sorcery, enmities, strife, jealousy, anger, rivalries, divisions, sects, envy, drunkenness, revelry and like things ... those who do such things will not inherit the kingdom of God."[612] (My translation.)

Not a word about oppressing the poor. Pauline Christianity is incredibly self-centered: obsessed with being saved, not with striving to make this a better world. It is in direct contrast to the ministry of Jesus and his Jewish followers. And the prophets who came before them.

For Paul, revelry was out. For Jesus, the life more abundant was the whole point. Not *just* for others, he shared in it too. When Luke's Jesus says, "The Son of man came eating and drinking, and you say: 'Behold, a glutton and a drunkard, a friend of tax-collectors and sinners,'"[613] neither

Matthew nor Luke nor Jesus rebut the charge. Considering all this reveling, Jesus would have been debarred from Paul's Kingdom of God.

Paul claims to have trained as a Pharisee,[614] yet his lack of concern for the poor is at odds with Judaism: the law,[615] the prophets, and Jesus all denounce oppression roundly. Yet aside from the passage about neglecting the hungry at the Lord's Supper and his response to James's request, Paul takes no interest. The proof text is this purple passage in first Corinthians 13: "And if I dole out all my goods to feed the poor … but have not love, it profits me nothing."[616]

In contrast, what does Jesus tell the rich man to do to inherit eternal life? "Go, sell what you own and give your money to the poor."[617] Black and white could scarcely be more opposite.

Now what are Paul's fruits of the spirit as opposed to the works of the flesh? These:

> "Love [*agape*, "spiritual love", not *eros*], joy, peace, longsuffering, kindness, goodness, faithfulness, meekness, self-control; against such things there is no law. Now those who belong to Christ Jesus have crucified the flesh with its passions and lusts."[618]

There are many admirable virtues there. Sadly, the church has poor record of living up to them.

In Paul's defense we should note that he expected Jesus's return within his lifetime, to end this evil age. After exhorting the Romans "love your neighbor as yourself," Paul writes:

> "Do this, knowing the time: the hour for you to be raised out of sleep; for now is salvation nearer to us than when we first believed. The night is far spent and the day has drawn near. Therefore, let us cast off the works of darkness and put on the armor of light. Let us walk properly, not in reveling and in drunken bouts, not in fornication and excesses, not in strife and in jealousy; but on the Lord Jesus Christ, and do not think of the flesh and its lusts."[619]

With the end of the world so close, why reform society? But two millennia later we are still waiting, while much of the church still obsesses over the flesh and its lusts while ignoring the dispossessed.

These were not Jesus's ideas. As a first century Jew, he would, of course, have frowned on sexual license, but he says precious little about it. Matthew's "Everyone seeing a woman with a view to desire her has already committed adultery in his heart,"[620] is suspect since it occurs only here. Yet he too, expected the immanent apocalyptic deliverance of Israel from this evil generation, as many sayings in the Gospels show. Actually the closest to Paul's thought is this:

> "And take heed for yourselves that your hearts don't become burdened with overeating and heavy drinking and life's anxieties and that day will come on you like a snare; for it will come on all those sitting on the face of the earth. But you, be watchful at all times, praying that you will be able to escape *all those things that are about to happen*, able to stand before the Son of man."[621] (Italics mine.)

Luke greatly admired Paul. Note the immediacy in both: "the day has drawn near" and "those things that are about to happen." Even the King James obscures this immediacy, hence my own translations.

For Jesus, the apocalypse would turn the world topsy-turvy: the poor and hungry would come first. He was a trendsetter: this has been the aim of many a revolution ever since. His Jewish followers, too, censured greed and lust for power while they sought to share the simple life.

The orthodox hierarchy, on the other hand, fell into the trap the devil set for Jesus on the mountaintop. Having seen the kingdoms of this world, it lusted to rule them; over the centuries, both the people and their secular rulers objected, which was one reason the Protestant reformation was so successful. It's a universal foible, however. Many (but by no means all) Protestants fell into the trap. Nevertheless, movements arose again and again over the millennia, inspired by the ethics of the early Followers of the Way, and they still inspire many people today. That's what Liberation theology is about and that's what Archbishop Romero died for.

The Yeshuites showed a surprising resilience. We have already seen it in tenth-century Iraq. But they didn't die there. There is evidence for them in sixteenth-century Russia, of all places. It, of course, borders Muslim lands. I quote the Qur'an:

> "Those who follow the Jewish religion, the Christians, the Sabeans, and whatever others believe in God and practice doing good, all these shall receive their recompense from the Lord ... Virtue does not consist in turning the face toward the East nor toward the West to pray, but in being tolerant."[622]

Ideally, Islam tolerated the "Peoples of the Book" (Jews and Christians), although that toleration was spotty, to say the least. Some Yeshuites apparently survived there, since they entered Russia from Asia Minor. We will hear more of that later.

The Disobedient Ones

As Paul approached the fateful climax of his career, he wrote:

> "Now I beg you, brothers, by our Lord Jesus Christ, and by the love of the Spirit, that you strive together with me in your prayers to God for me, that I may be delivered from those who are disobedient in Judea, and that my service which I have for Jerusalem may be acceptable to the saints."[623]

Those who are disobedient? Most translations render this as "unbelievers," but the World English Bible is faithful. Translators are not just trying to disguise Paul's arrogance. "Unbelievers" could mean Jews who did not believe that Jesus was the Meshikha. But the disobedient ones in Judea can only be Jesus's followers who rejected Paul's version of Jesus's mission. Since that belies the master narrative—Paul and the other apostles worked amicably together—it has to go. Actually, Jerome started it. He translates "disobedient ones" as "unbelievers" in the Vulgate. Although distressed by Paul's lying, Jerome could be duplicitous too.

Earlier Paul speaks of "what Christ worked through me for the obedience of the Gentiles ..."[624] Disobedience to him was disobedience to his Christ. Remember the silenced voices of the Yeshuites of the East: they said Paul had a passion for dominion.[625] That passion cast a long shadow over Christianity. His now familiar stricture, "But even if we, or an angel from out of heaven, should preach a gospel to you beside the one we preached, let him be accursed,"[626] eventually sanctioned the church's destruction of all its rivals.

There was also Paul's big stick to the Corinthians:

> "Now when I did not come to you, some were puffed up; but I will come shortly to you if the Lord wills, and I will find out not just the speech of the puffed up ones, but their power; for the kingdom of God is not in speech, but in power. What do you want? Shall I come with a stick or with love and a spirit of gentleness?"[627]

That's getting obedience out of the Gentiles. Jerusalem was another story.

Confrontation in the Mother of All Churches

Paul was taking the promised donation that he had gathered from Macedonia and Achaia for "the poor of the saints in Jerusalem" (Rom 15:26). The reader already knows about his confrontation with James. Paul had good reason for his fears. Let's follow him there.

But first, how reliable is Luke's account of the trip? According to Eusebius, Luke *composed* the *Acts of the Apostles "not from the accounts of others, but from what he had seen himself."*[628] (Italics mine.) Many claim that this is a pious lie. Heretic that I am, I disagree, certainly for the "we" passages. These are shark-infested waters over which I will lightly skim lest I be dismembered, but I believe he wrote the original "we" section—although later redactors tampered with it.

As I already pointed out in regard to the prayer about Pontius Pilate and Herod conspiring together, Luke drew on earlier sources in the first part of Acts. Some of those sources were in Semitic languages. For instance, in the second chapter of Acts, following a discussion of the enthusiasm of the early community of believers in Jerusalem, it concludes: "And day by day, the Lord added those who were being saved together."[629] Since that "together" makes no sense in either Greek or English, translators omit it. However, on the analogy of Hebrew usage in Qumran, the original word probably refers to the community. If so, the original might have run something like: "And day by day, the Lord added those who were being saved to the community," which makes perfect sense. In light of this, I think Luke was telling the truth when he claims to have "investigated from their source all things accurately in order to write to you."[630] His problems with his Aramaic sources help justify this claim.[631]

This isn't to say that he didn't have a bias, or that he wouldn't omit things that didn't suit his program. He recounts meeting Paul at Assos, where "we took him on board" before sailing to Miletus.[632] There, summoning the elders from Ephesus, Paul says: "The Holy Spirit testifies to me in every city that imprisonment and persecutions are waiting for me,"[633] that is, in Jerusalem. This accords with Paul's anxieties noted earlier. Yet Luke never tells us why Paul is going: it is Paul who says he is "going to Jerusalem in a ministry to the saints; for Macedonia and Achaia have been pleased to share their resources with the poor among the saints at Jerusalem."[634] You will remember James requesting it at the Jerusalem Council—the very thing Paul was "eager to do." Perhaps Luke wanted Paul to appear to be going on his own initiative to report his missionary successes.

But then why is Luke's account of the events in Jerusalem so embarrassing to Paul? It still is in the "we" portions of Acts, Luke's own voice:

> "When *we* arrived in Jerusalem, the brothers received us joyfully. The next day, Paul went in *with us* to James, and the elders came. And having greeted them, he related all the things God did through his ministry among the Gentiles. Hearing this, they glorified God, and said to him [Luke is fudging here. Surely they weren't all talking at once like a chorus line. "They" means "Bishop James"], You see, brother, how many ten thousands of Jews have believed, and all of them are zealots for the law. They have been informed that you teach apostasy from Moses to all the Jews who live among the Gentiles, telling them not to circumcise their children nor walk in the customs. What is to be done? They will hear that you have come. Do therefore what we tell you."[635]

James orders Paul not only to sponsor four men who are making a vow in the temple but to join them in their purification rites, adding: "Then everyone will know there is no truth in these reports *but that you yourself walk in the law*"[636] (italics mine).

Let's take a look at this. James demands that Paul recant and *prove* he is still observing the law—Paul, who claims that salvation comes through belief in Christ: the law is dead. Up until this point, Luke's narrative sweep has shown the slow acceptance of Paul's understanding of Jesus's ministry, even among Jesus's dim-witted disciples. So what does Paul do? The man who was going to take a big stick to the Corinthians humbly submits to James.

This time, pretending to be a Jew among Jews does not work. As in all good tales, just before his ordeal is finished, wouldn't you know it: some Jews from Asia see him in the temple and stir up a riot, crying: "This is the man who teaches all men everywhere against our people, our law and this place [the temple]."[637] This riot is the first protest against Christian anti-Semitism. Paul is arrested and never sees freedom again.

Consider the irony: Paul's last act as a free man is submission to the Law of Moses, a denial of everything he has striven for throughout his career. Could this be another reason the church gradually shoved James into the smoky house and forgot about him?

This is so embarrassing for Luke's thesis that he must have written it when these events were so well known that he could not falsify it. Remember Luke's report: "When [James and the elders] heard this, they glorified God."[638] Why did not he, or later redactors, simply remove the embarrassing material that followed? The narrative could have simply jumped to the Asian Jews seeing Paul in the temple compound (where he might have been for any reason) and the ensuing riot. How a passage recounting Paul recanting survived later Christian censors is a mystery. Had Luke written this after the destruction of Jerusalem in 70 CE, when Jesus's Jewish followers had been destroyed or dispersed and no longer wielded any power, he would surely have changed it. Therefore, he wrote this account sometime in the sixties. Those scholars who allege that Luke is late and unreliable need to explain this most inconvenient material.

Rome Houses Its Celebrated Saint

Eventually Paul appealed to the Emperor. Imprisoned in Eternal City, he continued to promote the religion he had created. Earlier, he had exhorted the Romans: "Let everyone be subject to the superior authorities, for there is no authority except from God, and the existing ones have been ordained by God."[639] Always obedience: yet the existing governing authority was Nero, a peculiar emperor for God to ordain if ever there was one. Though beloved of the religious right, this passage sticks in the craw of liberal theologians. Many claim it is an interpolation.

Why? It's perfectly in line with Paul's thought, actions, and relations. I am indebted to Eisenman for this insight. Not only does Paul recommend collaboration with Rome, but he claims to be on intimate terms with Caesar's household: "All the saints greet you, especially those of Caesar's household."[640] My goodness, what a name-dropper you are, Paul: "Especially those of Caesar's household." He even brags: "I want you to know, brothers, that my affairs have come rather to advance the gospel, so that my bonds in Christ have become known to all the Praetorian Guard and to everyone else."[641] Had he been a run-of-the-mill prisoner from the provinces, you can be sure that the palace guard would have known nothing of his existence.

With his connections, he may have had more pull with Herod's great-grandson, King Agrippa, than we might guess from their interview.[642] Again he mentions his kinsman, Herodion,[643] and you will remember that Acts lists Paul immediately after Manaen, the foster brother of Herod the Tetrarch in Antioch.[644] Cozy relations with the foster brother of the man who executed John the Baptist and "conspired" with Pilate to execute Jesus, in fact, with the whole Herodian family.

With this right-wing background, it becomes clearer why Paul persecuted the church in the beginning. As the henchman of Caiaphas, the tool of Rome, he destroyed those who were waiting for "the Son of man to come on the clouds of glory" and institute the millennial kingdom of justice. Paul never changed—just his tactics. Once inside the movement, he subverted it to his own purposes. As 'Abt al-Jabbar's Ebionite document puts it:

> It is a well-known [fact] ... that [the Christians] have abandoned the religion of Christ and turned toward the religious doctrines of the Romans, prizing and [seeking to obtain] in haste the profits which could be derived from *their domination and their riches*.[645] (Italics mine.)

Later, we will show how the church Romanized Christianity. Of course, the above was written after the church had prostituted itself to power under Constantine's benevolent eyes. Backed by the empire, it destroyed its rivals and burned their books: yes, Constantine did that and there is proof, although the worst burning times were under the Byzantine Emperor Theodosius II.[646]

Thus was Paul's curse on all other Gospels fulfilled. Only a precious few eluded it by escaping into the drifting sands of Egypt.

Chapter 9

The Two Ways: When the Church Was Jewish

The Teaching of the Lord, by the Twelve Apostles, to the Gentiles. There are two ways, one of life, the other of death ... Now the way of life is this: first, you shall love the God who made you; second, your neighbour as yourself, and everything that you would not have done to you, do not do to another. (*Didache*)[647]

Constantinople was a romantic spot, a standard stop on the Grand Tour. Lord Byron swam the Hellespont there, emulating Leander's amorous nightly visits to Hero, his ladylove. Afterwards, the poet wondered if its powerful currents might not have cooled Leander's lust.

A few decades later, an Orthodox Metropolitan discovered a dusty parchment volume in that fabled city. That crumbling work could not rival Lord Byron's mythic presence. Today such a find would spark international headlines, despite its drab title: *The Teaching (Didache) of the Lord, by the Twelve Apostles, to the Gentiles*, known simply as the *Didache*.

This slim manual has revolutionized our understanding of Jesus's early followers. The title "to the Gentiles" implies "from the Jewish followers of Jesus." Its Eucharist confirms its Jewishness: there's not a word about Jesus's body or blood. It gives thanks for the gifts of the earth.

The Lord's Prayer asks that God's kingdom come on earth. So does this Eucharist: "As this fragment lay scattered upon the mountains and has been gathered to become one, so gather your Church from the ends of the earth into your kingdom." No blood of the new covenant; no body broken for you. *Immediately afterward,* it says that if anyone "teaches another teaching, to destroy [the *Didache*'s teachings], do not listen to him,"[648] thus repudiating Paul's Eucharist.[649] I noted that the rite speaks of Jesus simply as God's servant, which, as we will see, is how Pope Clement understood him, a shocking view for that early head of the church.

The Way was a movement within Judaism—a most successful one—competing with the other sects: the Pharisees, Sadducees, and Essenes. The number of Paul's followers, scattered throughout the various cities of the empire, was still very small. This chapter deals with the period up to the destruction of Jerusalem in 70 CE. That event changed the balance irrevocably.

Yeshuites

I derived this word from Epiphanius. He tells us that before the disciples in Antioch began to be called Christians, they were known as Iessaeans.[650] He also says:

> When they were once called *Iessaeans* during a short period, some again withdrew at that time after the ascension of the Lord when Mark preached in the land of Egypt. *They were so-called followers of the apostles,* but I supposed that they were Nazoraeans who are described by me here.[651] (Italics mine.)

I italicized Epiphanius's sneer, "so-called followers of the apostles," since at one time no one questioned that they had inherited the mantel of those Jesus appointed to carry on his work. Just as Nazarene means followers of Jesus of Nazareth, *Iessaeans* could have meant followers of *Iesous*, the Greek form of Jesus, although Epiphanius waffles on that point, and the etymology is iffy. I will use Yeshuite for groups whose names we do not know, such as the Yeshuites whose Gospel quotations appear in the *Tathbit*. I will still use "Ebionites" and "Nazarenes" when the references are clear.

There are problems. First century Nazarenes were not the same as the Nazarenes of later centuries, and how much of the law should be observed covered a wide spectrum at various times and among various groups. Changes over time are why the historical records conflict.

Religions evolve. While anti-Semitism was the norm a hundred years ago, most churches now frown on it. Unlike progressive churches in the West, African Anglicans debar gays. There were many "Christianities" when they killed each other over who held the correct view.

The Paucity of Our Sources

Matthew has a saying that predates 70 CE: "The scribes and Pharisees sit on Moses' seat; do whatever they teach you and follow it."[652] After the destruction of the temple, neither scribe nor Pharisee sat there. The Pharisees had mutated into the rabbis of the coastal town of Yavneh, which was not "Moses's seat." The scribes had vanished, so the saying is no longer applicable on two counts. But note: this saying shows that Matthew's community was once a sect within Judaism.

This passage apparently reflects the growing conflict between that community and the temple. Later, the author condemns the Pharisees for nitpicking over swearing by both the temple and the altar.[653] No one could nitpick over either after 70 CE. They were gone.

There is a curious passage in Colossians whose reverberations will later echo into our story. The author charges some of the Colossians with submitting to "regulations, 'Do not handle, Do not taste, Do not touch.'"[654] These could be the forerunners of a "Jewish-Christian" sect later called the Athingians (touch-nots) who were to play a prominent role in medieval Byzantium.

For the first century or so, we have the New Testament, the *Didache*, the earliest layers of the Gospel of Thomas, snippets from Josephus, the first letter of Clement, and the Epistle of Barnabas. Later sources, such as the *Clementine Recognitions* and the *Tathbit*, must be used more critically— firstly, because all authors have a slant; secondly, their content may reflect later attitudes; thirdly, knowledge was inevitably lost; and lastly, later Christians amended texts to toe the orthodox line. It's like treading a maze. Which path leads to truth? And whose truth? Physicists have discovered that our observation determines the outcome of an experiment. Although this idea strikes me as a bit patriarchal, it hints at a wider application: every scholar's bent, including mine, determines the outcome of his research. Of course, I like to think that my bent arose from impartial study of the material.

Pacifism

Take pacifism. Matthew writes, "You have heard that it was said, 'You shall love your neighbor and hate your enemy,' But I say to you, love your enemies, and pray for those who persecute you ..."[655] How this pacifist saying fits in with Jesus's final days in Jerusalem is hard to say. If he loves the traders in the temple, it doesn't show.

Full pacifism probably developed later, at least in some branches of Jesus's followers, after the failed revolt in 70 CE and the total destruction of the Jewish state in 135 CE, a disaster that finally brought the political reality of Roman power home to all Jews. Scattered, humiliated, and persecuted, they were barred from their homeland. Zionism was not to raise its head again for well over a millennium and a half. In this situation, pacifism was not only the best, it was the only course.

Jesus's immediate followers can scarcely have been pacifists, as some allege. Let's recap the evidence. Pilate inscribed on the cross: "The King of the Jews." Firstly, crucifixion was only for crimes against the state. Secondly, the inscription stated the crime (that he had claimed to be the meshikha). Therefore Jesus was somehow involved in the insurrection that Mark so casually mentions—and Matthew and Luke so carefully delete. Secondly, there is that blank in the *Jewish War*, where we read in the Slavonic Josephus that the people expected Jesus to set the Jewish tribes free from the Roman hands. Thirdly, if Uncle Cleopas expected that "he was the one who was about to redeem Israel," that could only have meant "Rome out." Finally, when the disciples ask the risen Jesus if he will restore the kingdom to Israel right then,[656] do they think it can be done peaceably? Only by an act of God.

There's more. Remember that "Gamaliel's speech in Acts compares Jesus's followers to Theudas and Judas the Galilean, both of whom spearheaded nationalist movements ..."[657] Now we need to look at the political implications. Gamaliel says:

> "Keep away from these men and let them alone; because if this plan or this undertaking is of human origin, it will fail; but if it is of God, you will not be able to overthrow them—in that case, you may even be found fighting against God!"[658]

With those antecedents, he is talking revolution.

Now compare the *Clementine Recognitions*:

> "Gamaliel said, 'Be quiet for a little, O men of Israel, for ye do not perceive the trial which hangs over you. Wherefore refrain from these men; and if what they are engaged in be of human counsel, it will soon come to an end; but if it be from God, why will you sin without cause, and prevail nothing? For who can overpower the will of God?'"[659]

Not one word about Judas the Galilean. Gamaliel is defending Peter because he has predicted the coming destruction of the temple. That fits quite nicely with the pacifist stance of the *Clementines*. The scenario is totally different from that of Acts.

The Slavonic Josephus echoes Gamaliel's speech, attributed to not one but two procurators, Cuspius Fadus (44–46 CE) and Tiberius Alexander, (46–48 CE). Regarding the "servants of the previously described wonder-doer," the same people who were hauled in before the Sanhedrin:

> But when those noble governors saw the misleading of the people, they deliberated with the scribes to seize and put them to death, for fear lest the little be not little if it have ended in the great. But they shrank back and were alarmed over the signs, saying: "In the plain course such wonders do not occur. But if they do not issue from the counsel of God, they will quickly be convicted." And they gave [Jesus's followers] authority to act as they would.[660]

Could this be the Gamaliel tradition adapted to two procurators parroting away like the Bobbsey Twins? Compare the three passages. In Acts and the *Recognitions*, the temple authorities discuss the status of Jesus's followers. In the Slavonic Josephus, the governors consult with those same authorities. At issue is whether this little movement is going to become a big problem. Again in all three the caution is that if this movement has arisen through the agency of God, it should not be opposed. Because of that, all three sources free them. Surely these passages derive from a common source.

A little earlier, we learn the political thrust of Jesus's followers:

> And at the time of these two [procurators], many had been discovered as servants of the previously described

wonder-doer; and as they spake to the people about their teacher—that he is living, although he is dead, and that *he will free you from your servitude* [italics mine]—many from the folk gave ear to the above-named and took upon themselves their precept, not because of their reputation; they were indeed of the humbler sort, some just cobblers, others sandal-makers, others artisans.[661]

There is that familiar idea again: "*He will free you from your servitude.*" Clearly, in the forties, Jesus's followers expected him to return and free them, no doubt by restoring "the kingdom to Israel." Only an act of God could do that pacifically. It must still mean political servitude: the Slavonic Herod executed John the Baptist for just such promises.

These Jews were not looking for freedom from the law, as Paul would later proclaim. Another Slavonic passage may refer to him: "But if anyone diverged from the word of the Law, plaint was brought before the teachers of the Law. Often they expelled him and sent him to the Emperor's presence."[662] The emperor has no say about the law, but perhaps someone has a garbled memory of Paul appealing to the emperor and being sent to Rome. It is early for Paul, but scrambled dates plague our sources: Acts' Gamaliel has Theudas and Judas the Galilean backwards, for instance.

Although the identity of the author of the Slavonic material will always remain a mystery, no follower of Jesus would have used the term "noble governors." Only toadies like Josephus would have done so, but since Josephus was generally contemptuous of such movements, it seems unlikely that he wrote it as it stands. Someone could have, of course, adapted a passage now missing from all other redactions. Pagan Gentiles? Who would be interested enough to interpolate (or rewrite) this material? It is all quite mysterious. The crucial thing is that it is an independent witness to the life of Jesus's followers before the Jewish revolt. They had a reputation for healing (marvelous signs); their members were drawn from the masses of the people; and they taught that Jesus would "free them from their servitude," the essence of all these messianic movements.

The *Clementines* are strong on pacifism. In the head quote of the chapter on Paul, we saw it: "But, from their fear of God, [Jesus followers] rather suffered themselves to be killed by an inferior force, than they would kill others."[663] Later Peter maintains that he will not allow men to take up arms and fight, "and attempt whatsoever lust may dictate."[664]

Documents of such a later date cannot be used to prove the attitudes of Jesus or his followers in the first century. Neither can the Beatitude that blesses the peacemakers.[665] This saying, which is unique to Matthew (or a later interpolator), added new "blesseds" to Jesus's originals, ones that reward virtues. His community has, postrevolt, given up all hope of political deliverance. "Blessed are the poor *in spirit* for theirs is the kingdom of heaven,"[666] he consoles them. The destitute will just have to wait for their pie in the sky bye and bye. Luke's Jesus, on the other hand, still promises the rewards of the poor here on earth, which could only happen if the ruling powers were overthrown. The case for true pacifism in the earliest days of the movement is weak indeed.

Gentile Christianity was not pacifist until later either. The passage that Justin Martyr quotes about beating swords into plowshares proves nothing. He is showing that Micah prophesied the conversion of the Gentiles, and that passage just happens to be part of that quote.[667]

A few decades later the Christian-basher Celsus charges that if everyone emulated the Christians, the emperor would have no troops, and barbarians would overrun the empire.[668] Origen replies that pacifist Christians should be treated just as those who serve in shrines and are exempted from war to offer sacrifices with unstained hands for the well-being of the emperor.[669] Tertullian claims that the Lord banished the sword, and Christians may not bear army flags.[670]

It is not until the early third century that the *Apostolic Tradition of Hippolytus* bans soldiers (along with pimps, charioteers, and anyone "who does things not to be named") from becoming Christians.[671] Although this work is neither apostolic nor traditional nor by Hippolytus, it shows that, in the third century, soldiers and pimps and even those who do things not to be named wanted to become followers of Jesus. Maybe it was because Jesus liked to party with prostitutes and extortioners.

Relations between the Way and the Temple

We now have the same problem we had with James: the Sanhedrin versus the Way. Since Herod and Pontius Pilate conspired with the Jewish establishment to put Jesus to death,[672] Peter and John must have waited a considerable time before trying to attract new members. Otherwise, the Sanhedrin would have surely hauled them off to the Romans for crucifixion too. Yet since Gamaliel likened them to other rebel groups, their aims were known. They were probably quiescent, waiting for Jesus's return. Despite how dumb they all look in the Gospels, they could have been using Jesus's famous ploy—hide and reveal—to keep everyone guessing.

In the *Rise and Fall of Jewish Nationalism*, Doron Mendels points out that the high priestly houses controlled the temple during the first century just as they had under the Hellenistic priests. He fails to note that the situation was just the same as it was before the Maccabaean revolt: corrupt priests toadying to ruling powers. Few Jews could have missed the similarity. Likewise, the priestly establishment surely knew their history far too well to ignore the fate of their predecessors. At the first whisper of unrest, they would have investigated. The Gospels portray them doing just that with both John the Baptist and Jesus. Due to its late date, the *Clementine Recognitions* can portray the temple authorities meeting amicably with the disciples.

During the revolt, the various rebel groups splintered into warring factions. That sped up Rome's victory handily (which would later inspire the famous British tactic of divide and conquer). This tendency to splinter fits my Mount of Olives hypothesis: while Jesus and his committed followers waited for God to act, another faction, led by Barabbas and the two "thieves" who were crucified with Jesus, jumped the gun and revolted.

That also might be why Judas Iscariot did what he did (if he did it): to precipitate God's action. Since he was convinced the Jesus was God's chosen meshikha, it followed that God would not stand idly by while Jesus was arrested. He had fulfilled the prophecies: he had ridden into Jerusalem on an ass; he had cleared the traders from the temple; perhaps this would force the Mount of Olives to split.

If so, he was in the wing of Jesus's followers that expected God to be the prime mover in restoring the kingdom to Israel. From that probably flowed the later pacifism. That may be how the Way got away, for a short time at least, with promoting their cause in Jerusalem.

After his death, Jesus's followers focused on his return on the clouds bringing in the kingdom, spearheading a supernatural intervention in the style of Zechariah 14 that would conquer evil and reward the righteous. (Whether they would have to fight too is unclear.) Then God would renovate humanity and the luminous reign of justice would begin.

The Mystery of the Anointed Solved?

With their message that Jesus was the Meshikha, the disciples would have been suspect from the get-go. I dealt earlier with an item that long puzzled me: how could they refer to Jesus as the Meshikha, "the anointed," as though it were a *fait accompli*? I found Baukham's solution that Mary of Bethany anointed him helped.

Then we looked at the other passage in Acts' prayer of thanksgiving, where we read: "For in this city ... both Herod and Pontius Pilate assembled with the Gentiles and the people of Israel against your holy servant Jesus, *whom you anointed.*"[673] (Italics mine.) As pointed out earlier, this is a traditional Yeshuite prayer that Luke copied.

But the prayer states that *God* anointed Jesus. The Gospels record one event only that could be interpreted as God "anointing" Jesus: the spirit descending as a dove. Irenaeus alludes to this idea, sneering at heretics who believe that "Christ" descended upon Jesus as a dove after his baptism.[674] This is essentially the same idea as in Acts' prayer of the disciples. Thus there seem to have been two views: Mary of Bethany anointed him versus God anointing him at his baptism.

Despite centuries of heresy hunting, the latter proved a stubborn idea. In the early fifth century, John Cassian attacked a Gaulish heretic: "For he ... declared that our Lord *was made the Christ by His baptism* ...."[675] (Italics mine.) This belief was heresy; the orthodox faction was hooked on the idea of the preexistent Christ, an idea first stated in the moving and mysterious passage that opens John's Gospel:

> In the beginning was the Word, and the Word was with God, and the Word was God .... And the Word was made flesh and dwelt among us, (and we beheld his glory, the glory as of the only begotten of the Father) full of grace and truth.[676]

According to Irenaeus, John wrote that to combat those who believed that God adopted Jesus as his son at his baptism.[677] This Gospel is dated anywhere from the last decade of the first century to early in the second, long after the period we are looking at now.

The Mystery of the Martyrs

Convinced that God had chosen Jesus as his meshikha and that his plan had not died with him, the disciples sowed the seeds of the good news, ready to give their lives for it if necessary, as had their master. Thus bravely died Stephen and the shadowy James the so-called "greater," son of Zebedee. Many other unnamed Followers of the Way did likewise under the persecution of Saul/Paul.[678] Peter also risked his life, something he had wanted to do while Jesus was alive, had his courage not failed. So where did they get the courage?

There were two distinct events. First, the resurrection experiences. Although what actually happened must forever remain a mystery, something with profound implications for the future of humanity did occur. Mysterious sightings, numinous experiences, moments when the chills run up and down the spine; these are human universals. The disciples' memories of their leader's horrific death were likely to produce such phenomena. And so the resurrection stories started, and spread. Then as now, stories wield tremendous power. They speak to our innermost being in ways that "facts" do not. Jesus was still with them. Hope returned. Although Roman power seemed unstoppable, there was one thing it could not destroy: the human spirit.

And then came "Pentecost." Such a ragtag band would have needed some transforming experience like that to turn them into heroes. And a ragtag band they were, like so many others crushed by the Roman juggernaut in the ensuing forty years. Yet all the others, with the exception of John the Baptist's followers, left hardly a trace when their leaders foundered: just some smears on the pages of Josephus. This shows charisma, a charisma that has echoed down the centuries—the charisma that sparked the fireworks at Pentecost. And there were fireworks.

Although Acts is our only source, on the analogy of the very un-Lukan prayer we looked at earlier, he was drawing on old traditions:

> And there was suddenly a sound out of heaven like the rush of a violent wind, and it filled all the house where they were sitting. And it appeared to them that tongues of fire separated, coming to rest on each one of them. And they were all filled with the holy spirit and began to speak in other tongues, as the spirit gave them utterance.[679]

Rushing winds, loud noises, visionary fires, speaking in tongues: all familiar phenomena. Later, Peter (mis)quotes Joel: "In the last days ... I will pour out my spirit ... and they will prophesy ... before the coming of the great and notable day of the Lord."[680]

The original is quite different: "Before the great *and terrible* day of the Lord comes,"[681] (Italics mine) followed by: "All who call upon the name of the Lord shall be delivered ...and among the survivors shall be those whom the Lord calls." Joel was prophesying God's destruction of Judah's enemies and eternal peace in the land thereafter. That did not suit Luke's purposes.

Nonetheless, Peter's quote begins: *"In the last days."* Luke did not make that up fifty years down the road just to embarrass himself. Yet some scholars assert that Luke invented Pentecost to strengthen the Greek spiritual mode within Gentile Christianity. Why? There are perfectly good Biblical precedents. The Spirit of the Lord came upon David in power when Samuel anointed him.[682] Saul's pursuit of David, which I discussed earlier, is even more apropos. As in all good fairy tales, three messengers are sent, three messengers fall into trances, along with Samuel's prophets, and fail. Finally Saul decides that if you want something done, do it yourself, but unlike in fairy tales, he gets caught up into ecstasy too.[683] Mass possession best describes Samuel's prophets as well as the ecstatic trances of the king and his men. These are far more apt precedents than the vapor-induced spells of Delphi's priestesses. Those lonely ladies' trances were quite unlike mass possession among the early Christians. What about mad maenads and bacchants? I doubt Luke wanted to evoke their orgies!

Some sort of Pentecost event must have happened. Why else would the apostles risk their lives for a dead man's cause? Under the stress of hopes lost beneath the cross of Jesus and then stirred by mysterious visionary appearances, they met together. As sometimes happens, this high-tension situation sparked mass trance. Now they had fulfilled Joel's predictions: "Your young men shall see visions," "your sons and your daughters shall prophesy." That great and terrible day of the Lord must be at hand, therefore, confirming what Jesus had promised. The Pentecost event turned the cowardly disciples of the Mount of Olives into brave proclaimers of Jesus's mission. Assured that God was urging them on to greater deeds, they redoubled their master's efforts until, after being scattered in the persecutions, they took their message to the nations, even including India, as we shall see.

This impulse to bring the world to righteousness, and thus achieve that great and terrible day of the Lord, initiated the evangelical mind-set that has driven Christianity to this very day. One of the saddest chapters of history is its later perversion: trying to impose orthodox views on all followers of Jesus. This was a gross betrayal of the aims of both Jesus and his original followers. They strove to create a just world, not an orthodox one. It still infects many today. Two young men once told me I was going to go to hell because I went to Bathurst Street United Church and wasn't "saved." There was something quite disturbing about their fanatical gaze. If that was being saved, I wanted no part of it. That mind-set creates so much violence today, worldwide, no matter which religion thinks it has the only true revelation of its violent god.

There is one problem: the timing. The disciples are celebrating God giving of the law when they receive the gift of the Spirit. That fits too neatly the Pauline (and Lukan) program: the law has been superseded by salvation through Christ. God confirms it with the gift of the spirit.

Still, something like it must have happened although perhaps not so neatly timed. Since spirit possession was endemic in the early church (Paul mentions it several times, as does Acts), there had to be a first time. Whenever that was, Luke claims that, immediately after, there were mass converts in their thousands who "devoted themselves to the apostles' teaching and fellowship, to the breaking of bread and the prayers."[684]

Expanding the Operation

The *Clementine Recognitions* suggests a reasonable time frame for the growth of the movement. Peter says that a week of years had passed from Jesus's death to the confrontation with the Sanhedrin, after which time the church in Jerusalem "was most plentifully multiplied and grew ..."[685] And grow it did, exponentially. In fewer than thirty years it had reached Rome and many places in between. What was its attraction?

Of great importance was this:

> "Then Caiaphas attempted to impugn the doctrine of Jesus, saying that ... He said that the poor are blessed; and promised earthly rewards; and placed the chief gift in an earthly inheritance; and promised that those who maintain righteousness shall be satisfied with meat and drink ...."[686]

Thomas replies, pointing out that the prophets, in whom Caiaphas believes, taught these things.

Right! Thomas. One among a multitude: "But with righteousness he will judge the needy; with justice he will give decisions for the poor of the earth."[687] The next line states that God will slay the wicked. Caiaphas no doubt skipped over such passages with ears firmly shut, but let's dig deeper into his attempt to "impugn the doctrine."

Matthew had already declawed the promise: the poor in spirit will be rewarded in the great bye and bye. Not Luke: Jesus blesses the poor, because the kingdom of God is theirs.[688] Then he makes it quite explicit: "Blessed are the ones hungering now because you will be satisfied."[689] Saying that would have brought the wrath of the high priests down on his head in a hurry. If the disciples were preaching this, Caiaphas and company would have silenced them. But remember, when Fadus was governor (ten years after Caiaphas), they were still promising that Jesus would free them from their servitude.

Even the rarified John acknowledges the tradition: "I came that they may have life, and abundantly may they have it."[690] The here and now that must be, since the afterlife is surely all abundance. (Well, not for us damned, of course).

Who would not want to be freed from oppression? Small wonder they swarmed in according to both Acts and the *Recognitions*. The former claims that three thousand joined the movement.[691] The latter is even more dramatic: "The truth everywhere prevailed," it tells us. In just a few days, they, who had been very few, became "far more numerous" than their opponents. Consequently, the priests were afraid "lest the whole of the people should come over to our faith."[692] Exaggeration is a great human foible, then as now, but beyond any doubt, the movement grew large enough to threaten the temple regime—which precipitated the persecutions of Caiaphas and Saul.

If you promised freedom from oppression in any impoverished country today, you would soon have a following. Archbishop Oscar Romero did just that and, like Jesus, paid for it with his life. Typically, the church has not considered him for sainthood, yet he embodied, in the twentieth century, the ideals of Jesus and his Jewish followers. The same ideals and the same dynamics operate in contemporary Latin America as they did in first century Judea. That is why the high priests, whose power depended on the backing of Rome, persecuted the Way. Wealthy and powerful churches also want the poor kept in their place, thus betraying Jesus and his true heirs.

The *Tathbit* remembered the conflict too, telling us that Jesus's followers worshiped in the synagogues with other Jews but division arose over the Messiah.[693]

Then wider trouble. Paul met followers of John the Baptist, in particular one Apollos, on his travels.[694] His views differed from Paul's, who writes:

My brothers, some from Chloe's household have informed
me that there are quarrels among you. What I mean is
this: One of you says, "I follow Paul"; another, "I follow
Apollos"; another, "I follow Cephas"; still another, "I
follow Christ."[695]

Oh, oh. Here we are, perhaps twenty-five years after the crucifixion,
and the Way has already forked. That was only the beginning.

The Way Was Not Heretical; Orthodoxy Was

Although the earliest movement was made up of practicing Jews, the
competition for Jesus's name quickly grew fierce. For several centuries,
the Christianity we know was a distinct minority. This has been largely
ignored. But not by everyone. In the sixties, Georg Strecker wrote:

> Ecclesiastical historiography since Eusebius is not correct,
> *but that for broad areas the heresies were "primary." Jewish*
> *Christianity, according to the witness of the New Testament,*
> *stands at the beginning of the development of church history,*
> *so that it is not the gentile Christian "ecclesiastical doctrine"*
> *that represents what is primary, but rather a Jewish Christian*
> *theology.*[696] (Italics mine.)

Scholars are beginning to pay attention. In *The Ways Never Parted*,
John Gager writes: Jewish Christians do not quickly disappear from the
historical scene nor, in the regions of Syria and beyond, *are they even a tiny*
minority or a heresy.[697] (Italics mine.)

Some eminent scholars back my thesis. Thank you, John Gager and
Georg Strecker.

The Pitfalls of Radical Sharing

A just society: Jesus's followers both practiced and preached it. It was
Jesus who first sent them out with nothing but the clothes on their backs.
All sources agree on this, including Paul: "What soldier ever serves at his
own expense? The Lord ordained that those who proclaim the Good News
should live from the Good News."[698] Sending out the twelve, Jesus says

that the workman is worthy of his food.[699] The same idea is also found in Thomas and Mark. Later on, the Way, still following Jesus's ideals, endeavored to live the simple life and share everything.[700]

It never fails. Instead of yielding up all their goods to the common pool, a couple named Ananias and Sapphira withheld some proceeds from a property sale. Peter accused them of duplicity, at which they dropped dead, apparently from the judgment of God,[701] an unfortunate precedent. Should not offenders be given the chance to mend their ways?

The *Didache* eventually had to deal with freeloaders too; if someone arrived and wanted to settle down, it ruled: "See to it ... that no one lives among you in idleness because he is a Christian. If he is unwilling ... he is trading on Christ."[702]

Evangelism was a feature of the movement from the get-go. Traveling missionaries were off to marshal hearts and souls and earthly goods to transform the world and realize their vision. More problems. The *Didache* lays down rules for some of these:

> Let every apostle who comes to you be received as the Lord. He shall stay only one day, or, if need be, another day too. If he stays three days, he is a false prophet. When the apostle leaves, let him receive nothing but enough bread to see him through until he finds lodging. If he asks for money he is a false prophet.[703]

Communal sharing is prone to abuse.

The Ebionite name survived—if not the ideal. Around 630 CE, Isidore of Seville writes, "The Ebionites are named after Ebion or poverty."[704] In the twelfth century, Honorius Augustodunensis tells us that the Ebionites "are half Jews, keep the gospel, and serve the law carnally."[705] It's hard to imagine why Honorius would speak in the present tense about a sect that disappeared seven hundred years earlier (or why he would even bother to write about them anymore), yet Klijn claims that these authors are copying earlier works. That is, of course, the dogma that must not be challenged: the Ebionites disappeared in the early fifth century. I will disapprove that in a little while.

Early Christianity in Rome was Jewish

Simplicity, caring, and sharing: those who run the world detest those who live by these ideals, from Jesus's followers through the Flower Children of the sixties to Occupy Wall Street today, yet virtually every time they arise, they strike a deep chord. Again and again, we will see this as we trace the faint path of the Way down through the ages. The corruption endemic to power sparks such opposition. Small wonder its successes—and suppressions. Crushed by exploitation, the poor have little to lose. Simplicity, often destitution, is their lot anyway.

The Way was more successful than the Essenes, who were also living communal, righteous lives in anticipation of God's intervention in history. Why was the Way persecuted while the Essenes were left alone? Perhaps the Way was far more active than either Acts or the *Clementines* let on, and that is why I treasure the witness of the Slavonic Josephus, whoever that mysterious witness was. Why did Saul (or someone else) not lead a charge against the Essenes, well entrenched at the time and sharing the same revolutionary philosophy? Was the Way more active than we know?

That might be why Acts is utterly silent about events in Galilee. Having bad-mouthed the people of Nazareth at the beginning of his Gospel, Luke wanted them out of sight. Remember that Jesus's relatives went out from Nazareth and Cochaba (a name meaning "star" which might refer to the famous prophecy that a star will rise out of Jacob and a scepter out of Israel[706]), expounding their genealogy and teaching "from the book of daily records."[707] Could the land be that interested in their genealogy? Would people really sit and listen to them recite the list of their ancestors as they did to the bards of the Germanic kings? Does anyone (except the odd scholar) actually read those tedious genealogies in Matthew and Luke? There must have been something else going on.

There was. In Paul's rant at those who question his claim to be an apostle, we read:

> "Am I not an apostle? Have I not seen Jesus our Lord? ...
> This is my defense to those who would examine me ...
> Do we not have the right to lead about a sister/wife, as
> do the other apostles and the brothers of the Lord and
> Cephas?"[708]

Right. Jesus's brothers were leading their sisters/wives about in apostolic itineraries. And getting fed for it too. Obviously they were evangelizing yet all we have are these two tantalizing references. Why would the church not prize the daily records of Jesus's family? Why did they disappear? They kept enough nails from the cross to fill all the churches in Christendom. Jesus's foreskin(s) could be viewed in over a dozen different places, including the Vatican. Eighteen holy prepuces but no family records? Values are skewed here.

Clement of Alexandria tells us that those sister/wives weren't just along for the ride: "It was through them that the Lord's teaching penetrated the women's quarters without any scandal being aroused."[709] Thus women apostles continued to function in the church, just as they had during Jesus's ministry.

Yeshuites established the church in Rome at an early date. This doesn't make it into many studies of early Christianity, for obvious reasons:

> There were Jews living in Rome in the times of the apostles, and that those Jews who had believed passed on to the Romans the tradition that *they ought to profess Christ but keep the law* ... one ought ... to praise their faith; because ... without seeing any of the apostles, they nevertheless accepted faith in Christ, although according to a Jewish rite.[710] (Italics mine.)

We would never guess that from the Acts. We will never know how the faith got there; some commentators have wondered if Romans at the first Pentecost (Acts 2:10) took it back. It apparently caused considerable dissension in the Jewish community. Suetonius writes of Claudius: "Since the Jews constantly made disturbances at the instigation of Chrestus, he expelled them from Rome."[711] At that time, many of Jesus's followers would have been Jews, thus these disturbances were likely about whether Jesus was the Messiah. This happened in 49 CE.[712] When Paul came to Corinth, he met two recent refugees from that purge, Aquila and Priscilla.[713]

A surprising twist. In his first letter to the Corinthians, Clement of Rome writes: "Not in every place, brethren, are the continuous daily sacrifices offered, or the peace offerings, or the sin offerings and the trespass offerings but in Jerusalem alone ... and this through the high priest of the aforesaid ministers ..."[714] This Roman Christian is apparently unaware of Jesus's saving death since he still assumes that sin and trespass offerings are needed. This embarrassing passage is generally ignored, but note: it confirms Ambrosiaster's assertion that Jewish rites were the standard in Rome in the early days.

Christian liturgies grew out of Jewish practice. Many echoes can be heard, even today, by anyone who cares to listen: Amen, Hosanna,

Hallelujah, *In saecula saeculorum* (forever and ever) are all derived from Jewish sources, and that's only the tip of the iceberg in an almost invisible sea. *The Sacred Bridge* by E. Werner[715] presents a fascinating study of this subject.

The Roman Church originated as a Jewish movement. Although we can tell from Paul's letter to the Romans that there were some Gentiles in the movement by the 50s CE, Rome retained a Jewish complexion for a long time.[716]

Back to the hardening opposition in Acts: as noted earlier, the sources tell us that Stephen and James the son of Zebedee were martyred; after a hiatus of eighteen years, the pace picked up: James the brother of Jesus was assassinated in 62 CE. In 64, Nero turned Christians into living torches to illuminate his games in the forum. Soon thereafter, Rome made it a capital crime to be a Christian. Peter, according to church tradition, was martyred in the Eternal City then, as was Paul.

This new movement threatened the authorities. Since all followers of Jesus eagerly awaited Jesus's return to end the existing order, Rome would have seen them all as potential rebels. Nothing could be clearer than Paul's assertion that there is another king, Jesus.[717] That implies revolution. The Roman general, Titus, assumed that all followers of Jesus were insurgents, a fact that almost didn't make it to the twenty-first century. That's for later.

Now we are moving toward the revolt. I already discussed the insurgency under Judas the Galilean; then unrest around John the Baptist; then Theudas's abortive "revolt" on the Mount of Olives, followed by that of the Egyptian. Shortly after 50 CE, rebellion heated up. In Rome, while the vultures of palace intrigue circled, scenting the regicidal climax of Claudius's reign, he sent out that disastrous procurator, Felix, to govern Judea.[718] Later we read:

> And now these impostors and deceivers persuaded the multitude to follow them into the wilderness, and pretended that they would exhibit manifest wonders and signs, that should be performed by the providence of God.[719]

The turncoat, Josephus, typically ingratiating himself with Vespasian and family, spits venom on all these unfortunate men who truly believed that it was time for God to deliver Israel from the unbearable oppression of Rome and the temple priesthood. As has happened so often in history (including the twenty-first century), unrestrained greed could not see that it was sowing the wind and would reap the whirlwind. Recalled to Rome, Felix barely escaped punishment for his misrule.

This revolt profoundly affected the development of Christianity and Judaism. As noted earlier, mismanagement grew rife immediately after the assassination of James. Accepting bribes, the next procurator, Albinus, freed all imprisoned rebels, although one wonders how there were any left with Felix putting them to death every day. Albinus's successor, Florus, plundered cities and allowed the bandits (many would have been freedom fighters) free rein throughout the country. Greed carried away the temple priesthood too. They sent "their servants into the threshing-floors, to take away those tithes that were due to the priests" so that the poorest ones died for want.[720] Perhaps that is why Matthew's Jesus exclaims:

> "Woe to you, scribes and Pharisees, hypocrites! Because
> you cleanse the outside of the cup and the dish, but they
> are full of robbery and self-indulgence inside."[721]

Anyone not blinded by greed would have known that revolt was inevitable. Just like today.

Flight to Pella?

As a Tacitus fragment will show all later, many "Christians" (read that "Followers of the Way") stayed in the city and were active in the revolt. Yet Eusebius claims that they left before it happened. [*HE* III, 5] Although many suspect this claim, Eusebius is not alone. There are other traditions that make similar claims. This is not really a dilemma. All groups fracture. We saw the divisions between the conservatives and the liberals at the Council of Jerusalem. And just as there seems to have been on the Mount of Olives, there would have been both doves and hawks in 66 CE.

Those who stayed would have been the Zealots earlier headed by James. The revolt broke out only four years after his assassination. Perhaps an undocumented faction held the pacifist ideals that Jesus seems to have embraced. Those who don't get into trouble don't get into history. In the aftermath, such doves would have blamed those involved: the rebels for their futile bloodshed and the temple establishment for the abuse that is the concomitant of power.

If so, these pacifists would have seen the proverbial writing on the wall even before the revolt started. We hear in the *War* of another Jesus, "a very ordinary yokel." Around the time of James's death, he went about the city prophesying woe to Jerusalem.[722] Josephus tells us that he kept this up for over seven years. Then he uttered one last "woe" to himself before a siege engine hurled a stone that silenced his prophetic voice forever. Soon after, the city fell.

Those who left had been "commanded by a revelation, vouchsafed to approved men there before the war, to leave the city and to dwell in a certain town of Perea called Pella."[723] Could Jesus the yokel have been one of the "approved" who had a revelation? As the situation grew grimmer, many men (and women), approved or not, probably had had revelations, cried "woe!" and scurried away.

Much earlier in the revolt, just after the insurgents abolished the sacrifices for Rome and Caesar,[724] wiser Jews tried to talk sense into their heads. They could foresee the inevitable outcome—with plenty of time for the doves to fly away. If God intervened as the prophecies foretold, well, they could come back. If He procrastinated again, they still had their necks intact.

There is another factor: the Matthean community was probably centered in Galilee, perhaps even in Capernaum. The evangelist stresses that Jesus left Nazareth to begin his ministry in Capernaum so as to fulfill the prophecy of Isaiah. In this regard, Jerome's commentary on Isaiah 9:1 is illuminating:

> The Nazoraeans venture to explain this passage as follows: When Christ came and his preaching was glittering, especially the land of Zebulun and the land of Naphtali was delivered from the errors of the scribes and Pharisees, and he struck off from its neck the very burdensome yoke of Jewish traditions.[725]

Schoeps comments that the burdensome yoke may refer to the law of sacrifice.[726] The massive slaughter every day in the temple was a terrible burden on the produce of such a tiny country.

Matthew's prophecy runs: Zebulun ... *beyond Jordan* ... the people who sat in darkness saw a great light.[727] Pella (just beyond Jordan), a close place to flee the wrath to come, was an obvious refuge. They later saw themselves as fulfilling the prophecy there:

Jerome tells us that in the interpretation of Isaiah prevailing among both the Hebrews who believed in Christ (Ebionites) and the Nazoraeans (of Beroea) the passage is understood to mean that Jesus proclaimed the gospel first for the benefit of this land designated by Isaiah 9:1, i.e., the land in which they themselves then resided. And if Jesus's preaching, originating in Capernaum, caused the great light to dawn upon the land "beyond the Jordan," how much more obvious the fulfillment when his congregation settled down in that land![728]

Pella was also pagan, and was thus firmly among with those who sat in darkness.

Other sources add to the picture. The first occurs in the Syriac version of the *Recognitions*:

> And with these things [Moses] also set apart a place for [the Children of Israel] in which alone it was permitted to offer sacrifices. All of this was promulgated to them until a more convenient time should come, when they would be able to understand that God desires mercy and not sacrifices. Then that prophet who declares the things will be sent to them, and *those who believe in him will be led by the wisdom of God to the strong place of the land, which is for the living. There they will be preserved from the war* which will shortly come to their own destruction upon those who because of their division do not obey.[729]
> (Italics mine.)

Note the similarity in ideas. Here, however, God's wisdom leads them to safety. But then, who gives revelations to "approved men"?

There is another independent tradition, our third. Schoeps claims a connection between James's assassination and the Yeshuite flight to Pella:

> According to Hegesippus, they related the catastrophe of A.D. 70 to the murder of James and interpreted it as a divine judgment upon the Jews. From Symmachus' treatment of Ecclesiastes 12:5 we learn only that the death

of James occurred in tumultuous circumstances ... which preceded the Ebionite dispersion.[730]

Symmachus created a Greek Old Testament. Schoeps says that Symmachus "discovered the future destiny of his Ebionite church in Ecclesiastes 12:5."[731] That's tantalizing but Schoeps cites his *Theologie und Geschichte des Judenchristentums*,[732] which is beyond my linguistic abilities, and the fragments of Symmachus lie scattered among the fathers. I have to take Schoeps's word for it.

For a possible fourth, we return to that neglected source, the Slavonic Josephus. This author tells us that the governors "becoming pestered by them (Jesus's followers), they had them sent away, some ... to distant lands, for the testing of the matter."[733] This reference to distant lands, by a not unfriendly writer who, judging by all the inaccuracies, is drawing on rumors and dim memories, may well refer to the flight to the east rather than to any formal investigations.

There is a fifth. In that other muffled voice, the *Tathbit*, we learn that, after a struggle with the Christians (i.e., the Pauline faction), they fled to the districts of Mosul and the Jazirat al-'Arab.[734] Pines suggests that this term might refer to the Jazira region in Northeastern Syria, rather than the Arabian Peninsula. Even so, that is well north of Pella. Perhaps there were two flights.

This leads us to Pliny's enigmatic reference to the "Nazerini" who lived a little south of Antioch, a reference that has stimulated much scholarly speculation. However, Pliny assigns a "tetrarchia" (an administrative district much like that ruled by Herod Antipas) to them, which rules out a group of fleeing Nazarenes. In any case, Pritz claims that Pliny's sources date from the reign of Augustus,[735] so regretfully, we must dismiss this reference.

We have too many sources for the flight for it to be entirely fiction. Here is the sixth and last. An author named al-Qurtubi records Jewish followers of Jesus arguing with Christians who said, "God is three," pointing out that they had been Jesus's companions. A fight erupted. The Gentile Christians defeated the Yeshuites, who fled, finally reaching Jazirat al-'Arab, the same destination noted in the Tathbit. En route, "the Jews" captured them. They told their captors: "We have no need of (things belonging) to this world. We will stay in caves and cells and be wanderers upon the earth. Thereupon (the Jews) let them go."[736] The story has become garbled (it dates to the thirteenth century), but it shows the tenacity of the tradition of a flight. It also shows that living the life of the poor was still honored then. Curiously, a contemporary of al-Qurtubi, an inquisitor named Gregorius of Bergamo, fulminated against some wandering Yeshuites called the Pasagini ("wanderers"). They got around.

The Revolt

Summer, 66 CE. Greeks ignited violence in Caesarea while building a factory that would block a synagogue. The unrest spread to Jerusalem, where Florus was robbing the temple treasury. One lone voice tried to stem the flood. Noting that no one could defy Rome, Herod Agrippa II fruitlessly appealed to the Jews for peace. Ungovernable as storm, rage engulfed the land as it rose in revolt.

As in all good tragedies, there was a fatal flaw: no strong leader could unite the multitude of factions. Although I have studied the *War* many times, I'm still confused as to who's who. Jew fought Jew until the streets of the Holy City ran with blood. Even the temple was desecrated, to the unmitigated joy of the Roman general, Vespasian. The wonder is that it took him four years to crush such a rabble. Rome was, as usual, ill prepared. Events in the larger world interrupted the proceedings. It took almost a year for Vespasian and his son, Titus, to get the troops to Galilee; another year before they subdued most of the rest of the country. Following Nero's suicide the following year, Rome was in disarray, ruled successively by four emperors, with Vespasian coming out on top at last, thus fulfilling a prophecy Josephus had made to save his neck after his ignominious surrender.

It only delayed the inevitable, giving the rebels more time for mutual assassination. In the spring of 70 CE, Titus began the siege. Rome's forces needed another three years to wipe out the last stronghold, Masada, seven years to the month after hostilities first flared in Caesarea. Josephus claims that Titus took nearly a million prisoners, and over a million died in the siege, three times the number Tacitus estimates were there in the first place. Rome brought the enslaved survivors (along with the treasures of the decimated temple) to Rome for the Flavians' extravagant triumph, long remembered in the Eternal City and still viewable today on the arch of Titus.

To balance Josephus's sycophantic story, it is instructive to consult another source. The Roman Tacitus blames the blind, self-serving procurators for the outbreak of the Great War, highlighting Felix, who "practiced every kind of cruelty and lust, wielding the power of a king with all the instincts of a slave."[737] Happy Felix—killing insurgents every day.

Conspiracy haunts the fate of Tacitus's *Histories*. Only one incomplete copy survives. The fifth book breaks off at a crucial point: just as Titus is about to storm Jerusalem in 70 CE. This is most peculiar. The fall of Jerusalem (which the Christians attributed to God punishing the Jews for killing Jesus) should have been the most prized part of this work. Don't be silly, you say. In almost two millennia, there are many reasons why the ending could have been lost.

I disagree. There is a specific reason found in a fragment Suplicius Severus preserved:

> Titus is said, after calling a council, to have first deliberated whether he should destroy the temple, a structure of such extraordinary work. For it seemed good to some that a sacred edifice, distinguished above all human achievements, ought not to be destroyed, inasmuch as, if preserved, it would furnish an evidence of Roman moderation, but, if destroyed, would serve for a perpetual proof of Roman cruelty. But on the opposite side, others and Titus himself thought that the temple ought specially to be overthrown, in order that the religion of the Jews and of the Christians might more thoroughly be subverted; for that these religions, although contrary to each other, had nevertheless proceeded from the same authors; that the Christians had sprung up from among the Jews; and that, if the root were extirpated, the offshoot would speedily perish.[738]

That last phrase should read, "If the root were extirpated, the *branch* would speedily perish." I'm not nitpicking. It's an important distinction. A "branch" is still attached. An "offshoot" implies a separated descendant, i.e., Gentile Christianity. It would scarcely perish if the temple was destroyed.

Scholars attribute this fragment to the lost part of Tacitus's *Histories* although some claim that an interpolator added the Christian material. Did they actually read the content? No Christian would ever have dreamed up this notion: Titus believed that, by destroying the temple in Jerusalem, he would subvert the Christian superstition. Quite the opposite. For Severus and all other early Christians, the destruction of the temple was something to crow over, the just reward for the Jews.

Remember James and his Zealots for the law? What do Zealots do? They revolt against Rome. Only six years after James boasted about their numbers, the revolt began. Severus's fragment backs up James's allegation. Most of those ten thousand joined the revolt: *it was because of them that Titus decided to destroy the temple. They were the "Christians" who worshiped in the temple.*

Christians? Not Ebionites or Nazarenes? No mystery here. Both Titus and Tacitus were Romans: Christians was the only name they knew for Jesus's followers. Jerusalem still ruled with an iron hand, as the letters of Paul show. The movement only split after 70 CE, when the mother church's power was broken. For the Roman Titus and his chronicler, all followers of Jesus were Christians, their name in the Gentile world. Neither would have known—or cared—about factions.

Thus the *Histories* break off just as Titus is poised to storm Jerusalem. The ending blew the master narrative's cover. Remember Rufinus? He dealt with "offensive" material thus: "If, therefore, we have found ... any statement opposed to ... the Trinity, *we have ... omitted it, as being corrupt, and not the composition of Origen ...*"[739] (Italics mine.) Whoever preserved the lone copy of Tacitus out-Rufinused Rufinus: he dropped the offending ending into the garbage can. If they had garbage cans.

Another account, Orosius's *Seven Books of History against the Pagans,* also draws on Tacitus's lost material although the author reworked it more thoroughly than Severus. After deliberating over the fate of the temple, Titus decides that its continued existence is an incitement to the enemy (the Jews), so he destroys it. But Orosius's Christians are no longer the enemy; instead, he claims that the church flourished abundantly throughout the whole world,[740] obviously an interpolation. At that time it was a tiny sect with a few cells scattered across the empire. Orosius has conformed the text to his own time, the early fifth century. Since the church was flourishing, he declares, the temple was useless to anyone and so, "by the will of God," Titus destroyed it. Orosius whitewashes his hero as God's agent. In both versions, note, Titus chooses to destroy the temple.

Compare Josephus's account. Initial attacks failed so: "Titus, seeing that his attempts to spare a foreign temple meant injury and death to his soldiers, ordered the gates to be set on fire."[741] While fire raged through the colonnades, Titus summoned that council of war we read of earlier.

> Some insisted that ... there would be continual revolts
> while the Sanctuary remained as a rallying-point for Jews

all over the world .... Titus replied that ... he would not ... burn down such a work of art; it was the Romans who would lose thereby.[742]

After bringing several generals over to his view, he ordered soldiers to put out that fire. It was not to be. The God of both Josephus and Orosius had long ago condemned the temple to the flames.[743] Josephus's God, however, chose a lowly soldier:

> Then one of the soldiers, without waiting for orders and without a qualm for the terrible consequences of his action but *urged by some unseen force*, snatched up a blazing piece of wood and climbing on another soldier's back, hurled the brand through a golden aperture giving access to the north side to the chambers built round the Sanctuary. As the flames shot into the air the Jews sent up a cry ...[744] (Italics mine.)

Titus rushed to the sanctuary, hoping "to extinguish the blaze."[745]

Too late. The army was now a mob. "They pretended not even to hear Caesar's commands and urged the men in front to throw on more firebrands." After much confusion, God's mob won. "Thus the Sanctuary was set on fire in defiance of Caesar's wishes,"[746] Josephus glibly notes.

Rather, Caesar was whitewashed. Perhaps the Flavian emperors suggested the cover-up. (The trick Augustus pulled was not lost on them: he rid himself of Cleopatra and blamed it on an asp. Emperors eliminate threats to their power while maintaining, they hope, lily-white images.) In general, the accounts agree, although Titus's role varies, depending on how much toadying is going on. Only Severus's slim fragment gives the game away. Which is understandable. Christianity claimed its martyrs died for their religion, not their politics.

Chapter 10

The Smoke-Filled House

"For on this account Jesus is concealed from the Jews, who have taken Moses as their teacher, and Moses is hidden from those who have believed Jesus. For, there being one teaching by both, God accepts him who has believed either of these" (Clementine Homily 8.6).

[Paul] said: … "the whole of the Torah is evil …" Thus Paul abandoned the religious beliefs of Christ and adopted those of the Romans … you find that the Christians became Romanized and … you do not find that the Romans became Christianized (*Tathbit*, Pines, 1996, 116).

What a contrast between Peter and Paul! Although the above sources are late, they reflect reality. Peter happily ate non kosher food with Gentiles.[747] The Bible tells me so. Flexible is what I'd call him. The world needs more Peters. In the next paragraph[748] of the Homilies, he adds that they are "rich in God" who understand that the doctrines of Moses and Jesus are essentially the same.

Of course the *Tathbit* quote was written in Iran centuries after the fact. The authors had forgotten that Rome was originally observant of the law, as we showed earlier, and it continued to respect the Church of the Circumcision until at least the fifth century. Christianity, however, finally hardened against any other views but its own, betraying the harmony so dear to Peter's heart. The *Tathbit* highlights what we already know: Paul rejected the Torah.[749] And Christianity became "Romanized" by accepting his pagan dying god myth.

Had the Ebionite view prevailed—that Jesus was simply a human being God adopted at his baptism—then many of the crimes that blot history's pages might not be there. That view (adoptionism) was, in fact, a serious contender in the early days.

Historians claim that Theodotus the Tanner (excommunicated in 190 CE) created adoptionism. He did not. The Ebionites believed that from the beginning: "By the choice of God ... the Christ ... came into him from above in the likeness of a dove."[750] Theodotus got his idea from them, but the Yeshuites are right off the establishment radar screen. The *Tathbit* knows. It says their traditions claim that Joseph was the father of Jesus until his baptism when the heavenly voice said: "This is my son in whom my soul rejoices."[751] (No Muslim—or Christian convert to Islam—created this passage. Both Christians and Muslims believe that Mary was a virgin when Jesus was born. "People," therefore, are Yeshuites.)

After the Jewish Revolt, the Torah indeed seemed dead, at least within the empire. If I close my eyes, I can call up an image I saw in my youth (*LIFE magazine?*) that still haunts me: the camera looks down on some black-clad men with strange hairdos standing before a blank wall bewailing the lost glories of Jerusalem. If it still caused such pain in the twentieth century, how overwhelming it must have been for Jews, including Yeshuites, who lived through the catastrophe.

Zion was the uncontested font of authority for Jesus's followers, Jew or Gentile, until 70 CE. The destruction of Jerusalem broke Yeshuite power, despite attempts to reassert it as late as the fourth century—if the delegation of the *Desposyni* (the family of the Lord) to Pope Sylvester is not a myth.[752]

Power, like nature, abhors a vacuum. As waters follow the contours of the land, so command drained into the Gentile church when Jerusalem died. Now it had a deadly weapon: God had deemed Judaism wanting. Through Rome, He had destroyed its cult center, confirming Paul's claim that Gentile believers were now the inheritors of the promise. It was easy to ignore that, by the same token, God had judged Paul. The same imperial power destroyed them both—and in the same decade. Is that why Acts is silent on Paul's fate, ending with him triumphantly winning converts in Rome? His execution would have cast a long shadow over that triumph. And so Acts ends up in the air.

Gentile Christianity quickly spread its wings after desolation clipped those of mother church. Writing from what is now Turkey, Pliny the Younger reveals something startling. After he persecuted the Christians, the citizens of Pontus once again frequented the almost deserted temples, revived religious rites they had long neglected, while those who sold sacrificial animals began to thrive again.[753] Here early in the second century, a pagan coolly tells us that Christianity had almost swamped paganism in that corner of the empire.

Judea Capta (Legend on Roman Coins after Jewish Revolt)

> When the Romans conquered Jerusalem in 70 CE, they displayed their power in full. They stopped for all time Jewish sacrifice in the Temple, the sole place of Jewish sacrifice previously legal in the empire. They profaned the Temple area by sacrificing to their gods. They stationed in Jerusalem the Tenth Legion with the provocative emblem of a pig on its banner. The gold vessels of the Temple were rehoused in Rome in a specially built Temple of Peace–peace, by implication, from the Jews, currently seen as hostile and pernicious.[754]

Rome triumphant; Judea captive. For Jewish survivors in what Rome would later rename Syria Palestina, this was the new world order as they tried to rebuild their shattered lives, primarily in Galilee and Trans-Jordan. In their book, the Aberbachs vividly describe the depths of poverty and the torture the Jews endured in those years.[755] The psychological scars lasted much longer.

For the Yeshuites, the situation was even worse. They suffered, as did all Jews during those terrible times, but their fellow Jews now rejected them. Only ten years earlier, they had participated fully in the temple under the leadership of James.

Those days were gone. In an old *Birkat haMinim* (Blessing of the Heretics), we read:

> For the renegades let there be no hope, and may the arrogant kingdom soon be rooted out in our days, and the *Notzrim* [Nazarenes] and the *Minim* [heretics] perish as in a moment and be blotted out from the book of life and with the righteous may they not be inscribed."[756]

Eternal optimists! But God did not crush the wicked. Rabbi Gamaliel II, who presided over the new seat of Jewish religious power at Yavneh, inserted that sentence into the Eighteen Benedictions to smoke out any Nazarenes since, if they were invited to pronounce them, they would omit it.[757] Gamaliel II obviously found them a serious threat.

Gamaliel or his successors later sent out emissaries "throughout the world" condemning the "lawless heresy" of the Christians,[758] including Yeshuites. Parkes suggests that these emissaries distributed copies of the *Birkat haMinim.* It was known from Caesarea to Rome.[759]

Hatred breeds hatred. Jerome quotes from a Nazarene commentary on Isaiah: "And he will become … a stone of offense, and a rock of stumbling to both houses of Israel,"[760] adding that the Nazarenes saw the prominent families of Shammai and Hillel as the two houses because, by rejecting Jesus, they had brought destruction and shame on Israel.[761]

Centuries later, little had changed. Epiphanius tells us that the Nazarenes:

> Are very much hated by the Jews … Three times a day they say: "May God curse the Nazoraeans."[762]

A similar hostility is reflected in the Gospels. Mark's Jesus, for instance, predicts that his followers will be beaten in synagogues.[763]

The books attributed to John shed further light on the issue. In the Gospel we read: "Nevertheless many even of the authorities believed in him, but for fear of the Pharisees they did not confess it, lest they should be put out of the synagogue."[764] Revelation reflects a similar situation. Jesus's followers, Jew or Gentile, were hated throughout the empire. Hvalvik points out that a sect who worshiped a crucified Jew was a huge liability; other Jews who, at least in Asia Minor, were still accepted in the community despite the Jewish War, didn't want to have anything to do with them.[765]

The author of Revelation struck back. "I will make those of the synagogue of Satan who say that they are Jews and are not, but they lie—I will make them come and they will worship before your feet, and they will know that I have loved you."[766] Another prediction unfulfilled.

Although written later, Jewish sources reveal the tensions from their point of view. There is a witty story about Gamaliel II and his sister "making fun" of a Christian judge who was known for accepting bribes. Seeking part of an inheritance, Gamaliel's sister, Imma Shalom, sends the judge a lamp of gold. The judge cites an unknown saying in "the gospel" that the son and daughter inherit equally. After Gamaliel sends the judge a Libyan ass, he reverses his judgment: "I have looked further to the end of the [*Evangelion*], and in it is written, 'I am not come to take away from the Law of Moses and I am not come to add to the Law of Moses,' and in [the Law of Moses] is written, 'Where there is a son, a daughter does not inherit.' Imma Shalom says: Let your light shine as a lamp! R. Gamaliel said to her, "The ass has come and trodden out the lamp."[767]

Note how fluid the Gospel texts still were. The judge quotes a quite different version of Matthew 5:17: "Think not that I have come to abolish the law and the prophets …" Imma Shalom then seems to ironically allude to the preceding passage, "Let your light so shine before men that they may see your good works."[768]

Now let us turn to a Nazarene, a well-known healer. Early in the second century, Jacob of Kefar Sekaniah was a thorn in the side of the rabbis of Sepphoris. One Rabbi Eliezer bore the taint of heresy because Jacob once told him how to use a harlot's taxes, which could not be used by the temple. According to Jacob, Jesus had cited Micah: "For she gathered it of the hire of an harlot, and they shall return to the hire of a harlot,"[769] commenting, "Let them be spent on privies for the public." That pleased the rabbi and got him into trouble.[770] Trust Jesus to think up a witty use for a harlot's taxes. Too bad it didn't make the Gospels.

Another rabbi, Eleazar B. Dama, was less fortunate. After a snake bit him, Jacob came to heal him "in the name of Yeshu ben Pandira" (Pandira, or Pandera, was the putative seducer of Mary). Another Rabbi prohibited it. Although Eleazar tried to prove that the Torah allowed him to accept help from a *Min* (heretic), he died before he could finish expounding the law.[771]

Bagatti believes the bones of this prominent Nazarene lie in the tomb of the "just Jacob," which is found today in Saknin (the modern name of his town), just north of Nazareth.[772]

These Jewish writings are, of course, biased. Despite the bitter attacks in this literature, most ordinary folk got along peaceably, respecting each other just as Peter recommended: Jews consulting Nazarene healers, for instance. This mutual regard among ordinary folk would hold for centuries, not only between Jews of varying persuasions but between Christians and Nazarenes. It was the big wheels who got their shorts in a knot.

That was the world—with Judaism down but not out—in which the first versions of the Gospels appeared, 70 to 100 CE, according to the traditional dating. However, they did not reach their final form until much later. The early church fathers' "citations" vary widely, much like the quote from Matthew in the Gamaliel story.

In the first decade of the second century, the letters of Ignatius, which he wrote on his way to martyrdom, begin to shed more light on the infant (or maybe toddling by now) church. In one letter, he warned that to profess Jesus Christ and to Judaize was inconsistent.[773] Yeshuites likely inspired this warning: "They abstain from the Eucharist and from prayer because they do not confess that the Eucharist is the flesh of our Savior Jesus Christ …"[774] Since Yeshuites rejected the Eucharist, partaking of "the water of this world only," this early church father is preaching intolerance.

Rome left Egyptian Jews alone. "The first Christians … were Alexandrian Jews who had heeded the 'Good News' emanating from Jerusalem."[775] The author, Modrzejewski, is one of a small, devoted group who have studied the period. This quote illustrates the growing consensus among those scholars that the early Alexandrian church was Jewish in origin and makeup.[776] Apart from these lonely scholars, the story is almost invisible, usually a mere nod to the legend that Mark founded the church there.

Walter Bauer suggests why. He remarks that Eusebius "searched very diligently" in the sources.[777] Why the silence on the origins of Christianity in such an important center as Alexandria? he wonders. The follower of John the Baptist we met earlier, Apollos, whose teaching Paul "corrected,"[778] came from Alexandria. If the followers of John, why not the followers of Jesus?

Bauer's answer is that they were there, but either Jewish or Gnostic. Clement of Alexandria mentions both the Gospel of the Hebrews and the Gospel of the Egyptians. "If I am not mistaken," Bauer writes "the *Gospel of the Hebrews* was the 'life of Jesus' used by the Jewish Christians of Alexandria."[779] The Gospel of the Egyptians was the Gnostic text. Eusebius ignored both groups. Heretics were not welcome in his history.

Egyptians don't even use the word "Christian" until the second century.[780] We find it in the apocryphal *Preaching of Peter*, which also tells us that Peter called "the Lord *Law and Word*."[781] Peter's Jesus incorporates both the old, the Law, and the new, the Word, just as he asserts in the *Homilies* that both of God's covenants are valid. Pearson also points out that places mentioned in the apocryphal *Acts of Mark* are in Jewish, rather than Gentile, areas of that city.[782] Alexandria has an entirely different history than Antioch, where the name "Christian" originated.[783]

Pearson claims that Alexandrian followers of Jesus preserving the writings of Philo, and the Septuagint (the Greek translation of the Bible done in Egypt) points to its continuity earlier times despite Trajan devastating the Jewish community there in 117 CE.[784]

An exorcism in the *Paris Magical Papyri* suggests that Yeshuites still wielded influence in Egypt around 300 CE. A magician begins a spell, invoking "the God of the Hebrews, Jesus …," later calling on him who appeared to "Osrael in the pillar of light." It ends: "For the sentence is Hebrew and kept by men that are pure." Bauer remarks that this sounds "like an echo of those persons who oriented themselves around the *Gospel of the Hebrews.*"[785]

Back in Jerusalem, the Yeshuites struggled on. Visiting that city in 130/131 CE, the Emperor Hadrian found a very small "church of God," on the site of the upper room where the disciples had returned after the ascension. That part of Zion, Epiphanius claims, escaped destruction in 70 CE.[786] Hadrian had sinister plans: to turn Jerusalem into a pagan city. In response, Judea erupted in its final revolt. The Yeshuite church, along with the seven "poor" synagogues Hadrian also found there,[787] would be swept away in the debacle. The last Hebrew bishop of Jerusalem, Judas (surnamed Kyriakos, and therefore related to the Lord [*kyrios*]) presided over that small church, which was entirely Jewish in makeup, according to Eusebius.[788] Judas disappeared in that catastrophe. He was, perhaps, descended from Jesus's brother, Jude.

Yeshuite Symbolism: The Cross Controversy

Well over a century ago, an Arab found thirty ossuaries in a rock-cut tomb in the Mount of Scandal in Jerusalem. The mourners had inscribed some with "crosses." When the scholar Clermont-Ganneau ascribed a first century date to these ossuaries, it set off a debate that has raged down the years, including the controversial *The Jesus Family Tomb.* The problem was the crosses: early Nazarenes would hardly have treasured them. Only Gentile Christians saw them as symbols of salvation.

Bagatti[789] and Mancini[790] see the debate through theological blinkers. Discussing the famous ossuary bearing the inscription "Jesus, Son of Joseph," Bagatti finds "a complete theological thought." "There is a Greek *Tau*, symbol of the cross, then a Taw-cross of the old Hebrew form, and united to it a trinitarian delta."[791] A Trinitarian delta? The doctrine of the Trinity lay far in the future. Besides, Yeshuites rejected it even then.

Jesus quoted the Torah, "The Lord our God, the Lord is One."[792] Even Paul writes: "Yet to us there is one God, the Father."[793] If you consult the Athanasian Creed with that in mind, you will find that both Jesus and Paul "shall without doubt perish everlastingly."[794]

The Trinity, God in three persons, first appeared around 220 CE when Tertullian wrote: "In whom is the Trinity of the One Divinity—Father, Son, and Holy Spirit.[795] After Tertullian, the concept slowly became entrenched. It wasn't until the Council of Constantinople in 381 that the church formally promulgated the three persons in one God doctrine. Opposing factions bitterly fought it for centuries. Opposition still survives among such groups as the Unitarians and the Doukhobors.

The passage in Matthew "baptizing them in the name of the Father and of the Son and of the Holy Spirit ..."[796] makes no claim that they are one person. In any case, it is a later addition. Paul baptized only "in the name of the Lord Jesus."[797] Again, when Paul ended 2 Corinthians with this blessing: "The grace of the Lord Jesus Christ, the love of God and the fellowship of the Holy Spirit, be with you all,"[798] there is absolutely no indication that they are one person.

Jesus, being a Jew, would have been appalled at the idea that he was God. When John puts into Jesus's mouth the words: "I and the Father are one,"[799] the Jews try to stone him for blasphemy. Jesus most assuredly never said those words.

Scraping the Encrustations off the Cross

Few Christians know that making the sign of the cross originated with Ezekiel, two and a half millennia ago. In one of his wild visions, he sees a man whose loins are apparently burning up.[800] Grabbing the poor prophet by the hair, this specter drags him off to Jerusalem to show him the idols worshipped there. As if Ezekiel weren't terrified enough, the burning man summons the executioners. Preceding them, he sends a herald through the city to "put a mark upon the foreheads of the men who sigh and groan over the abominations that are committed in [the city]."[801] These marked men (no women?) will be spared in the coming destruction. The "mark" is literally a Hebrew *Taw*.

When the Nazarenes buried their dead, what would be more natural than to inscribe a *Taw* or its equivalent, a Greek *Tau*, in the tomb? (The early form of the *Taw*, (+) or (x), was still used.) It didn't signify "cross"; it meant that the dead had remained faithful. Compare Revelation 7.

As in Ezekiel, the day of wrath looms. One angel stays the hands of the avenging angels until "we have put a seal on the foreheads of the slaves of our God."[802] And who were sealed? One hundred and forty-four thousand of the twelve tribes of Israel. Only after that does John include the Gentiles who have washed their robes in the blood of the Lamb.[803] The seal on the forehead evolved into the practice of signing the cross there which, for Yeshuites, would have been the Hebrew *Taw*.

Back to the tombs. The Second Book of Esdras reads: "When you find the dead unburied, mark them with the sign and commit them to the tomb."[804] Written shortly after the destruction of the temple, this idea is related to the marks on Yeshuite ossuaries.

A passage in Origen (c. 185–264 CE) gives us further clues. He asked some Jews if they had traditions about the letter *Taw*. One referred to Ezekiel 9. Another said it symbolized those who observed the law, since it was the first letter of *Torah*. That could explain the symbol on ossuaries.

> Finally, a third, belonging to the number of those who had become Christians, said that the Old Testament writings show that the *taw* is a symbol of the cross and was a prototype of that sign which Christians are accustomed to make on their foreheads before beginning their prayers.[805]

Long before Origen, Justin Martyr saw the cross everywhere, for instance in a ship. The cross symbol—a sail against a mast—enables navigation, he notes.[806] The church was often likened to a ship.

The Clementine literature knew this concept. Voyaging through this stormy world, the ship of the church bears those who wish "to inhabit the city of the good kingdom."[807] "Clement" urges the reader to let God be his shipmaster, Christ his pilot—then elaborates this idea into a long allegory.

Excavating under the Shrine of the Annunciation in Nazareth, Bagatti found the remains of a third century synagogue. Someone had sketched a ship on the plasterwork, its sail divided into eight parts. He believes that this "Ogdoad ... recalls Christ, according to the ideas of St. Justin."[808] Justin claims that the eight passengers who escaped the flood on Noah's ark symbolized Jesus.

The ship of salvation has Jewish roots: Noah, the prototype. In the Testament of the Twelve Patriarchs, Naphtali recounts a dream of a storm that breaks up a ship. On it were Jacob and his sons. After Levi prays to God, the ship is magically restored. The Children of Israel reach land in peace. Levi is "the priestly messiah who will gather dispersed Israel at the end of time."[809] There is also Mark's tale of the storm that broke over Jesus and the disciples on the Sea of Galilee.[810]

The taw and the cross led us to the ship; now the ship leads us to the cosmic ladder via Hippolytus. "The ladder rising upwards to the sail yard is an image of the sign of Christ's passion leading the faithful to climb up into heaven," he writes.[811] A Jewish terra-cotta monument from Rome's St. Sebastian catacombs also speaks of the cosmic ladder.[812] Tombs have yielded inscribed amulets—one from Aleppo describes the "voyage beyond the tomb, according to the cosmic ladder".[813] This amulet was the deceased's passport to heaven. Yeshuite literature records people ascending through the various heavens (*The Testament of the Twelve Patriarchs, The Ascensions of Isaiah*).

Next Hippolytus leads us to the "cosmic cross": "The top-sails aloft upon the yard are the company of prophets, martyrs, and apostles, who have entered into their rest in the kingdom of Christ,"[814] a conceit that puts the top of the cross in heaven. The Gospel of Peter describes the cross following two angels who support a gigantic Christ whose head overtops the heavens.[815] They are returning to the paradise from which the angels earlier descended. In the Acts of Andrew, Jesus addresses the cross as though it were a person. He knows its mystery, he tells it; one part stretches toward heaven; its arms stretch to the right and to the left, and one part is planted in the earth so that it can join the things of the earth and under the earth to the things of heaven.

Yeshuites represented this cosmic symbol as enclosed in a circle, a haloed cross. Bagatti gives several examples.[816] Gentiles Christians also used it. Irenaeus sees the cross as illuminating the heavens, "calling together from every part the dispersed to the knowledge of the Father."[817]

Being in the cosmos leads us to one of the most famous prophecies in the Bible. In his oracle on the future of Israel, Balaam—he of the famous talking ass—said: "A star shall come forth out of Jacob, and a scepter shall rise out of Israel ..."[818] Beloved of the Qumran community, this prophecy was also treasured by Yeshuites, who believed that Jesus would return to establish the kingdom of righteousness. I will only mention two instances: the Jewish-Christian *Testament of the Twelve Patriarchs* applies it to Jesus, and in Revelation we read: "I am the root and offspring of David; the bright and morning star."[819]

Yeshuite symbolism is a vast topic we can only touch on here. For further information, consult Daniélou (1964) or Bagatti (1971).

Yeshuites Early History According to the Tathbit

Thanks to Shlomo Pines's translation of the *Tathbit*, we know what some Yeshuites wrote about the early period. Like everyone else, they had a bias. But that is the whole point of this work: their history, their biases, their views, have been silenced too long.

The *Tathbit* says that Jesus came to confirm the Torah. It, and the prophets, would guide his actions. He did not come to lessen but to fulfill. In God's eyes, heaven would collapse before anything was taken from the Torah. It's too bad the publisher won't allow me to quote the original but compare my summary to: "Don't think that I have come to destroy the law and the prophets ..."[821] and its last line with: "Whoever, therefore, shall break one of these least commandments ... shall be called least in the Kingdom of Heaven."[822] This *Tathbit* quote from a previously unknown apocryphal Gospel could be a fragment of the original Gospel of Matthew.

Next, Jesus's commission near the end of Matthew: "Go, and make disciples of all nations... teaching them to observe all things that I commanded you."[823] Compare the *Tathbit* where, just before he leaves this world, Jesus says to his companions: "Act as you have seen me act, instruct people in accordance with instructions I have given you ..."[824] Is this another quote from that lost Gospel?

Pines thinks so. He asserts that the "true Gospel" referred to in the historical section of the *Tathbit* is the Gospel according to the Hebrews known to Epiphanius and other church fathers.[825] As noted earlier, this material needs to be available for comparative study, but it is not. And if the establishment has its way, it never will be. This is a scandal.

The manuscript goes on to say that Jesus's companions and the first generation after them did obey Jesus's instructions. In the second generation, "they started to change the religion and initiate innovations in it ..."[826]

This passage echoes Hegesippus: the church was "a pure and uncorrupted virgin" until the generation after the apostles died; "then the federation of Godless error" began breeding heresies.[827]

Elsewhere he makes an astounding statement:

> On my arrival at Rome, I drew up a list of the succession of bishops down to Anicetus ... But in the case of every

> succession, and *in every city, the state of affairs is in accordance with the teaching of the Law and of the Prophets and of the Lord* ....[828]

Everything in accordance with the law? In every city? Around 170 CE? That would have lifted the eyebrows of Ignatius and Justin Martyr. Nevertheless, we saw in the previous chapter that the Roman church was born honoring the Law of Moses and still honored the Church of the Circumcision in the fifth century.

(Note: Hegesippus lists the bishops of Rome later, retrospectively, dubbed popes by the church. Not until the sixth century did the Emperor Justinian warn the bishop of Constantinople to acknowledge Pope John of Rome as "his supreme Holiness, the Pope of Ancient Rome."[829])

The church has always sidelined uncomfortable views, witness a rare quote of Pope Clement: "All nations shall know that you alone are God and Jesus Christ is your servant."[830] I say rare because some translations omit this;[831] others read: "Jesus Christ is thy son."[832] The correct rendering is perfectly in line with the Torah. Jesus is not the divine son of God. Clement was Peter's protégé, according to legend. Peter always referred to Jesus as God's servant.[833]

Justin Martyr does not consider Jesus's Jewish followers heretics. He thinks that, by observing the Torah, they are misguided but harmless so long as they don't try to force Gentiles to do likewise. It isn't until 180 CE that Irenaeus first calls the Ebionites "heretics."[834] That's ten years after Hegesippus found everything in accordance with the law and the prophets in every city he visited.

Since Hegesippus quoted the Gospel according to the Hebrews[835] and was Jewish in outlook, the church blotted out his writings. Seeing Christians living according to the law is one reason why. Yet his works contained invaluable information such as a memoir of apostolic traditions. Centuries ago, the Abbey of Corbie listed *The History of Hegesippus* in an inventory of books of uncertain date.[836] Since the treasures of its library were "loosed on the market" around the time of the French revolution (including some that went to Russia), it might yet resurface.

Eusebius probably mined Hegesippus's history for some of his early material, but if so, the rest is gone. Yet apparently three Eastern libraries still preserved the works of Hegesippus in the seventeenth century.[837] Book printing had long been flourishing, so why was this ignored? The earliest history of the church! Why did the powers that be let them molder away into dust in those cloistered libraries?

Back in the *Tathbit,* we find the apostles frequenting the temple until a dispute arises between them and the Jews regarding Christ. That's a good one-line summary of Acts 2–6, but the next passage sheds new light on our Western texts: to try and gain the sympathy of Rome, the Christians used to lament that they were weak compared to the Jews.[838]

The only Jew/Gentile conflict in Acts doesn't involve the Romans.[839] There the Hellenists (Gentiles) complain that their widows are being neglected in the distribution of food, after which the apostles appoint Stephen and six others to look after it.

The *Tathbit* paints a much grimmer picture: the Gentiles complain frequently of oppression. The Romans take pity on them. If they will abandon Jewish law, they tell them, they will make them powerful, and the Jews will not be able to harm them.[840] When the Christians agree, the Romans tell them to bring their companions and their book. No such luck. Their Jewish companions refuse; they will neither give up their Gospel nor associate with them any more. A violent quarrel breaks out. So back go the Gentile Christians to the Romans, asking them to take what they refer to as "our book" by force, at which the Yeshuites flee the country with *their* book, as noted earlier. The Romans contact their governors in Mosul and the Jazirat al-'Arab (either Arabia or possibly an area of Syria) who hunt them down and kill many of them.[841]

Garbled and late though it is, it recalls the accounts we examined earlier: i.e., Paul's admission that he persecuted the church and wasted it,[842] as well as the scattering of Jesus's followers in Acts and in *Recognitions.* Perhaps at that late date the authors confused two different flights: the first, corresponding more or less to that in Acts, and the second, the one just before the destruction of Jerusalem. Rome, however, never had governors in either Mosul or what we call Arabia. (Roman Arabia corresponded roughly to modern Jordan and the Sinai Peninsula.) However, Jazirat al-'Arab may refer to Syria (where there was later a large colony of Nazarenes). Rome did rule there.

Against all Odds—Survival in the East

Pines suggests that the main Yeshuite text incorporated in the *Tathbit* was written in the fifth or sixth centuries since it deals extensively with Constantine but knows nothing of the rise of Islam.[843] In that case, it may contain genuine memories of that early period, but it is too late to be reliable history. What it does is shine a light on the ideas, the attitudes, and the story of some Yeshuites in their own words—rather than in the attacks of their opponents.

Pines tells us that the writers of the non-Muslim sections of the Tathbit believe in Jesus as the Messiah but insist on observing the law. This, he points out, corresponds exactly to the sect of the Nazoraioi in Epiphanius, who writes that these Nazarenes differed from Christians in observing the law while their belief in Christ distinguished them from the Jews.[844]

Since 'Abt al-Jabbar used their records in the early eleventh century, they must have been still active then. Islamic scribes would have preserved neither apocryphal Gospels nor Yeshuite histories. 'Abt al-Jabbar uses them to shore up Islam by casting Gentile Christianity in a bad light. How long did they survive in the East? Did their survival influence the reform movements that were soon to disturb the complacent corruption of the church in the West? More research in Islamic records might show that they survived longer. I believe they did: in the fifteenth century, we are going to find bands of "Jewish Christians" roaming into southern Russia, apparently from the territories conquered by the Turks in Anatolia. In Russia, as we shall see, their ideas influenced the rise of various Christian sects including the Molokans and the more famous Doukhobors.

How the Gospels Were Born

According to the *Tathbit*, Gentile Christians created the canonical Gospels from what they remembered of the "true gospel." Perhaps Epiphanius had it backwards when he said that the Ebionites' Gospel of Matthew "is not whole and complete but forged and mutilated."[845] On the contrary, Jerome comments that many people believe that the Gospel which the Ebionites use is "the authentic text of Matthew."[846] I suspect that someone in Matthew's community reworked his Gospel after the destruction of Jerusalem. This community was beginning to accept Pauline Christology while still maintaining a Jewish outlook.

The *Tathbit* shines an interesting light on why Epiphanius was determined to belittle their Gospel. It tells us that many Gentile Christians remembered what was in the "true" Gospel (the Yeshuite Gospel) but in their desire to dominate, they were silent about this, adding that original said absolutely nothing about cross or crucifix.[847]

Pines notes that the Yeshuites opposed worshiping the cross. That fits the facts: neither the Gospel of Thomas nor other sayings gospels mention the crucifixion. The crucifixion is also absent from Q, the source of many sayings in Matthew and Luke.

Bereft of the Gospel, the Gentile Christians decided to create their own. It's weird. Their method exactly matches the claim of some modern pundits—a bunch of Bible nerds got together, mined the scriptures and cobbled together the Gospel on Old Testament patterns: the Bethlehem nativity, the flight into Egypt, the forty days in the wilderness (echoing the forty years on Sinai), and so on. That's just what the *Tathbit* Christians did: they decided that, since the Jewish Scriptures were made up of the lives of the prophets, they would write a Gospel on the same plan.[848]

Our manuscript then claims that there were eventually eighty Gospels. (Could Teabing, in *The Da Vinci Code,* have gotten his information here? It's hard to imagine Dan Brown reading such an obscure work, but he picked up the idea somewhere.)

The *Tathbit* then tells us that many Christians wrote Gospels. Later others decided that these contained errors, and the wrote new ones to correct them.[849]

This is just how Matthew and Luke combined Mark and Q, adding more material of their own. I earlier noted how differently Mark's and Luke's Jesus face death. Becoming "distressed and agitated," Mark's Jesus says, "My soul is deeply grieved, even to death."[850] Luke's Jesus is stoical even on the cross. The argument is much more complex.[851] Many scholars believe that Luke is here providing martyrs with a divine model for facing death.

Now thanks to Pines's work, we can recover another version of the original that is now lost. If the quote below is from the Hebrew Gospel, we have its record of the passion:

> And [Jesus] said in his supplication; for he feared death and did not cease to go on with praying, imploring, supplicating and weeping, "O God, if it is according to Your will that this bitter cup be turned away from any one, turn it away from me; but not as I wish, but as You wish." And he ejected as it were clots of blood from his mouth in his anguish in the face of death, and he sweated and was perturbed.[852]

This fits the scenario I earlier proposed for the agony in the garden. A verse in Luke must come from a similar source: "Being in agony he prayed more earnestly. His sweat became like great drops of blood falling down on the ground."[853] Although this passage (which clashes with Luke's serene savior) is absent from many early manuscripts, it might be a fossil of the original, rather than an interpolation. None of the canonical Gospels portray the depth of fear and anguish evident in the *Tathbit* although Hebrews records Jesus weeping and supplicating with loud cries, as noted earlier.[854] Again, this material would be useful in comparative New Testament studies—if anyone were to notice.

The Gospels Are Later than You Think

It's time to explode another myth: Gospel dates. Scholars say Mark wrote about 70 CE, Matthew: 80, Luke: 90, John: 100 (depending on the expert. Results may vary). Something was written around those times (and earlier) but much more primitive (and Jewish) than our texts. The Gospels were not born fully formed. These babies would mature into much different grown-ups.

Compare the *Tathbit* with Papias. In the former, the Christians write a Gospel from what they remember their Jewish companions saying about the Messiah.[855] This recalls John the Elder's comment to Papias: Mark had been Peter's interpreter (which makes sense since Mark was educated in Jerusalem, and Peter, the Galilean rube, would have had small Latin and less Greek—apologies to Ben Jonson.) Afterwards, Mark "wrote down accurately *whatsoever he remembered*" of what Jesus had said or done.[856] Papias tells us that Mark "neither heard the Lord nor followed him …"

John the Elder (not the son of Zebedee) likely knew Mark. Thus scholars should take these claims seriously. (Some are beginning to, for instance by Richard Bauckham in *Jesus and the Eyewitnesses*.) But the Mark of the New Testament did not write the Gospel we have now. He was a devout Jew who objected to eating Christ's body and drinking his blood. Mark's memoirs of Peter, probably dating to the 60s CE, were revamped by later Christians into our current Gospel, with the violent spirit possession after the baptism and a rebellion connected with Jesus still intact. If I had an anonymous Gospel, I wouldn't name it after Mark. Acts implies he's unreliable. That alone shores up Papias's claim.

Papias speaks of rewriting: "Matthew arranged in order the sayings in the Hebrew language, and each one interpreted/translated as he was able."[857] Some pooh-pooh this as "legendary at best."[858] It doesn't fit "the master narrative": Mark was written in 70 CE and Matthew in 80!

Why should we doubt Papias? He sought out people who had known the apostles and highly valued what they told him. Sneering scholars need to explain why people who knew Matthew and the other apostles would have lied to him. *I* see no motive.

Matthew could write. He was a tax collector. His collection of sayings would have resembled the Gospel of Thomas.

Surely this is the fabled Q!

The Ebionites would have based their Gospel on it. Some claimed it was the original Matthew.[859] Someone combined somebody's *logia* (the Q document) with Mark and molded it into the Gospel of Matthew we now know. It retains much of its Jewish focus, which agrees with Irenaeus's assertion that Matthew "published his Gospel among the Hebrews in their own language."[860] Thus were the Gospels born—but it's later than you think.[861]

"Gospels" are not even mentioned until the early second century (by Ignatius and Aristides). In the 140s, Justin Martyr still prefers Papias's term, "memoirs" (of the Apostles) although he sometimes uses the term "gospel." Not until 180 CE does Irenaeus list the four Gospels.[862]

Early Gospel "citations" are anything but exact. Clement, in his Letter to the Corinthians (circa 90 CE), quotes the "words of the Lord Jesus":

> [1]: Be merciful, that you may obtain mercy; [2] forgive, that it may be forgiven to you; [3]: as you do, so shall it be done to you; [4] as you give, so shall it be given unto you; [5] as you judge, so shall you be judged; [6] as you are kind, so shall kindness be shown to you; [7] with what measure you measure, with the same it shall be measured to you."[863]

Compare the analogous passages, sprinkled in some disorder through the Gospels. One occurs only in Luke. One is missing:

> [1]: Blessed are the merciful: for they shall obtain mercy. Mt 5:7; [2] For if you forgive men their trespasses, your heavenly Father will also forgive you. Mt 6:14; [3] Everything whatsoever you want, do that to other men ... Mt 7:12; [4] Give and it will be given to you ... Lk 6:38; [5]

> For with the judgment you make, you will be judged ...
> Mt 7:2; [6] ["Kindness" didn't make the Gospels]; [7] and
> with what measure you measure, it shall be measured to
> you ... Mt 7:2.[864]

Clement's quotes don't match any Gospel we know. He might, however, have used the "sayings" Matthew "arranged in order."

Around 110 CE, Ignatius also cites a Matthew-related phrase. Compare "Be in all things wise as a serpent and harmless always as a dove"[865] with Matthew's "Be ye therefore wise as serpents and harmless as doves."[866] These sayings draw on a common source, but the Greek texts are formulated quite differently.

In an epistle attributed to Barnabas dated to between 90 and 130 CE, the author says (literally): (as it is written) "For many called, but few found to be chosen."[867] The original translator, Schaff, comments: "It is worthy of notice that this is the first example in the writings of the Fathers of a citation from any book of the New Testament, preceded by the authoritative formula, 'it is written.'"[868] Not so. I translated it literally to show the difference. The Gospel reads: "For many are called, but few chosen."[869] (You can check the Greek in the footnotes.) Matthew has the word "are" and does not have "found to be." Barnabas is not citing the Matthew we know.

The apocryphal Clement II (140–160 CE?) renders Luke 16:10–12 fairly closely,[870] but it's not literal. Marcion (130–140 CE) renders some of Luke literally. Writing in the mid-second century, Justin Martyr never literally quotes the Gospels. Irenaeus is the first to quote them accurately. Thus until late second century, the "gospels" were in flux.

In the early days they were Jewish—Nazarene and Ebionite texts. Let's follow the Golden Rule. It first appears in the Old Testament Apocrypha: "And what you hate, do not do to anyone."[871] The great Hillel had his own version. A man once asked the famous rabbi to convert him but only if he could teach him the whole law while he stood on one foot. Hillel replied, "Do not do to others what is hateful to you. That is the whole of the law—the rest is commentary."[872] The Epistle of the Apostles quotes Jesus thus: "And what ye would not that man do unto you, that do unto no man."[873] Compare that with the *Didache*: "And everything that you would not have done to you, do not do to another."[874] Even the *Didascalia* (which means "instruction", related to *Didache*, "teaching") quotes the negative form,[875] apparently still unaware—in the third century—of the

Gospel version. We must not forget the Mandaean Right Ginza: "All that is hateful to you, do not do to your neighbor."

All these are "do nots." Since the three Yeshuite texts agree, I suggest that the evangelists had Jesus say: "Do to others as you would have them do to you"[876] to distance him from his Judaic roots. Remember Irenaeus adds the negative Golden Rule to the Jerusalem Council's rulings: "And what they do not wish to be done to themselves do not do to others."[877] Did redactors expunge that from the original Acts for the same reason they changed Jesus's words? The Jewish version is much more practical. But of course, Jesus could be quite impractical. Shed all your clothes in court?

Justin Martyr tells us that the memoirs of the apostles were read on Sundays. Some of the stories in the *Epistle of the Apostles* could well have come from one of these:

> And when we his disciples had no money, we asked him: What shall we do because of the tax-gatherer? And he answered and told us: Let one of you cast a hook into the deep, and take out a fish, and he shall find therein a penny: that give unto the tax-gatherer for me and you.[878]

Not only do we have the disciples' point of view, it is more primitive than Matthew's version. It lacks the Christological baggage about the Son of the king (God) not paying the temple tax.

The story of the Gadarene swine has a similar quality:

> The spirit which dwelt in a man, whereof the name was Legion, cried out against Jesus, saying: Before the time of our destruction is come, thou art come to drive us out. But the Lord Jesus rebuked him, saying: Go out of this man and do him no hurt. And he entered into the swine and drowned them in the water and they were choked.[879]

Matthew has two demoniacs, so fierce "that no one could pass that way." They cry out, "What have you to do with us, Son of God? Have you come here to torment us before the time?" Note the addition of the "Son of God," absent from the other text.[880]

The author of this epistle has drawn on the same source as Matthew for his tales, but they are in a more primitive form.

From the above, it is clear that the *Tathbit* knew whereof it spoke: people kept on reworking and rewriting the Gospels for well more than a century.

The classical world knew too. In the second century, Celsus charged Christians with corrupting "the Gospel from its original integrity, to a threefold, and fourfold, and many-fold degree."[881] This indicates that he had studied various versions. Many Christians complained likewise: Dionysius of Corinth (around the same time as Celsus), among many instances.[882]

Although the Gospels reached the form we know in the late second century, even then they were not immune. Originally Matthew 24:36 read: "But concerning that day and that hour, no one knows, neither the angels of the heavens, nor the Son, but the Father only" (my translation). After the council of Nicaea, how could Jesus, who was of "one substance with the Father," not know what the Father knew? So the Son disappeared from many copies of the text, including Jerome's Vulgate. Thus was the inerrant word of God tirelessly reworked, just as the *Tathbit* said.

This is where Christian anti-Semitism was born. After the revolt, Rome loathed the Jews. Trying to appeal to a Gentile audience, someone rewrote Mark's memoirs of Peter exonerating Rome and blaming the Jews for Jesus's death. Then they libeled Judas, the eponymous Jew, attributing treason to him. As we saw earlier, three untampered sources knew nothing of this and speak of the twelve as intact after the resurrection.[883]

I have only scratched the surface of this fascinating subject.[884]

Conservatism in the *Tathbit*

After complaining that the Gospels had abandoned the language of Christ,[885] the *Tathbit* alleges that these foreigners know neither God's books nor his commandments. They charge that the Christians gave up Hebrew because they wanted to deceive, quoting "counterfeit authorities in the lies which they composed ..." They did this so they could dominate all the others.[886]

Although the rigidity of these sectarians seems unpleasant, it is important to put it into context. Prior to the Jewish War, Hebrew had been in decline. Between that revolt and the revolt of Bar Kochba in 132–5 CE, Jews came increasingly to distrust Greek. It was universally used by Christians to proselytize among Hellenized Jews.[887] Yigael Yadin's team found a document in the desert caves in which the writer apologizes: "The letter is written in Greek as we have no one who knows Hebrew."[888]

Bar Kochba was probably trying to revive written Hebrew. In any case, the xenophobic attitude was based on real fears of being engulfed by the dominant Greek culture.

Back in the *Tathbit*, the author claims that the Gospels are full of absurdities, lies, and contradictions, which anyone who examines them carefully can see. You will find little of Christ's sayings there.[889] There are some today who agree, but their theories are beyond the *Tathbit*'s wildest dreams—Jesus as an incarnation of Horus, for instance.

The *Tathbit* charges that, if the Christians would consider all these things, they would realize that their Gospels are useless. Having abandoned what Jesus taught and practiced, they embraced Roman religious ways so they could get their share of the wealth Rome generated from dominating the world.[890]

A valid charge after the triumph of the church under Constantine, which fits the context.

Lust for domination runs like a *leit-motif* through the whole document. Jesus and his heirs prized cooperation.

Beliefs as to the Nature and Birth of Jesus

I was happy when the United Church left it to personal conscience whether one believed in the virgin birth or not. This dogma epitomizes the church's war against sex. Yeshuites scorned it; the church fathers sneered at the Ebionite belief that Jesus was conceived like everyone else.

Remember the Epistle to the Corinthians that Clement of Rome wrote toward the end of the first century: "You alone are God and Jesus Christ is your servant."[891] Meeting shortly after the death of Constantine, the Council of Laodicea must have been greatly relieved to ban that letter from the New Testament canon on the grounds that it was not written during the apostolic age, although the contemporary (or later) apocalypse of John squeaked in (as well as some pseudoepistles). I cite the Arnold version because it is honest. Others read "God's son" rather than "servant," but the word *paidos*, (which literally means "boy") is never translated "son" in the New Testament.[892] It occurs there twenty-four times—twelve are rendered as "servant." Clement's litany echoes Acts in which Peter says that God glorified "his servant Jesus."[893] That's one of the twelve times.

Most early Christians did not consider Jesus as "God" because of their ties to Judaism. Finally the Council of Nicaea imposed a creed—however incomprehensible—on the world that managed to make Jesus "God" and yet not break the first commandment.

Because the church could never exterminate it, we must take a further look at adoptionism, which came from Ebionite tenets. In spite of vicious suppression, it still flourishes today, Jehovah's Witnesses being a case in point.[894] This movement holds that Jesus was not God but was adopted by God at his baptism. The God-in-three-persons faction won the war, but its foes, the adoptionist guerillas, lurked in their hidden fastnesses and broke out from time to time, often taking on new forms but still holding that being "Christ" was God's gift and thus not intrinsic.

This idea is found in some versions of the *Liturgy of James the Apostle and Brother of God*: "By your will and favor, Christ is present in my person and I in truth am another Christ ..."[895] Could these words go back to Jesus's brother? Unlikely, but the idea flourished. Later we will meet it in the Doukhobor doctrines of the indwelling of the divine spirit and the incessant rebirths of Christ.

In a Smoky Syrian House

You may remember Peter telling his pupil, Clement, that God's will has been concealed. Bad instruction and other like evils

> "have filled the whole house of this world, like some enormous smoke ... preventing those who dwell in it from seeing its Founder aright ... What, then, is fitting for those who are within, excepting with a cry brought forth from their inmost hearts to invoke his aid ... that He would ... open the door ..., so that the smoke may be dissipated ..., and the light of the sun ... may be admitted."[896]

Yeshuites wrote this passage when a tidal wave of Gentile Christians threatened to swamp them. Had they not disguised Paul under the pseudonym Simon Magus, the Clementines would never have survived. In fact, they barely did.

After our stint with the rigid sectarians of the *Tathbit*, I wanted to remind the reader of the inclusive Clementine community in Syria. It is time to peer into a smoky house there.

The East Really Is Mysterious

Church history is incurably Eurocentric, yet its first historian lived in the Levant all his life. Although Eusebius studied in Antioch and was the bishop of Caesarea for over a quarter of a century, his writings face steadfastly West, ignoring what is behind his back. What *is* behind his back echoes Egypt—mostly blank. Well, he tells us that Jesus and King Abgar of Edessa were pen pals.

Walter Bauer remarks on a work from that city: "The older portion of the Chronicle certainly comes ... from a person who was still aware that the earliest history of Christendom in Edessa had been determined by the names of Marcion, Bardesan, and Mani"[897] (heretics all). He suggests that since the Chronicle speaks of these three but mentions no ecclesiastical bishop, then these heretical sects were the original "Christianity" in Edessa.

For centuries, the Marcionites monopolized the name "Christian." The latecomers, the Orthodox, had to wrest it from them. One wrote in some disgruntlement: "They even called us 'Palutians'"[898] (after Palut, the bishop who built the first church in Edessa in 313 CE).

Bauer illustrates this from the story of Mar Aba, patriarch of the Orient who died in 552. The patriarch asks a man what religion professes:

> "Are you a Jew?" The answer was "Yes." Then comes a second question: "Are you a Christian?" To this comes also an affirmative response. Finally: "Do you worship the Messiah?" Again agreement is expressed. Then Mar Aba becomes enraged and says: "How can you be a Jew, a Christian, and a worshipper of the Messiah all at the same time?" Here the narrator inserts by way of explanation: "Following the local custom he used the word Christian to designate a Marcionite." Joseph himself then gives his irate companion the following explanation: "I am a Jew secretly; I still pray to the living God ... and abhor the worship of idols. I am a Christian truly, not as the Marcionites, who falsely call themselves Christians."[899]

This recalls the broad-minded views of Peter, another example of how Yeshuites got along with Gentile Christians.

In the nineteenth century, a Scottish scholar-adventurer named William Ramsay unearthed a curious inscription in Turkey. It speaks of

Christians east of the Euphrates by the early third century. Traveling to Nisibis (a city not far from Edessa), the author of this tombstone writes that people fed him "with fish from the spring … whom a spotless Virgin caught."[900] This coded reference could mean either Jesus's teaching or the Eucharist, but he goes on to speak of having sweet wine and "the mixed cup with bread." This inscription has caused considerable controversy—some saying that these are not Christian references. Schoeps claims that Catholic Christianity did not penetrate the Yeshuite home base east of the Jordan "before the middle of the third century … Catholic bishops in Pella are mentioned for the first time in the fifth century."[901] Thus Roman Arabia, like Syria, was a hotbed of "heretics" in the early centuries.

Many scholars believe that the *Odes of Solomon* originated in Edessa. In this work, Jesus says:

> And the Gentiles who had been dispersed were gathered together,
> But I was not defiled by my love (for them)
> Because they had praised me in high places.[902]

Yeshuites who shared the broad-minded views of Peter must have written this, yet another example of how they got along with Gentile Christians.

The Syrian Church claims a disciple of the apostle Thomas named Addai as its founder. Legend says that Jesus sent him there to cure King Abgar V of Edessa. If you are going to invent a founder, why not choose a prominent apostle—like Peter—rather than a disciple who is not even named in the Gospels? Traditionally he was one of the seventy recorded in Luke.[903] Thus it seems likely that Addai truly founded Christianity in Syria. As so often happens, legends later grew up around him.

The liturgy attributed to him recalls the Jewishness of the early church there. In its original form, it does not have the words of the institution, "on the same night he was betrayed, etc.," which Yeshuites rejected. Only recently has the Catholic Church accepted it as a valid liturgy despite that omission (the right-wing faction still rejects it). One of the oldest rites still in use, it is called the "Holy Qurbana of Addai and Mari." *Qurbana* comes from the Jewish *"Korban,"* a sacrifice formerly made in the temple in Jerusalem.

Walter Bauer lists the early bishops of Ctesiphon-Seleucia on the Tigris, in what is now Iraq, which includes "Abris … (Ambrosius), a relative of Jesus who is elected in Jerusalem and consecrated in Antioch. Next comes

Abraham—related to James the Just—who also is ordained in Antioch." He concludes with the remark: "It is clear that we are dealing here not with history, but with legend."[904]

Richard Bauckham disagrees, believing that these chronicles had access to "accurate information."[905] I would lean toward Bauckham's view: this is in the general area where the rabbis fulminated against the *Notzrim*, but whether members of the family of Jesus actually came and led the church there is a question that can never be settled unless new material comes to light. Certainly the Jewish connection with Jerusalem was treasured in this area.

Westerners have seldom thought of Asia as enlightened (Greek "democracy" versus Persian tyranny, for instance), yet Syrian Christians cherished the ministry of women long after the West had silenced them in the church. The Eastern attitude, which may have come from the Yeshuites, began to flag as time passed.

One man was key to keeping it alive: Ephrem the Syrian. The mode in which he worked was song, writing hymns that celebrated the mysteries of the faith, which the "Daughters of the Covenant" sang. The women in this order were not nuns; they lived in the world performing religious duties, (among which was not washing up dishes for the male clergy.[906] The Canons of Rabula ruled against them performing such menial tasks— apparently men were up to their usual tricks.)

Joseph of Serug wrote Ephrem's biography. He tells us that the saint "founded these choirs explicitly to instruct the congregation of Edessa in right doctrine."[907] "[W]ho would not be astounded nor filled with fervent faith to see the athlete of Christ [Ephrem] amid the ranks of the Daughters of the Covenant, chanting songs, metrical hymns, and melodies!" he wrote.[908] A fascinating cameo of an athlete of Christ with his chaste harem.

This staunch supporter of women applied his considerable talents to songs about Biblical women. Eastern Christians treasure his poetry, yet the West hardly knows his name.

Some feminist theologians have become enamored of the saint. "Your [Ephrem's] teaching signifies an entirely new world; for yonder in the kingdom (of heaven), *men and women are equal*,"[909] (Italics mine.) Joseph rhapsodizes and then goes on to tell us that Ephrem prefigured that kingdom by treating them as equals here on earth, emulating the practice of Jesus. Recalling the role of Mary Magdalene among the Gnostics, these women were called "teachers among congregations." Unlike the Gnostics, men seemed not to have opposed their ministry. Here is a favorite among feminist theologians: "Uncover your faces to sing praise without shame to *the One who granted you freedom of speech by his birth*."[910] Ephrem openly defies the silencing of women in First Corinthians and Timothy. Jesus would have approved.[911]

After Ephrem died, a Synod ruled that every town should have Sons and Daughters of the Covenant to help maintain devotional life. Churches would choose one woman to be ordained a deaconess. This role continued in the East long after the Western Church had said to its women: "Get thee to a nunnery."

One deaconess, called Shirin, lived in what is now northern Iraq in the sixth century. An ascetic woman, she devoted her life to prayer, the liturgy, and ministering to others. A man she inspired to become a priest (she was over eighty at the time) wrote this:

> Monks and other strangers to the world who shared her reverence for our Lord used to come to visit her from all over the place, for they held her as a holy spiritual mother. They would gather ... as children coming for lessons in sanctity with her, wanting to receive her blessing and to gain benefit from her. She, for her part, would receive them lovingly and would minister diligently to their needs, providing both bodily sustenance as well as spiritual food: for while she saw to their bodily comfort, she would give joy to their souls at the same time, both by her words and by her actions ... they would depart from her, giving thanks to God and carrying with them all sorts of beneficial provisions as a result of what they had seen and heard.[912]

Such legendary wisdom once again recalls the Mary Magdalene of apocryphal literature. She also taught men.

Although the Syrian church claims that Edessa was the seat of the first Christian kingdom, the only "evidence" to support this is the legendary story of Jesus and King Abgar V. A later king of the same name, Abgar the Great (177–212 CE), did cultivate one of Jesus's followers: the heretic Bardesan. He was his intimate at court (the two had grown up together). Just because Julius Africanus describes Abgar as a holy man[913] does not mean he was a Christian (although some try to make it so).

Christians were a small minority, swamped by Marcionites, Yeshuites, and Bardesanites.

How heretical Bardesan was has caused much controversy. A basic Yeshuite tenet climaxes his only surviving work, *The Book of the Laws of Countries*: "At the establishment of that new world, all evil motions will cease … and there will be peace and safety, by the gift of Him who is the Lord of all Natures".[914]

What was the first Christian country? Armenia. It was born Jewish and retained many Jewish features for a long time.

An event during the reign of Marcus Aurelius (about 178–9 CE), illustrates how strong Christianity was there. Surrounded by German hordes, the emperor and his legions were desperate, suffering from many wounds and parched by a long drought. After a Christian division from Armenia fell on its knees and prayed, a huge rainstorm came. The Romans were refreshed, fighting off the enemy while drinking rainwater mixed with their enemies' blood from their shields. Suddenly great hailstones pelted the Germans. Lightning strikes burned them up. Miraculously, the Romans were spared. The pagan historian Dio Cassius tells this story with a straight face.[915] Since Marcus Aurelius depicted it on his column in the Piazza Colonna in Rome (where it can still be seen, including the upturned shields with leaping flames behind) this event did turn the tide against the Germans. No one contests that Marcus Aurelius had an Armenian Christian legion in his ranks.

Many scholars dismiss the traditional date of 301 CE for the conversion of the Armenian king Tiridates. M. Chahin writes: "A Gothic chieftain challenged the Roman Emperor Diocletian to meet him in single combat. Trdat [Tiridates] successfully stood in for the emperor. The latter gratefully gave Trdat an army with which to expel the Persians from Armenia, in his own right—not for Rome. The events influenced Rome to turn a blind eye to the introduction of the Christian faith by Trdat as the state religion of Armenia (301)."[916] Since Diocletian retired in 305 CE, this does suggest an early date.

The clinching argument is that the Armenians soundly beat Maximinus, a junior emperor in charge of the East when, in 311, he attacked them for abandoning paganism and embracing Christianity.[917] That flatly contradicts those historians who date the conversion of that country to 314. Obviously, they chose that date because it's one year after the Edict of Toleration in 313 CE, a silly attempt to rewrite history: it's only toleration. It wasn't until 380 CE that Theodosius declared Christianity the state religion of Empire, trailing Armenia by almost eight decades.

Not only was Armenia the first Christian nation, it was born among Yeshuites who left their distinct stamp on the nation. On the day before the feast of the Transfiguration of Christ, Armenians sprinkle each other with water on the streets, "an ancient allusion to the Temple feast of drawing water during Tabernacles week."[918] Armenians use a number of Jewish terms related to their worship: *kahana* for priest, from Hebrew *kohen*; *bema* (a raised platform), which recalls the structure in the temple in Jerusalem; the *bima*, from which the priest gave his blessing and read the Torah. This structure, the ancestor of the Christian pulpit as well as the Muslim *minbar*, is a reminder of the Jewish origin of these religions. (Many Eastern churches retain the Hebrew name: the *bema*.) The Old Armenians met not in churches but in synagogues.[919] They call their liturgy the *Soorp Badarak*, or Holy Sacrifice, harking back, like the liturgy of Addai, to the temple rites.

The Armenian Church retained its Jewish cast for a long time. In the eleventh century, the Syrian princes of the church accused their Armenian counterparts of retaining Jewish ceremonies, such as using unleavened bread in the Eucharist and sacrificing an actual Paschal lamb at Easter. The Armenians countered that the Syrians, "contrary to the account of the Gospels, mixed water into the wine of the Eucharist; that they used unclean foods and were *thus acting against the Law*."[920] (Italics mine.) The liturgical specialist Eric Werner claims that "we may safely assume that the tradition of the Armenian Church and its liturgy go back to the centuries when there was a well-established Jewish settlement, that is, between 100 and 380."[921]

Missionaries introduced "the Armenians to the Adoptionist or Ebionite type of faith which was dominant in the Far East"[922] long before Tiridates proclaimed the whole country Christian. Many Armenians continue to believe that Jesus was a man adopted by God as the Messiah, a view that would influence the heretics of the Middle Ages. We will look at them later

We will find many more Yeshuites in the East. "Heretics" overshadowed what we know as Christianity there. Bauer claims that that is why Eusebius writes so little about the Eastern Church. He wasn't going to write about "heretics." The history of orthodox Christianity was a blank. There was nothing to tell. Except for Jesus's pen pal, Abgar, of course.

The Nasara of Iran

Massoume Price is a social anthropologist currently living in Canada. Her "A Brief History of Christianity in Iran"[923] quotes a text the high priest Kirdir inscribed on the Kabah of Zartusht (late third century):

"And the Jews (Yahud), Buddhists (Shaman), Hindus (Brahman), Nazarenes (Nasara), Christians (Kristiyan), Baptists (Makdag) and Manicheans (Zandik) were smashed in the empire, their idols destroyed, and the habitations of the idols annihilated and turned into abodes and seats of the gods."

Backs went up. Someone who felt he knew better than an Iranian blogged that native believers were all called Nazarenes and that Kristiyan referred only to those who had been deported from Antioch. Another site, www.avesta.org, quotes Kirdir's complete text but translates Nazarenes as "Orthodox Christians" and Christians as "Gnostics." Nonsense! The Manichaeans (listed later) were *the* Gnostics in Persia. There were no others. Fascinating how far ignoramuses will go to blow a smoke screen across the Nazarenes.

Neusner, who points out that "Jewish-Christians" were a significant problem for the Talmudic Jews in the Sassanian Empire, supports Price's interpretation.[924] Further confirmation would come from Jerome around a hundred years later: "Until now a heresy is to be found in all of the synagogues of the East among the Jews; it is called 'of the Minaeans' and is cursed by the Pharisees until now. Usually they are called Nazarenes."[925] Those troublesome Nazarenes nettle some scholars who, to support their case, suggest that Jerome is a liar (in politer language than that).

And on to India

We will find the *Nasara* popping up in the Qur'an where there can be no question that they are Yeshuites, not Christians. That's for later. Now let us follow them to India, where they are called Nasranis. Although the legend of St. Thomas bringing the faith there may be just that—a legend—there is nothing impossible about it. A large Jewish Diaspora had settled in Cranganore (which Pliny described as India's chief trading city[926]) in Old Testament times. It maintained a brisk trade with the Mediterranean world. As early as Jesus's youth, Strabo found as many as 120 ships a year sailing from Egypt to India via the Red Sea.[927] They had recently discovered the secret of the monsoons and the "whole trip ... could now be accomplished in about ninety-four days."[928]

Such regular contact would have made it an attractive spot to drum up support. It was critical to bring the twelve tribes of Israel back to the

Holy Land for the messianic age. Jesus says the Son of Man will "gather his elect from the four winds, from the ends of the earth."[929] He also promises that his disciples will sit on twelve thrones judging the twelve tribes of Israel.[930] An embarrassment when the Evangelists wrote—it had not been fulfilled—it must go back to Jesus.

Since it is authentic, the disciples, too, looked for this outcome. An embassy to Cranganore to alert the Jews there that the kingdom was imminent would be essential. Whether Thomas, or some other, went, the native tradition that it happened early is true. Opinion now leans toward "probable" for it being Thomas. The evidence is far too extensive for me to present here.[931]

The Nasranis' called their religion "The Way" (*Margam)* and themselves "Followers of the Way" (Margavasis). Since that term disappeared early, someone must have brought it during the first century. A man named Pantaenus visited India circa 190 CE and found "persons there who knew of Christ" (he does not say *Christians*) using the Gospel according to Matthew in Hebrew. He claims Bartholomew brought the Gospel to them.[932] By 883 CE, the two saints had joined forces. The Anglo-Saxon Chronicle tells us that King Alfred sent two men "to India to St. Thomas and to St. Bartholomew."[933]

During the millennium and a half they lived unmolested, the Nasranis had many contacts with Syrian Christianity, during which time they assimilated many elements of that faith. Originally they observed the Sabbath rather than Sunday. Echoing Edessa, they call their service the Qurbana, from the Hebrew *Korban*, meaning "Sacrifice."

On Passover night, the Nasrani partake of Pesaha-appam (unleavened Passover bread) along with Pesaha-pal (Passover coconut milk).[934] These very Jewish traditions are much closer to Passover than our Maundy Thursday observances. They preserved other Yeshuite rituals, such as covering their heads during worship. The Nasrani Menorah, also known as the Mar Thoma cross, combines the menorah with the cross, a lovely symbol of Peter's dictum that both of God's covenants are valid.

Arriving in the sixteenth century, the Portuguese attacked. Describing the Nasrani as Sabbath-keeping Judaizers, they attempted to wipe out their traditions and force them into the Catholic fold. In 1599, nothing if not thorough, they burnt all their texts.[935] Feeding the Gospel of Thomas and the Acts of Thomas into the flames, they exulted in erasing all legacies of antiquity and Jewishness.[936] Then they tried to brainwash the Nasranis into believing that they were local people, not descendants of early Jewish settlers who Thomas converted to Christianity. It didn't work. The Nasranis never forgot.

Finally, the Portuguese burned the Nasrani Bible, which included *the Gospel of the Nazoraeans*. The Nasranis, who were, until then, "living fossils" of Yeshuite traditions, "lost their very defining ethos,"[937] and the world again lost precious documents.

Back in the West—Jesus's Grandnephews

I earlier mentioned the story of Jude's grandsons. It shines a brief light on Jesus's followers in Palestine, but first a prophetic digression. We turn to our trusty—or otherwise—Josephus who, in a former life, was the general of the Jewish rebel forces in Galilee. While hiding from his opponent, the Roman general Vespasian, our wily old historian dreamed up a plan to save his skin. As one of Judea's top brass, he could expect Vespasian to drag him through the streets of Rome, a prize trophy in a triumphal procession before a howling mob slavering for his blood (a fate some of his colleagues suffered shortly thereafter). The rebels cowering in the pit with him could expect a less dramatic, if no less sure, end. When Josephus suggested surrender, they vowed never to fall into the hands of the enemy. Enter an early, and possibly fixed, lottery. The stakes? Who would kill whom in what order. It is quite suspicious that Josephus managed to go last, "whether we must say it happened so by chance, or whether by the providence of God,"[938] he glibly remarks.

His comrades dead, he broke the pact. How much he knew about Rome's politics (volatile as Nero's reign approached its bloody climax) is anyone's guess, but, after surrendering, he arranged an audience with Vespasian and his son Titus. There he posed as a seer: he came as a messenger "of greater tidings." Vespasian should not send him to Nero for a triumph because he was, in fact, an emissary of God! His message?

> "You, Vespasian, are Caesar and Emperor, you and your
> son here, so load me with your heaviest chains and keep
> me for yourself, for you are master not only of me, Caesar,
> but of land and sea and all the human race ..."[939]

Treason—but what had he to lose? One wonders what the stolid-faced Vespasian thought of God's herald. Josephus notes that his captor suspected a cunning trick. How shrewd. Yet it may have influenced the general's march on Rome after Nero's assassination, where his successful coup fulfilled Josephus's prophecy. Lucky Joe! He had gambled twice and won—not only life, but ease.

This does have to do with why Domitian (Vespasian's son) hauled Jude's grandsons up before him, and it hinges on a mysterious oracle. Only in hindsight does Josephus claim that he—and he alone—understood this "equivocal oracle" found in Jewish sacred writings, prophesying that a man from their country would "become monarch of the whole world."[940] I'll say it was equivocal if the man from Judea was Vespasian! But oracles were notoriously tricky. Playing fast and loose with sources was also endemic (then as now).

When I researched this years ago, the favorite contender was the Star Prophecy: "A star will come out of Jacob. A scepter will rise out of Israel ..."[941] but there's no "monarch of the whole world" there. James Tabor argues that this was Daniel's "Seventy Weeks" prophecy: "And the people of the prince who is to come shall destroy the city and the sanctuary."[942] Vespasian and Titus certainly fulfilled that. Some Jews had computed the mathematics that showed that the prophecy would be fulfilled at that time, an important factor in the unrest in Judea during the first and second centuries. Nonetheless, no known prophecy truly fits Josephus's "equivocal oracle."

The Flavian emperors (Vespasian, Titus, and Domitian) were not so naïve as to imagine that all Jews were as accommodating as Josephus—not while such prophecies continued to rumble through the defeated country, with hopes, of course, placed on native contenders. Not only does uneasy lie the head that wears the crown; pretenders have sleepless nights too, in this case those who claim Davidic descent. And they rouse jealousy. After Domitian commanded "that the descendants of David should be slain," Eusebius tells us, some "heretics" brought accusation against the descendants of Jude, Jesus's brother, on the ground that they were of the lineage of David.[943]

Next Eusebius (quoting Hegesippus) tells how Domitian summoned Jude's grandsons (Zoker and James) for interrogation. They confessed, no doubt quaking in their sandals, that they were descendants of David. Next question: How much did they own? Well, they had about thirty-nine acres back there in Galilee but no money, they said, holding up calloused hands to prove lives of hard labor. Then the big question: What about "Christ and his kingdom?"

The brothers took a leaf from Paul's Gospel, possibly to save their skins: oh no. Domitian could sleep nights. Christ's was to be no earthly kingdom, but a heavenly one. Jesus would appear at the end of the world and judge the nations. That would have passed any Catholic tribunal with flying colors. Domitian passed them too. Simpletons, he decided: they were no threat to *his* throne.

Having faced the emperor and survived, back home they went where, despite calloused hands, they became "rulers of the churches."[944] The *Apostolic Constitutions*[945] tells us that their grandfather Jude was also a farmer. The family stayed put. Another descendant, Conon, who declared at his trial that he was born in Nazareth of Jesus's family, was still a farmer.[946] That was in 250, shortly after Julius Africanus, who wrote about their now lost chronicles, died. Then Jesus's family vanishes.

Archaeology to the rescue! When the Custody of the Holy Land decided to replace the old Shrine of the Annunciation at Nazareth, Fr. Bellarmino Bagatti excavated the site. No one was hopeful: scholarly opinion held that because Epiphanius said no Gentiles lived in Nazareth until the time of Constantine,[947] all the above material recounted by Eusebius was a pious fraud. It's a measure of how blind scholars are. They were Jews—Nazarenes—not Gentiles.

First, Bagatti found a previously unknown Byzantine church on the site of the shrine. The friar kept on digging and was rewarded when an earlier structure, a synagogue, emerged from the soil. Graffiti and monuments show that the shrine had been frequented by "Jewish-Christians" *until the end of the fifth century*.[948] (That's decades after the master narrative says they disappeared.) The church fathers were vindicated, and the pooh-pooh school of scholarship got a black eye. Zoker, James, and Conon would certainly have known where their ancestors had lived since they continued to farm the old property in an unbroken line from Jude. Did they remember where an angel startled their ancestors? Or did an old synagogue later acquire a myth?

135 CE: Jesus's Prophecies Fulfilled

> And as he went forth from the temple, one of his disciples said to him: "Teacher, look! What great stones and what great buildings." And Jesus said to him: "Not one stone will be left on another which will not be overthrown."[949]

In the early second century, the Emperor Hadrian desecrated Jerusalem, rebuilding it as the pagan Aelia Capitolina, with a temple to Jupiter on the site of Solomon's temple. The resulting revolt, led by Bar Kochba, was the ultimate debacle for Judea—and the Yeshuites. Curses in the synagogue gave way to persecution. Bar Kochba tortured Christians who would not deny Jesus.[950] Eusebius (as preserved by Jerome) claims that he murdered and tortured them because they would not help him against the Roman army.[951] The *Apocalypse of Peter,* written during this revolt, recounts a visionary Jesus telling Peter that one will come saying, "I am the Christ." The text continues: "And when they reject him he shall slay with the sword, and there shall be many martyrs."[952]

When so many hailed Bar Kochba as the "Christ" (Messiah), refusing to recognize him was perilous. He demanded total obedience:

> From Shimeon ben Kosiba [Bar Kochba] to Yeshua ben Galoula and to the men of the fort, peace. I take heaven to witness against me that unless you mobilize [destroy?] the Galileans who are with you, every man, I will put fetters on your feet as I did to ben Aphlul.[953]

What is that illegible word? "Mobilize" seems unlikely, considering the threat. And were these Galileans Yeshuites? Some think so. If so, it confirms Eusebius' report of murder. We will never know. Discord dogged Bar Kochba in life and in death: this letter is no exception.

Once Rome had put down its third Jewish revolt in less than a century (including the one in Egypt), Hadrian took out his fury on the Jews, debarring them from Jerusalem on pain of death. He merged Judea with Syria, renaming it Syria Palaestina, then banned Judaism throughout the empire.

Hadrian died soon after the war ended. His successor, Antonius Pius, so stingy they called him "the cumin-splitter," could be generous in some ways: his edict of toleration lifted the restrictions. In the interim, Jews practiced their religion covertly—the Mishnah cites rules for secretly putting on *tefillin* in the fields and blowing the *shofar* (the ram's horn) undetected in a pit.[954] All of this would have affected the Yeshuites. Those who had fled farther east were luckier; they still had freedom of worship under the Parthians.

One fugitive was the famous Rabbi Meir. On his return after the repeal of Hadrian's draconic laws, he dominated the new Sanhedrin in the city of Usha, captivating his hearers with fables, parables, and maxims. A parable that may refer to Jesus is about a man who took to "*listaia*" (in this context rebellion, not robbery since he was crucified). Passersby mocked him while he hung on the cross.[955]

Following this parable is a satirical account of the execution of five "disciples" of Jesus (not those in the Gospels).[956] Hereford says that the context implies a Jewish trial, not Roman, probably Christians persecuted under Bar Kochba. "So far as I know, there is no other period than this (132–5 CE) at which Christians were persecuted and even put to death by Jews,"[957] Hereford comments.

With the Essenes, Zealots, and Sadducees gone, Rabbinical Judaism's main rivals were Nazarenes. The enmity in Jewish sources reflects the power struggle between them. Nevertheless, Hereford records a passage, dated to the early fourth century, in which some Nazarenes hire a Jewish rabbi to teach them.[958] Peter's tolerance had not been entirely forgotten.

Attacked by both Jewish and church authorities, the Yeshuites in the West were slowly but surely crippled. The Gentile church would now prevail. This is why Christianity became a mainly Gentile religion so quickly after Jesus's death. Scattered, depopulated and stripped of their power, the sidelined Yeshuites stubbornly persisted. Although some still lived in Palestine, many remained beyond Jordan. In the latter half of the fourth century, Epiphanius locates them in a narrow strip stretching from Damascus in the north, through Caesarea Philippi, down the east side of the Jordan to the southern end of the Dead Sea. Here they apparently flourished for centuries. This was the area that had no Catholic bishops before the fifth century, as noted earlier.[959]

Here the *Didascalia Apostolorum* was written. Although the "teaching of the apostles" only in name, one passage tells us that the *Pascha* (Passover) fast commemorates "the disobedience of our brethren." "For even though they hate you, yet ought we to call them brethren," it commands. "For their sake therefore, and for the judgement and destruction of the (holy) place, we ought to fast and to mourn …"[960] That passage must be Yeshuite. If not, it is the sole instance of Christians grieving for the destruction of the temple.

Not content with destroying the temple, Hadrian profaned many sites the Yeshuites venerated. At Golgotha, he erected a statue of Astarte, the goddess who descended into the nether regions to rescue Tammuz/Adonis,[961] a deliberate mockery of Jesus's death and resurrection, as was the statue of Jove-Serapis on the site of the Holy Sepulchre. This God was identified with Osiris-Apis. "On his return victorious from the netherworld, he was … called 'the first-born of the dead.'"[962] Barred from Jerusalem, the Nazarenes would only have known about this secondhand.

Bethlehem did not escape. Jerome tells us that Hadrian desecrated it with a grove dedicated to Tammuz: "In the very cave where the infant Christ had uttered His earliest cry lamentation was made for the paramour of Venus."[963] Origen says that the locals pointed out this cave to visitors as the place of Jesus's birth.[964] Such caves were apparently sacred to the Nazarene community. In the fourth century, Cyril of Jerusalem remarks contemptuously: "The sects of the impious give this name (the House of God) to their caves."[965] When away from home, always ask for the Catholic Church, he adds, or you might fall in with heretics.

A Lost Opportunity

Among the phantoms haunting Peter's smoke-filled house are the "re-Judaizers." It is church dogma that Jesus started a new religion; his followers were Christians in the Pauline mode. Anyone who promoted Jewish values was a "re-Judaizer." Since they undermine this dogma, Yeshuites are seldom seen in Christian story. Closed minds do not want to hear the *Tathbit's* statement that Jesus's followers continured to worship in synagogues with other Jews after his death.[966] Yet Acts agrees: they spent much time in the temple.[967] People who haven't de-Judaized can't re-Judaize.

In his Dialogue with Trypho (a Jew who had just escaped the Bar Kochba debacle), Justin Martyr confronts Judaizing, writing: it is fine to observe the law of Moses so long as you don't impose it on other Christians. Such Yeshuites "will be saved," he grants, noting that others disagree, refusing all intercourse with them.[968] Such tolerance was rare among the church fathers.

Paul set the precedent: "You are alienated from Christ, you who desire to be justified by the law. You have fallen away from grace."[969] Confronting Peter, he asks why he compels the Gentiles to Judaize, bowing to Jerusalem's pressure to stop eating with them.[970] Fifty years later, Ignatius writes that it's better to hear Christianity from one who is circumcised than Judaism from one who is not.[971] Apparently, Gentile Judaizers were already at work. Earlier, he had ordered them: "Where the shepherd is, follow ye like sheep."[972] If only people were sheep, how idyllic for alpha males.

The church was emulating Rabbinic Judaism's attempts to curb Yeshuite influence. In first century Egypt, the Epistle of Barnabas condemns "certain people" who affirm that Judaism and Christianity belong in the same covenant.[973] (St. Peter, for instance?) That covenant is ours now, Barnabas writes, because the Jews lost it worshipping the golden calf even while God gave the law to Moses! Why the devil would an omniscient God waste his time? Was he so excited laying down the law that he failed to see the iniquities the Israelites were committing simultaneously?

A little later, Origen had a different problem: he castigated his listeners for referring back to what they had learnt the day before in the synagogue.[974] That would vex a preacher.

On to fourth century Spain, where the Council of Elvira prohibited Jews blessing the crops of estate owners because it made the church's blessing meaningless.[975] Far away in the Persian Empire, the church father Aphrahat warned his Eastern Christian listeners against observing the festivals of the Jews,[976] while Ephrem the Syrian saw "an imminent danger of Christians in Nisibis reverting to Judaism."[977] Soon after Constantine legitimized Christianity, the Council of Laodicea prohibited resting on the Sabbath or sharing in the feasts of the Jews.[978]

Then came John of the Golden Tongue. Scandalized by Christians who flocked to the synagogues on the Sabbath, he preached eight homilies against the Judaizers.[979] He asks his flock: why such zeal for Jewish practices? Then he asks the Jews why they are making trouble for the church.[980] (Jews in his church must surely have been Yeshuites.) He is forced, he claims, to say these things, because those who do not "use the Law as they should" are so contentious.[981] This faction was undermining his orthodox dogma—a power struggle, pure and simple. Finally, he bares his vulnerability, pleading, "Let us not show that they are strong and that our side is weak."[982]

How to do this? "If someone tells you that many have observed the [Jewish] fast," he boldly tells his parishioners, "stop him from talking so the rumor may not get around and become public knowledge.[983] Finally he even urges them to lie. The golden tongue, like the golden touch, is a treacherous gift.

In contrast to Chrysostom, Jerome refers to millenarian Ebionites as "our Judaizers," suggesting he viewed them as part of the church.[984] Paula Fredriksen writes, "We consistently find vigorous complaints of excessive intimacy between Gentile Christians and their Jewish neighbors."[985]

A pilgrim recorded people practicing such harmony in Palestine. Visiting Hebron in December around 570 CE, the anonymous pilgrim of Piacenza witnessed Christians and Jews worshiping together. The central atrium of the basilica, the pilgrim tells us, has a little screen; the Christians enter on one side and on the other the Jews, carrying a lot of incense. On that day, the people celebrate burial of Jacob and David "and Jews from all over the country congregate for this, too great a crowd to count. They offer much incense and lights, and give presents to those who minister there."[986] Jews along with Christians in a basilica? What kind of amity is this? O to know more.

Worthy of note *and* emulation. If God rejected the Jews for their sins, how much more would he have rejected a worldly church that betrayed Jesus from at least the time of Constantine? As to Paul teaching that God was faithless toward the People of his Covenant,[987] Peter refutes it better than I could: "If He is not faithful to His promises, who shall be trusted?"[988] Christianity might yet redeem itself by accepting that both covenants are a way to God and that God was faithful to his covenant with the Jews. Many Christians do, of course.

In their better moments, many church fathers agreed with Peter. Augustine once wrote that there is no one way to wisdom,[989] a remark that, sadly, he later withdrew: "I was wrong in saying that more than one way led to wisdom; there is none outside of Jesus, who says: 'I am the way.'"[990] Eusebius says the biblical patriarchs ought to be esteemed for observing the "first and most ancient form of religion," which has of late been published by the authority of Christ.[991] Justin Martyr went further: "Those who lived reasonably are Christians ... as, among the Greeks, Socrates and Heraclitus."[992] And what are we to make of Irenaeus: "Christ came not only for those who believed from the time of Tiberius Caesar, nor did the Father provide only for those who are now, *but for absolutely all men from the beginning*, who, according to their ability, feared and loved God and lived justly ..."[993] (Italics mine.) Can the great hammer of the heretics have lost his grip?

The echoes roll on: Clement of Alexandria, Origen, John Chrysostom. Even Pope Leo the Great: "So God did not take care of human affairs by a new plan, or by late mercy, but from the foundation of the world He established one and the same cause of salvation for all."[994] Not to be outdone, Mohammad writes: "If God had so willed, he would have made all of you one community, but [he has not done so] that he may test you ... *therefore compete in goodness*. To God shall you all return and He will tell you the Truth about what you have been disputing."[995] (Italics mine.) That's an inspiring thought. If we could all live up to that—Christian, Muslim, Jew—what kind of a paradise might we not create?

From the above, we see that, despite the control freaks, from Spain to Babylon, ordinary Christians, Jews, and Yeshuites were getting along just fine. Why did the Church fall from grace and promote hatred?

The Time for Sacrifice Is Past

We must revisit the Yeshuites, who rejected part of the Torah. Because the Israelites were addicted to idol sacrifices, Moses allowed them to continue the practice, but only to God. Moses's compromise left it to the "true prophet," Jesus, to fully wean them.[996] In the interim, nations defeated and exiled Israel, God's lesson that offering sacrifices led to foreign conquest but: "They who do mercy and righteousness are—without sacrifices—freed from captivity, and restored to their native land."[997] The *Clementines* echo a long line of prophets who quote God as rejecting "burnt offerings and grain offerings ... Away with the noise of your songs ... but let justice roll on like a river."[998]

These Ebionites blamed the destruction of Jerusalem on temple sacrifice: God is displeased with the practice, "therefore the temple shall be destroyed, and the abomination of desolation shall stand in the holy place ..."[999] The "abomination of desolation" was the temple of Jupiter, which Hadrian had erected on the ruins of the temple.

Our Homilitic Peter claimed that "the written law had added to it certain falsehoods contrary to the law of God."[1000] Did Peter know that the book of Leviticus, the prime source for sacrificial rules, was written after the Babylonian exile? He mentions it. Later, Peter explains some contradictions in the law.[1001] These Yeshuites were critical scholars, by no means ready to accept every word of scripture as the unalterable word of God, unlike some today who ignore such contradictions. Even in Ezekiel, there is the "devastating statement that the sacrificial system has statutes which are 'not good,' and 'commandments by which they cannot continue to live.'"[1002]

If sacrifice was evil, what about atonement? James asserted that baptism facilitates forgiveness, giving entry into the kingdom of God, "as the true Prophet [Jesus] taught ..."[1003]

If so, it never made it into the Gospels. Could it have anything to do with refuting Paul's doctrine: "For Christ *did not send me to baptize* but to proclaim the gospel ... so that the cross of Christ might not be emptied of its power."[1004] (Italics mine.) This elevation of Christ's death on the cross is a regression to a barbaric ethos—a blood-thirsty deity demanding victims, rather like Aztecs ripping out living, beating hearts to feed the sun god, or Druids burning victims in wicker cages. Yahweh had rejected such savagery many ages earlier when he prevented Abraham from sacrificing Isaac. How could he then demand that his own son sacrifice himself? Small wonder the Ebionites detested Paul.

Christmas

In third century Egypt, some Christians celebrated Christ's nativity on the twentieth of May[1005] (Clement lists other possible dates). But the old pagan Saturnalia with its wild orgies needed to be tamed. What better use for Christmas? If fact, it would hit two birds with one stone, eclipsing the Mithraic "Birth of the Unconquered Sun" on December 25. They thought.

It was an extended failure. Ordinary folk, bless them, kept Saturnalian revelry alive in their Feast of Fools, which even infected the lower hierarchy. In the eleventh century, we read of young subdeacons, splendidly arrayed in bishops' robes, leading the rest of the clergy into the sanctuary to perform a mock mass. The participants sang obscene songs, diced and gamed on the altar, and generally created an uproar. In spite of all attempts to suppress these celebrations, they persisted until the Reformation—and even after. Mathurin de Neure tells us in a letter written in 1645 that the cabbage cutters parodied the clergy, performing their rites with vestments inside out, books upside down, with orange peel in their spectacles instead of glass.[1006] Those cabbage cutters were a hoot.

Nor was superimposing All Saints Day on Halloween a great success. We still trick and treat to honor the All Hallowed dead who have gone to their reward—or have they crossed over into our world to haunt us?

The Romanization of Christianity wasn't altogether a bad thing. The Ebionites could have done with a bit more humor. May they rest in peace; they were fading from history when those antics began. But other Yeshuites had more staying power.

Easter Was Originally Passover

Communion (or the Mass) commemorates death—not resurrection. Likewise in earlier times, "Easter" celebrated Jesus's Passover, rather than his resurrection. Sadly, no Easter bunnies hopped around those early churches; no colorful Easter eggs lurked in their hidden nooks and crannies. In fact, such remnants of pagan fertility rites have caused considerable dissension down through the ages (although some Christians are reintegrating God and nature, God and sexuality, which, in earlier times, would have brought them to the stake).

In the first centuries, the date was the issue. Eusebius tells us that the parishes of all Asia observed the fourteenth day of the moon (the Jewish date) as *"the feast of the Savior's Passover" "according to their older tradition."*[1007] (Italics mine.) Victor, the bishop of Rome, was trying to force Rome's will on the world. An Asian bishop, Polycrates, objected that the apostles John and Philip, both of whom worked in Asia, had observed the proper date *"according to the gospel."*[1008] Bending the truth, Eusebius claimed that the churches everywhere else ended the fast on the day of the resurrection.

A fifth century passage in Socrates Scholasticus, long after Eusebius was dead, gives him the lie. It points out that Jesus did not tell us to keep Easter, adding that varying times and customs occur in different places. He concludes:

> *So also the feast of Easter came to be observed in each place according to the individual peculiarities of the peoples* inasmuch *as none of the apostles legislated on the matter.* And that the observance originated not by legislation, but as a custom the facts themselves indicate.[1009] (Italics mine.)

Really? Did this most sacred festival have such an offhanded origin? Born just as Christianity became the state religion, Socrates was a quite modern historian:

> Moreover, the Quartodecimans [those who observe the Passover] affirm that the observance of the fourteenth day was delivered to them by the apostle John: while the Romans and those in the Western parts assure us that their usage originated with the apostles Peter and Paul. *Neither of these parties however can produce any written testimony in confirmation of what they assert.*[1010] (Italics mine.)

Furthermore, Socrates notes that

> although the ancients who lived nearest to the times of the apostles differed about the observance of this festival [Easter], it did not prevent their communion with one another, *nor create any dissension* ... From these and many such considerations, they made the Indifferent Canon ... concerning Easter, whereby every one was at liberty to keep the custom which he had by predilection in this

matter ... *even though celebrating differently they should be in accord in the church.*[1011] (Italics mine.)

What a blissful situation! Note the echoes of St. Peter: different practices caused no dissension. This is not the picture Eusebius painted.

Socrates tells us about a presbyter in Constantinople who he calls a Jewish convert, but since he tried to bring the church into line with "Jewish Christian" practice, he may have been a Yeshuite. At first he was allowed to observe Passover on the fourteenth of Nisan, but because he influenced others to follow suit, there was uproar, and everyone was eventually brought to heel. Since he is talking about celebrating "the memory of the saving passion,"[1012] Socrates implies that, at this late date, *the high church festival was Passover,* either as in the sacrifice of Christ ("For indeed, our Passover, Christ, was sacrificed for us"[1013]) or in the traditional manner. In many countries to this day, the name for Easter is *Pasqua* (Passover) or some variant thereof. Easter is the name of an Anglo-Saxon goddess.

That was in the Orthodox East. In Rome, however, the church had already adopted a pagan resurrection festival, which confirms the *Tathbit*'s allegation that the Christians became Romanized, rather than vice versa.

This usage echoes down the ages. Instructing Abbot Mellitus, who was off to Britain to convert my ancestors, Pope Gregory I writes that, because the pagan Angles were used to slaughtering "many oxen in the sacrifices to devils," the abbot should, on church festivals, have them instead

> "kill cattle to the praise of God in their eating, and return thanks to the Giver of all things for their sustenance; to the end that, whilst some gratifications are outwardly permitted them, they may the more easily consent to the inward consolations of the grace of God."[1014]

In fact, Eostre or Easter, was once a pagan spring festival in Anglo-Saxon England, which the church adapted for its needs. Easter eggs and Easter bunnies were lots of fun when we were kids. Maybe Romanized Christianity wasn't all bad.

The Fate of Common Sharing

Before we turn to the millenarian hope, we must revisit radical sharing, its key component. Jesus instituted it. The early church lived it. It had a failure in Ananias and Sapphira yet communal sharing survived a lot longer than is generally supposed.

First, the Epistle of Barnabas. "Thou shalt share all things with thy neighbour and shall not say that they are thy own property ..."[1015] That was in first- or second-century Egypt.

A little later, Justin Martyr wrote in Asia Minor, "We, who loved the path to riches and possessions ... now produce what we have in common, and give to everyone who needs."[1016]

Around the end of the second century, Tertullian could still write: "One in mind and soul, we do not hesitate to share our earthly goods with one another. All things are common among us but our wives."[1017] This was in Carthage.

Murray Bookchin writes: "Although the church dealt with such descriptions, possibly such admonitions, very warily, these it probably could not expunge. [They] ... were too well-known to be suppressed ..."[1018] "Dealt warily" is probably mild. Much more was no doubt written about communal living in the early church, but it has vanished into the smoke.

Bookchin misses Syria, which just goes to show how Yeshuite records still fly right under the radar. In Peter's final speech before his death, he urges his listeners to: "Present your provisions in common to all your brethren in God, knowing that, giving temporal things, you shall receive eternal things."[1019] Thus when the Clementine literature reached its present form, communal sharing was still honored in principle. Peter echoes the second part of the quote from the Epistle of Barnabas that I omitted above: "For if ye are fellow-partakers in that which is imperishable, how much rather shall ye be in the things which are perishable." It is clear that both authors considered the Kingdom of God—which their communities embodied—paradise on earth. These communities were living Jesus's promise: "The Kingdom is inside of you, and it is outside of you,"[1020] that the kingdom is people living in right relations and sharing everything, as he and his disciples did. That did not suit the institutional church once it gained temporal power under Constantine.

Actually, it still lives. Whether monasticism began in Syria or in Egypt (both claim the honor), it ideally embodies Jesus's paradise on earth, as far as sharing everything is concerned. It, of course, early developed the hierarchy Jesus had prohibited. Is it too much to hope that people could live as equals? Like apes and seagulls, we love to dominate.

Millenarian Hope

Origen, commenting on the Apocalypse's multitude of Israelites who were to be sealed at the last trump,[1021] asserts: "But the number of believers is small who belong to Israel according to the flesh; one might venture to assert that they would not nearly make up the number of a hundred and forty-four thousand."[1022] Based on that, some scholars have decided that few Jewish followers of Jesus remained by the end of the second century.

I disagree. Considering Origen's cautious language ("one might venture to assert"), perhaps half that might be a reasonable figure. But he was familiar only with Lower Egypt supplemented by three brief excursions: one each to Rome, Caesarea, and the capital of Roman Arabia.

Alexandria was not typical: Trajan had massacred many of its Jews, as noted above. Most Yeshuites would have been new immigrants. Again, Caesarea had always been a Gentile city.

Add to that vast areas beyond his ken: Anatolia as well as the eastern empire (formerly Parthia, by then ruled by Sassanians,) Upper Egypt, the Sudan, Ethiopia, and the rest of North Africa. There was also Southern Arabia. Although he may have learned from Pantaenus about "persons who knew Christ" in India, he probably didn't know that they were Nazarenes. That's a lot of blanks.

Now Origen descends to sophistry: "It is clear that the hundred and forty-four thousand ... must be made up of those who have come to the divine word out of the Gentile world."

Not so. John lists *them* next: "A great multitude that no one could count, from every nation, from all the tribes and peoples and languages, standing before the throne and before the Lamb, robed in white ..."[1023] There are clearly two separate groups in this millenarian scenario: the hundred and forty-four thousand people of Israel and the countless multitudes of Gentiles.

One day, millenarians believed, God would destroy evil, and everyone would live in peace and right relations. This is classically expressed by Paul: "There cannot be Jew nor Greek, there cannot be a slave nor free, there cannot be male nor female: for you are all one in Christ Jesus."[1024] The early church took some of this seriously: in the letter to Trajan referred to earlier, Pliny tells us that he tortured two female slaves who were called deaconesses (the Latin says ministers; we don't know enough about early church structure to know exactly what role they played).[1025]

Later still, Clement of Alexandria would write "the virtue of man and woman is the same .... Common to them are love and training."[1026]

Thus even in the late second century, in an area still steeped in Yeshuite ideas (this is where Arianism, which derived some of its thought from the Ebionites, would arise), an ideal of male and female equality still held. It took the church a long time to stamp it out. In 383 CE, the church executed its first ever heretic, Bishop Priscillian of Avila. Not only had he studied with a woman called Agape, he treated women as equals in ministry. Of course, that wasn't why they executed him. Instead, they trumped up charges of magic and lewd conduct.[1027] After all, women shared equally in the movement. What would you expect?

Toward the end of the fifth century, Pope Gelasius sent off an angry missive to the episcopates in southern Italy:

> Nevertheless we have heard to our annoyance that divine affairs have come to such a low state that women are encouraged to officiate at the sacred altars, and to take part in all matters imputed to the offices of the male sex, to which they do not belong."[1028]

The master narrative claims that earlier in the century the Yeshuites had disappeared. Rather, both they and empowered women went underground only to resurrect again down the road.

By then millenarianism had fallen into disrepute. In the first centuries, however, both Jewish and Gentile followers of Jesus shared the hope that he would return to bring paradise on earth, generally for a thousand years. Unlike Christmas and Easter, this was solidly based on scripture.

Jesus predicted it:

> "No one who has left house or brothers or sisters or mother or father or children or fields …for the sake of the good news, who will not receive a hundredfold *now in this age*—houses, brothers and sisters, mothers, and children, and fields …"[1029] (Italics mine.)

Note, it was to happen *now*. All that's missing is the thousand years. Jesus never speaks of it. The millenarian text is:

> [The angel] seized … Satan … and threw him into the pit, and locked and sealed it over him … until the thousand years were ended … I also saw the souls of those who had

been beheaded for their testimony to Jesus ... They came to life and reigned with Christ for a thousand years.[1030]

Millenarianism permeated many early texts. One of its supporters was Justin Martyr.[1031] Another was that redoubtable foe of heretics, Irenaeus of Lyons.[1032] He had studied with Polycarp, who was believed to have been a student of John the Apostle—all chiliasts to the core. Although John living in Ephesus in his old age is likely just a tale, the actual apostle would have heard Jesus vow that he would never again drink of the fruit of the vine until he drank it new in the kingdom of God.[1033]

Such millenarian expectations contradict Paul's vision of the heavens opening, the archangels calling, and the last great trump blasting while Jesus descends with a cry of command to catch up the righteous into the clouds to meet the Lord in the air,[1034] a sweeping vision worthy of a Cecil B. de Mille epic. Michaelanglo decorated the Sistine Chapel with the outcome: Christ damning sinners to eternal torture, a doctrine the early church gleefully adopted to terrify its members into submission, borrowing pagan visions of the afterlife to flesh out terrors only hinted at in the New Testament. Paul, of course, expected to witness all this in his own lifetime. Still waiting.

The weight of two fathers, Jerome and Augustine, who opposed millenarianism, carried the day. That led to another conspiracy of the silencers. It robbed the world of an invaluable source for the early history of Christianity, the works of Papias that were written sometime between 115–140 CE. As noted earlier, he used to ask any visiting elders what the Lord's disciples had said because he felt "the voice which yet lives and remains," was worth more than the matter in books.[1035]

The establishment disagreed. The records of Papias vanished, every word of those disciples of Jesus! Why did the church not treasure them? Why did the church fathers ignore him? Eusebius gives us the clue (one that suggests that Jesus may have made a millenarian prediction):

"The same writer [Papias] gives also other accounts which he says came to him through unwritten tradition, certain strange parables and teachings of the Saviour, and some other more mythical things. *To these belong his statement that there will be a period of some thousand years after the resurrection of the dead, and that the kingdom of Christ will be set up in material form on this very earth.* I suppose he got these ideas through a misunderstanding of the apostolic accounts, not perceiving that the things said by them were spoken mystically in figures. For he appears to have been of very limited understanding, as one can see from his discourses."[1036] (Italics mine.)

Ouch. And oh to read those misunderstandings of Jesus's words! Papias's views were anathema to the church, so they ended up on the rubbish heap of history. Thus, if not Jesus, some of his disciples shared the hope of a millennial kingdom with the Apocalyptic John.

What about the Ebionites? Jerome, apparently forgetting that Jesus was a party animal, who came eating and drinking and dining with tax collectors and sinners, sneers at them. They expect:

Voluptuousness during a thousand years, horses and four in hands, coaches and palanquins or sedan chairs and bedrooms, mules, male and female, cars and vehicles of different kinds ...[1037]

Jerome sneers because the Ebionites "understand it in the way it has been written," "it" being the passage of Isaiah in which God promises a "*new earth* that will endure before me";[1038] (Italics mine.) then all nations as well as Israel will return "to my holy mountain in Jerusalem as an offering to the Lord—on horses, in chariots and wagons, and on mules and camels," says the Lord.[1039] I, too, would understand it the way it is written. Mules in filmy gowns flitting about the heavens? Surely you jest, Jerome.

There is also Gabriel's promise to Mary: "He will reign over the house of Jacob forever and of his kingdom there will be no end."[1040] This is an earthly kingdom, as Papias and the Ebionites believed. But their antichiliast foes would no doubt claim that even angels speak in mystical figures.

Allegory was the big stick the church took to the belief that Jesus would return to found a paradise on earth. Paul's last judgment was more its style as it obsessed over the vileness of the flesh. In contrast, one of the basic tenets of Jesus and his Jewish followers was that God looked upon his creation and found it good.[1041] Could joy, dining, and sex not be included in that?

Still the hope survived. In the apocryphal History of Joseph, popular in the East from the fifth to the seventh centuries, Jesus tells his disciples on the Mount of Olives that those who have given a cup of water or wine to a widow or orphan in Joseph's name will usher his adoptive father into "the banquet of a thousand years."[1042] This Yeshuite document survived among the fiercely independent Copts as well as farther east in an Arabic translation.

One sect that still cherishes the hope is the Doukhobors:

> The Lord said that it [the earthly paradise] would come some day, that there shall be a kingdom of holy ones.
> From all lands there shall gather blessed people in peace to dwell, in the Tsardom of Christ.[1043]

Jesus never says those precise things. In Mark, he does say:

> "Then they will see the Son of Man coming in clouds with great power and glory. Then he will send out his angels, and gather his chosen ones from the four winds, from the ends of the earth to the ends of heaven."[1044]

Close, but he never promised anyone would dwell in peace, although that might be a reasonable assumption. So where did the Doukhobors get the idea? I believe that they derived it from Ebionite belief, and I will try to trace the trajectory in the final chapter.

Most human cultures have apocalypses, followed by the rebirth of an earthly paradise–among them the Persians, who influenced both Judaism and Paul. Babylonians, Hindus, Buddhists, ancient Greeks and Romans, the Norse, various Africans, the Maya, and other Native Americans all have these myths, not to mention modern science with its big bangs and collapsing universes, followed by more big bangs—a sort of cosmic Valhalla. It's hardly surprising that in this world of war, abuse, and exploitation, hope springs eternal for a fresh new world of peace and justice.[1045]

That paradise was the primary focus of Jesus's mission. The two laws that mattered were loving God with all your heart and your neighbor as yourself. It follows that you would not do anything to hurt anyone. He also said you should not judge others. A society that actually lived those simple guidelines would be paradise indeed. Yet many followers of Jesus, both Jewish and Christian, later betrayed their founder, but that's not the end of the story. Again and again, inspired by how he and his early followers lived, people of good will revived his ideals. Again and again a power-obsessed church crushed them. And again and again those ideals resurrected—rather like Jesus himself.

Chapter 11

With Garments Soft

Constantine began to kill Pagan philosophers ... the philosophers' books were burnt and monks were lodged in their temples, which were transformed into churches (*Tathbit*).[1046]

N ow the smoke begins to billow in earnest. Received wisdom has it that Constantine burnt no books. Pines, consequently, suggests that the *Tathbit* confused the revered emperor with one of his successors. Wrong. In the case of the Burning Books, the *Tathbit*'s authors weren't in the least confused. The proof? This letter from about 333 CE.

"Victor Constantine Maximus Augustus, to the bishops and people. Since Arius has imitated wicked and impious persons, it is just that he should undergo the like ignominy. Wherefore as Porphyry, that enemy of piety, for having composed licentious treatises against religion, found a suitable recompense, and such as thenceforth branded him with infamy, overwhelming him with deserved reproach, *his impious writings also having been destroyed*; so now it seems fit both that Arius and such as hold his sentiments should be denominated Porphyrians ... And in addition to this, *if any treatise composed by Arius should be discovered, let it be consigned to the flames ...!*"[1047] (Italics mine.)

Porphyry was a Neo-Platonist philosopher who criticized the Church's antirationality. Just as the *Tathbit* says, he got his books burned for his trouble. Arius was a Christian heretic.

Reading between the lines, we find more. Late in life, Constantine issued one of his bombastic edicts against several heretical sects with jaw-busting names such as the Cataphrygians. That edict directed the authorities to seize the heretics' houses of worship and turn them over to the Catholic Church.[1048] (He did the same to pagan temples, confirming the *Tathbit*'s allegations.) Eusebius next discusses the "Discovery of Prohibited Books among the Heretics." The authorities detected them because "the law directed that search should be made for their books."[1049] Although he passes in silence over the fate of the books, keeping them for posterity is hardly an option. Bonfires are a good solution. Besides, they're fun. Later, Eusebius triumphantly claims that everyone returned to the church, and there were no more heretics! (He knows perfectly well that's a lie.)

So Constantine burned books and turned temples into churches (he also killed a philosopher). The *Tathbit* had some accurate information. Monks are problematic: since Constantine tossed all that real estate into Christian laps, one would expect that monks got their fair share. However, the first monasteries only appeared (in Egypt) in the last couple of decades of Constantine's life. Before that, monks haunted desert places in lonely austerity.

The emperor had scriptural precedent. In Acts, we learn about the seven sons of Sceva (the seventh son always has second sight). When they exorcised in the name of "the Jesus whom Paul proclaims," a demon-possessed man leapt on them, and they fled "naked and wounded." (There's so much nudity in the Bible.) The Ephesians were awestruck. As a result, other magicians brought out their scrolls and burned them, their value being "fifty thousand silver coins."[1050] That's one pricey pyre.

The Bible set the precedent for book burnings. Having decimated the Old World, the plague migrated to the New, destroying a precious heritage of Mayan codices. It is not dead yet. The twentieth century won many censorship battles, but fundamentalists still man the battlements. They tried to block the *Last Temptation of Christ* and would, no doubt, love to burn every last copy of *The Da Vinci Code*.

On the other hand, we can thank those early fanatics for the Nag Hammadi library. It was to foil the book-burners that heretical monks secreted their codices in the drifting sands of Egypt, only to have them discovered a millennium and a half later. If any Yeshuites did likewise, their treasures still lie undetected. They fared little better in the East. Those precious fragments in the *Tathbit* only survived because 'Abt al-Jabbar found them useful in showing the superiority of Islam over Gentile Christianity.

Constantine the Shrewd

Now for the man who began the suppression of dissent, pagan, Christian—and Yeshuite. Until Constantine backed it, Catholicism was only one among a bewildering selection of Christian flavors and with no power to suppress its "heretical" rivals who dominated Africa, Egypt, parts of Asia Minor, Armenia, Syria, and farther east. Little wonder the church called him the "Great": he began the process that eventually established its hegemony.

But he had a dark side—and beneath its shadow, the church hierarchy abdicated the ideals of both its God and The Poor, who were its original founders.

Heresies are just different points of view—"heretic" an insult to be hurled at opponents. Had the followers of burnt-book Arius won—which they nearly did—trinitarianism would have been the heresy to be reviled through the ages. The winners write history.

Many eminent churchmen were coerced into signing the Nicene Creed (the only known case of a father begetting a son who already existed). Although not consulted, the Yeshuites would never have agreed. It scarcely mattered. They had long struggled on the sidelines, long been labeled heretics, long maintained that Jesus had a human father like the rest of us and was not divine.

The *Tathbit* and St. Ambrose agree on the lowly origins of the emperor's mother, Helena. She was a maid at an inn, a *bona stabularia* (a good stablegirl), in the saint's words.[1051] The one English translation I was able to find renders Ambrose thus: "They claim that she was originally the hostess of an inn."[1052] More whitewash. (Or better, hogwash.) The hostess of an inn was a *caupona*. Anyone who called her a *bona stabularia* would have gotten a swift slap in the face.

Constantine's father, Constantius Chlorus, an able and ambitious general, had an affair with the pretty barmaid. The story is that about nine years later, Constantius learned by chance that Helena had borne him a boy. On summoning the two, he faced a problem: the law forbade any member of the equestrian class to marry a peasant. So he took her in a legal form of concubinage, its advantage being that his son became legitimate. This is the tale told by a monk centuries after the fact, too raunchy to be entirely fiction in the view of D. G. Kousoulas,[1053] ignoring the scads of raunchy monks the church has bred over the millennia.

Bastard births often spur the scions of the powerful. Constantine, son of stable-girl, and William the Conqueror, born of a tanner's daughter, both had outsized ambitions, outsized abilities, and huge impacts on history (distantly echoing Jesus's career, which began in a manger, if tales be true). But first, what stories the church fathers told.

Good Luck Signs in the Heavens

One of the more colorful Christian myths is the famous vision Constantine invented in hindsight. Eager to seize the throne yet facing the much larger army of his co-Emperor Maxentius at the Milvian Bridge, Constantine was praying fervently to God. Suddenly he saw "the trophy of a cross of light in the heavens, above the sun, and bearing the inscription, Conquer by this."[1054] Even Eusebius notes that, had a lesser mortal described this to him, he would scarce have believed it.

Indeed! This supermortal's memory romanticized his experience over the years. Lactantius, tutor to Constantine's son, Crispus, gives the earliest, and no doubt the most reliable, account. (We will hear more of poor Crispus anon.) Since Lactantius died less than a decade after the battle of the Milvian Bridge (312 CE), his tale lies close to the events. It also has the merit of being believable:

> Constantine was directed in a dream to cause the heavenly sign to be delineated on the shields of his soldiers, and so to proceed to battle. He did as he had been commanded, and he marked on their shields the letter *X*, with a perpendicular line drawn through it and turned round thus [a *chi-rho*] at the top, being the cipher of Christ. Having this sign, his troops stood to arms.[1055]

A dream, not a vision. Lactantius doesn't explain why the *chi-rho* was a "heavenly sign." For Constantine, a Greek-speaking pagan, it would have symbolized "*chreston,*" meaning "auspicious" or "good."[1056] An inscription from the Roman catacombs, dated 331, almost two decades after the battle of the Milvian Bridge, is the earliest Christian use (representing the first two letters of "Christ" in Greek). Perhaps Constantine Christianized this good luck sign later.

The Emperor's tendency for visions may date to his precarious youth. A hostage in the Emperor Diocletian's court (to keep any imperial ambitions of his father, Constantius, in check), he grew into an imposing young man, earning the nickname of "Bullneck" (of which he was apparently proud. Some of his coins portray perhaps the thickest neck in the history of coinage.). Shortly after Diocletian retired, his young hostage made a dramatic escape, forestalling pursuit by ham-stringing the post horses at every staging post (according to legend) until he reached safety with his father in Gaul.

His first vision was in 310 CE. A eulogist says that Constantine saw Apollo accompanied by Victory holding out crowns of laurel, which presaged thirty years of rule.[1057] The god was quite accurate: the legions proclaimed Constantine emperor in 306. His death in 337 just about fills the bill.

Apollo was the Greek avatar of the Roman *Sol Invictus*, the Unconquered Sun. The god of victories, he was close to Constantine's heart, even if in later years he kept him in the closet. Shortly after he became emperor of the West, the Roman senate erected a triumphal arch with no reference to Christ, who should have made at least an appearance had the traditional stories been true. There are images of Jupiter, Mars, and another sun god, Mithras. Elsewhere, topping a column Constantine brought from Heliopolis (City of the Sun), he placed a statue of Apollo, the sun's rays haloing the face, which he had reworked to evoke his own. Historian John Julius Norwich writes that in the Column of Constantine, "Apollo, Sol Invictus, and Jesus Christ all seem subordinated to a new supreme being—the Emperor Constantine."[1058] Except there's no sign of Jesus Christ.

Coinage tells a similar tale: on a bronze follis of about 316 CE, we see the emperor on the obverse with the sun god on the reverse surrounded by the inscription, SOLI INVICTO COMITI, meaning, "his companion, the unconquered Sun." A Christian? Hardly. No Christian would have acknowledged that pagan god, let alone claimed him as a companion.

Later on, such gods disappear from the coinage but are not replaced by Christian symbolism, one possible exception being a coin with a *Chi-Rho* banner. This symbol of Christ (or "good omen"?) is shown spearing a serpent, which represents Constantine's brother-in-law-turned-enemy Licinius.

First and foremost a pantheist, he did, however, favor the church more and more as his reign progressed. His motives were probably complex but certainly the church's hierarchy of obedience looked much more promising for imperial unity than the anarchy of paganism. He says as much in some speeches,[1059] which clearly hark back to his own struggle for power. As we saw earlier, Paul commanded Christians to be subject to the governing authorities because God has instituted them.[1060] How convenient for a ruthless emperor.

Master of the World

Lust for power is the curse of humanity. It was inevitable that Constantine would make himself master of the whole empire or go down trying. He was both lucky and an astute strategist. Lucky that while his troops lay in wait outside the city, the crowd in the Circus Maximus taunted Maxentius: "Are you a coward, afraid to fight Constantine?" Lucky that Maxentius was moved to consult the Sibylline Books; lucky in the reply that came: "Tomorrow, the enemy of Rome will perish."[1061] Ah, those ambiguous oracles! Lucky that Constantine had the dream about the *chi-rho* sign with which he heartened his troops. Then the brilliant strategist emerged. Seizing the advantage even though caught by surprise, he surrounded the enemy general and forced his troops back toward the river. Lucky once again that Maxentius's hastily constructed bridge collapsed under him. Dragged down by his armor, he drowned in the Tiber. Thus did the "enemy of Rome" perish. (Had Maxentius remembered the past, he might not have been condemned to repeat it. The oracle at Delphi once promised, "If Croesus crossed the Halys, a great empire shall be brought down." Crossing the river, Croesus lost his own.)

Again and again, fate dealt Constantine the right cards on the battlefield. He also knew how to build the confidence of his troops and drive them relentlessly to victory. It was a heady combination. Eliminating all rivals, he made himself master of the whole empire. Cultivating the new religion, he then released all captive Christians, restoring property that had been confiscated under his predecessor.

His proclamation reveals the inflation that had gripped him. Referring to the recent oppression of Christianity, he wrote: "What was the remedy which the Divinity devised for these evils? *I myself, then, was the instrument whose services He chose.*"[1062] (Italics mine.) Much like Paul—whom God chose from his mother's womb. The emperor, like Paul, saw himself as a new apostle.

This is not my fantasy. It's Constantine's. Shortly before he died, he built a splendid, gold-encrusted church in memory of the apostles.[1063]

Since it was to be his own mausoleum, he had twelve coffins set up inside, with the center reserved for his own, and six apostles on either side Shortly thereafter, Eusebius piously notes, at the climax of the feast of Pentecost, the emperor "was removed about mid-day to the presence of his God, leaving his mortal remains to his fellow mortals."[1064]

Soldiers laid these mortal remains in a golden coffin. Enveloping it in a purple pall, they removed it to the city called by his own name.[1065] The coffin was entombed in its appointed place. The last had become first; the bastard son of a casual amour had become the ruler of the world. Now he lay in state, apostles to left of him, apostles to right of him, outshining them all in funereal majesty.

Trying to Stabilize the Unstable

Constantine had striven to stabilize the empire. Ever since Nero's assassins extinguished the Augustan line, claimant after claimant to the purple, backed by their legions, had enthroned themselves in a sea of blood. He'd done it himself—he knew the dangers. Throughout the ages of empire, the wonder is that Rome maintained its hegemony despite its ceaseless bloody struggles.

Constantine reduced the legions from five to one thousand men to curb any generals eyeing the throne. Within a century, barbarian hordes broke through these weakened defenses, destroying the western empire and plunging Europe into the Dark Ages. Augustine's *City of God* argued that adopting Christianity had not plunged the world into chaos, yet the church's suppression of pagan science and philosophy helped precipitate that darkness. Had not Islam treasured the Greek philosophers, much of their work would be gone. Church histories don't mention that much.

Constantine also needed stability in the church. After seizing power, he was faced with a bewildering array of Christianities, all convinced they possessed the one true doctrine, all ready to fly at each other's throats to prove it. The original Zealot mindset had infected Christianity Triumphant: a jealous god had bred jealous devotees who tolerated no other views but their own.

The leading contenders were the Donatists in North Africa, the Arians in the East, and the proto-Catholics in the West. The Donatists refused to readmit lapsed Christians who, faced with martyrdom, had panicked and denied their faith. That split the North African church, setting the stage for centuries of violence on both sides. We will discuss the Arians later.

Hoping to find a consensus all could live with, the emperor convened the Council of Nicaea in 325 CE. He wrote to two of the largest factions, the Catholics and Arians:

> "Open then for me henceforward by your unity of judgment that road to the regions of the East which your dissensions have closed against me, and permit me speedily to see yourselves ... render due acknowledgment to God in the language of praise and thanksgiving for *the restoration of general concord and liberty to all.*"[1066] (Italics mine.)

"Concord and liberty to all" echoes St. Peter, but Michael Gaddis points out there were "two conflicting ideas of religious community. Was the congregation of the faithful to be inclusive, universal, built upon consensus—or was it to be marked off by firm boundaries from the known enemies, the exclusive preserve of the pure who saw compromise as the work of the devil?"[1067] Sadly, the latter won. That precedent would stain the church for almost two millennia. It still lives today.

Fighting over the Nature of God

> Your kings and your powerful ones ... wear garments which are soft upon them and they cannot know the truth.[1068]

The church had long since betrayed Jesus's ideals. Crossan paints an unforgettable picture of richly robed fathers reclining with the emperor as servants waited on them at an imperial banquet (Crossan, 1991, 424). They were celebrating the conclusion of the Council of Nicaea where they had disputed the substance of God. Arius claimed that the Father created the Son (a sensible idea: most sons come into being that way, although usually with mothers participating) and thus was only of similar substance with the Father. His Catholic opponents claimed Father and Son were the same substance (the Holy Spirit was still only a gleam in the eye of the original Nicene Creed). This ploy kept both Christ's divinity and the first commandment, as much paradox as orthodox.

This doctrine has caused endless dissension in the body of Christ, some limbs of which now ignore it. When we recited the Apostles' Creed when I was a child in Nova Scotia, I wondered why I believed in the "holy Catholic

Church." It said nothing about "being of one substance with the Father," a concept I don't remember meeting until I led my choir in singing the Nicene Creed. One choir member loved it. I hated it and eventually refused to conduct it—which was no big deal at Bathurst United. Latin masses were okay—I could get lost in the music and blissfully ignore the words.

Arius drew one of his tenets from the Ebionites: because of Christ's integrity, God adopted him as his son.[1069] The Arians pointed out that scripture portrays Jesus as an obedient servant who obeyed God's commands.[1070] It wasn't just the Ebionite view. Acts and Pope Clement concurred, as we saw earlier. Jesus was God's servant, most certainly not of the same substance.

As in all power struggles, skullduggery stalked Nicaea, enabling the orthodox faction to shakily win the day. Thus, under Constantine's auspices, the church adopted the Nicene Creed. Jesus would have been astounded, and many bishops regretted it—later. One wrote: "We committed an impious act, O Prince, by subscribing to a blasphemy from fear of you."[1071] That impious act echoed down the centuries as internecine bloodshed stained a bitterly divided Christianity.

Here I summarize the Tathbit on those men in soft garments: they approved "a symbol of faith". Those who disagreed with it were killed and all other professions of faith were crushed. Thus Christians began doing deplorable things such as bowing to the cross and practicing Roman religious ways.[1072]

The Trail of Blood

It was a bloodstained emperor who convoked that council:

> The Emperor Constantine, who lifted Christianity into power, murdered his wife Fausta, and his eldest son Crispus, the same year that he convened the Council of Nicaea to decide whether Jesus Christ was a man or the Son of God. The council decided that Christ was consubstantial with the father. This was in the year 325. We are thus indebted to a wife-murderer for settling the vexed question of the divinity of the Savior.[1073]

A snappy quip, but Ingersoll ignored many other victims. After the battle of the Milvian Bridge, Constantine beheaded the corpse of his brother-in-law, Maxentius, mounting it on a pike and parading this grisly trophy through the streets of Rome. No one recorded how Fausta (Maxentius's sister) felt.

Constantine's father-in-law, Maximian, was another victim, betrayed by that same Fausta for plotting against her husband. History disagrees as to why he scalded Fausta to death in his magnificent hot baths in Trier. He followed that up by murdering "innumerable friends. Constantine's court became as perilous as that of Henry VIII."[1074] Among those friends was Sopater, confirming the *Tathbit*'s allegation that he killed philosophers. There is a distinct irony: a blood-bespattered ruler tried vainly to halt the bloody struggles of the various Christian factions—and they were bloody indeed.[1075] All this mayhem stemmed from the same source: lust for power.

Constantine's brutal career did not go unnoticed. After he murdered Fausta and Crispus, a Roman consul fastened a satire to the palace gates:

> Who needs the golden age of Saturn?
> This one's of jewels—but Neronian![1076]

Overcome by remorse, Constantine "went to the priests to be purified from his crimes. But they told him that there was no kind of lustration that was sufficient to clear him of such enormities."[1077] The church was more forgiving. This pagan author sneers at it for turning a blind eye to the evils of his reign. The Orthodox Church even sainted him.

After Constantine's death, Eusebius, that former Arian/Catholic (depending on which way the wind blew) wrote this tribute:

> When I raise my thoughts even to the arch of heaven, and there contemplate his thrice-blessed soul in communion with God himself, freed from every mortal and earthly vesture, and shining in a refulgent robe of light, and when I perceive that it is ... honored with an ever-blooming crown ... I stand as it were without power of speech or thought and unable to utter a single phrase ...[1078]

Eloquent prose from one who has been struck dumb. One can only wonder what Jesus thought of this refulgent assassin in his ever-blooming crown.

Although the first "Christian" emperor administered the empire with great skill, he failed to resolve church disputes. Both Catholics and

Arians were adamant that there was only one way: theirs. Nonetheless, Constantine never stopped trying to make peace between them.

Finally, the failing emperor received the sprinkling that cleared him of all past sins, administered by Eusebius of Nicomedia—like his namesake of Caesarea, another Arian. (It was he who had written that he had committed a blasphemy at Nicaea.) Shortly thereafter, the redeemed sinner and baptized Arian went off to don his ever-blooming crown.

Constantine and the Ebionites

Malachai Martin claims that some Ebionites went to Rome in 318 to petition Pope Sylvester to appoint *desposynos* (Jesus's relatives) as bishops of Jerusalem, since they had always ruled there until the devastation of Hadrian in 135, and

> to revoke his confirmation of Greek Christian bishops in Jerusalem, in Antioch, in Ephesus, in Alexandria. Sylvester curtly and decisively dismissed the claims of the Jewish Christians. He told them that the mother church was now in Rome, with the bones of the Apostle Peter, and he insisted that they accept Greek bishops to lead them.[1079]

> It was the last known discussion between the Jewish Christians of the old mother church and the non-Jewish Christians of the new mother church. By his adaptation, Sylvester, backed by Constantine, had decided that the message of Jesus was to be couched in Western terms by Western minds on an imperial model.

> The Jewish Christians had no place in such a church structure. They managed to survive until the first decades of the fifth century. Then, one by one, they disappear ... But most of them die—by the sword (Roman garrisons hunted them as outlaws), by starvation (they were deprived of their small farms and could not or would not adapt themselves to life in the big cities), by the attrition of zero birthrate ... The *desposyni* have ceased to exist. Everywhere, the Roman pope commands respect and exercises authority.[1080]

Martin gives no references, but some, at least, were killed. Eutychius, a sixth century patriarch of Constantinople, claims that during Constantine's reign, as the congregations were leaving the church on Easter day, "they were forced to eat pork on pain of death,"[1081] an impossible dilemma for those who remained faithful to the law.

In faraway Teheran, in the tenth century, the *Tathbit* tells us that immediately after the Council of Nicaea, those who professed the religion of Christ adored the cross and ate pork. Anyone who refused was killed."[1082] Although both sources are late, that two such widely spaced accounts agree makes it likely that other historians simply glossed over this atrocity to preserve the emperor's good name.

Martin was wrong on one point though. "Jewish-Christians" did not disappear. We will find them flourishing many centuries after Constantine. Western scholarship has just turned a blind eye.

Around the end of the tenth century, a Coptic bishop, Severus ibn al-Muqaffa, recounts a story about Helena's vision of a luminous cross in Jerusalem (the family was big on portents in the sky). Her advisors said that it was one of "the prodigies of the cross which are worked among the Syrians, called Nazarenes."[1083]

Not only could they illuminate Helena's visions, they exercised power long after the Council of Nicaea. Cyril of Jerusalem says that Gentile Christians were still a novelty in that city. The name "Christians" is new,[1084] he tells his catechumens, and then tries to justify that name from scripture.

Gregory of Nyssa, in a letter from that city in 381, complains bitterly that Gentile Christians were a minority. He writes:

> Have any of ourselves dared to say "Mother of Man" of the Holy Virgin, the Mother of God, which is what we hear that some of them say without restraint? Do we romance about three Resurrections? Do we promise the gluttony of the Millennium? Do we declare that the Jewish animal-sacrifices shall be restored? Do we lower men's hopes again to the Jerusalem below, imagining its rebuilding with stones of a more brilliant material? What charge like these can be brought against us, that our company should be reckoned a thing to be avoided, and that in some places another altar should be erected in opposition to us, as if we should defile their sanctuaries?[1085]

Clearly, he was feeling oppressed. The Nazarenes still dominated the city. This passage shows that this faction still awaited Jesus's return to restore the glories of Jerusalem.

We earlier noted Jerome's sneers at the Ebionites for expecting the thousand-year reign with all the prosperity predicted by Isaiah. Visiting Jerusalem in 387, he mentioned the Nazarene custom, which he considered of apostolic origin, of the Easter worshipers staying until after midnight. They awaited the coming of the Lord till then. He also lamented that the Holy City did not live up to its "vision of peace" but was divided by what he calls heresy.[1086]

About fifty years after Gregory's visit, an artist created a fascinating mosaic in Santa Sabina in Rome. It contradicts the picture in the written sources, portraying two female figures: the one on the left embodies the Church of the Circumcision while on the right we see the Church of the Gentiles. (See cover illustration.) Note how the light brightly bathes the Church of the Gentiles while casting the figure representing the Church of the Jews in deep shadow. Here in Rome is a visual celebration of Peter's saying that both God's covenants are valid, defying the spite of the heretic-haters.[1087] The memory of its Jewish roots ran deep in the soil of Rome.

Religious Violence

The *Tathbit* implies that suppression began almost immediately under Constantine, as we saw with the book burnings at the start of this chapter. Yet soon after becoming emperor, he had guaranteed freedom of worship in the Edict of Milan: "The Christians *and all others* should have liberty to follow that mode of religion which to each of them appeared best ...[1088] (italics mine).

How quickly tolerance died in Nicaea! The Jews (and thus all Yeshuites) were among the victims, and Constantine was in the thick of the malevolence. The council reworked the Paschal schedule (Easter) so that it would never coincide with the Jewish date.

In his *Life of the Blessed Constantine*, Eusebius quotes a letter on this subject:

> "Let us then have nothing in common with the detestable Jewish crowd ... How should they be capable of forming a sound judgment, who, since their parricidal guilt in slaying their Lord, have been subject to the direction ...

of ungoverned passion, and are swayed by every impulse of the mad spirit that is in them?"[1089]

A milestone on the bloody anti-Semitic road the church took for millennia. At least the pope recently apologized, but, sadly, such attitudes live on among some Christians.

Malachai Martin's assertion that Yeshuites were killed gains some credence since, after Constantine, numerous Jews suffered that fate during the many persecutions.[1090]

In the rival empire farther east, Yeshuites also suffered. At about the same time Catholicism was consolidating itself under the Western emperors, "persecutors came to uproot the church" in the capital cities of the Sassanians. It was filled *"with the uncircumcised* and instead of the sound of prayer and splendor there was heard … the sound of … perturbation—with the roof of the church which was damaged—and instead of sweet incense the dust of the walls which were being uprooted ascended to the sky. There was a great commotion in fear for all the churches everywhere."[1091]

Since the invading persecutors were *"the uncircumcised,"* the church must have been largely made up of *the circumcised.* Earlier, a cryptic statement says that "members of the orders … and the flock were hidden." Becker suggests that the clergy and the congregation may have simply faded into the synagogues, since the authorities did not persecute Jews who did not believe in Jesus.[1092]

The whole Eastern question begs for a book that examines all the evidence.

Paganism Disguised: The Venerable Day of the Sun

We read in the *Tathbit*:

> However, Constantine, while professing to venerate the cross, did not put an end to the observance of the Roman religious rites; one of them was the custom to turn to the east when praying. Nor did he prohibit the worship of the stars. On the other hand, worship of the Christ and of Jesus and belief in the latter's divinity tended to spread. The Romans, who worshipped dead bodies such as the stars, did not find it difficult to worship a man.[1093]

The *Tathbit*'s charge that "the Christians became Romanized" is evident in Constantine's edict of 321: "Let all the judges and town people, and the occupation of all trades rest on the *Venerable Day of the Sun ...*"[1094] (italics mine). As a day of rest, it harks back to the Jewish Sabbath, yet Constantine does not call it "the Lord's Day" but "the venerable day of the sun."

Earlier, Christians celebrated the Lords' Day joyously. "We count fasting or kneeling in worship on the Lord's Day to be unlawful. We rejoice in the same privilege also from Easter to Whitsunday,[1095] wrote Tertullian. Constantine's edict, the first to dictate Sunday observance, was making big changes. Our Sunday has distinctly pagan roots.

Constantine's edict had limited effect. Sixty years or so later, Ambrose told Augustine that when in Milan, he observed the Sabbath, but when in Rome, he did as the Romans did: observed the Lord's Day.[1096] The Sabbath was honored in many places from Lyons to China.

An amusing Catholic caper attempted to force people to worship on Sunday. Eustace, the abbot of Flaye in Normandy, came to England in 1200 CE determined to discipline the stubborn English He failed. With the help of a little papal skullduggery, however, he returned the following year with a roll that had fallen from heaven onto the altar of Saint Simeon in Golgotha. In it was a celestial directive: "It is My will, that no one, from the ninth hour on Saturday until sunrise on Monday, shall do any work except that which is good."[1097] (One must treat the polemics of Seventh Day sects with caution: on consulting the source, I found that they weren't observing the Sabbath. They were simply doing business on Sunday like any other day. A lesson in always checking your sources.)

The Tathbit's View of Christmas

> The Romans and the Greeks had a feast, called the Nativity of Time, which celebrated the return of the sun in January. They introduced into it various modifications and called it the Nativity of Christ or the Nativity. This feast was unknown at the time of Jesus and of his companions.[1098]

It was not only the Yeshuites who disapproved; my own Puritan ancestors rejected Christmas as a pagan celebration, and would have no crosses in their meeting houses, believing images were a form of idol worship. Could those stubborn Nazarenes have influenced them?

The Killing Fields

The triumph of the church unleashed a murderous shadow. On coming to power, Constantine seized Donatist churches and handed them over to the Catholics. Michael Gaddis writes that, during an attempt to expel Donatist worshippers from a basilica, forcible eviction erupted into violence:

> "Finally, bloodshed marked the end of this hatred. Now the soldiers endorsed the contract and the covenant of crime in no other way than by the seal of blood. Everyone kept their eyes shut tight while each age group and sex was killed, cut down in the middle of the basilica. It is this very basilica, I say, between whose walls so many bodies were cut down and buried."[1099]

They agreed with the *Tathbit* that the Romans did not become Christianized.

> Having failed in his direct assault against the faithful, the Donatists feared, the Devil had simply chosen a more subtle method of attack. "Christ," said the Devil, "is a lover of unity. Therefore let there be unity."[1100]

Eventually Constantine backed off on church unity. Martyring Donatists was futile: his predecessors' persecutions had failed to stop Christianity. The emperor had two equally distasteful options: martyr them or tolerate disobedience. He chose the latter, even counseling bishops to turn the other cheek, "for it is a fool who would usurp the vengeance which we ought to reserve to God."[1101]

John Chrysostom's story about Constantine echoes that. When his counselors urged him to punish people who had pelted his statue with stones, he remarked: "I am quite unable to perceive any wound inflicted upon my face. The head appears sound, and the face also quite sound."[1102]

In act, his distaste for rigid sectarianism finally drove him into the arms of the Arians. The vindictive bishop of Alexandria, Athanasius, did the trick. While Constantine was trying to bring peace among the various factions, Athanasius refused to readmit Arius to communion. Constantine exiled him. And so the emperor who had burned Arius's books at the onset of his career was baptized an Arian on his deathbed. Flexible, like Peter, he was ready to believe that there is more than one way to God. He was no saint, but he certainly rose in my estimation as I researched this book. An astute politician and a brilliant strategist, he deserves the title "great" despite his many flaws. We all have them.

Over time, the devil on the mountainside won. Reared a Christian, the Emperor Julian turned against the church because of its bloodthirstiness. Gaddis tells us that in 362, the now pagan emperor brought the exiled Donatist bishops home. "Julian knew exactly what would happen: 'No wild beasts are as vicious to men as most Christians are to each other.'"[1103] The "apostate" was not disappointed.

Soon after Julian's death, the church began flexing its muscles. Only anonymous Romans protested when Constantine killed his wife and son. Fewer than sixty-five years later (in 390 CE), when the Emperor Theodosius massacred several thousand Thessalonians in reprisal for the assassination of his military commander, Ambrose, the Sabbath-observant bishop of Milan excommunicated him. The emperor did public penance for months before Ambrose reinstated him.

Theodosius will not occupy us long. Ten years before St. Ambrose excommunicated him, he made Christianity the official state religion. This new exclusivity sparked a famous instance of the abuse of power. Jealous of both the influence and brilliance of the pagan philosopher Hypatia, Cyril of Alexandria brought in a mob of desert monks, who assaulted her as she was leaving her academy. They dragged her into a church where Peter the Reader killed her with a club and then subjected her body to unspeakable indignities.[1104] The church made Cyril a saint.

This is only the most famous example of the fate of pagans to which the *Tathbit* refers. Thereafter pagan and Jew went in fear of their lives.

Dark times indeed. Hypatia was a martyr to science and philosophy. Christians created the Dark Ages by silencing pagan learning as viciously as they themselves had earlier been suppressed. With the deaths of Augustine and Jerome in the early fifth century, the West passed into an intellectual limbo that lasted for almost a millennium, finally broken by scholasticism in the thirteenth century. This was indeed the church founded by Paul—anti-Semitic, intolerant, obsessed with suppressing sexuality, having turned the social justice aims of Jesus into pious almsgiving. And so the Yeshuites seemed to slip into oblivion. Yet the dark forces did not kill them off, as the "master narrative" has it. We will see them resurrect in the next and final chapter.

Chapter 12

In the Fires of the Mountain Devil

> They were offended at [Jesus] ... and stumbled at Him as
> on a low stone. For He was as yet a small stone, already
> indeed cut out of the mountain without hands; as saith
> Daniel the prophet, that he saw a stone cut out of the
> mountain without hands ... "And that stone," saith he,
> "grew and became a great mountain and filled the whole
> face of the earth" (Augustine, On the Gospel of John,
> Tractate IV.4).

Nebuchadnezzar had a dream. The problem was he couldn't
remember what it was, and that troubled him. It troubled
the wise men of Babylon much more since Nebuchadnezzar
demanded they tell him what it was—or die.[1105]

The king's henchmen prowled the city looking for wise men. Enter
Deus ex machina: God grants Daniel a vision unveiling the enigma. Going
to the palace, he reveals the apocalyptic scenario the king had dreamed.
It began with a golden-headed statue with the feet of clay that gave us our
saying. A stone smote the statue. It crumbled to dust. The wind blew it
away, leaving not a trace. The stone then became a great mountain, filling
the whole earth. Daniel interpreted this dream as the many kingdoms that
would fall before God would set up a kingdom that would endure forever,
an early vision of a millennial kingdom of righteousness with Jerusalem
its center.

Not for Augustine. He claimed that Jesus was the stone. Since the thousand-year reign of Christ had failed to show up (making Jesus a false prophet), Augustine changed the whole ball game. Dropping the apocalyptic arrival of the one like a son of man, he claimed that the stone was the Catholic Church as it grew to fill the whole earth, embodying the thousand-year reign of Christ on earth. Thus did the saint steal Daniel's mountain of Israel!

But there was a problem. On that mythic mountain sat a power-besotted devil holding out his lures. Jesus saw the trap. His more fallible followers took the bait. Shortly after Augustine's death, Pope Leo I asserted the primacy of Rome, claiming that the pope should rule the entire church. The sad history of the papacy falling down and worshipping the devil climaxed during the reign of Pope Boniface VIII who, late in the thirteenth century, issued a bull declaring that every human being was subject to the pope. Could Jesus have ever imagined that God's vicar on earth would not only summer on a sumptuous estate but claim to rule the whole earth?

Unlike Augustine, Jerome was not fooled. In a summary of Christian history, he wrote: "After reaching the Christian Emperors … [the church] increased in influence and in wealth but decreased in Christian virtues."[1106]

Now let us turn to the East, which wasn't quite so dark.

The Fruitful Meetings of Mohammad and the Yeshuites

The Nazarenes were more resilient than history allows. You will remember that the *Nasrani* reached India in the first century (chapter 8). In Arabia, their co-religionists were known as *Nasara* (singular, *Nasrani*). Some of their tenets would reappear in Islam.[1107]

An in-law of the prophet became a *Nasrani*, having "learned from those that follow the Torah and the Gospel."[1108] (His mentors could not have been Christian; they did not follow the Torah.) Hearing of Mohammad's visionary experiences, this man predicted a glorious future for him as "the prophet of the Arabs." Islamic tradition claims that this cousin of Mohammad's wife was an Ebionite.[1109] He would have regarded Jesus as a prophet, the view of the Qur'an.

Traveling around Arabia with his caravan, Mohammad surely met many followers of Jesus. Al-Qurtubi relates one such meeting. The Gentile Christians and the Yeshuites fought over the doctrine of the Trinity. The latter lost and fled to Jazirat al-'Arab (the same place the *Tathbit* names).

Mohammad "made thirty monks from among them follow him."[1110] Although late, this account indicates that Mohammad knew Yeshuites and heard their doctrines.

There is more compelling evidence. According to the Qur'an, God tells Mary that she will bear a child although she is a virgin. He tells her that Jesus will teach "the scripture, wisdom, the Torah, and the Gospel." [1111] This is not Christian. It must have come from Nazarenes who accepted the virgin birth but still followed the Torah. Later on, speaking personally to Mohammad, God verifies his earlier announcement to Mary: "We" sent Jesus "confirming the previous scripture, the Torah. We gave him the Gospel ..."[1112] God obviously backs the *Nasara*.

The Qur'an never uses the Arabic word for Christians (*Masihiyya*). The fifth Sura, however, condemns Nicene doctrine: "Pagans indeed are those who say that God is the Messiah,"[1113] and "Pagans indeed are those who say that God is a third of a Trinity."[1114] Their "destiny is hell." Mohammad, then, calls Christians pagans. Yet just before, we read, "Those who believe, those who are Jews, the Sabians and the Nasara, any who believe in Allah and the Last Day, and work righteousness, on them shall be no fear ..."[1115] And a little later, "And you will find that the closest people in friendship to the believers are those who say, 'We are *Nasara*.'"[1116] God "will admit them into gardens with flowing streams. They abide therein forever."[1117] In this section, then, Mohammad distinguishes between the *Nasara* (usually incorrectly translated "Christians"), who will go to heaven, and the "pagans" who believe in a Trinity, who will go to hell.

Mohammad's views on helping the poor are reminiscent of those of Jesus: "If you publicize any acts of charity, it is quite worthwhile; while if you conceal them and give (directly) to the poor, *it will be even better for you*."[1118] (Italics mine.) Jesus's directive is wittier: "But when you give alms, do not let your left hand know what your right hand is doing."[1119] Surely some of his listeners smiled—although over-familiarity has masked the paradox. Mohammad's conclusion, that God knows what you do, echoes Jesus as well: "And your Father who sees in secret will reward you."

Since by both name and deeds the Ebionites cherished the poor, Mohammad may have seen it in action. In Homily XI, Peter says that anyone who loves his neighbor as himself "becomes poor by sharing his possessions with those who have none."[1120] We have evidence that the idea didn't die: before al-Qurtubi's monks join Mohammad, the Yeshuites tell their oppressors that they don't need the things of this world but will "stay in caves and cells and be wanderers upon the earth."[1121] Thus, even in the fourteenth century, authors remembered the Ebionites practicing poverty.

Back in the West

The Yeshuites mainly influenced dissenters; the apostles often inspired them. It is apt, therefore, to start with St. Anthony, back in the third century, the saint's youth. After his parents died, Anthony was pondering the selflessness of the apostles on his way to church. He was startled to hear about the rich man who would get treasure in heaven if he sold everything he had, gave it to the poor, and followed Jesus. It was an epiphany. Anthony did just that, retiring to the desert,[1122] where he founded Christian monasticism, although inadvertently, since he preferred the solitary life. If we are to believe his biographer, Athanasius, he chose a novel method to keep people away, neither bathing his body nor washing his feet.[1123] Like James, he died in the odor of sanctity.

Century after century, monastics practiced poverty and lived communally as Jesus taught, pricking the conscience of the church for its luxurious living and neglect of the poor, so beloved of their master. Time and again they too, falling into the nets of Satan, became wealthy and luxurious, until a new prophet would arise to reform the lapsed. It's human nature: around the same period in China, Buddhist monasteries were caught in like snares.[1124]

The church suppressed many reformers. Some it declared heretics and burned them. Such was the fate of the Spiritual Franciscans. It came to a head because of a public squabble between the property-owning branch of Franciscans (called the Conventuals) and the poor Spirituals. In 1317, Pope John XXII intervened: in the infamous papal bull, *Cum inter nonnullos* of November 12, 1323, he branded as a heretic anyone who claimed that the apostles were poor! Then he turned to persecution. When the Holy Roman emperor tried to protect friars who had been condemned to the stake, the pope excommunicated him. As de Rosa points out: "John XXII had triumphed. It was now official Catholic doctrine: Christ and the apostles did not live a life of poverty."[1125]

Popes John and Boniface were quite a pair.

Courageous people who dared stand up to the church hierarchy have continued struggling right up to our own time. I have noted Bishop Romero before. They are making headway: in the last fifty years, the liberal church has reawakened to Jesus's passion for justice. It calls not just for handouts but systemic change so that everyone may have adequate resources, instead of the grinding destitution that plagues so much of our world today. Jesus strove for just that. Likewise the Ebionites. Their vision flourished, often under bitter persecution, but with an inextinguishable flame. Censorship has tried to hide their lamp under a bushel basket for over a millennium. I am bringing it out.

The Mysterious Case of the Vanishing Yeshuites

The year is 1054. Change is stirring in the world. Soon hordes of Frenchified Viking pirates will invade Britain, turning it into a Norman kingdom whose aggressive descendants will one day conquer a third of the world. Events unfolding in Constantinople will dramatically impact history too. They will also shed light on our story.

The papal legate, Humbert, levels an astounding charge at the Patriarch Cerularius:

> Because you observe the Sabbath with the Jews and the Lord's Day with us, you seem to imitate in such observance the sect of the Nazarenes, who in this manner accept Christianity in order that they be not obliged to leave Judaism.[1126]

Mainstream scholarship has smudged that out of sight: standard histories want no truck with the Eastern Church observing the Sabbath in the eleventh century.

The hot potato for our study is that Nazarenes were active enough for Humbert to charge the Byzantine Church with imitating them. So much for the received wisdom that they all vanished in the fifth century. This is around the same time that al Jabbar incorporated Yeshuite material into his *Tathbit*. You may remember that, at this time, Bishop al Muqaffa also mentioned the Nazarenes in connection with a vision of Constantine's mother, Helena. Writing in the tenth century, he assumes that his audience knows perfectly well who the Nazarenes are.

There's more. A popular item in medieval Europe was Peter of Riga's rendering of the Bible in Latin verse! One copy bears a fascinating note in the margins regarding the cleansing of the temple: "In the Gospel books which the Nazarenes use it is written: From his eyes went forth rays, which terrified them and put them to flight."[1127] Not "used to use." The Nazarenes were using it in Northern Europe in the thirteenth century when someone wrote this note, someone who had access to their Gospel.

Jerome records a similar line in his Hebrew Gospel: "The people whom Jesus drove out did not resist him: 'For a certain fiery and starry light shone (radiated) from his eyes and the majesty of the Godhead gleamed in his face.'"[1128] Riga's text does not copy Jerome. This Gospel was in continuous use from the fifth to the thirteenth centuries.

Scholars (like the rest of humanity) can't see what they don't want to see: Nazarenes practicing openly in Peter of Riga's France, in the Byzantine Empire, in Islamic Egypt, and, as we saw earlier, in India, where the *Nasrani* followed the same rules as the Byzantine Nazarenes. There were also Yeshuites in Teheran. That's a broad swath of territory.

And only the tip of the iceberg.

Let us peer again into the frozen face of history. The icy silence around the Yeshuites masks the faith of an important emperor of Byzantium. Michael II (821–29 CE) endured the sneers of the Orthodox clergy because they despised his religion, calling him an ignorant peasant. That ignorant peasant founded a dynasty that brought stability to an empire that had not seen such for many a generation. Under his successors, Byzantium would rise to the height of its power as the mightiest state in the world. He sprang from a sect called the Athingians (meaning "touch-not"), a sect that "united baptism with the observance of all the rites of Judaism, circumcision excepted."[1129] The historian, Neander, who rose to prominence on his fresh insights, speculated that they had descended from the heretics that Paul condemned in the Epistle to the Colossians, the ones who practiced "touch not."[1130] Whence their nickname. In Michael's time, they were numerous enough to be an important part of the Byzantine army. He rose from a private soldier to the second-in-command of the imperial forces before he was fifty.[1131] Prelates scorned Michael's origins. Historians ignore it.[1132]

A turncoat is our next informant. Formerly a Cathar, Bonacursus wrote a tract, *Against the Heretics who are called Pasagii*:

> "First, they teach that we should obey the Law of Moses according to the letter—the Sabbath, and circumcision, and the legal precepts still being in force. They also teach that Christ, the Son of god, is not equal with God, and that the Father, the Son and the Holy Spirit—these three persons are not one God and one being."[1133]

Much like the tenets of the *Tathbit* in distant Teheran.

Gregorius of Bergamo, writing around 1250 CE, confirms Bonacursus:

> "The sect of the Pasagini … teach … that the Old Testament festivals are to be observed—circumcision, distinction of foods, and in nearly all other matters, save the sacrifices, the Old Testament is to be observed as literally as the New …"[1134]

This agrees with the Clementines, which, you will remember, rejected sacrifices. So who were these Pasagii or Passagini? There were actually Yeshuites, their name (from the Latin "passagieri" or "roamers"?) reflecting their roving lifestyle. Some writers believe that they sprang from the primitive church, a reasonable view considering the Clementine connection.[1135] They still emulated the early apostles, wandering about preaching their doctrine, thus rousing the ire of the church.

Pope Lucius III sealed their fate. In a meeting with Emperor Frederic Barbarossa in 1184, he issued a papal bull (which has been called "the founding charter of the inquisition")[1136] anathematizing the Passagines (the name is variously spelled), condemning them particularly for preaching "without any authority received either from the apostolic see, or from the Bishops of their respective dioceses."[1137] Lucius ordered no one to be burnt. He left that to the secular arm. They tackled it with gusto.

The Brush Fires Spread

That's a lot of Yeshuite history buried underground. Other sprouts are pushing up their heads in the fields about Byzantium.

Around 950 CE, a preacher named Bogomil (meaning "lover of God") kindled a fire under the deadwood of a complacent church using a volatile mixture of Ebionite and Gnostic ideas. He traveled about Bulgaria, teaching that an evil being created the world. Rich priests and nobles served him, he charged, their lavish lives betraying the simplicity of the first Christians. Practicing the frugality he praised, Bogomil soon won the loyalty of the country folk. The alarmed authorities, fearing that Bogomil was undermining their spiritual and political clout, instituted a violent persecution.[1138]

The Bogomils claimed to be the true heirs of the apostles, a claim taken seriously by some authors. One (Conybeare) even proposed an itinerary:

"They were probably the remnant of an old Judeo-Christian Church, which had spread up through Edessa into Siuniq and Albania."[1139] Albania here refers to a province of Armenia, where Jewish practices had survived for so long.[1140]

A grandiloquently named Orthodox preacher, Cosmas, roundly cursed the Bogomils: "Devils fear Christ's cross, but the heretics cut them up and make tools from them,"[1141] he fulminated, adding their reasons: "If someone killed the son of the king with a piece of wood, would that wood be dear to the king?" The Ebionites would have applauded.

The Bogomils shared many other views with the Yeshuites. Neither called Mary the mother of God. Both rejected the adoration of images, the intercession of saints, the sacraments (communion, baptism) and the Catholic apostolic succession. The Bogomils claimed that *they* were the true heirs of Jesus's disciples in a direct line of descent.

Although most believe that Bogomil sprang from the Gnostics (or Manichaeans or Paulicians; there are many conflicting views), his actions belie this. The Gnostics longed to escape this evil world; he tried to reform it. Living the simple life, he taught people to defy both worldly and churchly power.

Now we have a conundrum. Bogomil treated women and men alike. Cosmas said: "The heretics absolve themselves ... This is done not only by the men but by the women also, which is worthy of castigation."[1142]

Where did this equality come from? Both Bulgarian and Slavic society were patriarchal. It had to come from somewhere else. Since the Bogomils shared many Yeshuite traits, I wonder if women's equality survived among Jesus's Jewish followers, and they influenced Bogomil. (It's a big leap, I admit.) He lived around the time of the *Tathbit*. Like Bogomil, the *Tathbit*'s Yeshuites despised the Byzantine church. With Athingians, Nazarenes, and Pasagini populating the empire, Yeshuites could have moved into the Balkans, and thus their ideas could have reached Bogomil.

Formerly pagans, the Bulgars to whom Bogomil preached had been forcibly converted less than a century earlier. The oppression that followed sparked massive resistance among the peasantry, who were thus fertile ground for resisting the church.

There is some evidence. Reviewing Vidka Nikolova's book B*ogomilism, Images, and Ideas* (published in 2005 in Sofia), Dr. Lylia Kirova of the Institute of Balkan Studies in Bulgaria points out that Nikolova rejects the supposed dualism of the *Secret Book of the Bogomils*, defining it "as a strictly monotheistic work of the first Christians, dated to the first or the first half of the second century." (Thus agreeing with Conybeare that the Bogomils derived from the first Christians.)

Another Bulgarian, V. S. Kiselkov, believes that Bogomil's teachings were transmitted orally, since Cosmas mentions no writings, always stating "they say."[1143] Fear may have been a factor, as people hid "heretical" writings. The *Tathbit* material may also have been kept hidden. Pines believed that, for their own safely, his "Jewish Christians" often lived clandestinely under Islam.[1144]

Some of the Yeshuites fled to Harran on the borders of the Roman and Parthian empires to escape persecution,[1145] Others went to Arabia, where their descendants met Mohammad as described above. Still others moved east to Teheran. Roaming like the Pasagini, they could have carried their ideas west in those preinquisition days, as Conybeare alleged.

Sidelined under Islam, Christianity escaped many of the temptations that plagued the West, thus we hear less criticism of power abuse. In the al-Qurtubi passage quoted earlier, however, those who reject the things of this world, stay in caves and cells and wander the earth, implicitly criticize those who live in luxury (much like monks in the West). Wandering the earth is what the first apostles did, as did their heirs, the Pasagini. Perhaps this is how Yeshuites passed on their message of simplicity and equality to Bogomil, but a lot more research needs to be done.

It is time to fulfill my promise in the Barefoot Heralds—to reexamine the Lord's Prayer. Our petition for bread is not that of Jesus. Those who believe they are repeating the inerrant word of God are wrong. Jerome renders Matthew 6:11 as: "Give us today our supersubstantial bread."[1146]

"Supersubstantial bread?" What's that?

Actually Jerome tells us—and this is the connection to our topic: "In the Gospel according to the Hebrews for 'super-substantial' bread I found *mahar*, which means 'of the morrow' ..."[1147] In another place, he explains: "In the Hebraic gospel according to Matthew it has thus: Our bread for tomorrow give us this day, that is, the bread which you will give in your kingdom give us today."[1148]

Having learned his Hebrew from a Nazarene, Jerome knew what he was talking about. He tells us in his biography of Matthew that his source was a copy used by the Nazarenes of Beroea (modern Aleppo).[1149] They understood that this sentence was simply an extension of the previous one: "Your kingdom come, your will be done on earth as it is in heaven"[1150] (give us today the bread that you will give us in that kingdom). And that is why, when he later produced the Vulgate Bible, he translated the Matthew passages as "supersubstantial" for "*epiousion*," a mysterious word that appears only twice in the whole of Greek literature, Matthew's and Luke's Lord's Prayers. One of several suggestions is that it derives from *epienai*, meaning "bread for the future." Since *mahar* means just that, that's logical.

The church suppressed Jerome's decision. In the Middle Ages, only heretics used Jesus's actual words. A fiery death faced those who pled for "supersubstantial," not daily bread. The Bogomils prayed: "Give us our daily bread of another substance."[1151] The Cathars inherited this version. John Wycliffe, in his Bible translation, followed suit. His line reads, "Give us this day our daily bread over another substance." That line—among many other things—enraged the church. They dug up poor Wycliffe's bones and burned them. Take that, you dead heretic! Ironically, a few centuries later, the Catholic Douay-Rheims Bible rendered Jerome literally "supersubstantial" in Matthew, "daily" in Luke 11:3. Perhaps the doctrine of transubstantiation had rendered it acceptable by then.

The church failed to destroy Bogomilism. Too tough and too attractive, it lasted for almost eight hundred years. Despite massive and vicious attempts to suppress it, its ideas spread widely as wretched peasants flocked to join the critics of an oppressive elite and a church that neglected its laity. Christianity was ripe for rebellion, and rebellion it reaped in a gathering storm. From 950 till today, the spirit, at least, of the Ebionites has continued to flourish despite oppression and exterminations, the most famous being that of the Cathars. The church committed genocide, both depopulating Provence and destroying the high culture that had developed there. That story has always fascinated me since my great-great-great-great-grandfather came from the town of Alés in that region.

The inquisitors knew that Cathar roots burrowed deep into the Piedmont past. Egbert, writing in the second half of the twelfth century, noted the great multitudes of these heretics in all countries. He remarks, "They must have long existed as a people wholly distinct from the Catholic Church."[1152]

This leads us back to Bonacursus, the Cathar inquisitor who defected to Rome. Armed with inside facts, he attacked: the Cathars claim that the cross is Revelation's mark of the beast and that the blessed Pope Sylvester was the Antichrist, "for, from that time, they say, the Church perished."[1153] That blessed Pope Sylvester, you will remember, spurned Jesus's relatives during the reign of Constantine—just as the church was becoming a political power. Cathar memories went back many centuries. They knew about the devil on the mountaintop.

Bonacursus ends with this threat against his former friends: "I shall with the assistance of the grace of Christ stop their mouths, as David did Goliath's, with their own sword."[1154] The church lived up to the threat.

Catharism grew out of Bogomil practice: both followed Jesus's way of liberation—like the apostles living simple lives. That impressed the ordinary folk, who resented the rich tax-gathering priests. Both charged that the church preached only what it wanted people to hear. Since it controlled access to the Bible, it could do that. Of course, Bibles would have been useless in the hovels of illiterate peasants. They were in Latin anyway, which those who spoke the daughter languages, French, Provençal, Spanish, and Italian, no longer understood.

Better to Clothe the Poor than Decorate Walls[1155]

Now for a most unusual man who emerged in a most unusual time: Peter Waldo, a "heretic" from Lyons who lived until the ripe old age of seventy-eight years in an era when the average life span was around thirty. History claims that he founded the Waldensian sect, but they claimed a greater antiquity:

> "This religion we profess, is not ours only, nor hath it been invented by man of late years, as it is falsely reported; but it is the religion of our fathers, grandfathers, and great grandfathers, and other yet more ancient predecessors of ours, and of the blessed martyrs, confessors, prophets, and apostles ..."[1156]

Several authors claim that they were called Waldenses, or Vaudois, from the valleys in which they lived long before Waldo's time.[1157] These mountain people had long resisted Rome, which considered the area a hotbed of heresy.

There is other evidence. An inquisitor named Raynerus alleged that no one was more dangerous than the Waldenses "because it is the sect that is of the longest standing of any ..."[1158] Like the Cathars, they had an unusual grasp of church history for an illiterate people. Raynerus quotes them as saying that the Church of Rome "has ceased from being the true Church from the time of Pope Sylvester, at which time the poison of temporal advantages was cast into the Church."[1159] "Temporal advantages" refers to the bogus "Donation of Constantine," a fake document the Vatican concocted to increase its temporal power. (In it, Constantine supposedly made Sylvester head of all the churches of Christendom as well as temporal ruler of Italy and the Western provinces, while Constantine withdrew to his new capital, Constantinople, to rule the East.[1160] The devil on the mountaintop is always busy.)

Around 1175, Waldo changed history. He translated the Gospels into Provençal. A rich merchant, he once asked a priest how he could live like Jesus. The priest told him to obey Jesus's instructions to the rich young man: sell your possessions, give the money to the poor, and go and follow Jesus. [1161] To the astonishment of the priest, he did just that.

Waldo first provided for the women of his household. Putting his daughters in a convent, he left enough money for his wife, gave the rest to the poor, and set off through the dusty streets to follow Jesus. His need to ask a priest may have sparked his idea for the Bible in the vernacular.

His actions touched a nerve. His followers multiplied. In 1179, Pope Alexander III (who found no evidence of heresy) forbade them to preach except with the permission of a bishop, because they were laymen. Ordered by the archbishop of Lyons to stop preaching, Waldo quoted Peter's response to the Sanhedrin in a like situation: "We must obey God rather than men."[1162]

The church was not about to put up with such defiance. In the same bull in which he condemned the Passagines, Lucius excommunicated Waldo, but the movement had gotten out of hand. Trying to build a corral after the horses were loose, a council in 1215 forbade the reading of the Bible in the vernacular. In 1229 Council of Toulouse banned the possession of scripture by lay people, claiming that only priests could correctly interpret it.

The real problem was that, by reading it, ordinary folk could see how the church flouted the New Testament's commands. In 1234 a council ruled that those who owned Bibles must surrender them for burning within eight weeks. Bible-burning? Stung by the desire for spiritual knowledge, the Cathars soon imitated Waldo's followers, reading the vernacular Bible as well. The church never smothered the flame. Despite persecution, the Waldenses have survived to the present day, although many joined the Calvinists during the Reformation.

Either the Bogomils were tougher than the Cathars, or the Eastern Church held back from the genocide that stained the Church of Rome.

Bogomils slipped through the net since the heresy was so widespread. They reached England, flowering in both the Lollard movement and some major works of English literature: in *Piers Plowman;* in Wycliffe's Bible translation (the basis of the King James Version); in Milton's great epics *Paradise Lost* and *Paradise Regained*; as well as in the Robin Hood legends. To the world's eternal delight, Robin preyed on the rich, both ecclesiastic and lay, to give to the poor, as Jesus and the Lollards recommended. Milton, though inspired by the dualist strain of Bogomilism (God and Satan as almost equal forces in the cosmos), may have drawn on Ebionite ideas: some believed that the devil "has been entrusted with this age."[1163]

The Lollards are a Different Matter

Received tradition states that Wycliffe founded this movement. However, a Lollard is noted in Continental Europe as early as 1318,[1164] [1165] many decades before Wycliffe began preaching "heresy." The name of the sect seems to be of European origin.[1166] Like Wycliffe, the Lollards claimed that the wealth of the church was immoral. Hear the spirited Hawisia Moone:

> "Also that the temporal lordis and temporal man may lefully take alle possessions and temporel godys from alle man of holy Churche, and from alle bysshops and prelates bothe hors and harneys, and gyve thar good to pore puple."[1167]

A Robin Hood in spirit if not in action.

Bogomils, Cathars, and Lollards were unique in having women spiritual leaders,[1168] which harks back to the early church. A little-known disciple of Paul named Thecla is an instance. Much to the horror of the patriarchy, she baptized. For such presumption, she disappeared from Western history.

Comparing their writings shows how close Lollard and Bogomil-Cathar beliefs are, for instance: condemnation of bloodshed, disobedience to the feudal system, and rejecting oath taking. Under church ritual: spurning transubstantiation, the Crucifix, icons, and relics of saints.[1169] Note: these all correspond to Ebionite doctrines. Yeshuites also rejected the Eucharist. Compare the Bogomils: "They call the churches crossroads and the holy mass ... garrulity."[1170]

To summarize: the Lollards claimed that worshiping the cross was like worshiping the gallows. All three sects despised violence and bloodshed. (The apostles did not fight back when Paul's mob attacked them in the *Clementine Recognitions*.) All claimed the church was evil (the *Tathbit*'s Yeshuites were particularly virulent). They rejected the transubstantiation of Christ's body and blood, spurning the Mass according to their lights. They would worship neither virgin nor saint. That's five items shared by all three—not proof that the medieval heretics derived these from the Yeshuites, but suggestive, particularly the rejection of both communion and the worship of the cross.

The Nazarenes strove for equality, that no one should be called master or father. Both Bogomils and Lollards rejected the priesthood. We noted earlier that among the Bogomils, not only men, but women absolve themselves."[1171] Compare the Lollards, who stated that every good man and good woman is a priest.[1172] That honors Jesus's command for equality—no one is master, all are equal. Our Clementine Peter declares: "Thus, then, grateful service to Him who is truly Lord, renders us free from service to all other masters."[1173]

Bogomils might have drawn on the New Testament. James advises: "Confess your sins to one another, and pray for one another, so that you may be healed."[1174] This implies the equality practiced by the Bogomils (women were surely included in James's directive if he honored his brother's practice). As noted earlier, however, the Bogomils seem to have relied on traditions, not writings.

The Lollards went underground after the heresy act in 1401, another example of "heretics" surviving in secret: in the mid-sixteenth century, Bloody Mary burned some Lollards.

The Lollards derived many of their tenets from the Bogomils and Cathars. Although all three sects claimed the true succession going back to the apostles, any records are long gone. Bernard Gui (an inquisitor) notes they claimed that their faith was "as Christ and the apostles taught it."[1175] The apostolic succession is a tortuous maze riddled with lies, contradictions, and forgeries, which I will simply mention and drop like an ember from inquisitorial fires.

Doukhobors: Direct Heirs of the Ebionites?

Some decades ago, one branch of the Doukhobors, the Sons of Freedom, made headlines by stripping nude in court. Most are more traditional, although it is a radical sect. The evidence that they have a direct Ebionite link is much more persuasive than it is for the Bogomils, Cathars, or Lollards. Indeed, the Doukhobors' own traditions connect them with some sort of Yeshuites:

> In the fifteenth century in southern Russia there emerged a Christian sect known as the "Israelites" or "Old Israelites." Doukhobor tradition has it that the Israelites were descended from bands of early Christians who roamed into the area from Asia Minor.[1176]

Asia Minor was then in Muslim hands, and people of the book were, at least officially, tolerated. I know of only a few ambiguous records pointing to their presence in the Muslim East after 1000 CE, yet their reappearance around four hundred years later in southern Russia argues for a continuity for which we have little documentation. Remember that Pines sees them leading a clandestine existence (much like the Lollards after the heresy act in England). The Masons had to go underground during periods of suppression, yet they survived and even flourished. Pockets of Cathars survived far longer than was earlier believed: a man called Hans Thon was executed in Thuringia in the late sixteenth century for his Cathar beliefs.[1177] Thus the Yeshuites could have survived to roam into the memories of the Doukhobors. It is hard to imagine this Russian sect springing up spontaneously, particularly when they claimed influences from "bands of early Christians." With that tradition in mind, let us examine the common threads. The Ebionites and the Doukhobors shared twelve items—count them:

1. Both shared communal wealth (citations below).
2. Both strove to live the simple life (citations below).
3. The antagonists of both were "those in authority."[1178]
4. Both had a simple sacramental rite involving water and bread.[1179]
5. Both rejected the doctrine of Christ's death as redemption.[1180]
6. Both rejected the worship of the cross.[1181]
7. Both considered Jesus a good man only, born naturally.[1182]
8. Both rejected the doctrine of the Trinity.[1183]
9. Both believed that the "Christ" spirit was incessantly resurrected.[1184]
10. Both rejected the veneration of "holy" images.[1185]

11. Both held pacifist convictions, rejecting military service.[1186]

12. Both held millenarian beliefs.[1187]

Humans are not well suited to sharing communal wealth: freeloaders try to take advantage of it; witness the notorious Ananias and Sapphira of Acts 5. Nonetheless, monastics lived communally. The first item only shows a common ground with Jesus's first followers. Like them, Doukhobors sometimes failed in their commitment to communal practice. Nevertheless, in Canada, they fiercely resisted government efforts to force them to register separate homesteads. When these were confiscated, they moved to British Columbia, where they set up co-ops to remain true to their principles.[1188]

Number two is reflected in their motto: "Toil and the peaceful life."[1189] They were, for the most part, oppressed peasants with little choice. Nonetheless, over time, a few became wealthy, and the simple life grew luxurious.[1190]

Number three shows both groups resisting those who ruled. This could have arisen from the Ebionite view that God is the only legitimate ruler and Lord. However, at times, Doukhobor leaders fell prey to the lust for power, an almost universal failing when the devil on the mountain throws out his lures. But they were usually at odds with governments in both Russia and Canada.

The fourth through seventh items are entirely different matters. The Ebionites rejected the "heavenly wine" in favor of water. It is unlikely that substituting water for wine in this rite would spring up spontaneously in Russia, which is not famous for temperance.

This substitution leads to the fifth item: the rejection of Christ's redemption, anathema to the Ebionites. This is interconnected with the sixth item: refusal to venerate the cross, and the seventh: esteeming Jesus as a good man, not God. This presupposes the eighth item, the rejection of the doctrine of the Trinity. It stretches credulity that this complex of five related ideas could have arisen spontaneously. Add to this the belief that the "Christ" spirit was incessantly resurrected in those who were righteous, and it is even more persuasive.

Number ten, spurning icon worship (or for the Ebionites, idols), recurred at many other times and places and does not necessarily connect the two movements.

Pacifism. Many Yeshuites adopted it after the bar Kochba revolt when Hadrian so reduced and scattered the Jews that they were powerless anyway. The Doukhobors refused to serve in the army, burning arms in the Caucasus in 1895. The ensuing Tsarist persecution was "branded by suffering on Doukhobor memory."[1191] Tolstoy was so deeply impressed by them that he paid half of their passage to Canada (thirty thousand rubles) so they could escape persecution. Their commitment to nonviolence and communal sharing should excite anyone's admiration. I know of no other group that has maintained such a record for so long.[1192]

This leads us to the thousand-year reign of justice on earth. It is implicit in Jesus's teaching[1193] and explicit in the Revelation of John. The hymn below recalls some of the Gospel promises:

> God grants us life on this earth of His.
> We shall enter the land where there is no sorrow;
> The Lord shall help us with His saving grace
> To follow the path of all those who were holy.
>
> The Lord said that it would come some day,
> That there shall be a kingdom of holy ones.
> From all lands there shall gather blessed people
> In peace to dwell, in the Kingdom (Tsardom) of Christ.[1194]

The perennial vision of peace and justice that Jesus envisaged was a vision his followers strove for until the church declared it heretical. Now let us trace it to its roots.

The Doukhobors only emerge into the light of history in 1764, but their roots go back to another sect called the Molokans (Milk-drinkers), who broke away from the Russian Orthodox Church in the 1550s. The Molokans remained close to the Ebionite egalitarian ideals—ruled by a council of elders, rather than one leader. Denying the Tsar's divine right to rule, they too rejected military service, the Trinity, icons and saints' holidays, church fasts, and the rulings of synods and ecumenical councils. Like the medieval heretics execrated by the inquisitors, *they followed Jewish dietary laws,* rejecting unclean foods, although this is not strictly observed anymore.[1195]

Some scholars point to influential Judaizers who secured the patronage of Grand Duke Ivan Vassilyevich in the 1480s. N. I. Kostomarov, in his *Memoirs of the Molokans,* attributes the rise of that sect to the influence of these Judaizers. But there is something inexplicable here. Why would masses of Christians convert to Judaism, as these sources claim? The complications of Jewish dietary laws would discourage all but the most avid. A whole lot of people would scarcely have read the Torah and said, "Let's do that." There were two million Molokans in the early twentieth century,[1196] yet any sources I consulted passed over the oddity of Jewish food laws in silence.

Here the heretic in me comes out: I believe that heirs of the Yeshuites, living and supporting each other communally, attracted the oppressed masses, just as they had in Bulgaria, Provence, and England. The Judaizers, who were government employees, could not have sparked these radical movements. Such people don't bite the hand that feeds them. Where else could they have come from? The combination of Jewish law, communal living, resistance to the state, and the dream of a reign of justice points in the direction I have shown.[1197]

Despite all attempts to suppress the Yeshuites, their dream of a world where justice reigns remains unquenchable. Although they finally vanished, Jesus's promise: "He has sent me to proclaim release for the captives ... to free those who have been crushed ..."[1198] continues to inspire every person who has been oppressed and has yearned for the fulfillment of that promise.

I know I have.

Appendix

Women of Power among the Nazarenes and Beyond

(Much of this material appears in the main body of the text, but I thought some readers might appreciate having it gathered together in one place.)

Would you believe that the Gospel of Mary was discovered in 1896 but was not published until 1955? There were many excuses: for instance, two world wars delayed its publication.[1199] *I* suspect it languished in the dark because a woman apostle—rather than a male—plays a leading role.

That's almost sixty years! An awful lot of things managed to get published during that time. They only took a year to publish the Gospel of Judas. But Judas was a man defying the master narrative, not a woman.

Mary's Gospel is just one example of how the silenced women of the past are still sidelined. The church was, and still is, a major agent of that suppressed history. Some feminist scholars are trying to overcome that invisibility, but mainstream church historians have been slow to respond. I hope my work will help change that.

On a superficial reading, it's hard to see that Jesus included women in his ministry. He did, as I will show. Does this not seem revolutionary? Didn't men suppress and exploit women everywhere in the first century?

Women did have power in one area: religion. Priestesses had it made. Other Greek women were courtesans or closeted housewives.

Jewish women both attended, and participated in, synagogue activities. They were more fortunate than their Hellenic counterparts in their freedom of movement. Luke tells us that some women disciples not only traveled with Jesus, Mary Magdalene, Joanna, and Susanna, but supported them financially.[1200] Clearly, some Jewish women had independent means. Luke would never have made that up. And, of course, it was the women who went to Jesus's tomb, a story that no male writer dreamed up, we can be sure. If men had invented that story, the women would have been cowering in the upper room while the men bravely sallied forth to the tomb despite their fear of the Romans. Paul's list of those who saw the risen Jesus ignores women.[1201]

Luke's women were not alone—many inscriptions show Jewish women lavishly supporting synagogues in various parts of the Roman Empire. Some of these were "rulers of the synagogue," that is, they held administrative positions. Male scholars naturally claim that this was purely honorary, even that they were merely wives of rulers of the synagogue. Feminist scholars are challenging those assumptions.[1202] If the latter are right, Jesus and his followers weren't coming out of nowhere in having women in prominent roles. The evidence is persuasive, yet most male scholars resist or ignore it.

Remember Mary of Bethany? When she sat listening to Jesus's words, her sister Martha carped that she was not busy in the kitchen. In response, Jesus praised Mary.[1203] This story is so familiar we don't realize how radical it is. In most first century cultures (as still in some today), women's role was to serve men. Leave it to Jesus to turn expectations on their head. Waiting on men was unimportant compared to being his disciple.

To return to Mary Magdalene and the other women, Luke adds that these three accompanied Jesus and the twelve as they "journeyed through every city and village, proclaiming and preaching the kingdom of God.[1204] Thus like Mary of Bethany, they were disciples, not just supporters. This may be why people gossiped that Jesus was a friend of tax-collectors and sinners,[1205] "sinners" probably here meaning prostitutes. In his world, women traveling around with men who were not their husbands were considered such. Jesus retorts: "Wisdom is vindicated by her deeds." So what does that mean? Those who are wise are justified by their actions, not their words, the actions here being including everyone, women in this case, in the work of the kingdom.

Where did Jesus's revolutionary attitudes come from? For one thing, Matthew and Luke are unanimous that Mary and Joseph were not married when Jesus was born. He lived with that stigma—it left traces in the Gospels. The good folk of Nazareth call him "the son of Mary," a term used only for men whose fathers were not known. In the Gospel of John, Jesus's opponents sneer, "We were not born of fornication," implying that he was. Thus when Jesus heard that visionary voice at his baptism proclaiming him God's son (meaning the Messiah), he realized God was calling him to free the oppressed, such as he was, a poor bastard boy from a hick town, Nazareth. Jesus was a highly original thinker who routinely upset people's preconceptions. Women as disciples—as opposed to in the kitchen—fits the bill.

Let's take a deeper look at Mary Magdalene: the church has even called her an apostle—when not calling her a whore. In his commentary on the Song of Songs, Hippolytus calls her "apostle to the apostles,"[1206] the role she plays in both the Gospel of Mary and other works that did not make it into the Bible. But, since the risen Jesus sends her to announce his resurrection to the apostles,[1207] she has every bit as much right to be called an "apostle" as Paul, who was also appointed by a visionary Jesus.

As one might expect, the male disciples were not entirely happy. In the Gospel of Mary, which introduced this talk, the postresurrection Jesus commissions the disciples to go out and preach the gospel and then disappears.[1208]

The disciples are terrified. Weeping they say, "How are we going to go out to the rest of the world to announce the good news… If they did not spare Him, how will they spare us?"[1209]

Mary tells them not to be irresolute. Jesus's grace will protect them. Note that it is a woman who counsels bravery here, not a man.

Perhaps stalling for time, Peter says to Mary, "Sister, we know that the Savior loved you more than all other women. Tell us the words of the Savior … which you know that we don't …"[1210]

When Mary obliges him, Peter doesn't like what he hears. Forgetting his request, he exclaims, "Did he, then, speak with a woman in private without our knowing about it? … Did he choose her over us?"[1211]

Now it is Mary's turn to weep at Peter's abuse. Does he think she just thought these things up and is lying?

Defending her, Levi says: "Now I see you contending against the woman like the Adversaries."[1212] He concludes his speech by urging them to take Mary's advice and go and preach as Jesus commanded—and they do so. Thus it was Mary who inspired the disciples to overcome their fear in this Gospel.

Poor Mary. She struggled with jealous disciples as well as her demons during her life (Jesus perhaps cured her),[1213] but demons pursued her even after death. The patriarchy was uncomfortable with this prominent woman. In the sixth century, Pope Gregory the Great declared that she was the anonymous sinner who washed Jesus's feet in the Gospel of Luke.[1214] Not only that, he decided that "sinner" meant prostitute, which is not at all clear.[1215] The church enthusiastically took up this image, and it has prevailed to the present day—witness Mel Gibson's *The Passion of the Christ*. Nonetheless, in 1969, 1,378 years after Gregory libeled Mary Magdalene, the church finally corrected his mistake, but few noticed.[1216] Prostitutes make such juicy subjects for books, films, and gossips.

Pope John Paul II wrote, "Is it not an incontestable fact that women were the ones closest to Christ along the way of the cross and at the hour of his death?"[1217] Of course, the male disciples had scattered, since they risked being crucified by Rome for sedition along with Jesus. I know of no case where Rome thought women important enough to crucify them.

Women continued to minister in the early movement. Paul, in defending himself against his enemies, writes: "Do we not have the authority to lead a wife about, as do the remaining apostles and the brothers of the Lord and [Peter]?"[1218]

Clement of Alexandria tells us that these men weren't leading their wives about just for show: "It was through them that the Lord's teaching penetrated the women's quarters without any scandal being aroused," he writes.[1219] Thus women apostles continued to work beside men in the life of the church, just as they had during Jesus's ministry.

The epistle to Timothy disagrees: "Let a woman learn in quietness with all subjection. But I don't permit a woman to teach nor to exercise authority over a man, but to be in quietness."[1220]

That's revealing. Had women not been teaching or having authority over men in church assemblies, there would have been no need to rule against it. And if they were doing so, it lends weight to the inscriptions implying that Jewish women took leading roles in synagogues as well. However, the view in Timothy finally won, even though it took centuries.

But this is not the Paul we know from his authentic writings. Women appear there in roles where they could scarcely have been silent. The most famous was Junia. Her prominence profoundly impressed the great orator, John Chrysostom, who quoted Paul:

"Greet Andronicus and Junia ... who are outstanding among the apostles,"[1221] and then went on. "To be an apostle is something great. But to be outstanding among the apostles—just think what a wonderful song of praise that is! Indeed, how great the wisdom of this woman must have been that she was even deemed worthy of the title of apostle."[1222]

Typically, the church tried to take that honor away, but not until the thirteenth century, when one scholar decided that Junia was really Junias.[1223] His view took hold and still prevails, but, again, feminist scholars are challenging it. Bernadette Brooten searched all Greek and Latin texts and found not one instance of the masculine name Junias.[1224] But whether scholarship at large listens is another question.

Have you ever heard of a disciple of Paul named Thecla? She shocked her contemporaries by traveling about preaching and baptizing, all with Paul's blessing.[1225] For such presumption, she disappears from Western history, although the Orthodox Church kept her story alive even as they downplayed her ministry. Mary Magdalene, Junia, Thecla—all victims of the patriarchy.

Paul made one of the great inclusive statements of the New Testament: "There cannot be Jew nor Greek, there cannot be slave nor free, there cannot be male and female; for you are all one ..."[1226] It's too bad the church did not follow that side of the man.

In the early days, the church did take Paul's dictum seriously. Writing from what is now Turkey, Pliny told the Emperor Trajan that he had tortured two female slaves who were "called ministers."[1227] That was early in the second century. Women continued in official roles for a long time; their names appear on many epitaphs dating up till at least the fifth century, and documents speak of them much later than that.[1228]

As time passed, the forces of patriarchy began to suppress women's equal participation in the life of the church. In 383 CE, it executed its first ever heretic, the Bishop Priscillian of Avila. Not only had he studied with a woman called Agape, he treated women as equals in ministry. That wasn't the charge: instead, they trumped up the charge of lewd conduct. After all, with men and women interacting publicly, what might that lead to?[1229] The same smear tactics as those who accused Jesus of eating with prostitutes.

Eventually, the hierarchy banned women from singing in church. Late in the fourth century, Cyril of Jerusalem wrote: "Let the party of young women sit together ... either singing or reading quietly, so that their lips speak, but others catch not the sound: for I suffer not a woman to speak in the Church.[1230] (One wonders how women felt while men imposed these rules on them.) A little later, John Chrysostom took the opposite view. "For indeed," he wrote, "women and men ... have different voices, but ... the Spirit ... effects one melody in all."[1231] Obviously, they were all still singing together in Antioch.

Nonetheless, choirs of men and boys finally became the norm. The Epistle to Timothy had won, and the voices of women were silenced for centuries, at least in the choir lofts.

It was a long hard battle, most of which is lost to us. Toward the end of the fifth century, Pope Gelasius sent off an angry letter to the churches in southern Italy in which he wrote:

> We have heard to our annoyance that divine affairs have come to such a low state that women are encouraged to officiate at the sacred altars, and to take part in all matters imputed to the offices of the male sex, to which they do not belong.[1232]

That was the last squeak in the well-oiled patriarchal system for a long, long time.

Five hundred years pass. There is good reason for both the time and the place where a "troublemaker" challenged the system. The place: Bulgaria. In the ninth century, the king of that country forced his pagan subjects to convert to Christianity—against stiff opposition. Not only that, but the invading Bulgarian overlords had turned their Slavic subjects into serfs. As in the rest of Christendom, the ruling classes allied themselves with the recently imported church hierarchy. Soon the peasants detested both church and state, which had reduced them to poverty and servitude. To crown it all, the services were in Greek, which the peasants did not understand. Small wonder then, that when a man named Bogomil started wandering about the countryside criticizing the luxurious lives of the rulers, both lay and religious, the peasants flocked to him in droves.

Now we have a conundrum. Bogomil treated women as the equals of men. Where could such equality have come from? Since both Bulgarian and Slavic societies were highly patriarchal, it had to come from somewhere else. No patriarchal society I've ever heard of has ceded power to women voluntarily. In patriarchal societies, the thought does not even occur—unless women fight for it.

I am suggesting that, since the sect of the Bogomils had many Jewish-Christian traits, women's equality must have survived among Jesus's Jewish followers. But historians claim that these followers disappeared in the fifth century. Not true, as we saw earlier.

Jerome tells us that some Palestine Nazarenes accepted the divinity of Christ. The church may have persecuted them less than other Jewish-Christians who did not. In fact, Jerome's only problem with them was that they still practiced Judaism. Not only that, he tells us that they were to be found in "all of the synagogues of the East." That's peculiar! This is just about the time they are supposed to have disappeared. These are the lands that Islam would later conquer. Mohammad wrote extensively in the Qur'an about the Nasara (the Arabic word for Nazarene), and since these Nasara honored both the Law of Moses and the Gospel, guess what? They were the same Nazarenes that Jerome knew a couple of centuries earlier.

And thriving. Women in Islam had many rights and freedoms in the early years. Thus if women still took leading roles among the Nazarenes, no one would have noticed. That is a big if: I can find no documentation, but Nazarene literature was virtually all destroyed.

Historians ignore the evidence for Nazarene survival, with one exception. A woman named Patricia Crone discusses it in an article published in an obscure journal out of Jerusalem. Aiding and abetting the received truth that the Yeshuites perished in the fifth century, she decides that new groups of Jewish Christians must have sprung up later.[1233]

Really? Why? What's the attraction? Since there was always at least some anti-Semitism, it's hard to imagine a bunch of Gentiles suddenly saying, "Hey! Let's become Jewish Christians! We'll all study the Torah and follow the Law of Moses. We women will all learn to cook kosher, and all us men will go out and get circumcised. Won't that be fun!" (No anesthetics, of course.)

As for Jews, their criterion then as now is that the Messiah will institute a reign of peace and righteousness here on earth. Obviously, that has not happened; therefore Jesus could not have been the Messiah. If, as occasionally happens, a Jew decides to convert, there would be no point in becoming Jewish Christian because he would still suffer discrimination.

Since there is no conceivable motivation for a group of people to decide to become Jewish Christians (and some of these sects were quite large—at one time, they made up a good third of the Byzantine army), they have to have been direct heirs of the first disciples of Jesus.

Back to that Bulgarian sect in which women had equal roles. I'm not the only person who thinks that they at least partly derived from Jewish Christians. A little more than a century ago, an author with the cuddly name of Conybeare (actually, it's pronounced Ca-*nee*-ber) wrote that they were probably "the remnant of an old Judeo-Christian Church" that had spread up from the Middle East into Bulgaria. I discuss this more fully in the main text.

A man named Presbyter Cosmas tells us a lot about the Bogomils. Around the end of the tenth century, he got his shirt in a knot and preached an angry sermon about them: spurning priests, they absolve themselves, not only men, but women, which, he says is, "worthy of castigation."

Opposing the power of both church and state, they stirred the imagination of an oppressed peasantry and spread like wildfire. The sect influenced the Cathars of *The Da Vinci Code*, helping them establish their own organization in what is now southern France. There again, women shared equally in the ministry with men. The movement swept across Europe, finally reaching England, where its adherents were known as Lollards. I have become quite enamored of one of them, the spirited Hawisia Moone, a very modern lady and accomplished in debate. She said, "oonly consent of love betuxe man and woman, is sufficient for the sacrement of matrymony."[1234] (She had no use for all those church rites.) She also claimed that, "every man and every woman being in good lyf ... is a prest."

This was the standard view among the Lollards so the church suppressed them. It was a long, hard fight. Some of the Protestants executed by Queen Mary in the mid-sixteenth century were Lollards. One by one, however, these movements all disappear, and the voices for the equality of women are lost. And a lot of male-dominated scholarship wants to keep it that way.

I don't want to end on that note, so let's go back to sunny Provence, where women truly came into their own, partly under Cathar influence. In fact, the Cathars may have been the major reason why this area was far more pro-women than the rest of Christendom at the time. Here women troubadours flourished. I suspect few of my readers knew that.

There were other influences. Many lords of the Languedoc had gone crusading to the Holy Land, leaving their ladies in charge. Women in the Languedoc were accustomed to administering estates, dispensing justice, and defending castles. Writing songs could hardly have been a great leap for such women. Again, the Languedoc bordered Muslim Spain. And what do we find there? Women poets.

One of these was the wealthy and notorious princess Wallada. Wallada was the daughter of the Caliph of Córdoba. Recently, a Muslim woman spoke of sitting in the shadow of the medieval walls of that city just a few steps from a curious statue of two hands, which seem to be reaching toward one another.

"I knew from my studies in Damascus," she wrote, "that it pays tribute to a great Moorish poet and the Princess, also a poetess, whom he loved."[1235] Playing the dumb tourist, she asked the waiter about it.

"That statue is dedicated to *los enamorados*, the lovers," he said as he poured her coffee. The Princess Wallada hosted the finest poets and musicians of al-Andalus, who would sit around her on cushions and rugs, improvising ballads and epic sagas to the sound of the lute and zither.

Wallada not only refused to cover her face, she was also outspoken and free in her sexual behavior, thus becoming a symbol of liberation for the women of her time. She resisted all efforts to keep her in her traditional place and to prevent her from choosing the lovers she preferred. A most interesting period in Muslim culture.[1236]

Mutual influences flowed back and forth between Languedoc and Andalusia. Much like Princess Wallada, Eleanor of Aquitaine and her daughter Marie of Champagne cultivated troubadours at their court. Was there a reason that this Cathar area was also the homeland of secular women poets? Perhaps one day I'll research it further to find out more.

I am going to close this appendix on the empowerment of women through the influence of heretical movements with a look at Beatrice, the countess of Die, who lived around 1200. Her works include the only surviving lay by a woman troubadour for which we have the music. There is a marked difference between the songs of the male and female troubadours. The men languished over unattainable idols on their pedestals, almost always married women (whose husbands may, or may not, have been off crusading). Not Beatrice. Many of her songs are as racy as they get. Here is the first verse, the one for which we still have the music (this particular verse is not very racy):

I must sing of what I do not want,
I am so angry with the one I love,
Because I love him more than anything:
Mercy nor courtesy moves him,
Neither does my beauty, nor my worthiness, nor my good
sense,

For I am deceived and betrayed
As much as I should be if I were ugly.[1237]

You can find many versions of this song on the Internet.

I'd like to think that Beatrice's passionate song is an omen of more open times ahead; a man has now published a book on the subject: *The Hidden History of Women's Ordination*, by Gary Macy. The story of women in Christianity is slowly emerging from the shadows.

Afterword

How I Was Drawn to This Work

Know ye not that the unrighteous shall not inherit the kingdom of God? Be not deceived: neither fornicators, nor idolaters, nor adulterers, nor effeminate, nor abusers of themselves with mankind, nor thieves, nor covetous, nor drunkards, nor revilers, nor extortioners, shall inherit the kingdom of God (1 Cor 6:9–10, KJV).

I was a spiritual boy. It was not unusual for Sunday afternoons to find me sitting in my attic bedroom in the manse at Glenholme, Nova Scotia (formerly known as Folly Village because of its mosquito-bearing bog just up the road), reading the Bible. On one of those occasions, I had the misfortune to read the above passage from 1 Corinthians. I can still physically feel the shock of that moment. In spite of the convoluted language and my tender age—thirteen—I understood what Paul was saying—and I was sexually attracted to boys. Closing the Bible, I did not voluntarily open it again for decades. With no one to turn to for counseling and support, I buried the memory in my unconscious, where it festered until, at the age of sixteen, I was hospitalized with a bleeding ulcer. At twenty-six, the ulcer burst; only the miracles of modern surgery saved me. And how I cursed the surgeon who did so. I slowly sank into the personal wasteland of the manic-depressive, accompanied by substance abuse, alcoholism, and periodic madness, one bout of which precipitated a suicide attempt.

I was about thirty-five when the first steps toward healing began. One night during a gut-wrenching depression, I literally beat my head against the wall, the physical pain somehow distracting me from my mental agony as I cried out to God for relief. Except for my drumming head, the answer was silence. Yet that night I dreamed that a nurse came to me, stroked my forehead, and comforted me. That dream was a sign that I had summoned my own inner healing powers. They would, however, heal in their own way and in their own time.

The next step came about a year later. Shortly after my suicide attempt, I yelled at my psychiatrist, "I've got to get back the faith of my childhood. I can't live without meaning."

"You'll never get back the faith of your childhood," he replied. "Read Jung."

I immersed myself in the work of Carl Jung, reading such books as *Modern Man in Search of a Soul*, attending seminars and even a course at the University of Toronto. I began to do Jungian dream work and active imagination, which, over time, began to show me new and hopeful paths through this desert. As well, Jung's spiritual ideas began to help me toward a new perspective on religion.

Also at my psychiatrist's urging I wrote music every day. That positive activity helped change my focus. After an explosion of creativity in which I wrote a lot of music that I really liked, I told my psychiatrist that my depressions could never be as bad again.

Soon after that exchange I had another dream: I was standing before a trench. As I looked down into it I became aware that it had once been an abyss. Now it was only a few feet deep and workers were filling it in.

I immediately recognized that the abyss was my depression, and my inner healing powers were hard at work "making the rough places a plain" (Is 40:4).

I shared that dream with several people at Bathurst Street United Church in Toronto, where I was the music director. That congregation has been a rock to me in my trials. They knew I was suffering and struggling, and through it all I knew that people cared. That gave me the courage to keep on through many a dark night of the soul.

When I was in my early fifties, a feminist member of Bathurst Street United helped me up onto the next step. During one memorable church service, I sat gaping as she vented her anger at Paul, the man who ruled that women should be silent in church and wait until they got home to ask their husbands to explain anything they didn't understand. It was almost an epiphany: no bolt of lightning struck her down. I don't have to take Paul's judgments meekly either, I thought.

Shortly thereafter I began to write a novel about Paul as a kind of therapy. During that project, I learned that he waged a bitter battle with Jesus's original disciples. I began to feel that this man had no authority to rule on whether or not I could enter the kingdom. It was illuminating and freeing.

For the purposes of the novel I also took a hard look at Jesus's life and teaching. Slowly, cutting through the brambles of my personal wilderness, I noticed that Jesus hung around with extortioners and prostitutes and lepers, all—like me—the rejects of society.

Then came another memorable Sunday. The lectionary reading was from Luke 4:18: "The spirit of the Lord is upon me, for he has anointed me to preach good news to the poor, He has sent me to proclaim release for the captives … and freedom for the oppressed." Again it felt like an epiphany, for who was more oppressed than I, always ashamed, and fearful of rejection if anyone ever found out what I was? It is still a passage I treasure.

As I slowly but surely healed, I began to take more interest in Paul's opponents, Jesus's Jewish followers who, like me, had been sidelined by the establishment. During this time I was inspired by gays wrestling with the church for acceptance, a struggle that has continued to this day and has, in the United Church, won many battles. The more I learned about the Ebionites, the more I felt that they, too, needed to be accepted back into their proper place in the history of the church—they who nurtured the hope that, one day, a just society would be established here on earth. Finally they became almost an alter ego; I wanted to shout their story from the rooftops in a way I could not shout my own. Their story became my story. Their anger at Paul, my anger. Their hope for a just world, my hope.

The Author's Research

Not going to theological college is one of my greatest assets. I look at theology and scripture with fresh eyes rather than through the lens of two thousand years of church dogma. Thus I have a unique perspective as well as my passion to right a wrong. No one is without bias, but I have striven to remain faithful to my sources. One example: I was excited to find Pliny's reference to *Nazerini* living in Syria, but further study revealed that these could not have been Nazarenes, which, regretfully, I had to note.

When I began my research, I relied heavily on the works of S. G. F. Brandon (Jesus as a revolutionary) and Hyam Maccoby's *The Mythmaker, Paul and the Invention of Christianity*. Over time, I discovered a wealth of material, the Internet being a great asset, although one must use it with care. In my book, I note a Seventh-Day author "bending the truth." That taught me always to go to the source and check. The works of the church fathers were invaluable—I could study the original texts at home. The beauty of the Internet is that when looking for one thing, your find leads to others. In this way, I discovered virtually all the material that the church has suppressed.

I have been steeped in scripture since birth, hearing it read and expounded every Sunday. I have been a lay preacher at Bathurst United Church for over ten years and have for decades served on worship committees, all of which added to my knowledge of scripture. I researched this book for twenty-four years. Because of my scholarly inclinations and my determination to uncover truths that others have missed or distorted, they were rewarding years.

Anyone who examines my footnotes (all 1,237 of them) and my nine-page bibliography will realize that I have done my homework.

This study covers a period of over two millennia and stretches from India to the New World. No one can be an expert on such a vast time span and geographical area. Despite all my checking and rechecking of primary sources, mistakes will have crept in. For these I apologize.

About the Author

Lawrence Goudge has spent twenty-four years researching and writing this book. He was driven to this topic because he was convinced that St. Paul's obsession with the life hereafter was in direct contradiction to Jesus's passion to make this world a better place.

He has a BA in anthropology from the University of Toronto.

He has published articles in many journals and was formerly a reporter for the *Bluffs Monitor* in Scarborough, Ontario.

Mr. Goudge lives in Toronto. He sings in choirs, plays marimba in a band, and writes.

Acknowledgments

I have some big thank-yous to make: one is to my speaking agent, Cathleen Fillmore; the other is to my cousin Colette Malo. My thanks go to Cathleen because she never lost faith either in my abilities or in this project. She organized support groups and gave me all sorts of wonderful advice on how to get my book out there. She freely gave of her time to help me develop my public speaking skills. Colette volunteered her time to proofread some of the manuscript and has given me many helpful suggestions. Another cousin, Carole Hart, proofread the second half. My heartfelt gratitude to them.

I would also like to thank Richard Partington, whose help in bringing my book proposal up to snuff went well beyond the call of duty. Another helper, Elena Anisovits, gave me invaluable leads in my research on Jewish-Christian influences on the Doukhobors and the Molokans.

I would like to thank Lee Graves, who nurtured my writing skills while I was a cub reporter at the *Bluffs Monitor.*

Many other people gave me encouragement: Ken McAvoy and Judi McCallum, Joanna Manning, and Lee David.

Frances Combs, the former minister of Bathurst United, greatly influenced my understanding of Christianity as did the entire community of that church.

During my season in hell, I saw a psychiatrist, Dr. Orchard ("Man was not made for inaction!"), who spurred me on to the creative activities that had such a role in my (ongoing) healing. Without him, I probably wouldn't be here.

The same is true of Bathurst Street United Church, but my debt to them is covered more fully in my bio.

Finally, my thanks to Muriel Anderson whose outburst at St. Paul's sexism freed my soul to write this book.

Abbreviations

AJ Josephus, *Antiquities of the Jews*, (Whiston, 1737)
ANF *Ante-Nicene Fathers*. Ed. A. Cleveland Coxe Christian Literature Company, 1885
CCSL *Corpus Christianorum Series Latina,* Turnhout, Belgium: Brepols Publishers
CH *The Clementine Homilies*; *ANF*, vol. 8 (*The Clementia*)
CR *The Clementine Recognitions*; *ANF*, vol. 8 (*The Clementia*)
CR-SY The Syriac version of *Clementine Recognitions*
HE *The Ecclesiastical History* of Eusebius
MTB my translation of biblical passages
NEB the New English Bible
NH Pliny, *Natural History*
NIV New International Version
NPNF *Nicene and Post-Nicene Fathers*, series 1, trans. and ed. Alexander Roberts and James Donaldson, Edinburgh: T. & T. Clark, 1885
NPNF2 *Nicene and Post-Nicene Fathers*, series 2, trans. and ed. Alexander Roberts and James Donaldson, Edinburgh: T. & T. Clark, 1885
NRSV New Revised Standard Version Bible
PG *Patrologia Graecae* 1857–66
RSV Revised Standard Version
WEB World English Bible (public domain)

Endnotes

1. *CH* 8.6.
2. Phil 2:5–7 MTB.
3. Dt 6:4.
4. Jn 2:14, 15, cf Mk 11:15–17.
5. *CR* 1.37.
6. *CR* 1.64.
7. Mt 8:4.
8. Mk 8:31, 9:31, 10:33–34; copied by Matthew in 16:21, 17:22, 20:18, 26:1. Luke borrows from Mark in his own way: Lk 9:22, 43–45; 18:31; 17:25.
9. Mk 14:22, 24.
10. Ehrman, 2005, 166.
11. Jn 6:53, NRSV.
12. Lev 17:10–12.
13. Jn 6:66.
14. Staniforth, 1968, 231 (language modernized).
15. Irenaeus, *Against Heresies*, 5:3.
16. 1 Cor 11:25, WEB.
17. Acts 21:24.
18. 1 Cor 9:20–22.
19. Jerome, "Letter LXXV," ch. 3.10 (to Augustine).
20. Pines, 1966, 46, folio 66b.
21. Ibid., 9, folio 70a-b.
22. Acts 21:26.
23. 1 Cor 11:23–25.

24. *CH* 8:6.
25. Gal 1:8–9.

Chapter 2

26. Josephus, 1959, 54.
27. Ibid., 66.
28. Ibid., 69–70.
29. Josephus, 1959, 126, Ant. XVII, x, 5; x, 9.
30. Josephus, 1959, 127.
31. Tabor, 2006, 40.
32. Josephus, 1959, 371.
33. Ibid., 1959, 384.
34. Mk 3:18.
35. Lk 6:15.
36. Num 25:11, 13.
37. Josephus, 1959, 393.
38. Antiq. XVIII, i, 6.
39. 1 Sam 8:7, NRSV.
40. Josephus, 1959, 393.
41. Josephus, 1959, appendix 462.
42. Acts 21:20.
43. AJ. XVIII, I, 1. (peri hês oliga boulomai dielthein, allôs te epei kai tôi kat' autôn spoudasthenti tois neôterois ho phthoros tois pragmasi sunetuche.)
44. AJ XVIII, 1.
45. Josephus, 1959, 133.
46. Ibid., 393.
47. Acts 5:37.
48. Josephus, 1969, 406.
49. *Martyrdom of Polycarp*, 8:2.
50. Josephus, 1959, 167.
51. Josephus, 1959, 192.
52. Reed, 2002, 83.
53. *Anacephalaiosis*, in Klijn and Reink, 1973, 169.
54. Reed, 2002, 133.
55. Crossan and Reed, 2001, 36.
56. *CR* 3:67.

57. For a breezy, *National Geographic*-style account of this, try *Jesus & the Forgotten City,* by Richard A. Batey, CenturyOne Media, 2000.

Chapter 3

58. Is 9:7, KJV.
59. Mead, 1924, 104.
60. Mt 3:1, 2, MTB.
61. Jn 3:25–30, MTB.
62. Vermes, 1962, 74.
63. Ibid., 64.
64. Mt 3:7–8 NRSV.
65. Crossan, 1992, 231–32.
66. *Wars of the Jews*, II, viii, 7, Whiston, 1737.
67. 1QS, V, Vermes, 1962, 67–68.
68. 2 Macc 5:27.
69. 1 Macc 2:26.
70. 1QS, IX, G. Vermes, 1962, 74.
71. Josephus, *Vita*, 2, Whiston, 1737.
72. Dunkerley, 1957, 41.
73. *Anacephalaiosis,* 30 1 13.
74. Jer 35:6–7, NRSV.
75. Lk 1:13–15.
76. Lk 1:80, MTB.
77. Jer 35:14, 17, MTB.
78. Jer 35:19, MTB.
79. Orion-list Enochian Sects, http://www.mail-archive.com/ orion@panda.mscc.huji.ac.il/msg01050.html.
80. Vermes, 1962, 86–87.
81. Ibid., 71.
82. Wise, 1999, 129.
83. Lk 1:43, MTB.
84. *Panarion* 30.16.4–5, 1994.
85. Lk 1:68.
86. Lk 1:69–75, MTB.
87. *CR* 1.60.1.
88. 1 Sam 2:10.
89. 1 Sam 16:13, NIV.
90. Mead, 1924, 104.

91. Ehrman, 2005, 139–44.
92. Mead, 1924.
93. Vermes, 1962, 89.
94. Finegan, 1997, 280.
95. Is 1:27.
96. Is 1:13, KJV.
97. Jer 50:20, NIV.
98. Is 40:3, NIV.
99. Lk 3:15.
100. Vermes, 1962, 73.
101. Ibid., 74.
102. Josephus, 1959, 133.
103. Vermes, 1962, 62.
104. Ibid., 118.
105. Ibid., 116, 289.
106. Lk 3:11, NIV.
107. *CR* 1.54.6 in Stanley, 1995, 88.
108. Mk 11:32, MTB.
109. Acts 19:3–7.
110. *CR* 1.54.
111. Howard, 1995, 51.
112. Mt 11:13, NRSV.
113. Mt 11:11, NRSV.
114. *The Truth of Troy*, BBC program on TV.
115. Jn 3:23, MTB.
116. Jos 3:15–17.
117. Acts 5:36, RSV.
118. Lk 3:19–20 NRSV.
119. Not to be confused with Herod Philip, Herodias's first husband, who was also her uncle, inbred bunch that they were.
120. AJ XVIII, iv, 5; v, 1.
121. AJ XVIII, v.
122. AJ XIII, iv, 2.
123. Lk 3:19–20, NIV.
124. Jn 1:18, MTB. Most modern translators get upset over a 'bosom" so they take it out.

Chapter 4

125. Josephus, 1959, 116.
126. Lucian of Samosata in Meyer, 1984, 132.
127. Is 53:3–4, KJV.
128. Lk 24:19–21, MTB.
129. Lk 1:54, 55 MTB.
130. Spong, 1992, 108.
131. Lk 1:52.
132. 1 Sam. 2:7, WEB.
133. Lk 23:18–24.
134. Acts 28:23–28.
135. *CH* II, XLIV.
136. Lk 1:53, NRSV.
137. Lk 6:21, 24, NRSV.
138. Lk 2:29–32, MTB.
139. Lk 2:1–2, MTB.
140. Josephus, 1959, 133.
141. Mic 5:2, KJV.
142. Jn 7:42, NIV.
143. Mt 2:6, MTB.
144. *HE* I, vii. 13, NPNF.
145. Pines, 1966, 1.
146. Reynolds, 2004.
147. Reynolds, 2010.
148. Leviticus 18:21.
149. Becker and Reed, 2007, 366.
150. Ibid., 367.
151. Pines, 1966, 51.
152. *NH* XXX.
153. Lk 1:33.
154. *Panarion* 30.16, 4; Williams, 1994, 132.
155. Is 1:23.
156. Jn 8:31–32.
157. Jn 8:37–38, RSV.
158. Jn 8:41, RSV.
159. Mk 6:3, RSV.
160. Mt 13:55, RSV.
161. Ibid., 1:24–25, NRSV.
162. Gal 4:4, NRSV.

163. Tabor, 2006, 49–72.
164. Mk 1:40–41, NRSV.
165. Mt 2:19–20.
166. Lk 11:27–28, MTB.
167. Mk 12:29, RSV.
168. Dt 6:6–9, RSV.
169. Ag. Ap. II: 173–5, in Zeitlin, 1988, 8.
170. *Against Apion.* II, 19, Whiston, 1737.
171. Reed, 2000, 45.
172. Hezser, 2001, 41.
173. Ibid., 41 (*y. Ket.* 8:11, 32c).
174. Ibid., 46.
175. 1QSa 1:6–8.
176. See Vermes, 1962, 1990, 100.
177. Hezser, 2001, 48.
178. Ibid., 50.
179. Ibid., 68.
180. *Against Apion.* 2.26, 204 corrected: Hezser erroneously cites
     2.25, 204.
181. Hezser, 2001, 68.
182. Ibid., 54 (Martial 9, 68).
183. Ibid., 52.
184. *Protevangelion of James,* 13:1.
185. Lk 2:41–52.
186. Folio 94b, Pines, 1966, 51.
187. Jn 7:15, KJV.
188. Jn 8:6.
189. *HE* 3:39.
190. Th 20:1–4.
191. Funk and Hoover, 1993, 484.
192. Ibid., 485.
193. Ez 17:22–23, KJV.
194. Dt 30:11–14, NIV.
195. Th 3, MTB. Cf. Lk 17:21–22.
196. See Flusser, 1987, 7, 19.
197. *HE* 2, 23, 169, Loeb.
198. *HE* 1.7.14.
199. 1 Cor 9:5–6.
200. Jas 4:9, KJV.

201. Mk 3:32–35, KJV.
202. Funk and Hoover, 1993, 53.
203. Josephus, 1959, 393.
204. Mead, 1924.
205. Reed, 2000, 88.
206. Ibid., 84–89.
207. Lk 3:15.
208. *Panarion* 30.16, 4 in James, 1924, 8.
209. Lk 3:21–22, NRSV.
210. Ehrman, 2005, 159.
211. Mk 1:9–12, MTB.
212. Mt 4:1, NRSV.
213. Lk 4:1, NRSV.

Chapter 5

214. 1 Sam 19–24, MTB.
215. Mk 1:13, MTB.
216. 1 Cor 2:4, MTB.
217. Gal 1:15, MTB.
218. 1 Cor 2:16, NRSV.
219. Gal 2:20, MTB.
220. Mk 3:21, KJV.
221. Origen, "Against Celsus," I, vi. *ANF*04.
222. See *Jesus and the Eyewitnesses* by Richard Bauckham, a book that supports my thesis.
223. *HE* 3.11.1 as quoted in Eisenman, 1996, 394.
224. Stanton, 2004, 101.
225. *HE* 3.39, *NPNF*.
226. *HE* 3.39.
227. See Lk 22:28–30.
228. Ps 2:7, RSV.
229. Ibid., 2:2.
230. Ezek 17:24.
231. Mt 4:12.
232. Mt 13:33, MTB.
233. Gn 18:6.
234. Funk and Hoover, 1993, 195.
235. Lk 18:2–8, WEB.
236. Maccoby, 1986, 52–53.

237. Acts 17:7, NRSV.

238. Jn 1:46.

239. Jn 7:52, WEB.

240. *Anacephalaiosis* 29 1 5.

241. *Mishnah Taanit* 3:8, 1933.

242. For a fuller treatment of Galilean eccentrics, see Geza Vermes (1981:72–80) and John Dominic Crossan (1991:148–56).

243. *b. Berakoth*, 34b.

244. Mead, 1924, 106. This follows Josephus's report on Pilate bringing the ensigns into Jerusalem (*Jewish War*, B. J. II. ix. 3) precisely where one would expect to find it by analogy with the Antiquities.

245. Mk 1:14–15, MTB.

246. Tabor, 2006, 178.

247. Zech 13:7, WEB.

248. Mk 1:21.

249. Lk 4:19, MTB.

250. Is 61:2, RSV.

251. Lk 4:21, MTB.

252. Lk 4:24–27.

253. *HE* I, vii.

254. Acts 28:25–28, RSV.

255. *CH* 2.44.

256. Lk 3:15, NRSV.

257. Dan 9:24.

258. Pines, 1966, 46.

259. Ibid.

260. See Gager, 2007, 367.

261. Mt 12:39, 41, RSV.

262. Jon 3:4.

263. Jon 3:8.

264. Josephus, 1959, 166.

265. Mt 6:12.

266. Lk 6:30, 35, WEB.

267. Th 95, my rendition.

268. *The Five Gospels*, 1993, 149.

269. Lk 16:1–8, NRSV.

270. Hezser, 2001, 133.

271. Dt 15:2.
272. We'll look at that shortly.
273. Mt 6:1–4.
274. Lk 6:20, RSV.
275. Mk 10:17–22.
276. Vermes, 1962, 70.
277. Josephus, 1959, 133.
278. *Hypothetica* 11:2; *Every Good Man is Free* 12:86–87.
279. *Hypothetica* 11:1.
280. Josephus 1959, 133.
281. *Vita* 2; Whiston, 1737.
282. *NH* V, ch. 15:17.
283. Vermes, 1962, 92.
284. *Politics*, Bk II, Pt. vii, 1931.
285. *Every Good Man Is Free*, 12:79.
286. *Hypothetica*, 11:12.
287. Lk 3:11.
288. Mt 5:40, MTB.
289. Mt 5:43.
290. Lk 8:1, MTB.
291. Mt 11:19.
292. Mk 2:17, NIV.
293. For a fascinating account of women in the early church, see Griffith, 2008, 92–101.
294. Jn 20:18.
295. Mt 20:25–26, MTB.
296. Lk 16:13, MTB.
297. Ibid.
298. Th 47; Cameron, 1982, 30.
299. Th 64; Ibid., 33.
300. Howard, 1995, 27.
301. Mt 23:8–10, MTB.
302. *Against Apion*, 17; Whiston, 1737, 630.
303. Pines, 1996, 197.
304. *CR*, "Epistle of Clement to James," Chapter IX.
305. Mt 6:25–30, MTB.
306. Mt 9:36.
307. Josephus, 1959, 192.
308. Lk 6:20–21, MTB.

309. Lk 6:24–25, MTB.
310. *CR* III, 66.
311. Mt 8:19–20, MTB.
312. Prov 30:7–9, NIV.
313. Mt 10:5–10, MTB.
314. Josephus, 1959, 133.
315. Lk 4:5–8, MTB.

Chapter 6

316. Lk 23:8–9, MTB.
317. Lk 13:32–33, MTB.
318. Lk 6:1–5; Mk 2:23, Mt 12:1–8.
319. 1 Sam 21:1–6.
320. Pines, 1966, 5.
321. Mk 5:1–20.
322. Mk 6:31, MTB.
323. Mk 7:24–30.
324. Mk 8:15, MTB.
325. Lev 2:11.
326. *HE* 3:39.
327. Josephus, 1959, 138.
328. Ibid.
329. Ibid., 139.
330. AJ XVIII, iii, 3.
331. Lk 13:1.
332. Dan 9:27, RSV.
333. Lk 13:22.
334. Lk 17:11.
335. Sicker, 2001, 168.
336. Mt 21:10–11, MTB.
337. Mt 21:2.
338. RSV. Hebrew poetry uses parallelism.
339. Mt 21:1–7.
340. Th 47.
341. Mk 11:9–10, MTB.
342. Jn 12:13, MTB.
343. Lk 19:37–38.
344. Mk 10:25, MTB.
345. Mk 10:27, NIV.

346. Lk 22:38, NRSV.
347. Funk and Hoover, 1993, 391.
348. Is 53:12. While checking my manuscript, I found a site that translates this passage correctly—"rebels": the Net Bible. Can scholarship be changing?
349. Lk 22:37, MTB.
350. Is 53:12.
351. Lk 22:37.
352. Mt 7:7–8, MTB.
353. Th 2, 92, 94; Cameron, 1982.
354. Mk 11:20, MTB.
355. Lk 13:6–11.
356. Mk 11:22–24, NIV.
357. Jn 14:13–14, NRSV.
358. Jn 15:7, 15:16, 16:23–26.
359. Lk 18:7–8, WEB.
360. Ex 14:13–18, NIV.
361. Jo 3.
362. Jo 6.
363. Ezra 1:1–4.
364. 1 Sam 2:9–10, NIV.
365. Is 40, 9–10, KJV.
366. Jer 10:10, NIV.
367. Crossan, 1992, 164–65, quoting Josephus, *Jewish War* 2.258–60.
368. Josephus, 1959, 147.
369. Vermes, 1962, 105.
370. Dn 9:24, WEB, italics mine.
371. Bauckham, 2006, 194–97.
372. Mt 26:6–11, Mk 14:3–9, Lk 7:36–50, Jn 12:1–8.
373. Mk 11:11.
374. Mk 11:15, MTB.
375. Zec 14:21, RSV.
376. Zec 14:9.
377. Zec 14:16, RSV.
378. Th 64; Cameron, 1982, 33.
379. AJ, XVIII, iii, 2.
380. Jn 2:13–16.
381. Jn 11:47–48, RSV.

382. *CR* 1.65.2.
383. Mk 14:25, NRSV.
384. Lk 22:18, NRSV.
385. Mk 9:1, NRSV.
386. Mk 1:5.
387. For a thorough study of Jesus's prophecies of the kingdom see: Bart D. Ehrman, 1999, 125–206. A more compact assessment is found in his *Truth and Fiction in the Da Vinci Code* (Oxford: Oxford University Press, 2004), 126–33.
388. Mead, 1924, 106–7.
389. Ibid., 101.
390. Jn 11:45–8, 53, RSV.
391. Cameron, 1982, 81.
392. "The Apology of Aristides," *ANF*, vol. X.
393. 1 Cor 15:5.
394. Maccoby, 1982, 121–33.
395. Jn 6:2, MTB.
396. Jn 6:4, MTB.
397. Jn 6:11, MTB.
398. Jn 6:14–15, NRSV.
399. Zec 14:3–4, 5b, 9, RSV.
400. Crossan, 1992, 232.
401. Pines, 1996, folio 52b, 214.
402. Heb 5:7, RSV.
403. Maccoby, 1973, 147.
404. Mk 15:7, MTB.
405. Mt 27:16, RSV.
406. Lk 23:19.
407. Brandon, 1968, 1988, 97–98.
408. Ibid.
409. Mk 14:61–62.
410. Lk 22:71.
411. Lk 23:2, RSV.
412. Jn 18:33.
413. Jn 18:28–34.
414. Acts 4:27.
415. Lk 23:2, RSV.
416. Lk 20:25, MTB.

Chapter 7

417. *The Divine Liturgy of James the Apostle and Brother of God.* Anastasis, Copyright to Archimandrite Ephrem ©, November, 2008. http://www.anastasis.org.uk/lit-james. htm
Monastery of St Andrew the Apostle. Archimandrite Ephrem. Tel: 0161–881–5774. Fax: 0870 77063279. E-mail: ephrem@chorlton.com.

418. Pope John Paul II, 1997, http://www.ewtn.com/library/PAPALDOC/JP2HLYCT.HTM

419. Mk 6:1–4, NRSV.

420. Lk 3:15, MTB.

421. Cameron, 1982, 71.

422. Pines, 1996, 61.

423. Jn 2:4, NIV.

424. NIV, paperback edition, 1984, ix.

425. Ibid.

426. Jn 7:3–5.

427. Acts 1:12–14, NIV.

428. "Lives of Illustrious Men," *NPNF*, ser. II, vol. III.

429. *HE* III.xxxii.

430. Gal 2:11ff.

431. *HE* I.xii.

432. Acts 1:15–26.

433. Acts 2:14–42.

434. Acts 3:1–26.

435. Acts 4:1–22.

436. Acts 5:1–11.

437. Acts 5:27–32.

438. Acts 8:14, RSV.

439. Acts 12:17, MTB.

440. AJ, XIX.8.

441. Mt 16:18, KJV.

442. Cameron, 1982, 26.

443. *HE* II.i.

444. *HE* IV.v.

445. Jas 2:10, NIV.

446. *CH* 11.35 *ANF*08.

447. Acts 15.

448. Irenaeus, *Against Heresies,* 3.14.
449. *CR* 1:43.
450. Ibid., 1:64.
451. Ibid., 1:66.
452. *Anacephalaiosis* 30.16.7 in Klijn and Reinink, 1973, 186.
453. *HE* II.xxiii.
454. *Panarion,* 78.13.2, quoted in John Painter, *Just James: The Brother of Jesus in History and Tradition* (Columbia, SC: University of South Carolina Press, 1998), 211.
455. *Summa theologica,* 3, q. 28, a. 3, ad 6; Opera 11, 527. The church had earlier morphed Jesus's brothers into cousins and Mary into a perpetual virgin.
456. AJ XX, viii, 5.
457. Gal 3:10, MTB.
458. Gal 3:6, NIV.
459. Jas 2:21, RSV.
460. *HE* II.xxiii.
461. Jas 1:1, MTB.
462. Jas 4:11–12, NIV.
463. Yadin, 1971, 130.
464. Brown, 1982.
465. Hezser, 2001, 288.
466. Jas 2:2–5, MTB.
467. Jas 2:7, WEB.
468. *HE* 3:27.
469. Jas 1:22, MTB.
470. Jas 1:26–27, MTB.
471. Jas 1:17, MTB.
472. Jas 3:4–5, MTB.
473. 2 Cor 11:5, 13–15, MTB.
474. Jas 4:1–2, MTB.
475. Mt 5:28.
476. Jas 5:4, NRSV.
477. Jas 5:6, MTB.
478. Jas 5:8, MTB.
479. Mk 1:14.
480. "Lives of Illustrious Men," *NPNF,* ser. II, vol. III.
481. Origen, *de Principiis,* "Prologue of Rufinus," *ANF,* vol. IV.
482. AJ XIV:ii:2.

483. AJ. XI.vii.1.
484. *IIE* II:xxiii.
485. *CR* 1:44.
486. Acts 5:38–39, NRSV.
487. *CR* 1:65.
488. Acts 7:40–43.
489. Acts 5:40.
490. Acts 7:1–3.
491. Acts 9:21, MTB.
492. *CR* 1:71.
493. Acts 8:2, NIV.
494. *CR* 1:71.
495. AJ XX.ii.5.
496. AJ XX.viii.5.
497. Ibid.
498. Acts 24:7.
499. Acts 17:7, MTB.
500. Acts. 25:8, MTB.
501. *HE* II, xxiii.
502. Ibid.
503. Vermes 1962, 1987, 52.
504. 1QM, Vermes, 1962, 123–24.
505. Mk 13:24–27, 30, MTB.
506. AJ, XX, ix, 1.
507. Ant. XX.ix.1.
508. *HE* II.xxiii.
509. *HE*, VII, 18.
510. Ibid., 19.

Chapter 8

511. *CR* 1.70–1.
512. *CH* 17:19.
513. Ibid., 17.17.
514. Gal 2:11, MTB.
515. *CH* 17.19.
516. Ibid., 17.19–20.
517. Schoeps, 1969, 54.
518. Gal 1:13.
519. *CR*-Syriac version 1.73–4 in Jones, 1995, 108.

520. I suspect that Rufinus, who translated the *Clementines* into Latin, "smoothed and corrected" them to conform more closely to Acts.

521. Acts 6:14, MTB.

522. Mk 14:58, Jn 2:19, Th 71.

523. Gal 1:15–23, MTB.

524. Gal 1:18.

525. 1 Cor 15:3–8, MTB.

526. The Greek implies, "as you are intended to be" (that is, good) rather than "without flaw."

527. Mt 5:48.

528. Rom 7:4–6, MTB.

529. Maccoby, 1986.

530. Rom 7:7–8, MTB.

531. Ex 20:17, RSV.

532. Rom 7:14–25, MTB.

533. *Confessions*, III.6.

534. *Anti-Pelagian Writings*: "On Marriage and Concupiscence."

535. *Didache* 1.4a, Garrow, 2004.

536. Pines, 1996, 156–57.

537. Ibid., 334.

538. Acts 9:3–8, 22:6–11, 26:12–18.

539. Acts 9.

540. Gal 1:17.

541. For an excellent study of Acts' "creative history" in making Paul an accepted part of the Jerusalem movement, see Wilson 2008, 138–49.

542. Mt 27:25, NRSV.

543. Reynolds, 2004, quotes from it extensively yet frustratingly does not list it in its bibliography.

544. Pines, 1966, 51.

545. 'Abd-al-Jabbar's *Tathbit Dala'il al-Nubuwwa*, 1966.

546. Reynolds, 2004, 4.

547. Acts 9.

548. Pines, 1966, 26.

549. Gal 1:9, MTB.

550. 1 Cor 4: 21.

551. Rom 16:7.

552. Brooten, 1977, 142.
553. Acts 13:2–3, MTB.
554. Gal 2:9, MTB.
555. Acts 13:1.
556. Gal 1:1, MTB.
557. 1 Cor 9:1–2, WEB, italics mine.
558. 2 Cor 11:4–5, MTB.
559. *CR* 4.35. My thanks to Hans Joachim Schoeps, 1969, 51.
560. 2 Cor 11:12–15, MTB.
561. 1 Cor 1:1, MTB.
562. *CR* 4.34.
563. Ibid., 4.35.
564. 2 Cor 2:17, MTB.
565. 2 Cor 3:1, NRSV.
566. Pines, 1966, 46.
567. 2 Cor 6:8.
568. Pines, 1966, 47.
569. Betz, 1968, 62–80.
570. Meyer, 1984, 205.
571. "Life of Pompey," chap. 28 in *Parallel Lives*.
572. *First Apology*, chap. LXVI, 7.
573. *Dialogue with Trypho*, LXX.
574. 1 Cor 15:20, NIV.
575. *Didache* 9:4.
576. 1 Cor 2:7–10, MTB.
577. Coffman, *Commentary*: 1 Cor 2:7.
578. Pines, 1966, folio 52a.
579. Pines, 1996, folio 52b, 113.
580. Acts 15:36–40, NIV.
581. Jn 6:66.
582. *Panarion* 51.6.10–11; Williams, 1994.
583. *HE* III, 39.
584. Mk 14:51.
585. Acts 12:5.
586. Lk 10:1–17.
587. Jn 6:66, MTB.
588. Acts 13:13, NIV.
589. In the authentic epistles, Paul refers to Mark once—in Philemon, where he calls him a fellow worker, along with

Luke. Was there reconciliation just before Paul's death? Or was this another Mark? It was a common name. Turning to I Peter 5:13, that apostle calls him, "my son, Mark," but Peter and Mark worked together, according to all sources.

590. *Panarion* 51.6. 11.
591. Acts 13:5.
592. 2 Cor 11:25.
593. Gal 2:2.
594. Gal 2:2, Douay-Rheims Bible.
595. Gal 2:9, MTB.
596. Acts 15.
597. 1 Cor 6:13, MTB.
598. Acts 15:29.
599. 1 Cor 8:4, 7–8, MTB.
600. 1 Cor 9:16, MTB.
601. Ibid., 9:19, MTB.
602. Ibid., 10:19–21 MTB.
603. 1 Cor 11:23, 25, NRSV.
604. Acts 15:31, K JV.
605. 1 Thes 2:14–16, MTB.
606. 2 Cor 3:15.
607. 2 Cor 3:15–17, MTB.
608. 1 Cor 9:20–21, NRSV.
609. Gal 5:12, NRSV.
610. Gal 2:10, MTB.
611. 1 Cor 11:20–22, MTB.
612. Gal 5:19–21, MTB.
613. Lk 7:34, RSV.
614. Phil 3:5.
615. Ex 22:22.
616. 1 Cor 13:3, my rendition from the Vulgate.
617. Mk 10:21, NRSV.
618. Gal 5:22–24, MTB.
619. Rom 13:11–14, MTB.
620. Mt 5:28, MTB.
621. Lk 21:34–36, MTB.
622. *Qur'an*, ix, 59, 76, from the Spanish text. Quoted in Wheless, 1930.

623. Rom 15:30–1, WEB.
624. Rom 15:18–9, MTB.
625. Pines, 1966, 25.
626. Gal 1:8, MTB.
627. 1 Cor 4:18–21, MTB.
628. *HE* III, iv, 6–8.
629. Acts 2:47, MTB.
630. Lk 1:3, MTB.
631. My thanks to Payne, 1970, 143–44.
632. Acts 20:14, NRSV.
633. Acts 20:23, NRSV.
634. Rom 15:25–26, NRSV.
635. Acts 21:17–23, MTB.
636. Acts 21:24, MTB.
637. Acts 21:28, NIV.
638. Acts 21:20, MTB.
639. Rom 13:1, MTB.
640. Phil 4:22, MTB.
641. Phil 1:12–13, MTB.
642. Acts 25:23–26, 32.
643. Rom 16:11.
644. Acts 13:1.
645. Pines 1996, 19.
646. *The Theodosian Code*, 1952, lib. XVI, tit. 5, *De Haereticis.*

Chapter 9

647. Garrow, 2004.
648. *Didache* 11.1,2, Garrow, 2004.
649. 1 Cor 11:23–26.
650. *Anacephalaiosis*, 29.1.3., Klein, 1973, 169.
651. Ibid., 29.5.4.
652. Mt 23:2–3, MTB.
653. Mt 23:16–18.
654. Col 3:20–21, NRSV.
655. Mt 5:43–44, NRSV.
656. Acts 1:6.
657. Maccoby 1986, 52.
658. Acts 5:35–39, NRSV.
659. *CR* 1:65.

660. Mead, 1924, 108.
661. Ibid.
662. Slavonic *B. J.* II.2–3, in Mead, 1924.
663. *CR* 1.71.
664. Ibid., 3.42.
665. Mt 5:9.
666. Mt 5:3 NRSV.
667. *Dialogue with Trypho,* 109.
668. Origen, *Contra Celsus,* VIII, 68.
669. Ibid., VIII, 73.
670. *The Chaplet* XI.
671. Canon 16, 11.
672. Acts 4.
673. Acts 4:27, MTB, italics mine.
674. *Against Heresies,* 1:26.
675. Cassian, "Seven Books," VII.xxi.
676. Jn 1:1, 14, KJV.
677. *Against Heresies,* 3.11.1.
678. Acts 22:4, *CR* 1:71.
679. Acts 2:2–4, MTB.
680. Joel 2:28–32, Acts 2:17–18, 20, MTB.
681. Joel 2:31, RSV.
682. 1 Sam 16:13.
683. 1 Sam 19:19–24.
684. Acts 2:42, RSV.
685. *CR* 1:43.
686. *CR* 1:61.
687. Is 11:4, NIV.
688. Lk 6:20.
689. Ibid., 6:21, MTB.
690. Jn 10:10, MTB.
691. Acts 2:40–41.
692. *CR* 1:43.
693. Pines, 1966, 14, folio 71a.
694. Acts 18:24ff.
695. 1 Cor 1:11–12, NIV.
696. Georg Strecker, in Bauer, 1971, 241.
697. Becker and Reed, 2007, 367, note 35.
698. 1 Cor 9:7, 14, WEB.

699. Mt 10:10.
700. Acts 4:32.
701. Acts 5:1–11.
702. Garrow, 2004; *Didache* 12.4, 5.
703. Ibid., 11:3–6.
704. *Etymologiae*, VIII VI 37, in Klijn, 1973, 263.
705. Klijn, 1973, 273.
706. Num 24:17–18.
707. *HE* I.vii.
708. 1 Cor 9:1:5–6, MTB.
709. Clement, "Stromata" III, 53, *ANF*02.
710. Ambrosiaster, *Prologue to the Commentary on Romans*, as quoted in Skarsaune and Hvalvik, 2007, 186.
711. Suetonius, *Claudius*, 25.4, in *The Lives of The Twelve Caesars*. Reprint of the 1915 Cambridge edition, Project Gutenberg, 2004. www.gutenberg.org/files/6400/6400-h/6400-h.htm.
712. Benko, 1986, 18.
713. Acts 18:2.
714. Clement of Rome, "To the Corinthians," 41: *ANF*01.
715. Werner, 1959–84.
716. I must express my debt to Reidar Hvalvik for this material. His chapter in Skarsaune and Hvalvik, 2007, 179–216 is well worth reading.
717. Acts 17:6–7.
718. AJ XX, viii, 5.
719. Ibid., XX, viii, 6.
720. Ibid., XX.8.8.
721. Mt 23:25–26. cf. Lk 11:39–40, MTB.
722. Josephus, 1959, 361–62.
723. *HE*, III, v.
724. Josephus, 1959, 164.
725. Quoted in Schoeps, 1969, notes 12, 26.
726. Ibid.
727. Mt 4:15–16, MTB.
728. Schoeps, 1969, 26.
729. *CR* 1.37.1–2; Voorst, 1989, 52–53.
730. Schoeps, 1969, 21.
731. Ibid., 15.

732. Tübingen, 1949.
733. Slavonic *B. J.* II. xi. 11 in Mead, 1924, 108.
734. Pines, 1966, 15.
735. Pritz 1988, 17.
736. Pines, 1996, 266.
737. *Histories* 5.9.
738. "The Sacred History," 2:30:6.7, *NPNF2*, vol. 2.
739. *de Principiis*, "Prologue of Rufinus," *ANF*, vol. IV.
740. Orosius, 1964, 302.
741. Josephus, 1959, 355.
742. Ibid., 356.
743. Ibid., 357.
744. Ibid., 357.
745. Ibid., 358.
746. Ibid., 358–59

Chapter 10

747. Gal 2:12, Acts 10:9–48.
748. *CH* 8.7.
749. Gal 2, 3.
750. *Panarion*, 30, 16, 3.
751. Pines, 1966, 63.
752. Martin, 1983, 30.
753. Pliny, *Letters*, Book 10, Letter 96, 1915, 313.
754. Aberbach and Aberbach, 2000, 86.
755. Ibid., 93–94.
756. Published by Solomon Schechter in Genizah Specimens, *Jewish Quarterly Review* 10, 1898.
757. Parkes, 1979, 78.
758. Justin Martyr, *Dialogue with Trypho*, Ch. CVIII.
759. Ibid., 80.
760. Jerome, *On Isaiah* 8.14, RSV.
761. See Pritz, 1988, 58.
762. *Panarion* 29.9.2; Klijn and Reinink, 1973, 175.
763. Mk 13:9.
764. Jn 12:42, RSV.
765. Skarsaune, 2007, 221.
766. Rv 3:9, MTB.
767. Travers, 1903, 146–47.

768. Mt 5:17, RSV.
769. Mi 1:7, KJV.
770. Travers, 1903, 138–39.
771. Midrash Rabbah, *Eccles.* I:8.
772. Bagatti, 1971, 95.
773. Ignatius, "To the Magnesians," 10:3, *ANF.*
774. Ignatius, "To the Smyrnaeans," 6, *ANF.*
775. Modrzejewski, *Jews of Egypt*, 228. Cited in Pearson, 2007, 100.
776. Ibid., 99.
777. Bauer, 1971, 51.
778. Acts 18:24ff.
779. Bauer, 1971, 51.
780. Pearson, 2004, 99.
781. Clement of Alexandria, *Stromata* I.29.
782. Pearson, 2004, 98.
783. Acts 11:26.
784. The interested reader can further pursue the subject in "Christians and Jews in First-Century Alexandria," chapter 2 in Pearson, *Gnosticism and Christianity in Roman and Coptic Egypt.*
785. Bauer, 1971, 53.
786. Epiphanius, *Treatise on Weights and Measures* 14. Reprint of the 1935 University of Chicago edition, Tertullian. com, 2005. www.tertullian.org/fathers/epiphanius_weights_03_text.htm.
787. Ibid.
788. *HE* 5.4.
789. Bagatti 1971, 1984.
790. Mancini 1970.
791. Bagatti, 1971, 1984, 211.
792. Mk 12:29, WEB.
793. 1 Cor 8:6, WEB.
794. Schaff, 1877, 66–71.
795. Tertullian, "On Modesty," 21, *ANF*, vol. IV.
796. Mt 28:19, WEB.
797. Acts 19:4, WEB.
798. 2 Cor 13:13, WEB.
799. Jn 10:30, WEB.

800. Ezek 8:2.

801. Ezek 9:4, RSV.

802. Rv 7:3, MTB.

803. Rv 7:14.

804. II Esdras 2:23, NEB.

805. Origen, *Selecta in Ezechielem*; *PG* 13, 799–802. Quoted in Mancini, 1970, 25.

806. *First Apology*, LV.

807. *CR*, "Epistle of Clement to James," XIV.

808. Bagatti, 1971, 221.

809. Daniélou, 1964, 63.

810. Mk 4:35–41.

811. Daniélou, 1964, 60.

812. Bagatti 1971, 26.

813. Ibid., 25.

814. *On Christ and Antichrist*, 59.

815. *Gospel of Peter* 39–42.

816. Bagatti, 1971, 225, 227.

817. Ibid., 226.

818. Nm 24:17, RSV.

819. Rv 22:16, WEB.

820. Pines, 1966, 5.

821. Mt 5:17, WEB.

822. Mt 5:19, WEB.

823. Mt 28:19–20, WEB.

824. Pines, 1966, 25.

825. Pines, 1996, 237.

826. Ibid., 261–62.

827. Ibid., 261.

828. *HE* IV.xxii, italics mine.

829. *Body of Civil Law*, Codices lib. I tit. I.

830. Clement: the Epistle to the Corinthians 59:4, Arnold, 1926, my translation.

831. *ANF*, vol. I.

832. J. B. Lightfoot, 1891; C. H. Hoole, 1885.

833. Acts 3:13, 4:27.

834. Strecker, 1971, appendix.

835. *HE* IV, xxii.

836. G. Becker, *Catalogi Bibliothecarum* Antiqui. Reprint of the Bonn, 1885 edition. (Excerpt: §136, pp 277-285), Tertullian.org, 2001. http://www.tertullian.org/articles/becker_catalogi_79_corbie.htm.

837. Zahn, *Zeitschrift für Kirchengeschichte*, II (1877–78), 288, and *Theologisches Litteraturblatt* (1893), 495.

838. Pines 1966, 14.

839. Acts 6:1–6.

840. Pines 1966, 15.

841. Ibid., 15.

842. Gal 1:13.

843. Pines, 1966, 35.

844. Pines, 1966, 11.

845. *Panarion* 30.13; James, 1924, 8.

846. Jerome, *In Matth* 12, 13, in Klijn, 1973, 217.

847. Pines, 1966, 16.

848. Ibid., 15.

849. Ibid., 16.

850. Mk 14:34, MTB.

851. Ehrman, 2005, 139–44.

852. Pines, 1996, 214–15, folio 52b–53a.

853. Lk 22:44, WEB.

854. Heb 5:7.

855. Pines, 1966, 16.

856. *HE* III, 39, italics mine.

857. Brown, 1997, 158.

858. Kloppenborg and Verbin, 2000, 80.

859. Jerome, *Lives of Illustrious Men*, III.

860. *HE* V.8.

861. This assessment is highly simplified. The arguments are complicated and contradictory and far beyond the scope of this book to go into in any detail.

862. *Against Heresies*, III, 11, 8.

863. Clement, ch.13.

864. My literal translations from the Greek for proper comparison.

865. "Epistle to Polycarp," II, *ANF*, vol I.

866. Mt 10:16, KJV.

867. πολλοι κλητοι, ολιγοι δε εκλεκτοι ευρεθωμεν. Ep. Bar. IV:14. Compare Matthew below.

868. "Epistle of Barnabas," IV, note 1480, *ANF*, vol I.

869. Mt 22:14, πολλοι γάρ εισιν κλητοι ολιγοι δε εκλεκτοί.

870. Clement, II:8.

871. Tobit 4:15, NRSV.

872. *The Talmud*, tractate Shabbos 31a.

873. *Epistle of the Apostles*, 18.

874. *Didache*, 1.2e.

875. *Didascalia*, ch. 1.

876. Mt 7:12, Lk 6:31, NRSV.

877. *Against Heresies*, book 3, 14.

878. *Epistle of the Apostles*, 5.

879. Ibid.

880. Mt 8:28–34, NRSV.

881. Origen, "Contra Celsus," II.xxvii, *ANF*, vol IV.

882. *HE* 4.23.12.

883. See Maccoby, 1982, 121–33 for a fuller discussion.

884. See Bart Ehrman, 2005.

885. Pines, 1966, 16.

886. Ibid., 17.

887. Aberbach and Aberbach, 2000, 103.

888. Yadin, 1971, 130.

889. Pines, 1966, 18.

890. Ibid., 19.

891. *First Epistle of Clement*, 59.4; Arnold, 1926.

892. Houle (1885) and Lightfoot (revised, 1990).

893. Acts 3:13, MTB.

894. *Historical dictionary of Jehovah's Witnesses*, George Chryssides, (Scarecrow Press, 2008), 80.

895. The Divine Liturgy of James the Apostle, accessed August 29, 2008, http://www.apostle1.com/liturgies1/liturgy_of_james_the_apostle.htm.

896. *CR* 1.15.

897. Bauer, 1971 17.

898. Segal, 1970, 81.

899. Bauer, 1971, 29.

900. Quasten, 1966, I:172.

901. Schoeps, 1969, 30.

902. *Odes of Solomon,* 10:5.
903. Lk 10.
904. Quoted in Bütz, 2009, 29.
905. Bauckham, 2004, 68–70.
906. Harvey, 2005, paragraph 4.
907. Ibid., paragraph 10.
908. Ibid.
909. Ibid., section 17.
910. Ibid., section 19.
911. I'm indebted to Susan Harvey for this material.
912. Martyrios (Sahdona), quoted in Brock, 1987.
913. Jerome, *Chronicle,* 296. Translated and edited by Roger Pearse. Ipswich, UK, 2005. http://www.tertullian.org/fathers/jerome_chronicle_03_part2.htm.
914. *The Book of the Laws of Countries,* final paragraph.
915. Dio Cassius, *Roman History,* Epitome of Book 72:9.
916. Chahin, 1987, 253.
917. *HE* 9.8.2–4.
918. Werner, 1984, 38.
919. Ibid., 41.
920. Ibid., 39.
921. Ibid., 40.
922. *Gregory the Illuminator.* Reprint of the Encyclopedia Britannica, 1911, Internet Archive, 2010, http://www.archive.org/stream/encyclopaediabrit12chisrich/encyclopaediabrit12chisrich_djvu.txt.
923. Price, 2002.
924. Neusner, 1990, 77–81.
925. Jerome Ep. 112:13, in Pritz, 1988, 105.
926. *NH* 6.96–111.
927. Strabo's *Geography,* II.5.12. Reprint of the 1917 Cambridge edition, LacusCurtis Project, 2009. http://penelope.uchicago.edu/Thayer/E/Roman/Texts/Strabo/2E1*.html.
928. Moffett, 1992, 31–2.
929. Mk 13:27, NRSV.
930. Mt 19:28; Lk 22:28–30.
931. For an excellent study, see Moffett, 1992, 29–44.
932. *HE* V, chap. x.
933. *Anglo-Saxon Chronicle*: entry for the year A.D. 883–84.

934. http://nasrani.net/2007/12/11/cultural-similarities-of-syrian-christians-and-jews/
935. Geddes, 1694.
936. Buchanan, 1811.
937. Ibid.
938. *Wars of the Jews*, III.8.7, Whiston, 1737.
939. Josephus, 1959, 221.
940. Ibid., 362.
941. Num 24:17–18, WEB.
942. Tabor 2006, 143–44; Dan 9:26.
943. *HE* 3.19.
944. *HE* 3.20.
945. *Apostolic Constitutions*, bk. II.8.
946. Bagatti, 1971, 20.
947. *Panarion* 30.11.9–10.
948. Mancini, 1970, 64–70.
949. Mk 13:1–2, MTB.
950. Justin Martyr, *First Apology* 31, 6.
951. Jerome, *Chronicle*, 228th Olympiad.
952. *Apocalypse of Peter,* James, 1924. See Bauckham, 1998, 228–38 for an analysis of this fascinating material.
953. Yadin, 1971, 136.
954. Ibid., 95.
955. *Talmud Sanh.* ix. 7.
956. Hereford 1903, 90.
957. Ibid., 1903, 94.
958. Ibid., 266–67.
959. Schoeps 1969, 30.
960. *Didascalia,* Ch XXI.
961. Mancini, 1970, 170.
962. Ibid., 171.
963. Jerome, "Epistle," LVIII:3 *NPNF2*, 1893.
964. *Contra Celsus,* 1:51.
965. Bagatti, 133, citing *Patrologia Graecae* 33, 1047–48.
966. Pines, 1966, 14.
967. Acts 2:46–47.
968. *Dialogue with Trypho*, XLVII.
969. Gal 5:4, WEB.
970. Gal 2:11–14.

971. "To the Philadelphians," 6:1, *ANF*, vol I.
972. Ibid., 2:1.
973. "Epistle of Barnabas" 3.6, *ANF*, vol I.
974. *Homily on Leviticus* 5:8; *Selecta on Exodus* 12:46, in Dunn, 1996, 102.
975. Council of Elvira, ca. 306, Canon 49, accessed March 19, 2008. http://faculty.cua.edu/pennington/Canon%20Law/ ElviraCanons.htm.
976. Dunn, 1996, 102.
977. Murray, 1975, 19.
978. Council of Laodicea in PhrygiaPacatiana, 364 A.D. Canons 29, 37, accessed May 5, 2008. http://reluctant-messenger. com/council-of-laodicea.htm.
979. John Chrysostom, *Eight Homilies Against the Jews*.
980. Homily IV:iv:5.
981. Homily II:ii:5.
982. Homily VIII:v.1.
983. Homily VIII:iv.5.
984. Jerome, *In Isaiam* 35 (CCSL 73a, 427); *In Isaiam* 49.14 (CCSL 73a, 543); *In Ezekielem*11 (CCSL 75, 525 and 543). The usual phrase is *"Iudaei et nostri iudaizantes."*
985. Becker and Reed, 2007, 60.
986. Wilkinson, 1977, 85.
987. Acts 28:28.
988. *CH* 2.44.
989. *The Soliloquies of Augustine* I.xiii.23.
990. The Retractions, I, chap. 4.
991. *HE* 1:4.
992. *First Apology*, 46.
993. *Against Heresies*, 4. 22. 2.
994. *Sermon* 23.4.
995. *Qur'an* 5:48.
996. *CR* 1:36.
997. Ibid., 1.37.
998. Am 5:22–24, NIV.
999. *CR* 1:64.
1000. *CH* 2.38.
1001. *CH* 16.13.
1002. Schoeps, 1969, 119.

1003. *CR* 1:69.
1004. 1 Cor 17.
1005. Clement of Alexandria, *Stromata*, Bk. I, xxi, "In the twenty-eighth year of Augustus, and in the twenty-fifth day of Pachon."
1006. Chisholm, Hugh, ed., entry for "Feast of Fools." Reprint of 1911 Encyclopedia Britanica, accessed July 12, 2008. http://spanish.studylight.org/enc/bri/view.cgi?n=11089.
1007. Eusebius, *HE* V, xxiii.
1008. In the synoptic Gospels, Jesus celebrates the Passover on that date.
1009. Socrates Scholasticus, "Ecclesiastical History," XXII.
1010. Ibid.
1011. Ibid., XXI.
1012. Ibid.
1013. 1 Cor 5:7, MTB.
1014. Bede, *Ecclesiastical History of the English Nation*, Book I, Chapter XXX, 1910.
1015. Epistle of Barnabas 19:8, Lake, 1912.
1016. *First Apology*, reprint of G. J. Davie, ed. (Oxford: J. H. and Jas Parker, 1861), 10. Internet Archive, accessed July 6, 2010, http://www.archive.org/stream/cu31924050431844/cu31924050431844_djvu.txt.
1017. Tertullian, *Apology*, Ch. 39.
1018. Bookchin, 1991 276.
1019. *CH*, "Epistle of Clement to James," IX.
1020. Th 3.
1021. Rv 7:5–8.
1022. Origen, "Commentary on the Gospel of John," 1.2, *ANF*, vol I.
1023. Rv 7:9, NRSV.
1024. Gal 3:28, MTB.
1025. Letter to Trajan, 10.96. Pliny, 1915.
1026. *Paedagogus*, 1:4, *ANF*, vol II.
1027. Severus, *The Sacred History* II, Ch. XXX.
1028. Otranto, trans Rossi, 1991, 81.
1029. Mk 10:29–30, NRSV.
1030. Rv 20:2–4, NRSV.
1031. *Dialogue with Trypho* LXXX.

1032. *Adversus Haereses* V, 33.
1033. Mk 14:25.
1034. 1 Thes 4:16–17.
1035. *HE* III, 39.
1036. Ibid.
1037. Jerome, *In Esaiam,* 66, 20, in Klijn, 1973, 227.
1038. Is 66, 22, NIV.
1039. Ibid., 20.
1040. Lk 1:33, NRSV.
1041. Gen 1:12–31.
1042. *History of Joseph the Carpenter,* 26.
1043. Peacock, 1970, 114–15.
1044. Mk 13:26–27, NRSV.
1045. Nicholas Campion's *The Great Year* is a fascinating study of this phenomenon.
1046. Pines, 1966, 30.

Chapter 11

1047. Socrates Scholasticus, *Ecclesiastical History,* Bk I, Ch. IX.
1048. Eusebius, "Life of the Blessed Constantine," *NPNF* II, vol. I.III.65.
1049. Ibid., ch. 66.
1050. Acts 19:13–19.
1051. Ambrose, *De obitu Theodosii* 42, Patrologia Latina, 1844– 55, vol. 16.
1052. Liebeschuetz, J. H. W.G. and Hill, Carole, trans. *Ambrose of Milan: Political Letters and Speeches.* Liverpool: Liverpool University Press, 2005, p. 198.
1053. Kousoulas 1997, 11.
1054. Eusebius, *Life of the Blessed Constantine,* 1.28.
1055. Lactantius, *Of the Manner in which the Persecutors Died,* ch. LXIV.
1056. Pitt-Rivers, 1966.
1057. MacMullen, 1969, 66–67.
1058. Norwich, 1988, 66.
1059. Gaddis, 2005, pp. 42–3, note 60.
1060. Rom 13:1.
1061. Prophecy from the Sibylline Books to Maxentius, Emperor of Rome, October 27, 312.
1062. Eusebius, *Life of the Blessed Constantine,* 2.28.

1063. Ibid., 4.63.
1064. Ibid., 4.64.
1065. Ibid., 4.66.
1066. Eusebius, *Life of the Blessed Constantine*, 2.72.
1067. Gaddis, 2205, 61.
1068. Thomas, 78 (My rendering from the Coptic).
1069. Gregg and Groh, 1981, 24).
1070. Ibid., 24.
1071. Wilson, 1984, 168.
1072. Pines, 1966, 31.
1073. Ingersoll (1833–99) in *Ingersollia*, 1882.
1074. Frend, 1984, 496.
1075. See Gaddis, 2005, 68–130.
1076. *Saturni aurea saecula quis requirat? Sunt haec gemmea, sed Neroniana*. Sidonius Appolinaris. *Letters* 5:8. Translated by O. M. Dalton. Reprint of the 1915 Oxford edition, Tertullian.org, 2003. www.tertullian.org/fathers/sidonius_letters_00_0_epreface.htm.
1077. Zosimus, *New History*, bk. 2, reprint of the 1814 edition. Tertullian.com 2002. http://www.tertullian.org/fathers/zosimus01_book1.htm
1078. *Life of the Blessed Emperor Constantine*, 1.2.
1079. Martin, 1983, 30.
1080. Ibid., 31.
1081. Bagatti, 1984, 14.
1082. Pines, 1966, 31.
1083. Bagatti, 1984, 13.
1084. Cyril of Jerusalem, *Catechetical Lectures*, X:16.
1085. Gregory of Nyssa, *Letter XVII, to Eustathia*.
1086. Bagatti, 1984, 12.
1087. Ibid., viii.
1088. Lactantius, *On the Manner in which the Persecutors Died*, ch. 48.
1089. *Life of the Blessed Constantine* 3.18.
1090. Gaddis, 2005, 189.
1091. Bedjan, 1968, 2.143–45, as quoted in Becker, 2007, 379.
1092. Becker, 2007, 379.
1093. Pines, 1966, 30.

1094. *Corpus Juris Civilis Cod.*, lib. 3, tit. 12, Lex. 3, in Philip Schaff's *History of the Christian Church*, vol. 3, chapter 7, sec. 75, note 692.
1095. *The Chaplet*, III.
1096. Augustine, Letter 36, Ch. 14—perhaps the most turgid, long-winded letter I've ever read—or rather skipped over.
1097. Roger Hoveden, *Annals*, vol. ii, 526–28, in Andrews, 1887, Ch. 20.
1098. Pines, 1996, 31.
1099. *Sermon on Avioccala,* 6–8 (trans. Tilley) as quoted in Gaddis, 2005, 54.
1100. *Sermon on Avioccala* 3; Gaddis, 2005, 57.
1101. Gaddis, 2005, 57.
1102. "Homily on the Statues," 21:11. *NPNF*, vol. IX.
1103. Gaddis, 2005, 119.
1104. Socrates Scholasticus: *Ecclesiastical History*, Bk VI. Chap. 15.

Chapter 12

1105. Dan 2.
1106. "The Life of Malchus," 1, *NPNF2*, vol. 6.
1107. Schoeps, 1969, 37.
1108. Goddard, 2000, 20.
1109. Ibn Hisham, 1998, vol. 1, pt. 2, 73.
1110. Pines, 1996, 401.
1111. *Qur'an* 3:48.
1112. Ibid., 5:46.
1113. Ibid., 5:72 Khalifa, 2009.
1114. Ibid., 5:73.
1115. Ibid., 5:69.
1116. Ibid., 5:82 Khalifa, 2009.
1117. Ibid., 5:85.
1118. Ibid., 2:271.
1119. Mt 6:3.
1120. *CH* 12, 31.
1121. Pines, 1996, 401.
1122. Athanasius, *Life of Anthony*, 2.
1123. Ibid., 47.

1124. Philip, 1998, 125.
1125. de Rosa, 1988, 298.
1126. Joseph Hergenröther, *Photius Patriarch von Konstantinopel, sein Leben, seine Schriften, und das griechische Schisma* (Ratisbon, 1867–69), I, 643. Quoted in Andrews, J. N., *History of the Sabbath*, 1887, 1998. Also in Migne, *"Patrologia Latina,"* vol. 145, 506.
1127. Throckmorton, 1936, 1979, 139.
1128. Jerome, *on Matt.*, xxi. 12.
1129. Neander; 1850–58.
1130. Col 2:20, 21.
1131. *The Oxford Dictionary of Byzantium*, Oxford University Press, 1991.
1132. Hergenröther, (1876, I, 527), for instance, said the Athingians stood in intimate relations with the emperor, Michael II. At least, he mentioned them.
1133. Luc d'Achery, *Spicilegium sive collectio veterum aliquot scriptorum qui in Galliae bibliothecis delituerant*, Montalant, Paris, 1723, I, f. 211–14. Quoted in Andrews, 1873, Ch. 21.
1134. *Collectio Rev. Occitan*, in the Royal Library of Paris, quoted in Dollinger, 1890, vol. 2, 375.
1135. Neander, 1852, 403–4.
1136. Edwards, 1989, 47.
1137. Allix, 1692, 164.
1138. George, 1995, entry on Bogomil.
1139. Conybeare, 1898, clxii.
1140. Conybeare, Chapter 10.
1141. www.bogomilism.eu/Other authors/Cosma.html, 61.
1142. Vasilev, 2000, 326.
1143. *Presbyter Cosmas's Sermon Regarding the Newly Appeared Bogomil Heresy*, T. Butler, 156.
1144. Pines, 1996, 470.
1145. Pines, 1966, 29.
1146. *panem nostrum supersubstantialem da nobis hodie.*
1147. *On Matt*, vi.11, in James, 1924, 4.
1148. *Commentary on Psalm 135*, The Jewish-Christian Gospels, Text Excavation, 2012, http://www.textexcavation.com/hebrewmatthew.html.

1149. "Lives of Illustrious Men," 3.
1150. Mt 6:10, NRSV.
1151. Yordan Ivanov, *Bogomil Books and Legends*, quoted in Etudes balkaniques, 2001, No. 1, http://www.bogomilism.eu/ Studies/John%20Wycliffe-and-the-Dualists.html.
1152. Jones, 1812, 9.
1153. Allix, 1690, 169.
1154. Ibid.
1155. An assertion of a heretic according to an inquisitor, in Jones, 1812, ch. 5.
1156. Mitchell, 1853, 104.
1157. Allix, 1690, 108.
1158. Ibid., 113.
1159. Ibid., 136.
1160. Johann Peter Kirsch, "Donation of Constantine," The Catholic Encyclopedia, vol. 5 (New York: Robert Appleton Company, 1909).
1161. Mt 19:21, NRSV.
1162. Acts 5:29.
1163. Epiphanius *Anacephalaiosis*, 30.16.2; Klijn, 1973, 183.
1164. Vasilev, 1993, 98.
1165. Ibid.
1166. From the Middle Dutch *loellen*. *New Schaff-Herzog Encyclopedia of Religious Knowledge*, 1908–14, 15.
1167. Vasilev, 1993, 102. Depositions of Hawisia Moone, uxor Thome Moone de Lodne: "Also that the temporal lords and laymen may legally take all possessions and temporal goods from all churchmen, and from all bishops and prelates, both horse and harness, and give their goods to poor people."
1168. Ibid., 105.
1169. Ibid., 99.
1170. Ibid., 103 *(Tract against Bogomil)*.
1171. Vasilev, 2000, 2.
1172. Vasilev, 1993, 101.
1173. *CH* 17.12.
1174. Jas 5:16, NRSV.
1175. Wakefield and Evans, 1969, 383.
1176. Peacock, 1970, 121.

1177. Harris, 1995, 69.
1178. Woodcock and Avakumovic, 1977, 20.
1179. Ibid., 18.
1180. Ibid., 18.
1181. *Last Days of the Georgian Dukhobors?* Doukhobor Genealogy Website, 2012, Www.doukhobor.org/Grigorian.htm.
1182. Woodcock and Avakumovic, 1977, 25.
1183. Baron Haxthausen, *A Visit to the Dukhobortsy*, 1843, Doukhobor Genealogy Website, 2012, www.doukhobor.org/Haxthausen.htm
1184. Woodcock and Avakumovic, 1977, 19.
1185. Ibid., 18.
1186. Ibid., 20.
1187. Ibid.
1188. Woodcock, 1977, 41.
1189. *Dukhobors History to 1930*, http://edocs.lib.sfu.ca/projects/Doukhobor-Collection/history.html
1190. Woodcock, 1977, 20.
1191. Ibid., 25.
1192. Ibid., 20; *Lev Tolstoy and the Doukhobors*, by Larry Ewashen, www.doukhobor-museum.org/lae/var/sep-22-2010.htm
1193. Mk 13:26.
1194. Peacock, 1970, 114–15.
1195. The Molokan and Prygun Home Page, updated April 30, 2011, http://molokane.org/molokan/.
1196. *Religion as an Instrument of Culture Change: the Problem of the Sects in the Soviet Union,* by Ethel and Stephen P. Dunn. *Slavic Review,* vol. 23, No. 3, Sep., 1964 Association for Slavic, East European, and Eurasian Studies.
1197. Much more research is needed. Perhaps someone fluent in Russian will take up the challenge.

Appendix: Women of Power among the Nazarenes and Beyond

1198. Lk 4:18, MTB.
1199. King, 2003, 7–11.
1200. Lk 8:1–3.
1201. 1 Cor 15:3–8.
1202. Brooten, 1982, 9–10; Kraemer, 2004, 241.
1203. Lk 10:38–42.

1204. Lk 8:1–3, MTB.
1205. Mt 11:19.
1206. de Boer, 2007, 108.
1207. Jn 20:18.
1208. King, 2003, 14.
1209. Ibid.
1210. Ibid., 15.
1211. King, 2003, 17.
1212. Ibid.
1213. Lk 8:2.
1214. Gregory the Great, sermon 33.1, in de Boer, 2007, 172.
1215. Sermon 25.10, in de Boer, 2007, 181.
1216. Katherine Ludwig Jansen, *Making of the Magdalen: Preaching and Popular Devotion in the Later Middle Ages* (Princeton: Princeton University Press, 2000), 335–36.
1217. Pope John Paul II, Letter to Priests for Holy Thursday, 1995. http://www.vatican.va/holy_father/john_paul_ii/letters/documents/hf_jp-ii_let_25031995_priests_en.html.
1218. 1 Cor 9:5, MTB.
1219. *Stromata* III, 53.
1220. 1 Tm 2:11–12, WEB.
1221. Rom 16:7.
1222. *In Epistolam ad Romanos,* Homilia 31, 2, *PG* 60, 669f, quoted in Brooten, 1977, 141.
1223. Brooten, 1977, 141.
1224. *Women Priests*, Arlene Swidler & Leonard Swidler (eds.), Paulist Press 1977, 141–44.
1225. Acts of Paul and Thecla in James, 1924.
1226. Gal 3:28, MTB.
1227. "Letter to Trajan," 10.96.
1228. Kraemer, 2004.
1229. Severus, *The Sacred History,* II, 46–51.
1230. Cyril of Jerusalem, "Catechetical Lectures; Procatechesis," 14 *NPNF2*.
1231. 22 John Chrysostom, *Homily on Psalm 14, 2* on Psalm 46:2–3, in *Inheriting Wisdom: readings for today from ancient Christian writers,* by Everett Ferguson (Hendrickson Publishers, 2004), 243.
1232. Otranto, trans. Rossi, 1991, 81.

1233. Crone, 1980, 93–95.
1234. Vassilev, 2000, 107.
1235. Wijjie, Great Moors of al-Andalus, accessed May 9, 2008 www.vivagranada.com/greatmoors/index.htm.
1236. Nichols, J. M. "Arabic Women Poets in al-Andalus." *Maghreb Review* 4 (1979): 114–17.
1237. Pray, Fight, Dream, June 4, 2005, http://dreams-of-enfilade.xanga.com/276964357/item/.

Bibliography

Ancient Sources

Andrew, The Acts of. In *The Apocryphal New Testament*. Translated by M. R. James. Oxford: Clarendon Press, 1924.

Ambrose. "De obitu Theodosii." In Migne's *Patrologia Latina*, vol. 16.

Ambrosiaster. "Prologue to his Commentary on Romans." Translated from John Knox, "The Epistle to the Romans," in the Interpreters Bible, 9:362. Nashville: Abingdon Press, 1952-57.

Anglo-Saxon Chronicle. Translated by Rev. James Ingram, London: Everyman Press, 1912.

Apollinaris, Sidonius. *Letters*. Translated by O. M. Dalton, 1915.

"The Apology of Aristides the Philosopher." *ANF*, vol. X.

"Apostolic Constitutions" (or "Constitutions of the Holy Apostles, lat. Constitutiones Apostolorum"). *ANF*, vol. VII.

Aristotle. *Aristotle's Politics*. Translated by Benjamin Jowett. Oxford: Oxford at the Clarendon Press, 1931.

Athanasius. "Life of Anthony." *NPNF* 2, vol. 4.

Augustine. "Anti-Pelagian Writings." *NPNF*, vol. 5.

_____. "Confessions." *NPNF*, series I, vol. 1.

_____. "Letters." *NPNF*, series I, vol. 1.

_____. "On the Gospel of John." Tractate IV. *NPNF*, vol. 17.

_____. *Soliloquies of Saint Augustine*. Translated by Rose Elizabeth Cleveland. Boston: Little, Brown, 1910.

_____. "The Retractions." Translated by Sister Mary I. Bogan, in *The Fathers of the Church*, vol. 60. Washington, Catholic University of America Press, 1968.

_____. "Tractates on John." *NPNF*, vol. VII.

Bardesan. *The Book of the Laws of Countries*. Reprint of the 1855 edition, Tertullian.org, 2003. http://www.tertullian.org/fathers/spicilegium_3_bardesan.htm.

"Barnabas, the Epistle of." Translated by J. B. Lightfoot, in *The Apostolic Fathers*. London: MacMillan, 1891.

"Barnabas, the Epistle of." *ANF*, vol. I.

"Barnabas, the Epistle of." Translated by Kirsopp Lake, 1912. Loeb Classical Library.

Bede. *Ecclesiastical History of the English Nation*. London: J. M. Dent; New York: E. P. Dutton, 1910.

Cassian, John. "Seven Books on the Incarnation of the Lord, Against Nestorius." *NPNF* 2, vol. XI.

Chrysostom, John. "Eight Homilies against the Jews (Adversus Judeaus)." *Patrologia Greaca*, vol. 98. Internet Medieval Sourcebook. Public domain.

"First Epistle of Clement to the Corinthians." Eberhard Arnold translation. 1926.

"Second Epistle of Clement." Translated by Kirsopp Lake in *The Apostolic Fathers*, v. I, 125-27. London: 1912.

Clement of Alexandria. "Stromata." *ANF*, vol. II. (The Ante-Nicene Fathers is too prudish to translate chapter 3; it stays in Latin for scholars only.)

"The Clementine Homilies." *ANF*, vol. 8.

"The Recognitions of Clement." *ANF*, vol. 8.

"The Presbyter Cosmas's Sermon Regarding the Newly-Appeared Bogomil Heresy." Reprint from *Monumenta Bulgarica*, T. Butler, ed. Michigan: Univ of Michigan, 1998. http://www.bogomilism.eu/Other%20authors/Cosma.html.

Cyril of Jerusalem. "Catechetical Lectures." *NPNF* 2, vol. VII.

Didascalia Apostolorum. Edited by R. Hugh Connolly. Oxford: Clarendon Press, 1929.

Dio Cassius. *Roman History*. Translated by Earnest Cary. Loeb Classical Library. Harvard UP: 1914.

Epiphanius. "Anacephalaiosis." In A. F. J. Klijn and G. J. Reinink's *Patristic Evidence for Jewish-Christian Sects*. Leiden: E. J. Brill, 1973.

Epiphanius, Saint, Bp. of Constantia in Cyprus. *The Panarion of Epiphanius of Salamis.* Translated by Frank Williams, Leiden: E. J. Brill, 1994.

The Panarion of St. Epiphanius, Bishop of Salamis: Selected Passages. Translated by Philip. R. Amidon, S J. New York: Oxford University Press, 1990.

"Epistle of the Apostles." In Montague Rhode James's *The Apocryphal New Testament.* Oxford: Clarendon Press, 1924.

Eusebius. "The Ecclesiastical History." *NPNF* 2, vol. I.

———. "The Life of the Blessed Emperor Constantine." *NPNF* 2, vol. I.

Gospel of Peter. *The Other Gospels.* Edited by Ron Cameron. Guildford: Lutterworth Press, 1982.

Gregory of Nyssa. "Letter XVII, to Eustathia." *NPNF* 2, vol. V.

Hippolytus. "On Christ and Antichrist." *ANF*, vol. IV.

Hippolytus of Rome, the Apostolic Tradition of. Translated by Kevin P. Edgecomb, accessed January 23, 2012, www.bombaxo.com/hippolytus.html

"History of Joseph the Carpenter," *ANF*, vol. VIII

Hoveden, Roger. *Annals*, vol. II. London: H. G. Bohn, 1853.

Ibn Hisham. *The Life of Mohammad.* 3rd ed. Beirut, Lebanon: Dar-al-Jil, 1998.

Ignatius of Antioch. In Lightfoot & Harmer's *The Apostolic Fathers.* London: MacMillan, 1891.

Irenaeus of Lyons. "Adversus Haereses" ("Against Heresies"). *ANF*, vol. 1.

Jerome. "The Letters of Saint Jerome." *NPNF* 2, vol. VI.

———. "The Life of Malchus." *NPNF* 2, vol. VI.

———. "Lives of Illustrious Men" (*de vir*). *NPNF* 2, vol. III.

Josephus. "Antiquities of the Jews." In William Whiston's *The Works of Flavius Josephus.* London and Edinburgh: William P. Nimmo, 1737.

———. *The Jewish War.* Translated by G. A. Williamson. Harmondsworth: Penguin Books, 1959.

———. "Vita." In William Whiston's *The Works of Flavius Josephus.* London and Edinburgh: William P. Nimmo, 1737.

Justin Martyr. "Dialogue with Trypho." *ANF*, vol. I.

———. "First Apology." *ANF*, vol. I.

Justinian I, Emperor. *Body of Civil Law*. Translated by S. P. Scott. Cincinnati: The Central Trust Company, 1932.

Lactantius. "Of the Manner in Which the Persecutors Died." *ANF*, vol. VII.

"Leo the Great, Sermons of St." *NPNF* 02, vol. XII.

The Mishnah. Translated by Herbert Denby. Oxford: Oxford University Press, 1933.

"The Martyrdom of Polycarp." *ANF*, vol. I.

"The Preaching of Peter." In Montague Rhode James's *The Apocryphal New Testament*. Oxford: Clarendon Press, 1924.

The Odes of Solomon: The Syriac Texts. Edited with translation and notes by J. H. Charlesworth. Oxford: Clarendon, 1973.

Origen. "Contra Celsus." *ANF*, vol. IV.

———. "de Principiis, Prologue of Rufinus." *ANF*, vol. IV.

———. "Commentary on the Gospel of John." *ANF*, vol. X.

Orosius, Paulus. *The Seven Books of History against the Pagans*. Washington: Catholic University of America Press, 1964.

Patrologia Latina, Edited by J. P. Migne. Paris: Excudebat Migne, 1844–65.

Philo of Alexandria. *Every Good Man is Free*. Translated by C. D. Young. London: H. G. Bohn, 1854–90.

———. *Hypothetica*. Translated by C. D. Young. London: H. G. Bohn, 1854-90.

Pliny the Elder. *The Natural History*. Edited by John Bostock and H. T. Riley. Reprint of the 1855 edition, Tufts University: Perseus Digital Library, 2009. www.perseus.tufts.edu/hopper/text?doc=Plin.+Nat.+toc

Pliny the Younger. *Letters*. Cambridge: Loeb Classical Library, 1915.

Plutarch. *Parallel Lives*. Cambridge: Loeb Classical Library, 1915.

"Polycarp to the Philippians." *Apostolic Fathers*. Translated by Kirsopp Lake. Cambridge: Loeb Classical Library, 1912.

"Protevangelion of James." M. R. James. *The Apocryphal New Testament*. Oxford: Clarendon Press, 1924.

Quran: The Final Testament. Authorized English Version translated from the original by Rashad Khalifa, PhD. Islamic Productions, 2009. http://submission.ws/index.php/quran-koran-the-final-testament.html.

Socrates Scholasticus. "Ecclesiastical History." *NPNF* 2, vol. II.

Sulpicius Severus. "The Sacred History" ("Chronica"). *NPNF* 2, vol. XI.

Tacitus. *Tacitus III: Histories 4–5 and Annals 1–3*. Translated by C. H. Moore. Loeb Classical Library. Cambridge: Harvard University Press, 1931.

Tertullian. "Apology." *ANF*, vol. III.

———. "The Chaplet." *ANF*, vol. III.

The Theodosian Code and Novels and the Sirmondian Constitutions. Translated by Clyde Pharr. Princeton: Princeton University Press, 1952.

Modern Works

Aberbach, Moshe and David. *Roman-Jewish Wars and Hebrew Cultural Nationalism*. New York: St. Martin's Press, 2000.

Akenson, Donald Harman. *Saint Saul*. Montreal: McGill-Queen's University Press, 2000.

Akers, Keith. *The Lost Religion of Jesus*. New York: Lantern Books, 2000.

Allix, Peter. *Some Remarks upon the Ecclesiastical History of the Ancient Churches of Piedmont*. Reprint of the 1690 edition, Classic Works of Apologetics Online. Accessed May 5, 2008. http://www.classicapologetics.com/a/Alecclesiastical.pdf.

———. *Remarks upon the Ecclesiastical History of the Ancient Churches of the Albigenses*. Reprint of the 1692 edition, Princeton Theological Seminary, E-book and Text Archive. Accessed May 20, 2008. http://www.archive.org/details/remarksuponeccle00alli.

Andrews, J. N. *History of the Sabbath*. Battle Creek, MI: Review & Herald Publishing Assn., 1887. Adventist Bible Truths, 2004. http://dedication.www3.50megs.com/historyofsabbath/hos_contents.html

Bagatti, OFM Fr. Bellarmino. *The Church from the Circumcision. History and Archaeology of the Judaeo-Christians*. English translation by Fr. Eugene Hoade, OFM. Jerusalem: Franciscan Printing Press, 1971, 1984.

———. *Excavations in Nazareth*. Jerusalem: Franciscan Printing Press, 1969.

Bagatti, B. *Excavations in Nazareth*. Vol. I, *From the Beginning till the XII Century*. Translated from Italian by E. Hoade. Jerusalem, 1969.

_____. *Ancient Christian Villages of Galilee.* English translation by P. Rotondi. Jerusalem 2000.

Barrett, C. K. *The New Testament Background: Selected Documents.* London: SPCK, 1956.

Batey, Richard A. *Jesus and the Forgotten City: New Light on Sepphoris and the Urban World of Jesus.* Pasadena: Century One Media, 2000.

Bauckham, Richard. *Jesus and the Eyewitnesses: The Gospels as Eyewitness Testimony.* Grand Rapids: Wm. B. Eerdmans, 2006.

_____. "Jews and Jewish Christians in the Land of Israel at the Time of the Bar Kochba War, with Special Reference to the Apocalypse of Peter." In *Tolerance and Intolerance in Early Judaism and Christianity,* edited by Graham Stanton and G. G. Stroumsa, 228-38. Cambridge University Press, 1998.

_____. *Jude and the Relatives of Jesus in the Early Church.* T&T Clark Int'l, 2004.

Bauer, Walter. *Orthodoxy and Heresy in Earliest Christianity.* Philadelphia: Fortress Press, 1971.

Becker, Adam H. and Annette Y. Reed, eds. *The Ways that Never Parted: Jews and Christians in Late Antiquity and the Early Middle Ages.* TSAJ (Texts and Studies in Ancient Judaism) 95. Tübingen: Mohr Siebeck, 2003.

Becker, Joachim. *Messianic Expectation in the Old Testament.* Philadelphia: Fortress Press, 1977.

Bedjan, Paul. *Acta Martyrum et Sanctorum.* Hilderheim: George Olms, 1968.

Benko, Stephen. *Pagan Rome and the Early Christians.* Bloomington: Indiana University Press, 1986.

Betz, Hans Dieter. "The Mithras Inscriptions of Santa Prisca and the New Testament." In *Novum Testamentum* 10 (1968): 62–80.

Blasi, Anthony J. *Early Christianity as a Social Movement.* New York: Peter Lang, 1988.

Bookchin, Murray. *The Ecology of Freedom.* Montreal: Black Rose Books, 1991.

Boyarin, Daniel. *Border Lines: The Partition of Judaeo-Christianity.* Philadelphia: U Penn Press, 2004.

Brandon, S. G. F. "Saint Paul and his Opponents." In *Horizon* X, no. 1 (winter, 1968): 106–11.

_____. *The Trial of Jesus.* New York: Dorset Press, 1968, 1988.

Brock, Rita Nakashima, and Rebecca Ann Parker. *Saving Paradise: How Christianity Traded Love of This World for Crucifixion and Empire.* Boston: Beacon Press, 2008.

Brock, Sebastian P., and Susan Ashbrook Harvey, eds. *Holy Women of the Syrian Orient.* Berkeley: University of California Press, 1987.

Brooten, Bernadette. "Junia. Outstanding among the Apostles." In *Women Priests: A Catholic Commentary on the Vatican Declaration.* Leonard Swidler and Arlene Swidler, eds. New York: Paulist Press, 1977.

———. *Women Leaders in the Ancient Synagogue: Inscriptional Evidence and Background Issues.* Chico, CA: Scholars Press, 1982.

Brown, Raymond E. *The Epistle of James: A Commentary on the Greek Text.* New International Greek Testament Commentary. Grand Rapids: Wm. B. Eerdmans, 1982.

Brown, R. E. *An Introduction to the New Testament.* New York: Doubleday, 1997.

Bütz, Jeffrey J. *The Brother of Jesus and the Lost Teachings of Christianity.* Rochester: Inner Traditions, 2005.

———. *The Secret Legacy of Jesus.* Rochester: Inner Traditions, 2009.

Buchanan, Claudius. *Christian Researches in Asia: With Notices of the Translation of the Scriptures into the Oriental Languages.* 2nd ed. Boston: Samuel T. Armstrong, Cornhill, 1811.

Cameron, Ron, ed. *The Other Gospels.* Guildford: Lutterworth Press, 1982.

Campion, Nicholas. *The Great Year.* London: Arkana, 1994.

Chahin, M. *The Kingdom of Armenia.* New York: Dorset Press, 1987.

Charlesworth, James H. *Jesus within Judaism: New Light from Exciting Archaeological Discoveries.* New York: Doubleday, 1988.

Conybeare, Frederick Cornwallis. *The Key of Truth, a Manual of the Paulician Church of Armenia,* Oxford: Clarendon Press, 1898.

Crone, Patricia. "Islam, Judeo-Christianity and Byzantine Iconoclasm." *Jerusalem Studies in Arabic and Islam* II, 59-95. Jerusalem: The Magnes Press, 1980.

Crossan, John Dominic. *The Birth of Christianity.* New York: HarperSanFrancisco, 1998.

———. *The Historical Jesus; the Life of a Mediterranean Jewish Peasant.* New York: HarperCollins, 1991.

Crossan, John Dominic and Jonathan Reed. *Excavating Jesus, beneath the Stones, behind the Texts.* San Francisco: HarperSanFrancisco, 2001.

_____. *In Search of Paul.* New York: HarperSanFrancisco, 2004.

d'Achery, Luc. *Spicilegium sive collectio veterum aliquot scriptorum qui in Galliæ bibliothecis delituerant.* Paris: Montalant, 1723.

Daniélou, Jean, S.J. *Primitive Christian Symbols.* Translated by Donald Attwater. Baltimore: Helicon Press, 1964.

de Boer, Esther. *The Mary Magdalene Cover-Up.* London: T and T Clark, 2007.

de Rosa, Peter. *Vicars of Christ.* London: Corgi Books, 1988.

Dollinger, Johann Joseph Von. *Reports on the History of the Sects of the Middle Ages.* Munich, 1890.

Dunkerley, Roderic. *Beyond the Gospels.* Harmondsworth: Penguin, 1957.

Edwards, Peter. *Inquisition.* California: University of California Press, 1989.

Ehrman, Bart D. *Lost Christianities: The Battles for Scripture and the Faiths We Never Knew.* Oxford: Oxford University Press, 2003.

_____. *Jesus: Apocalyptic Prophet for the New Millennium.* Oxford: Oxford University Press, 1999.

_____. *Misquoting Jesus: The Story behind Who Changed the Bible and Why.* San Francisco: HarperSanFrancisco, 2005.

_____. *Truth and Fiction in the Da Vinci Code.* Oxford: Oxford University Press, 2004.

Eisenman, Robert and Michael Wise. *The Dead Sea Scrolls Uncovered.* New York: Penguin Books, 1992.

Eisenman, Robert. *James the Brother of Jesus.* New York: Viking, 1996.

Ferguson, John. *The Religions of the Roman Empire.* Ithaca: Cornell University Press, 1970.

Finegan, Jack. *The Archaeology of the New Testament.* Princeton: Princeton University Press, 1992.

_____. *Myth and Mystery: An Introduction to the Pagan Religions of the Biblical World.* Grand Rapids MI: Baker Academic, 1997.

Flusser, David. *Jewish Sources in Early Christianity.* New York: Adama Press, 1987.

Frend, W. H. C. *The Rise of Christianity.* Philadelphia: Fortress Press, 1984.

Funk, Robert W. and Roy W. Hoover. *The Five Gospels; What Did Jesus Really Say?* New York: Macmillan, 1993.

Gaddis, Michael. *There Is No Crime for Those Who Have Christ.* California: U of Cal. Press, 2005.

Gager, John. "Did Jewish Christians See the Rise of Islam?" In *The Ways that Never Parted: Jews and Christians in Late Antiquity and the Early Middle Ages.* Edited by Adam H. Becker and Annette Y. Reed. Philadelphia: Fortress Press, 2007.

Garrow, Alan. *The Gospel of Matthew's Dependence on the Didache.* Edinburgh: T&T Clark International, 2004.

Geddes, Michael. *A Short History of the Church of Malabar together with the Synod of Diamper.* London: 1694.

George, Leonard. *Crimes of Perception: An Encyclopedia of Heresies and Heretics.* New York: Paragon House, 1995.

Gibson, Shimon. *The Cave of John the Baptist: The Stunning Archaeological Discovery that has Redefined Christian History.* New York: Doubleday, 2004.

Goddard, Hugh. *A History of Christian-Muslim Relations.* Chicago: New Amsterdam Books, 2000.

Gregg, Robert C. and Dennis Groh. *Early Arianism—A View of Salvation.* Philadelphia: Fortress Press, 1981.

Griffith, Brian. *Different Visions of Love; Partnership and Dominator Values in Christian History.* Parker, CO: Outskirts Press. 2008.

Handford, Thomas W., ed. *Ingersollia: Gems of thought from the lectures, speeches, and conversations of Col. Robert G. Ingersoll, representative of his opinions and beliefs.* Belford: Clarke & Co., 1882.

Harris, Lynda. *The Secret Heresy of Hieronymus Bosch.* Edinburgh: Floris Book, 1995.

Harvey, Susan Ashbrook. "Revisiting the Daughters of the Covenant: Women's Choirs and Sacred Song in Ancient Syriac Christianity." In *Hugoye: Journal of Syriac Studies*, July, 2005. http://syrcom.cua.edu/Hugoye/Vol8No2/HV8N2Harvey.html.

Hereford, R. Travers. *Christianity in Talmud and Midrash.* London: Williams and Norgate, 1903.

Hergenröther, Joseph. *Handbuch der allgemeinen Kirchengeschichte (Manual of General Church History).* Freiburg: Herder, 1876.

_____. *Photius Patriarch von Constantinopel, sein Leben, seine Schriften, und das griechische Schisma.* Ratisbon: 1867–69.

Hezser, Catherine. *Jewish Literacy in Roman Palestine.* Tübingen: Mohr/Siebeck, 2001.

Horsley, Richard A. *Archaeology, History, and Society in Galilee: The Social Context of Jesus and the Rabbis.* Valley Forge, PA: Trinity Press International, 1996.

Horsley, Richard A., with John S. Hanson. *Bandits, Prophets and Messiahs.* San Francisco: Harper and Row, 1985.

Howard, George. *The Hebrew Gospel of Matthew.* Macon: Mercer University Press, 1995.

Hurtado, Larry W. *Lord Jesus Christ, Devotion to Jesus in Earliest Christianity.* Grand Rapids: William B. Eerdmans, 2004.

Ibn Hisham. *The Life of Mohammad.* 3rd ed. Beirut, Lebanon: Dar-al-Jil, 1998.

Jackson-McCabe, Matt, ed. *Jewish Christianity Reconsidered: Rethinking Ancient Groups and Texts.* Minneapolis: Fortress Press 2007.

James, Montague Rhode. *The Apocryphal New Testament.* Oxford: Clarendon Press, 1924.

Jenkins, Philip. *The Lost History of Christianity: The Thousand-Year Golden Age of the Church in the Middle East, Africa, and Asia.* New York: HarperOne, 2008.

Pope John Paul II. *Holy City Is the Mother of All Churches: Letter to the Patriarch, the Auxiliary Bishops, the Priests and Deacons, the Men and Women Religious, and the Faithful of the Patriarchal Diocese of Jerusalem for Latins,* 1997.

Jones, F. Stanley. *An Ancient Jewish Christian Source on the History of Christianity: Pseudo-Clementine Recognitions L.27–71.* Atlanta: Society of Biblical Literature, 1995.

Jones, William. *The History of the Christian Church from the Birth of Christ to the Eighteenth Century including the Very Interesting Account of the Waldenses and Albigenses.* Reprint of the 1812 edition. Internet Archive, Accessed January 8, 2012. http://www.archive.org/details/historyofchris01jone.

Kee, Howard Clark. *Medicine, Miracle and Magic in New Testament Times.* Cambridge: Cambridge University Press, 1986.

King, Karen L. *The Gospel of Mary of Magdala: Jesus and the First Woman.* Apostle Santa Rosa, CA: Polebridge Press, 2003.

Klijn, A. F. J. *Jewish-Christian Gospel Tradition,* E. J. Brill, 1992.

Klijn, A. F. J. and G. J. Reinink. *Patristic Evidence for Jewish-Christian Sects.* Leiden: E. J. Brill, 1973.

Klinghoffer, David. *Why the Jews Rejected Jesus*. New York: Doubleday, 2005.

Koester, Helmut. *Ancient Christian Gospels: Their History and Development*. London: SCM Press 1990.

Kloppenborg, Verbin, J.S. *Excavating Q: The History and Setting of the Sayings Gospel*. Edinburgh: T&T Clark, 2000.

Kousoulas, Dimitrios George. *The Life and Times of Constantine the Great*. Danbury: Rutledge Books, 1997.

Kraemer, Ross Shepard. *Women's Religions in the Greco-Roman World: A Sourcebook Book*. Oxford: Oxford University Press, 2004.

Kuhn, Alvin Boyd. *Shadow of the Third Century: A Revaluation of Christianity*. Whitefish, MT: Kessinger Publishing, 1992.

Levine, Amy-Jill. *The Misunderstood Jew*. San Francisco: HarperSanFrancisco, 2006.

Lieu, Judith, John North and Tessa Rajak. *The Jews among Pagans and Christians in the Roman Empire*. London: Routledge, 1992.

Lüdemann, Gerd. *Opposition to Paul in Jewish Christianity*. Minneapolis: Fortress Press, 1989.

———. *Paul, the Founder of Christianity*. Amherst: Prometheus Books, 2002.

Maccoby, Hyam. *The Mythmaker; Paul and the Invention of Christianity*. London: Weidenfeld and Nicholson, 1986.

———. *Revolution in Judea: Jesus and the Jewish Resistance*. New York: Taplinger, 1973.

———. *The Sacred Executioner*. London: Thames & Hudson, 1982.

MacMullen, Ramsay. *Constantine*. New York: The Dial Press, 1969.

Mack, Burton L. *The Lost Gospel. The Book of Q and Christian Origins*. San Francisco: HarperSanFrancisco, 1993.

Mancini, Ignazio. *Archeological Discoveries Relative to the Judaeo-Christians*. Jerusalem: Franciscan Printing Press, 1970.

Martyn, J. Louis. *History and Theology in the Fourth Gospel*. 3rd ed. Louisville, KY/London, UK: Westminster John Knox Press, 2003.

Martin, Malachi. *The Decline and Fall of the Roman Church*. New York: Bantam, 1983.

Maude, Aylmer. *A Peculiar People, the Doukhobors*. New York: Funk and Wagnalls, 1904.

Mead, G. R. S. *The Gnostic John the Baptizer; Selections from the Mandaean John-Book Together with Studies of John and Christian*

Origins, the Slavonic Josephus' Account of John and Jesus, and John and the Fourth Gospel Proem. London: Watkins, 1924.

Mendels, Doron. *The Rise and Fall of Jewish Nationalism.* New York: Doubleday, 1992.

Meyer, Marvin W. *The Ancient Mysteries.* San Francisco: Harper and Row, 1984.

Millard, Alan. *Reading and Writing in the Time of Jesus.* New York: New York University Press, 2000.

Mitchell, A. W. *The Waldenses: Sketches of the Evangelical Christians of the Valley of Piedmont.* A reprint of the 1853 edition. Scholarly Publishing Office of the University of Michigan Library (no date) http://quod.lib.umich.edu/cgi/t/text/text-idx?c=moa&cc=moa&view=text&rgn=main&idno=AJH3867.

Moffett, Samuel Hugh. *A History of Christianity in Asia.* San Francisco: HarperSanFrancisco, 1992

Murray, R. *Symbols of Church and Kingdom: A Study in Early Syriac Tradition.* Cambridge: Cambridge University Press, 1975.

Neander, August. *General History of the Christian Religion and Church.* Translated by Torrey, Joseph. London: H. G. Bohn, 1852.

Norwich, John Julius. *Byzantium: The Early Centuries.* Harmondsworth: Viking Penguin, 1988.

O'Shea, Stephen. *The Perfect Heresy: The Revolutionary Life and Death of the Medieval Cathars.* Vancouver/Toronto: Douglas and McIntyre, 2000.

Otranto, Giorgio. "Note sul sacerdozio femminile nell'antichità in margine a una testimonianza di Gelasio I." *Vetera Christianorum* 19 (1982): 341–60. Translated by Mary Ann Rossi as "Priesthood, Precedent, and Prejudice: On Recovering the Women Priests of Early Christianity." *Journal of Feminist Studies in Religion* 7 (1991): 73–94.

Parkes, James. *The Conflict of the Church and the Synagogue.* New York: Atheneum, 1979.

Payne, D. F. "Semitisms in the Books of Acts." In *Apostolic History and the Gospel. Biblical and Historical Essays Presented to F. F. Bruce.* Edited by W. Ward Gasque and Ralph P. Martin. Exeter: The Paternoster Press, 1970.

Peacock, Kenneth. *Songs of the Doukhobors.* Ottawa: National Museums of Canada, Bulletin No. 231, Folklore Series No. 7, 1970.

Pearson, Birger Albert. *Gnosticism and Christianity in Roman and Coptic Egypt.* Edinburgh: T&T Clark International, 2004.

Pelikan, Jaroslav. *The Christian Tradition.* Vol. 1, *The Emergence of the Catholic Tradition* (100–600). Chicago: The University of Chicago Press, 1971.

Pendle, Karin. *Women & Music: A History.* Bloomington: Indiana University Press, 1991.

Pharr, Clyde. *The Theodosian Code and Novels and the Sirmondian Constitutions.* Princeton: Princeton University Press, 1952.

Philip, T. V. *East of the Euphrates: Early Christianity in Asia. India.* India: CSS & ISPCK, 1998

Pitt-Rivers, George. *The Riddle of the 'Labarum' and the Origin of Christian Symbols.* London: George Allen & Unwin Ltd, 1966.

Pines, Shlomo. *The Jewish Christians of the Early Centuries of Christianity according to a New Source.* Proceedings of the Israel Academy of Sciences and Humanities II, no.13. Jerusalem: The Israel Academy of Arts and Sciences, 1966.

Price, Massoume. *Christianity in Iran, a Brief History.* December 2002. http://www.iranchamber.com/religions/articles/history_of_christianity_iran1.php.

Price, S. R. F. *Rituals and Power: The Imperial Cult in Asia Minor.* Cambridge: Cambridge University Press, 1984.

Pritz, Ray A. *Nazarene Jewish Christianity: From the End of the New Testament Period until Its Disappearance in the Fourth Century.* Jerusalem: Magnes Press, 1988.

Quasten, Johannes. *Patrology.* Vol. 1. Utrecht: Spectrum Publishers, 1966.

Ramsay, W. M. *The Church in the Roman Empire.* Grand Rapids: Baker Book House, 1954.

———. *St. Paul the Traveller and Roman Citizen.* London: Hodder and Stoughton, 1895.

———, ed. *Studies in the History and Art of the Eastern Provinces of the Roman Empire.* Aberdeen: Aberdeen University Press, 1906.

Reed, Jonathan L. *Archaeology and the Galilean Jesus.* Harrisburg: Trinity Press International, 2000, 2002.

Reynolds, Gabriel Said & Samir, Samir Khalil Samir, eds. and trans. *Critique of Christian Origins: A Parallel English-Arabic Text*; (*Tathbīt dalā' il al-nubūwah*) Selections. Provo, Utah: Brigham Young University Press, 2010.

Reynolds, Gabriel Said. *A Muslim Theologian in the Sectarian Milieu: Abd al-Jabbar and the Critique Of Christian Origins.* Leiden: E.J. Brill, 2004.

Ross, Steven K. *Roman Edessa: Politics and Culture on the Eastern Fringes of the Roman Empire,* 114–242 C.E. Routledge, 2001.

Rothschild, Fritz A., ed. *Jewish Perspectives on Christianity: Leo Baeck, Martin Buber, Franz Rosenzweig, Will Herberg, and Abraham J. Heschel.* New York: Crossroad, 1990.

Schaberg, Jane. *The Illegitimacy of Jesus.* San Francisco: Harper & Row, 1987.

Schaff, Philip. *Creeds of Christendom, with a History and Critical Notes.* Vol. II of *The History of Creeds.* Harper & Brothers, 1877.

_____. *History of the Christian Church.* Charles Scribner's Sons, 1910.

Schoeps, Hans-Joachim. *Jewish Christianity: Factional Disputes in the Early Church.* Translated by Douglas R. A. Hare. Philadelphia: Fortress Press, 1969.

Segal, J. B. *Edessa, 'The Blessed City.'* Oxford: Clarendon Press, 1970.

Sicker, Martin. *Between Rome and Jerusalem.* Westport: Praeger, 2001.

Simon, Marcel. *Verus Israel: A Study in the Relations between Christians and Jews in the Roman Empire, AD 135–425.* Translated by H. McKeating. Oxford: Oxford UP, 1986.

Skarsaune, Oskar, and Reidar Hvalvik, eds. *Jewish Believers in Jesus: The Early Centuries.* Peabody, MA: Hendrickson Publishers, 2007.

Skarsaune, Oskar. *In the Shadow of the Temple: Jewish Influences on Early Christianity.* Downers Grove, IL: InterVarsity Press, 2002.

Smith, Morton. *Jesus the Magician.* San Francisco: Harper and Row, 1978.

Spong, J. S. *Born of a Woman.* San Francisco: Harper Collins, 1992.

Staniforth, Maxwell, ed. *Early Christian Writings.* Harmondsworth: Penguin Books, 1968.

Stanton, Graham. *Tolerance and Intolerance in Early Judaism and Christianity.* Cambridge, Mass.: Cambridge University Press, 1998.

Stark, Rodney. *The Rise of Christianity; a Sociologist Reconsiders History.* Princeton: Princeton University Press, 1996.

Stoyanov, Yuri. *The Other God: Dualist Religions from Antiquity to the Cathar Heresy.* New Haven: Yale University Press, 2000.

Strecker, Georg. "On the Problem of Jewish Christianity." In *Orthodoxy and Heresy in Earliest Christianity*. Philadelphia: Fortress Press, 1971.

Stroumsa, Guy G., ed. *The Collected Works of Shlomo Pines*. Vol. IV, *Studies on Jewish Christianity*. Gospel Quotations and Cognate Topics. Jerusalem: The Hebrew University, Magnes Press, 1996.

Tabor, James D. *The Jesus Dynasty: The Hidden History of Jesus, His Royal Family and the Birth of Christianity*. New York: Simon and Schuster, 2006.

Throckmorton Jr., Burton H., ed. *Gospel Parallels*. Nashville: Thomas Nelson, 9th ed., 1936, 1979.

Van Voorst, Robert E. *The Ascents of James: History and Theology of a Jewish-Christian Community*. Atlanta: Scholars Press, 1989.

Vasilev, Georgi. "Bogomils and Lollards, Dualistic Motives in England during the Middle Ages." *Etudes Balkaniques*, no. 1 (1993). http://www.bogomilism.eu/Studies/John%20Wycliffe-and-the-Dualists.html.

―――. "Bogomils, Cathars and Lollards and the High Social Position of Women during the Middle Ages." Series Philosophy and Sociology, *Facta Universitatis* 2, no. 7, University of Nis, Yugoslavia (2000): 325–36. http://facta.junis.ni.ac.rs/pas/pas2000/pas2000-02.pdf.

Vermes, Geza. *The Dead Sea Scrolls in English*. London: Penguin Books, 1962.

―――. *Jesus the Jew*. Minneapolis: Fortress Press, 1973.

Vernadsky, George, Ralph T. Fisher Jr., Alan D. Ferguson, Andrew Lossky, and Sergei Pushkarev, eds. *A Source Book for Russian History from Early Times to 1917*. New Haven, Conn.: Yale UP, 1972.

Wakefield, W. L. and A. P. Evans, eds.. *Heresies of the High Middle Ages*. New York and London: Columbia UP, 1969.

Werner, Eric. *The Sacred Bridge: The Interdependence of Liturgy and Music in Synagogue and Church during the First Millennium*. London: D. Dobson, 1959–84.

Wheless, Joseph. *Forgery in Christianity*. New York: Alfred A. Knopf, 1930.

Wilken, Robert L. *The Christians as the Romans Saw Them*. New Haven: Yale UP, 1984.

Wilkinson, John. *Jerusalem Pilgrims before the Crusades*. Warminster, England: Aris & Phillips, 1977.

Williams, Stephen and Gerard Friell. *Theodosius: The Empire at Bay.* London: B. T. Batsford, 1994.

Wilson, Barrie. *How Jesus Became Christian: St. Paul, the Early Church, and the Jesus Cover-up.* Toronto: Random House Canada, 2008.

Wilson, Ian. *Jesus the Evidence.* London: Weidenfeld and Nicolson, 1984.

Wise, Michael O. *The First Messiah.* San Francisco: HarperSanFrancisco, 1999.

Woodcock, George and Ivan Avakumovic. *The Doukhobors.* Toronto: McClelland and Stewart, 1977.

Yadin, Yigael. *Bar-Kokhba: the rediscovery of the legendary hero of the Second Jewish Revolt against Rome.* New York: Random House, 1971.

Zeitlin, Irving M. *Jesus and the Judaism of his Time.* Oxford: Polity Press, 1988.

Zwemer, Samuel. *The Moslem Christ: An Essay on the Life, Character, And Teachings of Jesus Christ According to the Koran and Orthodox Tradition.* Oliphant, Edinburgh, and London: Anderson & Ferrier, 1912.

Index

Christianity; Pauline Christianity
    birth of, 156
    effect of Jewish revolt on, 201
    in India, 237–239
    in Iran, 236–237
    as mainly Gentile religion quickly
        after Jesus's death, 243
    Protestants, 167, 176, 300
    Romanization of, 210, 248, 271
    Syrian Christians, 233, 236, 238
    tragedies of, ix
Christmas, 248, 271
Chrysostom, John, 245–246, 272,
    296, 298, 352
church in Jerusalem, rapid growth
    of, 194–196
Church of the Circumcision, 209,
    220, 269
Church of the Gentiles, i, 269
Church of the Jews, 269
the Church, as promoting hatred,
    246
Cilicia, 166
Circle of the Unbelievers (*Gelil ha-
    Goyim*), 83
circumcision, 51, 54, 56–57, 138,
    170–171, 173, 179, 244, 270,
    280–281, 299
City of God (Augustine), 263
Claudius, 148, 199
Clement, 136, 185, 225–226
Clement (pupil of Peter), 230
Clement II, 226
Clement of Alexandria, 199, 214,
    246, 252, 296, 352
Clement of Rome, 1, 199, 229
Clementine Homilies, 209, 352
Clementine literature, 251
Clementine Recognitions (CR), as
    source, 1, 4, 7, 34, 41, 52, 56, 67,
    119, 137–139, 146, 153–154,

156, 164, 185, 187, 190, 194–
    195, 203, 217, 247
Clementines, 230, 281
Cleopas (uncle of Jesus, brother of
    Joseph), 50–51, 77, 81, 186
Clermont-Ganneau, Charles S., 215
Cochaba, 198
Coffman, James B., 167
coinage, Roman, 261
Colossians, 185, 280
Column of Constantine, 261
common sharing, 250–251, 290
communal society, launching of
    first, 91
communion, 167, 248–249, 272,
    282, 288
communism, 92–93
Community Rule, 30, 32, 40
Conon, 241
conservatism, in *Tathbit*, 228–229
conspiracy
    to betray Jesus's conviction, 89
    and fate of Tacitus's *Histories*, 206
    of Luke, 84, 87
    of proto-Catholicism, 132
    of the silencers, ix, 2, 26, 55–56,
        254
    to smother beliefs of Jesus's Jewish
        followers, 51
    that stole the God of the Jews, 87
Constantine, 15, 101, 132, 181,
    222, 245, 251, 257–273, 286
Constantinople, 183
Constantius Chlorus, 259
Conventuals, 278
Conversion of St. Paul, 72
Conybeare, Frederick Cornwallis,
    281, 283, 300, 357
Coponius, 17
Corban (offering), 107–108
1 Corinthians 6:9–10, 135, 175,

303
Corinthians, Epistle to the, 229, 280
Cosmas the Presbyter, 282, 300
cosmic ladder, 218
Council of Constantinople, 216
Council of Elvira, 245
Council of Laodicea, 229, 245
Council of Nicaea, 132, 229, 264, 268
Council of Toulouse, 286
Cranganore, 237, 238
Crispus, 260, 266
Crone, Patricia, 56, 299, 357
cross
    controversy, 215–216
    sign of the cross, origin of, 216–219
    worshipping of, 222–223
Crossan, John Dominic, 20, 28, 42, 61–62, 116, 264, 357–358
Ctesiphon-Selecuia, 232
Cumanus the Procurator, 173
Curse of the House of Herod, 45
Cuspius Fadus, 187
Custody of the Holy Land, 241
Cyril of Alexandria, 273
Cyril of Jerusalem, 244, 268, 297, 352
Cyrus, 38, 115

D

The Da Vinci Code (Brown), 43, 223, 258, 300
Damascus, 147, 243
Damascus Rule, 32, 92
Daniel
    9:24, 23
    9:26, 110
Daniel (prophet), 24, 88, 107, 116–117, 240, 275

Daniélou, Jean, 219, 358
Dark Ages, 263, 273
Daughters of the Covenant, 233–234
David, 33, 54–55, 68, 104, 193
de Neure, Mathurin, 248
de Rosa, Peter, 278, 358
Dead Sea Scrolls, 27, 29, 92
Decapolis, 42–43, 84, 104, 105, 123
DeMille, Cecil B., 115, 254
demons, 76–77
Desert of Judea, 28
Desposyni (king's relatives), 132, 210, 267
Didache, 6, 20, 89–90, 160, 167, 170, 183-184, 197, 226
Didascalia Apostolorum, 226, 243,
Dio Cassius, 235, 352
Diocletian (emperor), 235, 261
Dionysius of Corinth, 228
disciples, as dim, 3
"disobedient ones," 177–178
The Divine Liturgy of James the Apostle and Brother of God, 131–132, 230
Domitian (emperor), 240
Donatists, 263, 272
Douay-Rheims Bible, 284
Doukhobors, 216, 222, 230, 256, 289–292

E

earthly kingdom, 23, 46, 110, 118, 240–241, 255
Easter, 248–250, 269
Eastern Church, 231–236, 279, 286
Ebionim, 41
Ebionite Gospel, 57, 71, 117, 128
Ebionites, 2, 6, 20, 25, 33, 37, 52, 58, 72, 77, 88, 92, 94, 96, 100,

122, 141–143, 160, 173, 197, 204, 209, 220, 222, 225, 245, 247–248, 253, 255, 265, 269, 281, 287, 289–292
Ecclesiastes 12:5, 204–205
Edessa, 231–232, 234, 238
Edict of Milan, 269
Edict of Toleration, 235
Egbert, 284
Egypt, 57–58
Egyptian Jews, 214
Egyptians, Gospel of the, 214
Ehrman, Bart, 5, 18, 71–72, 358
Eighteen Benedictions, 212
Eisenman, Robert, 44, 142, 181, 358
Eleanor of Aquitaine, 301
Eleazar, 19
Eleazar B. Dama (rabbi), 213
Eleazar ben Boethus, 36, 37, 53
Eleusis, 166
Eliade, Mircea, 76
Eliezer (rabbi), 213
Elijah, 85
Elisha, 85
Elizabeth (wife of Zechariah), 31, 33, 35–37
Elizar, 35–36
Endnotes, 313–350
England, 250, 271, 287, 289, 292, 300
Enron, 90
Ephesians, 76
Ephrem the Syrian, 233–234, 245
Epiphanius, 20, 33, 83, 139, 168–170, 184, 212, 215, 219, 222, 241, 243, 352–353
Epiphany, 72
Epistle of Barnabas, 185, 226, 244, 251, 352
Epistle of James, 68, 140–142, 357

Epistle of the Apostles, 226–227, 353
Epistle to the Corinthians, 229, 280
Epistle to the Hebrews, 125
Epistle to Timothy, 296, 298
Epistles of Paul, 140, 154, 163–164, 171
Epistula Apostolorum, 47, 124
Eretz Israel, 70
Esau, 10
Esdras, Second Book of, 217
Essenes, 16, 28–30, 32–33, 36, 39–41, 82, 87, 92–93, 99–100, 113, 184, 198, 243
Ethiopia, 252
Eucharist, 5–6, 9, 131, 165–170, 172, 214
Eurocentric, church history as, 231
Eusebius, as source, 65, 67, 77–78, 136–137, 139–140, 142, 144–145, 151, 178, 201, 214–215, 220, 231, 236, 240–242, 246, 248–249, 254, 258, 260, 263, 266, 269, 353
Eusebius of Nicomedia, 267
Eustace (abbot), 271
Eutychius (patriarch), 268
evangelical mind-set, 193–194
evangelism, 197
Excavating Jesus, Beneath the Stones, Behind the Texts (Crossan and Reed), 62, 358
Exodus 24:7–8, 7
Ezekiel, ix, 58, 66, 80, 216, 247
Ezekiel 17:22–23, ix
Ezra, 38

F
Fadus, 195
Fausta, 266
Feast of Fools, 248

Feast of the Baptism of Our Lord, 72

Felix the Procurator, 116, 140, 148–149, 200–201, 205–206

feminist scholars/theologians, 233–234, 293–294, 297

Festival of Booths, 135

Festus, 149

First Corinthians, 7. *See also* 1 Corinthians

Flavians, 145, 205, 208, 240

Florus, 201, 205

Followers of the Way, 2, 38, 92, 147, 176, 191, 201, 238

Fourth Gospel, 34, 46, 71, 88, 114, 119, 170

Franciscans, 278

Frederic Barbarossa (emperor), 281

Fredriksen, Paula, 245

fundamentalist Christians, 27, 40, 43, 137–138, 258

G

Gabriel, 58, 255

Gadarenes, 43

Gaddis, Michael, 264, 272, 273, 359

Gager, John, 56, 196, 359

Galatians, 162

1:11, 9

1:13–17, 7

Galileans, 11–21

Galilee, 11–21, 45, 50, 79, 99–100, 110

Gamaliel, 17, 43, 81–83, 86, 117, 119, 146–147, 155, 186–187, 189

Gamaliel II, 212–213

Gaulanitis (Golan), 43, 84, 105

Gentile Christianity, 1–2, 47, 87, 97–98, 143, 189, 193, 196, 204, 206, 211, 215, 218, 221–223,

230–232, 245, 259, 268, 276

Gentile Judaizers, 244–245

Germanicus, 109

Gibson, Shimon, 29, 359

Gnostic material, 89

Gnostics, 233, 237, 282

The Gnostic John the Baptizer (Mead), 69, 361

"God-fearers," 141

Golden Rule, 37, 139, 226

Golgotha, 243, 271

Gospel of John, 27, 46, 58–59, 65, 105, 110, 113–114, 116–117, 119, 122–125, 134, 169, 191, 195, 212, 216–217, 224, 229, 252, 295

Gospel of Judas, 293

Gospel of Mary, 293, 295

Gospel of Peter, 124, 218, 353

Gospel of the Egyptians, 214

Gospel of the Hebrews, 135, 214

Gospel of Thomas, 67, 77, 87, 89, 95, 98, 110, 113, 118, 137, 185, 194, 197, 223, 232, 238

gospels, origination of, 222–228

Greek (language), 6, 14–15, 24, 36–37, 47, 60, 117, 120, 124, 129, 134, 140–141, 144, 151, 158, 178, 184, 215–216, 224, 226, 228, 233, 260, 297–298

Gregorius of Bergamo, 204, 281

Gregory of Nyssa, 268, 353

H

Hadrian (emperor), 39, 215, 241–244, 247, 267, 290

Hallelujah, 200

Halloween, 248

Handel, George Frideric, 50

Hanina ben Dosa, 83

Hannah, 33–35, 52, 115

61:1–2, 84
Iscariot, 47
Isidore of Seville, 197
Islam, 177, 210, 222, 263, 276, 283, 299
Isle of Capri, 44
Israel, 14, 31, 33–35, 37–38, 41, 50–54, 66, 79–82, 84–85, 88, 100, 104, 115–118, 126, 128, 150, 176, 186–188, 190–191, 198, 200, 212, 217–218, 237–238, 240, 247, 252, 255, 276. *See also* Children of Israel
Israel Academy of Sciences and Humanities, x
Israelites, 9, 14, 58, 83, 91, 114–115, 245, 247, 252, 289
Ivan Vassilyevich (Grand Duke), 291

J

Jacob of Kefar Sekaniah, 213
Jacob/Israel, 10, 33, 58, 213, 218
James (brother of Jesus), 2, 7–8, 15, 19, 26, 64, 67–68, 77, 81, 86, 95, 119, 135–143, 145–149, 152, 180. *See also* Epistle of James
James (grandson of Jude), 240, 241
James the greater, 191
"James the Less," 135, 151
Jazirat al-'Arab, 204, 221, 276
Jehovah's Witnesses, 230
Jeremiah (prophet), 31, 38
Jericho, 115
Jerome, as source, 46–47, 50, 112–113, 135, 177, 202, 212, 222, 228, 237, 242, 245, 254–255, 269, 273, 276, 280, 283–284, 299, 353
Jerusalem, 12, 15, 24, 29, 31–32, 36–39, 42, 45–46, 49–51, 54,

56–57, 62, 64–65, 67, 77, 80, 95, 104–113, 115–119, 131–132, 134–141, 143, 147–150, 155–157, 160–165, 169–170, 172, 177–179, 186, 190, 194–196, 199, 202, 207, 214–216, 224, 232–233, 236, 242–244, 255, 267–269, 275, 299
Jerusalem, destruction of, 4, 39, 144–146, 151–152, 173, 184, 206–207, 210–211, 221–222, 241, 247
Jerusalem Council, 138, 170–172, 201, 227
Jesus
    as adept at turning the world topsy-turvy, 129
    as adopted by God at baptism, 210, 230
    bastardy of, 58–60
    birth of, 53–58
    charisma of, 73, 83, 133
    childhood of, 60–61, 68–70
    competition for name of, 196
    conviction that God had chosen him, 115
    crucifixion of, 124
    education of, 61–68
    family of, 79, 241
    family records, 85, 132, 198–199
    as God, 230
    as God's son, Joseph's son, or bastard? 58–60
    grandnephews of, 239–240
    and healing, 83, 133
    humor of, 68, 94
    on idea that he was God, 216
    inheritance of mantle of, 136–137
    as inventive, 94
    as itinerant *tekton*, 133

Jewish followers of, ix, 2, 8, 10,
51–52, 54, 56–58, 69, 72, 137,
151, 156, 164–165, 174, 176,
180, 183, 195–196, 199, 204,
220, 244, 252, 255, 282, 299,
305
as king of the Jews, 11–12, 57–
58, 128, 129, 186
as mustard weed, 73
as partying, 97–98, 255
versus Paul on social justice,
173–177
as possessed, 76
prayers of, for "God's chosen
ones," 81
revolutionary relations with
women, 94, 294–295
sexless and spiritual, according to
Luke, 33
and strategy of parables, 80, 82
trial of, 126–127
as well versed in scripture, 65–67,
100, 114
as witty, 69
Jesus and the Eyewitnesses
(Bauckham), 224
Jesus Seminar, 66, 69, 80, 90, 112
Jesus the Magician (Smith), 73, 364
The Jesus Family Tomb, 215
Jewish Christianity (Schoeps), ix, 364
*The Jewish Christians of the Early
Centuries of Christianity according
to a New Source* (Pines), x, 55, 363
Jewish Diaspora, 237
Jewish Kingdom of God, 105
Jewish revolt/Jewish war, 13, 51,
89, 150, 188, 200–202, 205–208,
210, 211, 228, 242
The Jewish War (Josephus), 16–18,
24, 26, 69–70, 84, 144, 186, 353
"Jewish-Christians," x, 2–3, 51, 55–

56, 185, 196, 214, 222, 237, 241,
250, 267–268, 283, 299–300
Joanna, 294
Joel, 192–193
John, 5–6
6:15, 122
6:35, 5
11:45–8, 53, 123
John (apostle), 108, 128, 135–137,
145–146, 163–164, 168, 169,
171, 189, 249, 254–255. *See also*
Gospel of John
John (brother of James), 147, 151
John (Mandaean), Book of, 35
John Mark, 136, 169–170
John of the Golden Tongue, 245
John the Baptist, 20–39, 41–47,
51, 54, 65, 70, 72–74, 76–78,
80, 82–84, 87–88, 92–93, 95, 97,
99, 103, 105, 109–111, 116, 121,
133, 145, 181, 188, 190, 192,
195, 200, 214
John the Elder, 65, 224
John the Evangelist, 46,
Jonadab, 31
Jonah, 88–89
Jonathan, 148, 149
Jordan River, 24–25, 28, 42–43, 60,
71–74, 104–105, 115, 133, 232,
243
Joseph (father of Jesus), 49, 54, 56,
58–60, 64, 68, 70, 73, 79, 256,
295
Joseph of Arimathea, 117, 119, 155
Joseph of Serug, 233
Josephus
life of, 70, 239–240
as source, 11–19, 24, 27–30, 35,
42, 44, 53, 55, 61–62, 82–83,
92, 96, 99, 101, 106–107, 109,
118, 120, 123, 125–126, 129,

Leviticus, 5, 247
Liberation theology, 176
Licinius, 261
Life of the Blessed Constantine (Eusebius), 269, 353
Lilyukh, 36
Lives of Illustrious Men: James, the Brother of our Lord (Jerome), 135, 144, 353
Lollards, 287–288, 290, 300
Lord Byron, 183
Lord's Day, 271
Lord's Prayer, 67, 89–91, 100, 184, 283
Lucius, 286
Lucius of Cyrene, 163
Luke
  2, 14
  3:3, 27
  4:18, 305
  4:32, 135
  6:35, 89
  6:38, 225
  7:31–34, 97
  8:5–8, 87
  11:3, 284
  13:31, 103
  16:10–12, 226
  22:14–19a, 5
Luke, as source, 3, 5, 14, 31, 33–37, 39, 46, 50–54, 58–59, 68, 71–73, 76, 80–82, 84–90, 94, 103–104, 111–113, 117, 120, 126–129, 133, 136, 138, 147, 149–150, 161, 163, 169–170, 172, 174–176, 178–180, 186, 189, 191, 193–195, 198, 223–226, 232, 284, 294–296
Luther, Martin, 140
Lyons, 45
Lystra, 170

M
Maccabaeans, 29, 107, 190
Maccabees, 30, 38, 104, 115
Maccoby, Hyam, 55, 82, 158, 306, 361
Macheras, 44
Macy, Gary, 302
Magi, 54, 58–59, 72
Magnificat, 51, 52
Manaen, 163, 181
Mancini, Ignazio, 215, 361
Mandaean Book of John the Baptizer, 29
Mandaeans, 28, 35–37, 39, 41, 227
Manichaeans, 237, 282
Mar Aba, 231
Mar Thoma cross, 238
Marcion, 226
Marcionites, 231, 235
Marcus Aurelius, 235
Marie of Champagne, 301
Mark
  1:4, 27
  6:3, 21
  10, 168
  12:29–32, 3
  13:24–27, 30, 4
Mark, as source, 4–5, 13, 15, 27, 35, 41, 46–47, 50, 58–61, 72–73, 76–78, 80, 83–84, 87, 91, 104–105, 110–111, 113, 116–118, 125–126, 129, 143, 168–169, 184, 186, 197, 212, 214, 218, 223–225, 228, 256
Martha, 294
Martial, 63
Martin, Malachai, 267–268, 270, 361
martyrs, 26, 191–193, 272, 273. *See also* Polycarp; Stephen (martyr)

Marx, Karl, 95, 100
Mary (mother of Jesus), 33, 49, 51,
 54, 58–59, 64, 79, 134, 143, 210,
 255, 277, 282, 295–296
Mary (queen), 300
Mary, Gospel of, 293, 295
Mary Magdalene, 94, 234, 294–296
Mary of Bethany, 116–117, 128,
 191, 294
Masada, 17, 205
Masons, 290
Mass, 248
massacre (in Bethlehem), 54–55
Mattathias, 30
Matthew
 3:4, 30
 5:7, 225
 5:17, 213
 6:11, 283
 6:14, 225
 7:2, 226
 7:12, 225
 11:16–18, 97
 13:55, 21
 24:36, 228
 27:19, 124
Matthew, as source, 3, 5, 27, 39, 41,
 46, 54–55, 57–60, 67–68, 73, 76,
 80, 88, 91, 95–96, 98–99, 104,
 110–111, 117–118, 124, 126–
 127, 136–137, 143, 161, 168,
 175–176, 185–186, 189, 195,
 198, 201–202, 214, 216, 219,
 222–227, 238, 283–284, 295
Maxentius (co-emperor), 260, 262,
 266
Maximian, 266
Maximinus (emperor), 235
McCarthy, Joseph, 40
Mead, G. R. S., 69, 120, 361
Meir (rabbi), 242

Mellitus (abbot), 250
Memoirs of the Molokans
 (Kostomarov), 291
men in soft garments, 265
Menahem, 19
Mendels, Doron, 190, 362
menorah, 238
Meshikha, 50–51, 71, 73, 80, 125,
 128, 134, 149–150, 186, 190, 191
Messiah, 23, 34, 39, 41, 50, 106,
 117, 127, 195, 199, 224, 236,
 242, 299
Messiah (Handel), 50
messiahs, 32, 43
Micah, 54, 189, 213
Michael II (emperor), 280
Michaelanglo, 254
mikveh (ritual bath), 20
millenarian hope, 252–256
millenarianism, (see also chiliasts),
 253–254
millennial kingdom, 255
Milton, John, 287
Milvian Bridge, battle of, 260, 265
Minaeans, 237
Mishnah, 39, 40, 63, 242, 354
*Misquoting Jesus: The Story behind
 Who Changed the Bible and Why*
 (Ehrman), 18, 358
Mithraeum, 165
Mithraism, 166
Mithras, 165
Modern Man in Search of a Soul
 (Jung), 304
Modrzejewski, Joseph M., 214
Mohammad, 168, 276–277, 283,
 299
Molokans (Milk-drinkers), 222,
 291–292
monasticism, 251, 258, 278, 290
Moone, Hawisia, 287, 300

Moses, ix, 7, 14, 58, 114, 155, 161, 173, 179, 185, 203, 209, 245, 247
Mosul, 204, 221
Mother of God, 268, 282
Mount of Olives, 112, 116, 124, 126, 190, 201, 255
Mount Scopus, 80
mustard seed, parable of, 65–66
The Mythmaker, Paul and the Invention of Christianity (Maccoby), 306, 361
myths
  of apocalypses and rebirth, 256
  "barren" mothers, 33
  betrayal as, 47, 124
  Christian myth, 69
  Constantine's vision invented in hindsight, 260
  dispersing haze of, 11
  of Epiphanius, 139
  founding myths, 43
  Galilee, 18
  of Gospel dates, 224
  Greek, 10
  of Herodias, 46
  Hippolytus calling Mary Magdalene "Apostle to the Apostles," 94
  of John the Baptist, 103
  of Luke, 85
  of a mob of Jews lusting for Jesus's death, 161
  Paul's pagan dying god myth, 210
  raising of Jesus to mythical proportions, 58, 66
  of relations between original apostles, 171

N
Naaman the Syrian, 85
Nag Hammadi library, 258

Naphtali, 217
Nasara, 236–237, 276–277, 299
Nasrani, 276, 280
Nasrani Menorah (Mar Thoma cross), 238
Nasranis, 237–239
Nathaniel, 83
Nazarene, 19–20
Nazarenes, 2, 68, 70, 77, 82, 85, 94, 131, 132, 148, 184, 212, 215, 237, 243, 269, 276, 277, 280, 282, 288, 299
Nazareth, 12, 18–20, 54, 64, 70, 79–80, 83, 133, 198, 241, 295
Nazerini, 204, 306
Nazirites, 19, 31, 143, 145
Nazoraioi, 222
Neander, August, 280, 362
Nebuchadnezzar, 275
Nero, 58, 180, 200, 205, 263
Neusner, Jacob, 237
New International Version (NIV), 73, 75, 134–135, 167
New Testament, 33, 36–37, 41, 46, 77, 185, 196, 226, 229, 254, 286, 288, 297
Nicaea, 72
Nicene Creed, 259, 264–265
Nicene doctrine, 277
Nicodemus, 117, 119, 155
Nikolova, Vidka, 282
Nineveh, 88–89
Nisibis, 232
NIV (New International Version), 73, 75, 134–135, 167
Noah, 217
Noahide rules, 86, 138, 171
North Africa, 71, 252, 263
Norwich, John Julius, 261, 362
Notzerim, 20
Notzrim, 211, 233

Numbers, Book of, 14
Numbers 6:2–21, 31

O
Odes of Solomon, 232
Old Testament, 76, 204, 217, 223, 226, 281
Olympus, 165
Origen, 144, 207, 217, 244–246, 252, 354
Orosius, Paulus, 208, 354
Orthodox, 231
Orthodox Church, 266
orthodox views, 193
Osiris-Apis, 243

P
pacifists/pacifism, 186–189, 201–202, 290
pagans/paganism, 5, 11, 25, 30, 33, 36, 42–43, 45, 50, 58, 60, 86, 93, 104–105, 107–108, 125, 138, 167, 188, 203, 210–211, 215, 235, 241, 248, 250, 254, 257–263, 266, 270–271, 273, 277, 282, 298
Paget, Carleton, 56
Palm Sunday, 111
Palut, 231
Palutians, 231
Paneas (Caesarea Philippi), 151
Pantaenus, 238, 252
Papias, 65, 73, 77, 105, 169, 224–225, 254–255
parables
of manager caught squandering property, 90
of mustard seed, 65–66
of Rabbi Meir, 242–243
of the reluctant guests, 95
strategy of, 80, 82

of wasted seed, 87
Paradise Lost (Milton), 287
Paradise Regained (Milton), 287
Paris Magical Papyri, 215
Parkes, James, 212, 362
Parthia, 109, 252
Pasagii, 281
Pasagini (wanderers), 204, 282, 283
Passagines, 281, 286
Passagini, 281
Passion Week, 77, 117
The Passion of the Christ (movie), 296
Passover, 109, 114, 119–120, 124–125, 134, 173, 238, 243, 248–250
patriarchy, 287, 297, 298
Patristic literature, 168
Paul, 1–3, 6–10, 15, 20, 30, 41, 52, 59, 67–68, 72, 76, 82, 86, 94, 108, 124, 131–132, 135–136, 138, 140–143, 146–149, 151, 153–182, 184, 188, 192, 194–196, 198–200, 207, 209–210, 214, 216, 221, 230, 240, 244, 246–247, 249, 252, 254–256, 258, 262, 273, 280, 287–288, 294–297, 303–305. See also Epistles of Paul; St. Paul
Paulicians, 282
Pauline Christianity, 46–47, 56, 110–111, 132, 165, 174, 194, 222
Pauline grace, 158
Pearson, Birger Albert, 215, 363
Pella, 202–203, 232
Pentecost, 76, 156, 192–193, 199
"People of the Book," 177, 289
Perea, 42, 202
Peter (apostle), ix, 1, 3–4, 7, 9–10, 19–20, 52, 56, 73, 76–78, 82, 86, 98–99, 105, 111, 118, 126, 128, 135–139, 146–147, 151, 154,

Matthew's prophecy, 202
God's hosts in the Scrolls, 150
of Simeon, 52
star prophecy, 198, 218, 240
of Zechariah, 34–35, 51, 84, 110,
118, 125–126
prophets. *See specific prophets*
Protestants, 167, 176, 300
Protevangelion of James, 64
proto-Catholicism, 101, 132, 140,
263
Provence, 284, 292
Proverbs, 67, 100
pseudoepistles, 229

Q

Q (*Quelle,* German for "source"),
88, 95, 98, 113, 223, 225
Qaraites, 8
Quirinius, 14, 16, 17, 36, 53
Qumran, 23–24, 28–29, 32, 38,
40–41, 62, 82, 92, 94, 150, 155,
178, 218
Qur'an, 177, 237, 276, 277, 299
Qurbana, 238

R

radical sharing, 91–95, 97, 196–
197, 250–251
Ramsay, William, 231, 363
Raynerus (inquisitor), 285
Rechab, 31
Rechabites, 31, 32
Reed, Jonathan, 20, 62, 358, 363
Reformation, 286
"re-Judaizers," 244
resurrection, 50, 78, 94, 108, 124,
146, 157, 192, 228, 243, 248–
250, 254, 268, 295
Revelation, 212, 291
revolt

among Jesus's followers, 126
census revolt, 70, 109
failed revolt, 186
against foreign taxation, 69–70
against James, 140
Jewish revolt/Jewish war, 13, 51,
89, 150–151, 188, 200–202,
205–208, 210, 211, 228, 242
of Judas the Galilean, 69
Judea's final revolt, 215
led by Bar Kochba, 36, 63, 242,
290
Maccabaean revolt, 190
messianic revolt, 125
Theudas's abortive "revolt," 200
Reynolds, Gabriel Said, 55–57, 162,
363–364
Right Ginza, 37, 227
righteousness, kingdom of, 18, 23,
129, 175, 193, 218, 275
Rise and Fall of Jewish Nationalism
(Mendels), 190, 362
ritual bathing, 20, 62
River Jordan. *See* Jordan River
Robin Hood, 287
Roman Church, origin of, 200
Romans
7, 158
15:26, 178
Rome, 12–13, 15, 17–18, 38–39,
53, 84, 87, 100–101, 107–110,
116, 129, 132, 149, 180–182,
199, 205, 210, 221, 269
Romero, Oscar (archbishop), 176,
195, 278
Rufinus, 7, 144, 207
Rule of the Congregation, 62
Russia, 177, 220, 222, 288–291
Russian Orthodox Church, 291

S

Sabbath (Jewish), 8, 38, 66, 79, 83, 104, 133, 238, 245, 271, 273, 279–280

Sabians, 277

The Sacred Bridge (Werner), 200, 365

sacrifice

  God's banning of, 56, 247

  as irrelevant, 28

  Jesus's opinion on, 3–4

  as norm until became repugnant, 166

Sadducees, 16, 39, 184, 243

saints. *See specific saints* under St.

Salome, 44, 46

Samaria, 12, 104, 108

Samaritans, 45, 104

Samuel, 15, 33, 34–35, 52, 77, 193

Sanhedrin, 12, 43, 117, 119, 123, 128, 139, 146, 147, 150, 155, 187, 189, 242

Santa Maria delle Grazie, 164

Santa Sabina (Rome), 269

Sapphira, 136, 197, 251, 290

Sarah, 33

Sassanian Empire, 237, 252, 270

Saturnalia, 248

Saul, 15, 75–76, 77, 104, 148, 153, 195, 198

Saul/Paul, 192

Sceva, seven sons of, 258

Schaberg, Jane, 59, 364

Schliemann, Heinrich, 41

Schoeps, Hans-Joachim, ix, 154, 202–204, 232, 364

scholasticism, 273

scientific materialism, 43

Scribes, 149

scripture verses. *See* Acts; 1 Corinthians; Daniel; Ezekiel; Galatians; Isaiah; John; Luke; Mark; Matthew; Zechariah

Second Book of Esdras, 217

Secret Book of the Bogomils, 282

Secret Gospel of Mark, 134

Seleucid, 29–30, 38, 107, 115

Sepphoris (city), 12–13, 18, 21, 64, 68, 70, 79, 99

Septuagint, 215

Sermon on the Mount, 98, 113

Seven Books of History against the Pagans (Orosius), 207, 354

Seventh Day sects, 271

"Seventy Weeks" prophecy, 240

Severus, 208

Severus ibn al-Muqaffa (bishop), 268, 279

sex, church's war against, 229

sexual abuse, as shame of the church, 160

sexual neurosis, 33

sexuality, church's hatred of, 159–160

Shamanism (Eliade), 76

Shammai (rabbi), 39–40, 212

Shavuot (Pentecost), 45

Shimon ben Shetach, 62

ship of salvation, 217–218

Shirin (deaconess), 234

Shlomo Pines Society, 162

Shrine of the Annunciation, 217, 241

Sicarii, 13, 18–19, 53, 148, 149

Sicker, Martin, 109, 364

Sidon, 50, 85

silences

  another conspiracy of, 254

  author's experience of, 304

  of Christian scholars, 56

  of Eusebius, 258

  of Evangelists, 118

in *The Jewish Wars* (Josephus), 24
of Josephus, 70, 120
of Judas's fate by Josephus, 16
on oddity of Jewish food laws, 292
on origins of Christianity, 214
of prehistory, 166
Tathbit Dala'il Nubuwwat Sayyidina Mahammad (Pines) silenced, 55
two-thousand-year conspiracy of, ix
of women's voices in church, 27, 233, 293, 298
of Yeshuites, 177, 219, 280
Simeon, 51, 52
Simeon (Jesus and James's cousin), 77
Simeon (Niger), 163
Simeon ben Shetah, 83
Simon (brother of Jesus), 134
Simon (scribe), 25
Simon Magus, 230
Simon the Zealot/Simon the Cananaean, 13–15, 26
Sion, 132
Sistine Chapel, 254
Slavonic passages, 24, 26, 28, 122, 188. *See also* Josephus, as source
Smallwood, E. Mary, 15
Smith, Morton, 73, 364
Socrates Scholasticus, 249–250, 354
Son of God, 3, 11, 33, 71–72, 127, 135, 220, 227, 265, 280
Sons of the Covenant, 234
Sons of Freedom, 289
Soorp Badarak (Holy Sacrifice), 236
Sopater, 266
Southern Arabia, 252
Spain, 245
Spiritual Franciscans, 278
Spong, J.S. (bishop), 51, 56, 364

St. Ambrose, 259, 271, 273, 351
St. Anthony, 95, 278
St. Augustine, 139, 159. *See also* Augustine
St. Bartholomew, 238
St. Francis, 95
St. Helena, 20
St. Jerome, 8
St. Joseph, 139
St. Justin, 217
St. Paul, 1, 72
St. Peter, 168, 250, 264
St. Simeon, 271
St. Thomas, 237, 238
St. Thomas Aquinas, 139
Star Prophecy, 198, 218, 240
Stephen (martyr), 147, 153, 155–156, 191
Strabo, 237
Strauss, Richard, 46
Strecker, Georg, 196, 365
Suda Lexicon, 32
Sudan, 252
Suetonius, 199
Sulpicius Severus, 206–207, 354
super-apostles, 164, 171
Susanna, 294
Swaggart, Jimmy, 160
Symeon bar Cleopas, 151
Symmachus, 203–204
synagogue, 64, 141
synoptic Gospels, 9, 88
Syria, 12, 45, 53, 147, 156, 196, 204, 221, 230, 232, 242, 251, 259, 305
Syria Palestina, 211, 242
Syrian Christians, 233, 236, 238

T

Tabernacles Week, 236
Tabor, James, 13, 59, 84, 88, 119,

240, 365
Tacitus, 201, 205, 206, 207, 355
Talmud, 62, 162
Tammuz, 244
Tammuz/Adonis, 243
Tarsus, 166
Tathbit Dala'il Nubuwwat Sayyidina Mahammad (Tathbit) (Pines), 9, 55–56, 64, 88, 97–98, 125, 134, 160–162, 167–168, 173, 184–185, 195, 204, 209–210, 219, 221–224, 228–229, 257, 259, 265–266, 268–273, 279
Tau (Greek letter), 216
Taw (Hebrew letter), 215–217
Teacher of Righteousness (Qumran's), 32
Teheran, 88, 134, 268, 280–281, 283
tekton (carpenter), 21, 60, 64, 90, 133, 145
temple traders, 119
Tertullian, 189, 216, 251, 271, 355
Testament of the Twelve Patriarchs, 217, 218
Thecla (disciple of Paul), 94, 287, 297
Theodosius (emperor), 235, 273
Theodosius II, 181
Theodotus the Tanner, 210
Thessalonians, 82, 148, 273
Theudas (prophet), 28, 43, 116, 146
Thomas. *See* Gospel of Thomas
Thon, Hans, 290
Tiberias (city), 42, 70, 84, 90, 99, 133
Tiberius (emperor), 44–45
Tiberius Alexander, 187
Tiberius Caesar, 246
Timothy, Epistle of, 296, 298
Tiridates (king), 58, 235, 236

Titus (emperor), 13, 200, 205, 207, 208, 240
Tolstoy, Leon, 291
Torah, 3, 36, 39–40, 49, 62–64, 93, 151, 209–210, 213, 216–217, 219–220, 236, 247, 276–277, 292, 299
Trajan (emperor), 252, 297
trances, 72–76, 193
Transfiguration of Christ, 236
Trdat, 235
trinitarianism, 259
Trinity, 216, 276
Trypho, 244
Tyre, 43, 105

U
Unitarians, 216
United Church, 229, 305
Upper Egypt, 252
Usha (city), 242

V
Varus, 53, 79
Vaudois, 285
Vespasian (emperor), 13, 15, 205, 239, 240
Victor (bishop), 249
virgin birth, 58–59, 71, 132, 210, 229, 277
vision quest, Jesus into the desert as, 76
Vitellius, 44–45
Vulgate Bible, 177, 228, 284
Vulgate Jews, 46

W
Waldenses, 285
Waldensian sect, 285
Waldo, Peter, 285–286
Wallada (princess), 301